Freud's Wizard

Freud's Wizard

*Ernest Jones and the
Transformation of Psychoanalysis*

BRENDA MADDOX

A MERLOYD LAWRENCE BOOK
LIFELONG BOOKS • DA CAPO PRESS
A Member of the Perseus Books Group

Typeset in Monotype Bembo by Rowland Phototypesetting Ltd.,
Bury St. Edmunds, Suffolk, England

Cataloging-in-Publication data for this book is available from
the Library of Congress.

First Da Capo Press edition 2007
Reprinted by arrangement with John Murray,
a division of Hodder Headline
ISBN-13 0-306-81555-3
ISBN-10 0-306-81555-9

Published by Da Capo Press
A Member of the Perseus Books Group
www.dacapopress.com

Da Capo Press books are available at special discounts for bulk purchases
in the U.S. by corporations, institutions, and other organizations. For more
information, please contact the Special Markets Department at the
Perseus Books Group, 11 Cambridge Center, Cambridge, MA 02142,
or call (800) 255-1514 or (617) 252-5298, or e-mail
special.markets@perseusbooks.com.

10 9 8 7 6 5 4 3 2 1

For Laura

Contents

Illustrations

Picture credits: 1, 2, 11, 19, 25 and 27, Estate of Ernest Jones; 4, Derys Maddox; 5, Llandovery College; 6, 16 and 24, BPAS; 7, Freud Museum; 8, Centre for Addiction and Mental Health, Toronto; 9, Museo Casa Anatta, Monte Verità and Harold Zeemann; 10, Clark University Archives, 12, 14 and 32, Jackie Jones; 13, John Wilsey; 15, Mrs J. G. Jones; 17, 18, 30 and 31, Sigmund Freud Copyrights; 20, 22 and 35, Brenda Maddox; 23, National Portrait Gallery, London; 26, Melanie Klein Trust; 28, Brecht; 29, National Archive; 33, Bibliothèque Sigmund Freud; 34, John Hannam.

Acknowledgements

Many people helped me prepare this book on the rich, complex life of Ernest Jones. My warmest personal thanks must go first to his family. Not only did they give me permission to quote freely from his letters and personal records, but also they supplied unpublished memoirs of family history. I am particularly grateful to Jones's sons, Mervyn, who talked with me in spite of formidable ill health, and Lewis Jones, and also to Mervyn's daughter, Jackie Jones.

For reading the manuscript and making valuable comments from his own unique perspective, my thanks go to John Forrester, professor of history and philosophy of science at Cambridge University, and to R. Andrew Paskauskas, editor of *The Complete Correspondence of Sigmund Freud and Ernest Jones, 1908–1939*, published in 1993, without which this book would not exist. Paskauskas's richly annotated volume of the 671 surviving letters exchanged between Jones and Freud gives new insight into both men. I benefited also from reading Dr Paskauskas's unpublished thesis written for the University of Toronto: 'Ernest Jones: A Critical Study of His Scientific Development' which contains much new information and corrective interpretation on Jones's years of exile in Canada. I am grateful also to the poet and historian Philip Kuhn, who has made a special study of the troubled pre-psychoanalytic years of Jones's medical career.

Throughout, the archives and library of the British Psycho-Analytical Society at the Institute of Psychoanalysis in London have provided ideal working conditions. I am indebted to Kenneth Robinson, honorary archivist, and to Allie Dillon and her predecessor Polly Rossdale for masterly and swift production of papers from the storehouse, whose excellent classification system was the work of a previous honorary archivist, Pearl H. M. King.

I received help and encouragement from Don Maddox in researching Jones's Welsh background, from Dr Tony Maddox through his historical perspective on British medical education and treatments, and from Derys

Maddox, who photographed Gower locations. From Paul Ferris, biographer of Freud and Dylan Thomas, and from his wife, Mary Ferris, I received an invaluable loan of papers and interview notes relating to Jones, which they gathered while preparing Ferris's excellent biography, *Dr Freud*, which appeared in 1994. These contained material and quotations I could have found nowhere else, as did Ferris's recording of his broadcast on Jones done for the BBC Home Service in March 1959 in the year following Jones's death.

I had the privilege also of the background notes of the psychoanalyst Dr Eric Rayner, gathered in the preparation of his book *The Independent Mind in British Psychoanalysis* (Jason Aronson, 1991). Dilys Daws also kindly assisted, as did Drs Hugh and Joan Freeman. Dr Joseph Schwartz was generous and helpful with his comments; his 1999 book *Cassandra's Daughter: A History of Psychoanalysis in Europe and America* was essential reading.

Not for the first time, Asheley Johnston of Data Management Ltd offered patient and lucid technical support. Dr Dougal Goodman of the Foundation for Science and Technology also provided invaluable assistance, as did Sarah Marr of Imperial College. Once again Dr Walter Gratzer was an unfailing source of erudition and translation. From the Freud Museum, Michael Molnar, its director, made available its fine archive and answered many questions. His predecessor, Erica Davies, gave me great encouragement when I embarked on my Jones quest.

I could have wished for no better introduction to the beauty and serenity of The Plat, Jones's seventeenth-century home in West Sussex, than the pleasant day I spent there with the present owners, Mr and Mrs David Marlow, both very conscious of the Jones heritage. Equally hospitable in the village of Llanmadoc on the Gower peninsula was Sally Rees, the present tenant of Jones's old cottage, Ty Gwyn, who generously accepted an influx of visitors for an afternoon. For information and memories of Jones's first wife, my thanks go to Janet Lewis-Jones and to Mrs J. G. Jones, whose mother shared a flat in London with the musician Morfydd Owen.

In Berlin, the analyst Regine Lockot gave me her own perspective on the still-controversial issue of psychoanalysis during the Third Reich and the part in keeping it alive played by Ernest Jones, then president of the International Psychoanalytic Association. In Amsterdam, the late Dr W. H. M. Möller, before his untimely death in March 2005, unearthed much information on the family background and wealth of Loe Kann, Jones's common-law wife from *c.*1907 to 1913.

From Toronto, Professor Cyril Greenland offered his own valuable papers on Jones's under-examined and important years there. In Cambridge, Massachusetts, the sudden death of the psychoanalytic historian Paul Roazen in late 2005 deprived me of a new friend and a valuable critic.

I met Peter Gay, author of *Freud: A Life For Our Time*, when we were fellow nominees for the US National Book Award in 1988. He provided assistance and helpful comment for this present book.

Many others helped in many different ways, and my thanks go also to Anne Alvarez, Lisa Appignanesi, Ann Casement, Andrea Chandler, Dr T. G. Davies, Professor Paul Doty, Derek Fordham, Charlotte Franklin, Professor Warwick Gould, Vanessa Hannam, Ronald Higgins, Dr Brett Kahr, Dr Muriel and Paul Laskin, Bernard McGinley, Mim Reece, Michael and Virginia Rush, John F. Turner, the Revd John Whettleton of St John the Evangelist, Gowerton; Ben Whitaker and Baroness Whitaker, General Sir John Wilsey, GCS, CBE, and Dr Dorothy Zinberg.

To Roland Philipps, managing director of John Murray Publishers, I am grateful for his sharing my enthusiasm for the Jones story, and my warm thanks go also to Rowan Yapp and Lucy Dixon of John Murray, and to Bob Davenport for scrupulous editing. As always, I have relied on the unfailing support of my literary agent, Caradoc King; I have been exceedingly lucky in having him and all at A. P. Watt Ltd shepherd me through many books.

As always, I have been bolstered by the interest and support of my children, Bronwen and Bruno Maddox, and of my husband, Sir John Maddox. He has been the first and perceptive reader of these pages, and supplied the Lloyd George doggerel that includes the racial epithet with which Freud mocked Jones. My granddaughter Laura has helped by reminding me of the questions children ask when life is new. A surprising and touching aid to my work has been *The American Pocket Medical Dictionary*, twelfth edition, of my late father, Dr Brendan W. Murphy, who trained in medicine at McGill University in the decade after Jones made his mark on Canada. This small red-leather book has provided me with the 1920s definitions of many of the now unheard-of medical terms that peppered Jones's pages.

Jones's interests were, to say the least, eclectic. I am grateful to the following organizations for helping me retrace his intricate path: The Athenaeum (Jonathan Ford); Bank of England Information Centre; BBC Wales (Huw Roberts); Bibliothèque Sigmund Freud, Paris (Cécile Marcoux); Cardiff University Library Archives (Peter Keelan); Centre for Addiction and Mental Health, University of Toronto (John P. M. Court, archivist); Clark University Archives (Mott Linn); Llandovery College (Peter A. Hogan, warden, and J. Hugh Thomas, Llandovery Association); Mumbles Historical Society; National Ice Skating Association of UK Ltd (Dennis L. Bird, historian); Public Record Office, S4C (Iona Jones); the Royal Society; St John the Evangelist, Gowerton (the Revd John Whettleton); Swansea Reference Library; University College London Library Services, Special Collections (Dan Mitchell); Welsh Music Information Centre (Ruth Jones); Westminster City Archives; University of Wales; Museum of Welsh Life; Wellcome Trust for the History of Medicine (Dr Sonu Shamdasani).

The Estate of Ernest Jones kindly gave permission for the use of quotations from Jones's work and from his archive. I would like also to thank Sigmund Freud Copyrights for permission for use of quotations from the Freud archive and from the Freud-Jones letters as published by The Belkap Press of Harvard University, Freud Correspondence Copyright © 1953 by Sigmund Freud Copyrights, Jones Correspondence Copyright © 1993 by the Estate of Ernest Jones, Editing Copyright © 1993 by R. Andrew Paskausas by arrangement with Mark Patterson and Christine Bernard, Introduction Copyright © 1993 by Riccardo Steiner.

For granting other permissions, I am grateful to the Melanie Klein Trust for the use of quotations from the letters of Joan Riviere; to the Estate of Anthony Burgess, 2006, for quotations from *The End of the World News*; to the Random House Group Ltd. for quotations from *Bloomsbury/Freud: The Letters of James and Alix Strachey*, edited by Perry Meisel and Walter Kenrick and published by Chatto & Windus.

I must also thank the many who provided me with photographs or helped me locate them and search out copyright owners. Every effort has been made to trace copyright holders; if any have been missed, I would very much like to hear from them.

Freud's Wizard has been an enjoyable book to write. Buoyed by so much assistance, I hardly need add that any errors that remain are my own.

Introduction

'It is statistically demonstrable that the odds are heavy against anyone achieving distinction in life if he has to share his surname with hundreds of thousands of his contemporaries.' So wrote Ernest Jones in his autobiography, *Free Associations*, published in 1959, the year after his death.

Would his reputation be greater if he had expanded 'Jones' with another name from his family line and become 'Beddoe-Jones'? He proposed making this 'amplification' in 1922, when his first son was born. But his mentor and idol Sigmund Freud talked him out of it. 'I only know that you will continue to be Dr Ernest Jones to us,' said Freud. Perhaps. But to those not part of 'us', the world of psychoanalysis, Jones's achievement as the man who did more than any other to introduce Freud's ideas into the English-speaking world may have been obscured by the common surname carried by so many, including a chain of high-street jeweller's shops.

How he emerged from the land of Joneses, Wales, to become the colossus of the international psychoanalytic movement is a gripping story. After a near-ruinous start to his professional career, including brushes with the law, Jones piloted himself to become Freud's second-in-command. He did so through prodigious energy, administrative skill and literary ability – bolstered by wide reading and an acerbic wit. His vast output of books and articles, capped by the three-volume *Sigmund Freud: Life and Work*, is astonishing. As the *British Medical Journal* said in its obituary of him, 'Whatever he wrote was worth reading.' A later historian of psychoanalysis, Paul Roazen, declared that 'his expositions of Freud's ideas are unmatched in their clarity.'

Jones also had the gift of making things happen. He founded not only the British Psycho-Analytical Society, but also the *International Journal of Psycho-Analysis*, and edited it for many years, writing a good part of it himself. He held together the International Psychoanalytic Association when schism threatened. In the 1930s, as the Association's president, he organized the rescue of many Jews – Freud among them – from the Nazi threat and arranged their resettlement in England and elsewhere.

I

The book I have written is not concerned with the comparative merits of Freudian and Jungian psychoanalysis, nor with the future of psychoanalysis in the twenty-first century. Rather, it is the life story of an extraordinary man – one of the shapers of the twentieth century and a controversial figure who, in his lifetime and after, drew much criticism for his alleged arrogance, autocracy, dishonesty and, not least, hagiography. Insults, such as 'Freud's Rottweiler', abound. Freud himself commented to his good friend Sándor Ferenczi, 'Jones makes trouble all the time, but we know his worth well enough.'

For me, one attraction of Jones was the way his life touched the others about which I have written. I was not surprised, when I considered that all my subjects lived in the first part of the twentieth century and that, with the exception of Nora (Mrs James) Joyce, they spent much of their time in the social and intellectual circles of London. For that matter, Jones's early book on Hamlet and the Oedipus complex found its way to the Joyce household in Trieste and influenced the writing of *Ulysses*.

From Jones's autobiography, I knew of his acquaintance with D. H. Lawrence and his German wife, Frieda, and of how Jones gave her a sarcastic diagnosis of their marital difficulties. Following the Lawrence trail led me to the library of the Institute of Psychoanalysis. There, looking up Lawrence's Hampstead connections, I met a young woman who said she was writing a biography of 'the first wife of Ernest Jones'. At the time this seemed an implausibly esoteric subject. But that was before I learned the tragic story of the beautiful Welsh musician Morfydd Owen, who was Mrs Ernest Jones for a little over a year.

As far as I know, the Irish poet Yeats (the subject of a later biography) never met Jones. Their periods of membership of their London club, the Athenaeum, did not coincide. Nevertheless, they had a common interest in the British Society for Psychical Research – Yeats as an avid believer, Jones as a scornful sceptic. Moreover, as a Celt and as a psychoanalyst, Jones was alert to the significance of the event that drew Yeats back from London to Dublin – the Anglo-Irish Treaty of 1922, which gave Ireland independence from Britain. To me, 'The Island of Ireland', written in 1922 and including a discussion of the cult of the Virgin Mary, is one of Jones's best papers.

I went on to write *Rosalind Franklin: The Dark Lady of DNA*. The family of Rosalind Franklin, prominent among London's Anglo-Jewry, were, like Jones, vigorous in attempting to bring Jewish refugees into Britain during the early years of Hitler's rule, and, also like him, indefatigable in demanding that the Home Office relax its reluctance to admit refugees who had no sponsorship or means of support. The Franklins, who traced their ancestry back to King David of Jerusalem, would have not recognized Jones as Jewish. Yet all his adult life he believed in the similarity between the Welsh and the Jews, and convinced himself that he was an honorary Jew – or, in the joke he like to make about himself, a *Shabbes-Goy*: a Gentile who does the work Jews are not allowed to perform on the Sabbath.

Working on the Franklin book brought me in contact with the physicist and biochemist Francis Crick, co-discoverer of the double helix of the DNA molecule. It interested me that Crick, in his later life, should move from the study of the gene to the study of consciousness, a problem with a far less definable solution. He concluded, in *The Astonishing Hypothesis* (1998), that 'the self' is 'no more than the behaviour of a vast assembly of nerve cells and their associated molecules: a pack of neurons'. He pronounced Freud not a scientist, 'but rather a physician who had many novel ideas and who wrote persuasively and unusually well'.

That sounds right to me. I should say, at the same time, that I have undergone psychoanalysis in the form now called 'classical' – couch; five days a week; August off – and found it very helpful, especially in dealing with my problems with my young stepchildren. Analysis was beneficial to me as a writer too. What might seem its greatest drawback – the dailiness – was welcome. With little time lapsed since the previous session, I found it easy to keep the continuity of the narrative without having to summarize and recapitulate. When I turned to writing biography, I found that analysis reinforced my convictions that the early years of a life deserve serious attention and that there is no such thing as a casual remark.

Jones held a further attraction for me in coming from a part of Britain I know very well. He was born in Gowerton, South Wales, in the village adjacent to my husband's birthplace, Penllergaer. I was intrigued by the spectacle of a boy rising from this industrial heartland to stride around Vienna, Zurich and Budapest, as confident as if he were in Swansea.

I was fascinated too by the saga of a man who conquered what he described to Freud as 'various wrong tendencies in myself' and who went on to achieve a happy and productive marriage. The transition from near-ruin to towering accomplishment is part of the fascination of his life story.

There has been a previous full-length biography of Jones, *Freud's Alter Ego*, by Vincent Brome, a scholar and a friend of Jones's. Brome died in 2004 at the age of ninety-four. His book appeared in 1982, long before the publication in 1993 of the complete correspondence between Freud and Jones, edited by the Canadian historian R. Andrew Paskauskas, and before the appearance of Philip Kuhn's articles giving precise details of the sexual scandals that clouded Jones's early career. Not until 1984, moreover, did Jones's full archive pass to the Institute of Psycho-Analysis, making available many more letters from Jones's lifetime correspondence. These letters offer ample evidence of the fierce feuding among early psychoanalysts, and are also dramatic testimony to the powerful effect that Jones had on many women.

In 1919 one of his smitten analysands, later his collegue, Joan Riviere, accused Jones of knowing that he was 'irresistible to women'. I must confess that, as a biographer, I have found him captivating.

Prologue
March 1938

———

O N 15 MARCH 1938, one day later than Hitler, Ernest Jones arrived in Vienna. For a British doctor, getting there took some ingenuity. Once the Germans had entered Austria and the *Anschluss* had been declared, all commercial flights from London were cancelled. But Jones knew his way around central Europe. He chartered a monoplane in Prague, and flew in. The British Foreign Office knew of his mission and asked its ambassador in Vienna to do all it could to help. Jones was 'an eminent psychoanalyst, a personal friend of the Lord Privy Seal' and representative of the many people worried about 'the fate of Dr Freud'. President Roosevelt took a personal interest in the case.

Anxiety was justified. Freud was eighty-one, and suffering from cancer of the jaw. In 1933, when the Nazis came to power, his books had been publicly burned in Berlin and 'the practice of psychoanalysis of the Jew Sigmund Freud' condemned. From Zurich, Carl Gustav Jung, Freud's former adherent, intoned against Freud for his Jewish ignorance of 'the Germanic soul'. Freud then feared that the whole psychoanalytic movement was about to perish; but Jones reassured him. 'Nothing', he wrote to him, 'can lastingly set back the progress of our work.' Now, with Jews being beaten on the streets of Vienna, what might happen to Freud?

Jones had been a personal friend of Freud's for three decades. He had made it his life's work to teach and popularize Freud's psychoanalysis, in Britain, in the United States and around the world. The two men had engaged in a long, prolific and vivid personal correspondence, in which they exchanged thoughts not only on their profession and its vicissitudes, but also on their private hopes, frustrations and griefs.

In 1938, upon arriving in Vienna, Jones had a bad hour when, visiting the *Verlag*, Freud's international psychoanalytic publishing house, of which Jones was a director, German soldiers arrested him. But, quick-tongued and fluent in German, drawing on his diplomatic connections he talked his way free. He made his way to Freud's flat, well known to him, at Berggasse 19 and found a harder task: he had to talk Freud into leaving.

Freud was very reluctant to abandon, in their blackest hour, the country and city where he had lived since he was four. It took Jones five days to win him over. He succeeded by reminding Freud of the second officer of the *Titanic*. Blown clear when the ship sank, he was later interrogated about deserting his post. 'I never left the ship, Sir,' he replied; 'she left me.'

Charm, determination and obstinacy were Jones's stock in trade. But his work was not done. Freud insisted on bringing a large entourage with him to London: his whole family, as well as his doctor and his doctor's family. Jones worked to grant the Master's wish, but was besieged, while manoeuvring, by other Viennese analysts wanting to come to Britain too. The Vienna Psychoanalytic Society had decided that all must leave and settle in any city chosen by Freud as the Society's new seat.

Jones was a fixer. On 22 March, back in London, he wrested from the Home Office permits for the entire Viennese contingent not only to enter, but also to work – an almost impossible achievement at that time of high unemployment, when British resentment of refugees was intense. His success was achieved with the aid of the Lord Privy Seal, known to their mutual friends in the Bloomsbury Group as 'Buck', otherwise the Earl de la Warr.

In his warm letter of thanks to Jones, Freud apologized for putting into words feelings that 'between beloved friends' should be 'obvious and remain unexpressed'. On 6 June, to much attention from the London press, Freud and his family arrived at Victoria station. The next day's newspapers carried photographs of Freud, various members of his family, and the small, dapper, triumphant figure of Dr Ernest Jones.

I

The Celt
1879–1892

He is a Celt and consequently not quite accessible to us, the Teuton and the Mediterranean man.

Sigmund Freud to Carl Gustav Jung, 18 July 1908

ERNEST JONES WAS born in South Wales on New Year's Day 1879 in a town his father would soon rename. The village, six miles west of Swansea, was originally Rhosfelyn – 'Yellow Moorland'. As the population grew, the Great Western Railway in 1852 altered the name to something easier on the English eye and tongue: Gower Road. In 1886 Thomas Jones, a rising young colliery surveyor annoyed by the constant confusion of the place with Gower Street in Swansea, persuaded the authorities to change its name to Gowerton. Neither he nor the railway bothered to alter the name of the parish and census district: Llwchwr. (As the 'w' is pronounced 'oo', the name is sometimes written as 'Loughor'.)

Both of Ernest Jones's parents were Welsh-born of Welsh stock, his mother the more tenaciously so. The family of Mary Ann Lewis originated in the county of Carmarthenshire on the northern side of the Llwchwr estuary. As a girl she was sent for a year to a farm in a remote part of mid-Wales, where she learned to speak Welsh. The Lewises later settled in the seaport Swansea, in the county of Glamorgan.

Jones was descended on his father's side from the Beddoes who moved from Shropshire to Gorseinon, near Gowerton, and from a greatgrandfather Jones who tended pit ponies at the coal mines of Merthyr Tydfil before moving to Swansea to work in a livery stable. His son, John Jones, worked as a self-employed ship's carpenter, and sometimes went on long sea voyages. John's son Thomas – Ernest's father – was born in Swansea in 1853.

Thomas Jones and Mary Ann Lewis were young and well suited. They met at the Baptist Bethesda Chapel in Swansea, and married there in 1877, when he was twenty-five and she twenty-three. Ernest, their first child, was born a decorous eighteen months after the wedding.

The tussle over Ernest Jones's cultural identity began at the cradle. His mother wanted to call him Myrddin (pronounced 'Merthyn'), a variant of the name of Merlin the Magician. But her husband, looking to England and the House of Windsor, chose Alfred Ernest, the name of Queen Victoria's second son and second in line to the throne. There was no christening, as their Church did not practise infant baptism.

Ernest's birth coincided with the surge of industrial expansion and coal production that was turning south-west Wales into a centre for heavy industry, in Europe second only to the German Ruhr. Gowerton, equidistant from Swansea on Glamorgan Bay to the east and from Llanelli on Carmarthen Bay to the west, and at the junction of two railways lines, was at the heart of this growth. It lay above the anthracite field of the Swansea Valley and eastern Carmarthenshire; anthracite, which yielded a non-bituminous variety of coal, was suddenly in demand for its smokeless qualities (owing to its high carbon content). Gowerton boasted two collieries as well as the Elba steelworks, the biggest employer, and a factory for manufacturing tinplate, a product essential for the new process of preserving food in cans. These products left Gowerton by rail for Swansea, now a major port, for export.

Gowerton was no picturesque 'How Green Was My Valley' mining village, with winding rows of grey stone cottages of the kind found in the Neath and Rhondda valleys to the east. Rather, with a population trebled to nearly 2,000 by 1891, it was a vibrant, if straggling, industrial town with tall chimneys flaring orange against the night sky.

Thomas Jones rode the crest of this wave of prosperity. In a short time the carpenter's son rose from clerk at the Cory colliery in Gowerton to the position of accountant and general secretary at Messrs Wright, Butler & Co., a large steel company with international connections. Thomas, a diligent autodidact, owned a set of *Popular Education* volumes. He read books on astronomy and navigation for pleasure, as well as the English classics, and much poetry. But his real passion was for administration. He dealt with company business with a feeling that things went better if he were in charge. His little son, Ernest (as his family called him – the 'Alfred' was never used except in school registers and formal documents), watched with admiration as his capable father handed out the pay packets at the end of the week.

The Joneses were Baptists who believed in regular church attendance.

Yet all four of Gowerton's chapels conducted their services in Welsh, and Thomas insisted on praying in English. Because, under Wales's strict Nonconformist Sunday observance laws, no trains ran on Sunday, he would lead his family on foot over the six miles to and from the chapel in Swansea where he and his wife had been married.

By the time Ernest was nine, this trek was no longer necessary. Thomas Jones, like many other Welsh people rising in the social scale, shifted allegiance to the Church of England. (His pious wife from then on chose to read her Bible in private.) By then Gowerton had acquired its own Anglican church – St John's, built in 1882 in a Gothic style, with a stained-glass window donated by a local industrialist. Young Ernest turned this theological shift to his advantage. When at school he was pressed to join the class for Anglican confirmation, he protested that his parents were Baptists and would object. Thus he avoided confirmation as well as baptism – a sacramental omission which he was later both proud of and grateful for.

Soon after Ernest's birth, Thomas Jones, in keeping with his increasing income, moved his family into a small but comfortable four-bedroom, semi-detached house called The Woodlands, within walking distance of the steelworks. The house was lit by oil lamps, not candles, and before long it had acquired an enclosed cooking stove – an appliance far superior to the *sospanbach* of the Welsh song which celebrates the kettle boiling merrily over the hearth. Another sign of rising status was a piano, and with it a teacher who came from Swansea twice a week to give lessons. Even so, The Woodlands had no running water, and the supply for the house, apart from rainwater, had to be carried in heavy jars from a well a mile and a half away in the woods.

All in all, the Thomas Joneses were a family of modest sophistication and mobility. They preferred London musicals to the National Eisteddfod, the annual Welsh festival of bards and singers. Ernest was taken on his first trip to London at the age of three, and remembered being carried round the Zoo. At six his parents – Liberals – took him to hear William Gladstone, then in his second term as prime minister, speaking at Singleton Park in Swansea. At nine they took him again to London, to see *The Mikado* at the Savoy. That same year, 1888, Thomas Jones made his first trip abroad, to Paris, and the following year he took his wife to see the Paris Exhibition. It was Mary Ann's first and only trip out of Britain; she was not inspired to try again, as their return took twenty-four hours – fourteen of these spent moored on the Goodwin Sands.

★   ★   ★

Thomas Jones had avoided the Welsh church services for a reason. Welsh-speaking was something to grow out of, like thumb-sucking. It had been strongly discouraged by a stern 1847 parliamentary report into education in Wales, which managed to associate the use of the Welsh language with Welsh immorality. For many years after, some schools would force any child who spoke Welsh to carry a stick or a plaque saying 'Welsh Not'. The stick was passed from one offender to the next; the pupil left holding it at the end of the day was punished. In any case, it was obvious that English was the language of commerce, and most parents believed that their children could get better jobs if they spoke English. The Jones family, however, employed a servant who spoke the vernacular tongue. She taught young Ernest (according to his autobiography, *Free Associations*) only two words in Welsh: those to distinguish the flaccid from the erect penis. He did not say what the words were.

The English language suited Ernest Jones very well. As soon as he learned to talk, it was clear that he was both clever and fluent. His mother would jab her finger towards his tongue to indicate to her talkative son that once again his cutting words had gone too far. His sharp tongue possibly reflected the assertiveness of the firstborn – or of the small male. Full-grown, he was no more than five feet four inches tall. As a boy he could see that his father was tall, handsome and golden-haired – 'evidently a Celt', he said in retrospect – whereas his mother was short, dark and pale – 'the "Iberian" type of Welsh' – and he took after her.

That the Welsh came in two sizes was a recognized anthropological fact. In his introduction to *The Life of Lloyd George with a Short History of the Welsh People*, written in 1913, J. Hugh Edwards, MP, describes how the Iberians, from the Basque country and the Iberian peninsula, held sway over Wales until the fifth or sixth centuries BC, when they were conquered by 'a new race', the Celts, from northern Europe, with fair complexions, round heads, overhanging eyebrows and high cheekbones. The invaders also had bronze weapons, superior to the Iberians' stone axes and spears. Even so, according to Edwards, 'the Iberian race determined in the main the general physical trend' and 'is still represented by the small, dark, clever, and generally alert Welshman, capable of holding his own against all comers'. Edwards might have been describing Ernest Jones.

The combined tribes known collectively as the Welsh were gradually driven west until they inhabited a long mountainous region from the River Dee in Scotland to the Severn Estuary. Thus isolated, after 44 BC they were less influenced by Roman domination than any other part of the Roman Empire. Their apartness was secured in the eighth century by

Offa, the king of Mercia, who constructed an earthen dyke 168 miles long from the River Wye in the south to the Dee in the north, and who vowed to cut the arm off any Welshman found east of his line. Even so, the Welsh still felt they had independence, and a succession of romantically named kings defended it until the conquest by the English king Edward I in 1283. Edward formally created his son (later Edward II) the first English Prince of Wales.

Wales's hopes of regaining independence rose in the fifteenth century under the banner of the scholar-warrior Owen Glendower (whose name is variously rendered in Welsh as Owain Glyndwr or Owain Glyn Dwr). In 1400 Glendower initiated a war against English rule, and his supporters proclaimed him as Prince of Wales. But after his defeat, in 1415, he disappeared. Glendower's death is reported as good news in Shakespeare's *Henry IV, Part 2*, as Prince Henry of England acquired the title of Prince of Wales.

In 1536 Wales was forced into union with England, under Henry VIII. Bringing Wales under English administration, Parliament passed a law forbidding any further attempts at Welsh independence, and began the official discouragement of the use of the Welsh language. From then on the Welsh preserved their ancient traditions through ceremony, myth and song.

The lengthy shared border with the conqueror gave the Welsh an entirely different relationship to the English from that of their fellow Celts in Ireland and in Scotland. When David Lloyd George, Britain's first – and only – Welsh prime minister, became a young Member of Parliament for the Liberal Party in 1890, he scolded the Welsh for their ingratiating adaptability towards the English. 'We have never quarrelled with tyranny as the Irish have done,' said Lloyd George. 'We have rather turned the cheek to the smiter.'

By the last decades of the nineteenth century, the Welsh – numbering nearly 1.8 million – felt neither neglected nor isolated. At a time when the Irish campaign for Home Rule was at its height, Wales's thriving mines, steelworks and tinworks soaked up the agricultural workers driven off the land and spared Wales the desperate poverty that sent the Irish and the Scots emigrating in their millions. Indeed, Wales drew immigrants from other parts of Britain in numbers large enough to be called 'the coal rush'. This influx anglicized Wales even further.

If the Welsh lacked the sense of class exploitation felt by the Scots and the Irish, they also lacked the corresponding puritanism about the body.

They were, and remain, at ease with their sexuality. It was a minister's son who asked the schoolboy Ernest Jones if he believed that men ever thought about anything but their cocks when they were alone.

Ernest's mother was prudish enough to tell him when he was three-and-a-half that his new baby sister was a gift from Queen Victoria. He had concluded otherwise, having heard his mother's cries during labour and noticed the attendance of the doctor. The doctor – the first doctor to move into the growing village – was the Joneses' lodger for a time. Ernest remembered him as a 'handsome dashing fellow, with lurid stories of his harum-scarum medical student days in Dublin', and would later attribute his own choice of profession to this heady early role model.

At the age of three, Ernest entered the village school and learned the alphabet and how to count. A few years later at school, he learned where babies came from and that 'fuck' was the operative verb. In *Free Associations*, written at the end of his life, he makes the extraordinary claim that he first experienced sexual intercourse 'at the ages of six and seven'. The plural seems deliberately chosen.

This sexual achievement, he insists, was by no means precocious. 'Coitus', he maintains, was 'a common enough practice among the village children', and he recalls that the same minister's son who was so preoccupied with his male organ complained one day of having a bellyache so severe that 'I don't think I could fuck a girl even if she was under me at this minute.'

Wales's new prosperity brought a need for a new trained technical class to run the new commerce and industry. After the Intermediate Education Act of 1889, Welsh boys were encouraged to try for the professions. Whereas previously only a small minority of Welsh children had more than elementary education, now there was a growth in secondary education, giving Wales a network of instruction superior to that of England's county schools. The same impetus led to the creation of the University of Wales, with university colleges at Cardiff, Aberystwyth and Bangor.

Ernest Jones's parents, seeing his sharp intelligence and wanting him to get on in life, decided when he was nine that he should go to the Higher Grade School in Swansea. Thus, twice a day he took the train between Gowerton and Swansea – a difficult journey, during which he was often bullied for his small size. Twice a week he lunched with one of his grandmothers; the other days he bought his lunch at a tavern. He knew his way around Swansea because as a child he had occasionally had the task of fetching his maternal grandfather, Benjamin Lewis, home from the pub; the old man drank too much, but always obeyed his grandson's summons. The two were very attached – to Ernest's mother's anxiety. However, of the temptations of the flesh to which her son would later succumb, excess of alcohol was never one.

After he fell ill with scarlet fever, his parents decided that the Higher Grade School was too rough and transferred him to the Swansea Grammar School – a two-hundred-year-old school with high social standing. (It was the school that the Swansea-born poet Dylan Thomas was to attend thirty years later.) There Jones met English boarders who spoke with correct received pronunciation. For the first time he became aware that he had a Welsh accent – and a working-class accent at that – and strove to eradicate it.

A fact of Welsh life was – and remains – the paucity of surnames. To distinguish one Jones from another, Roman numerals were used: Alfred Ernest became 'Jones VI' on his school reports. He chafed at his inherited handicap: a surname that did not distinguish him from many of his schoolmates.

English surnames tend to have been taken from a trade – Smith, Baker, Miller – or a location – Bridge or Hill – but the Welsh followed the patronymic tradition, their names deriving from those of a father or grandfather. The prefix 'Ap', like the Irish 'O', indicated 'son of'. When, between the sixteenth and eighteenth centuries, the Welsh began to adopt the English custom of surnames, the final 'p' of 'Ap' was often elided with the father's Christian name. Thus Ap Huw became Pugh; Ap Rhys, Price; Ap Richard, Prichard; Ap Roberts, Probert. A simpler adaptation was to add an 's' to the father's Christian name. As Christian names were fairly few in number, Wales was soon full of Edwardses, Evanses, Davieses and Williamses. As John was the most common Christian name of all, there was soon a particular surfeit of John's sons – Joneses all.

The need to distinguish one individual from another gave opportunity for merry and sometimes sardonic nicknames, from the straightforward Jones the Shop and Mrs Jones Bridge to Mrs Chocolate House (from the colour of her house) to Dai the Death (for David the Undertaker). When the Scottish Conservative Sir David Maxwell Fyfe was made the first Minister for Welsh Affairs, in 1951, the Welsh, aware of the Fyffe label on every banana they bought, thanks to the company that was Britain's principal importer of fruit from the Caribbean, disregarded the difference in spelling and dubbed him 'Dai Bananas'.

Jones VI, to judge from his Swansea school reports, was a bright little boy. He was 'very good' in mathematics, 'excellent' in English and 'very good' in classics, and the headmaster summed up, 'His work is thoroughly well done at all times, & deserves great praise.' However, his reports several times contained the comment 'too talkative'. Not surprisingly, he was often near the top, and once at the top, of the top form. He was too small for team sports, but he found his exercise in tennis and skating. At ten he taught himself Italian from his father's *Popular Education* series, and he also managed to acquire the skill of Pitman shorthand.

East to school, but west to wilderness. Gowerton, standing on the dividing line between smoky industry and ancient landscape, liked to be known as the 'Gateway to the Gower'. The succession of geological forces that formed the layers of coal also sculpted the rocks and caves of the promontory jutting out into the Irish Sea. The Gower's pillowing green moors, wide bays and high cliffs made it, many decades later, Britain's first designated Area of Outstanding Natural Beauty. Rhossili Bay, at its westernmost tip, is a four-mile crescent of white sand that would be one of the most celebrated beaches in Europe were it blessed with sun more often than rain. At as young an age as nine, Ernest could wander the Gower the entire day with his dog – a gift from their doctor and lodger, of whom he was very fond.

From the top form at Swansea Grammar School, when he was thirteen Ernest won a Carmarthen county scholarship to the respected Welsh public school Llandovery College. The scholarship derived from the administrative nicety that the subdistrict of Llwchwr where his birth was registered was 'in the Counties of Carmarthen and Glamorgan'.

Jones saw himself as faithful to both counties – and to both countries, Wales and England. This facility for swivelling between contraries – Glamorgan and Carmarthen; Baptist and Anglican; industry and wilderness; England and Wales; and, not least, father and mother – served him well as he rose to become commanding wizard over the warring tribes of psychoanalysis. Few of his later critics in the psychoanalytic world – and they were many – felt any of the ingrained English distrust of things Welsh. Rather, bossed about by this 'small, dark, clever, and generally alert Welshman, capable of holding his own against all comers', they interpreted his capacity for double allegiance as duplicity.

2

'For Wales, See England'
1893–1898

⌐~~⌐

I T WAS TIME to leave home. Winning the Llandovery scholarship gave Ernest Jones independence from his father. Equally opinionated and argumentative, father and son kept falling into fierce disputes about small points of fact, such as how the siphon pump works; neither would give in. Obstinacy was a trait each retained to the end of his days.

Thus in 1893 Jones found himself, at fourteen, a boarder at a public school in mid-Wales, a day's journey from Swansea. Llandovery College had been founded in 1847 by a distinguished Welsh surgeon turned wealthy businessman, and was boosted by a handsome gift from the six-year-old Prince of Wales (Prince Albert, the future Edward VII). Originally called, from the name of its founder, The Thomas Phillips Foundation, the college had as its initial purpose the encouragement of the study of the Welsh language, history and literature, 'especially for young men desirous of qualifying themselves to be efficient Ministers of the Church in (the) Principality'. The location, in a thriving town close to the Roman road from Brecon to Carmarthen, was chosen for its healthy air, absence of factories and scenic beauty; the surrounding hills were dotted with picturesque ruins, such as a twelfth-century Norman castle and a first-century Roman marching camp. Soon the school acquired the accoutrements of a proud public school – Gothic-style buildings centred around a high tower, a chapel, a wood-panelled hall and a library.

By the time that Jones entered, any attempt to encourage Welsh cultural and literary traditions had vanished in the face of the school's determination to distinguish itself in the number of pupils passing the Oxford and Cambridge Schools Examinations. In 1887 Llandovery ranked a proud third on the published list of Britain's twenty-two first-grade public schools, and noted that all the other public schools mentioned, from Eton and Harrow on down, were double its size.

In the *Encylopædia Britannica* of the time, the entry for Wales read, 'For

Wales, see England.' That might have been Llandovery's motto. The Welsh language was not in the curriculum. Although most of the pupils – and the warden too – were Welsh, the teachers were Oxbridge to a man. Englishmen, from English public schools, they inculcated a respect for the English language, written and spoken, and, recalled Jones, 'never let us forget their opinion of our native inferiority'. Only Welsh surnames distinguished Llandovery from any other public school. In later life Jones was to write, 'The English are notoriously hard to understand – they really are a peculiar people – and I must be one of the few foreigners who have entered into their arcana.'

Arcana? In common with all the other Joneses, Jenkinses, Pritchards and Lewises (including one Lewis Lewis) registered in January 1893, Jones was well taught. In neat handwriting (nothing less was tolerated), he continued the classical curriculum begun in Swansea and studied Latin (for six years), Greek, Scripture, much mathematics and chemistry, and acquired both a clean prose style and an opulent vocabulary. His schoolboy notebooks, headed 'The College, Llandovery', show that at sixteen his lessons included the study of 'Relation of English to Other Languages: Indian, Iranian, Armenian, Celtic, Italian, Hellenic, Teutonic'.

In his notebooks, he also copied down impressive words from the mathematician, Darwinist philosopher and friend of Darwin, W. Kingdon Clifford: 'As never man loved life more, so never man feared death less.' Forty years later he would find good use for this sonorous quotation.

The dark meandering River Towy running through the town ('Llandovery' means 'Church among the Waters') served the school according to season. In warm weather masters and boys bathed naked and tested themselves by swimming upstream to the nearby bridge. In the three winters when Jones was a pupil, the Towy froze over and, already a skater, he taught himself figure-skating. Tracing the small, precise figures suited his form and temperament. He delighted in gliding for miles up and down the river, dreaming (so he later claimed) that he was ice-waltzing with a beautiful Viennese maiden. The romance of Austro-Hungary, it would seem, had already lodged in his imagination. Too small for the school's main sport, rugby, he played halfback at football.

Young Jones was quickly aware that the warden, the Reverend Owen Evans, a native of Cardiganshire with a degree in classics and natural science from Jesus College – the Oxford college known for its Welsh associations – was working to bring the school into line with great English public schools. To have his pupils gain entry to Oxford and Cambridge was his supreme goal. Evans looked down on the new Welsh university colleges as doing mere 'educational work'.

As Victorian public schools went, Llandovery was strict but not cruel. There was no corporal punishment. In the hall when the boys sat down to breakfast, the formidable French master gave his standard grace: 'Those who were late this morning will write 100 lines.' Naming the monarch to whose reign the lines were to be devoted, he continued, 'For what we have received may the Lord make us truly thankful.'

For the boys, a popular entertainment after hours was to suspend a rope from a window at the top of the tower, slide down, pick mushrooms, and climb back up to cook them over a gas jet. Another was to push someone face down and pile half a dozen others on top of him. There was also the traditional public-school prank of thrusting a boy's head into the toilet.

Was Jones bullied because of his small size? His sarcastic recollection hints that he was. In his autobiography he wrote that Llandovery had prepared him for his career in psychology and psychiatry by teaching him 'the depths of cruelty and of obscenity to which human beings can descend'. He had observed the phenomena objectively – 'except of course when I was a personal victim'. As for obscenity, he declared that in his long career in psychiatry he had failed to find any sexual practice or perversion that his schoolmates had not heard of. All the same, he acknowledged that neither homosexuality nor mutual masturbation had 'serious vogue' at the school.

In his second year, when he had to choose a career, Jones resurrected his old dream of being a doctor. He was all the more determined because the romantic figure of his Gowerton childhood had told him when he was eight that he was too delicate for such a demanding profession. However, that doctor had set a poor example, dying not long after from an overdose of morphia. Jones preferred to believe his father's maxim: 'There is plenty of room at the top.'

His decision brought him into conflict with his school. When he showed ability in mathematics in passing the Lower Oxford and Cambridge examinations, the authorities placed him in the sixth form in mathematics, with a view to his taking the Higher exams and competing for a scholarship to Cambridge. Here Jones baulked. This course of action would require him to spend three years more at school. He chose to take instead the less distinguished set of examinations of the University of

London. Passing these would allow him (after special classes in chemistry and Anglo-Saxon) to leave school and begin his medical studies in Cardiff at the age of sixteen. He had to go to Cardiff to sit the papers. While on holiday with his family in the mid-Wales spa town of Llandrindod Wells, he received a telegram telling him he had passed in the first division.

To his surprise, when he returned to Llandovery for his final month he found the warden still expecting him to sit the Higher exams for Oxford and Cambridge. Jones flatly refused, and was scolded for disloyalty to the school.

Inspirational though the doctor may have been, some of the credit for Jones's ambition to prepare for a profession belongs to the new educational provision for Wales and the establishment of the Welsh universities. The federal structure of the University of Wales was recognized in 1896, the year after Jones's arrival at the institution whose full name was University College of South Wales and Monmouthshire at Cardiff. He registered as a medical student, and began the serious study of science. The thorough grounding he received, in physics, electricity, biology, botany and chemistry (organic and inorganic) sustained him as he followed his interests into neurology and beyond.

Once again he was supported by a county scholarship – this time from his father's county of Glamorgan. With free tuition plus £40 year as an allowance, he again was independent of his father.

Those years, which took him from sixteen to eighteen, were the most stirring and formative of his life. Cardiff had not yet been declared the capital of Wales, as it would be in 1955, nor had it the self-consciously monumental buildings it acquired in 1914. But it was cosmopolitan and mercantile, with theatres, growing suburbs and good transport. One of the anatomy professors would invite students to parties at his country house; Jones much enjoyed these – and also the rowdy sing-songs on the late-night ride back to town.

Impressed with his teachers, he encountered for the first time three letters that would loom very important in his future life: FRS, for Fellow of the Royal Society, Britain's leading scientific academy. His lectures in physics and electrical research came from the brilliant scientist John Viriamu Jones, FRS, Cardiff's first principal, who held the post from 1883 until his death in 1901.

Jones lived in lodgings, with a furnished sitting room, a bedroom and a bathroom, plus meals, for eight shillings a week, and enjoyed his new freedom from supervision. Full of energy, he would cycle, alone or with a girl companion, the twelve miles to Newport – though his claim to ride there and back 'before breakfast' is hard to believe.

This was a girlfriend for early morning but not for late at night. Jones says he fell deeply in love in Cardiff and that the relationship lasted 'a year or two', but he maintains that it was not physical but rather of 'an exceedingly romantic and adoring order'. In his autobiographical claim of childhood coitus, he adds, 'after which I did not resume it till I was twenty-four'. That dating places the resumption well beyond his Cardiff years.

His sexual outlet seems to have been masturbation, but his conscience troubled him badly about this. He prayed for help, but soon decided that religion was a cover for his personal problems. The alternative to faith was readily available. At the end of the nineteenth century the post-Darwinian debate (which continues) was at its height. Did a belief in evolution rule out belief in God? If 'mind' was a property of the brain, was there such a thing as free will?

Jones did not hesitate long in coming down on the rationalist side. He devoured the works of T. H. Huxley. Huxley, who had recently died, had led the rationalist side in the arguments about ethics and evolution. Jones much admired Huxley for his lucid arguments against religion. He saw him as the man who gave Darwin to the world, and in time he decided that, his father apart, Huxley was the man who most influenced his mental development. He also read further into the anti-metaphysical works of W. Kingdon Clifford, who dared to relate consciousness and morality to an inner ethical sense of self rather than to an immortal soul.

Jones's notebooks from his Cardiff years show him absorbed in the late-Victorian preoccupation with the significance of Darwin's evolutionary discoveries for religious belief and morality. As he moved into agnosticism, he fortified himself with copious notes from the thinkers he admired, not least Darwin and his *The Descent of Man*.

An enduring benefit from extensive reading far outside the medical curriculum was a wide knowledge of the literature on ethics, socialism and theories of the mind – a knowledge that would be displayed again and again in the extraordinarily large numbers of references cited in the many papers that Jones was to write.

Through this wide reading, he solved his (undescribed) sexual problems. A paper he wrote in 1909, analysing why boys had more trouble with speech than girls do, concludes with an 'every-day observation' that 'the well-observed awkwardness and shyness of pre-pubescent boys' is due to 'the more frequent and intense feeling of shame, or even guilt, that boys experience as a consequence of the nature of their early sexual emotions'.

If this shame blighted Jones's post-adolescence, it cannot be said to have affected his speech. He enjoyed public speaking. While he lacked a Welsh singing voice, he made up for it in rhetorical force. He began with recitations at the boisterous medical-student shows called 'smoking concerts', held in the dissecting room once a term. His set piece – delivering selections from Kipling's *Barrack-Room Ballads* – was much in demand. These poems, first published in 1892, were immensely popular, and made Kipling rich. They celebrated the ordinary soldier who found himself 'somewhere east of Suez', and to do justice to 'An' they're hangin' Danny Deever in the mornin'' or 'By the old Moulmein Pagoda, lookin' eastward to the sea' required something of a Cockney accent. However, Jones met the vocal challenge, and was good enough to be invited to recite before an audience of 2,000 at Cardiff's Park Hall. To his embarrassment, on that occasion he twice forgot his lines. The first time the audience was forgiving; the second time less so. He took pains to be sure he never failed on a public platform again.

At Cardiff, Jones had one of what was to become a series of ruinous brushes with authority, to which he responded with a profound sense of injustice. In his second year he was one of a group of medical students who made a formal protest against the indifferent attitude of their organic-chemistry professor. The man took his revenge, or so it seemed to Jones, by slapping 'irregular attendance' on Jones's term report. But all Jones had done, he protested, was to be absent for a couple of days through illness, without supplying a medical certificate. The excuse did not work. The black mark on his record cost him a temporary suspension in his scholarship, and a row with his father.

Relations with his father nonetheless had improved. Ernest could appreciate that his father read widely and was achieving a continual rise in managerial status. In 1897, joining them from Cardiff, he accompanied his father and some friends on an excursion train to Portsmouth to see the naval review celebrating Queen Victoria's diamond jubilee. He was struck by the gentle beauty of the Hampshire countryside.

At the end of his first year at Cardiff, in the summer of 1896, Jones went to London with a medical-student friend, J. F. Jennings, for six weeks of intensive coaching at the University Tutorial College in Red Lion Square.

H. G. Wells was on the staff, in transition from teacher of biology to novelist. For Jennings and Jones, it was their first taste of London life. They mastered the Underground, and learned to hop on and off moving horse-drawn trams without waiting for the stop. More often, to save the fare, they walked from their rooms above a cigar factory in Camden Town – whether to their college in Holborn, to Hyde Park, or to open countryside north of London. Jones admired Jennings's wit and raconteurship; Jennings, for his part, appreciated Jones's complete self-confidence. Their efforts were rewarded when they returned to Cardiff and each passed the preliminary scientific (Bachelor of Medicine) examination in the first division.

In the autumn of 1896 they then entered 'the Cardiff medical school proper', to prepare for examinations two years hence, with lessons in dissection and in dispensing medicine. The medical classes were co-educational. (Women medical students were a rarity at the time: most colleges did not allow them. First admitted to Trinity College, Dublin, in 1904, women were allowed to study medicine only provided that they lived out of college, kept apart from male students during college hours, went home by six o'clock, and practised dissection separately from the men.) At Cardiff the ladies were asked to withdraw on the occasion of a special men-only lecture on the harmful consequences of the evil practice of masturbation. Jones found the lecture 'lurid'.

Sexual subjects were generally avoided, even though the students were doctors-in-training. Jones managed to embarrass the new professor of anatomy ('a red-haired Irishman with a habit of blushing') when asked to describe the direction of the vagina: Jones replied from the male point of view – 'upwards and backwards' – rather than giving the expected answer, 'downwards and forwards'. That the functioning of the sexual organs was not part of the curriculum did not concern Jones. (His interest had fastened on the brain and its control over the rest of the body.)

By the summer of 1898 he had completed the first part of his medical course. To his dismay, he received no better than a second-class degree in the examination. But his close friends Jennings and Herbert 'Bertie' Ward got no higher, and all three were rewarded with their names in the newspaper. His father's reward was to take him on his first trip abroad. Switzerland delighted him, as did northern Italy. From the wider world, Wales began to look parochial and petty. Jones was ready to put it behind him and take on England.

3

Thus Far and No Further
1898–1904

Opinionated, tactless, conceited
Ernest Jones's retrospective view of himself as a young doctor

IN THE AUTUMN of 1898, at the age of nineteen, Jones moved to London to begin three years of clinical training at University College Hospital. Feeling from the start that he could get anything he wanted if he wanted it hard enough, he was determined, after taking his degree, to secure a permanent post at this distinguished London teaching hospital. He was financially dependent on his father for the first time since he left grammar school.

UCH, as it was called, was closely allied with University College London across the street. The college, UCL, was the original University of London. It had been founded in 1826 by Dissenters under the influence of the ideas of the utilitarian philosopher and social reformer Jeremy Bentham (1748–1832), who wanted wider access to university education. For admitting Roman Catholics, Jews and other non-Anglicans, the college was dubbed the 'Godless Institute of Gower Street' and was denied a royal charter. Eight years later, out of the college dispensary, University College Hospital was created.

By the end of the nineteenth century, no other medical school in London could match UCH in its scientific outlook in all branches of medicine, owing to its close association with the great physiological laboratories at the college. Many of the hospital's staff were Fellows of the Royal Society. Hospital and college fitted well into the intellectual neighbourhood, which included the British Museum, the British Library and many other hospitals. The environment suited Ernest Jones very well, for he was by then an affirmed atheist – or, as he preferred to think of himself, a philosophical materialist.

London at that time had eleven medical schools, as distinct as separate universities: St Bartholomew's, Charing Cross, Guy's, King's, London,

Middlesex, St George's, St Mary's, St Thomas's, University College and Westminster. 'Bart's', the oldest (opened in 1123), considered itself the best, though Jones would later sarcastically dismiss it as 'where all the upper class dilettantes go'. He did not feel that way in 1898, when his two best friends from Cardiff, John Jennings and Bertie Ward, were Bart's men. He happily accompanied them to lectures and demonstrations at the venerable institution next door to the Smithfield cattle market.

Jones shared lodgings with Jennings – in Lansdowne Place, overlooking the old Foundling Hospital in Bloomsbury. Tasting for the first time the delights of seeing his thoughts in print, he wrote an article for the Cardiff college magazine about their adventures while hunting for 'digs' in London. They saw about thirty unsuitable places, including a dubious one run by a young and pretty landlady who, he reported, 'gracefully reclined in a lounge chair and a tea gown'. Then they suddenly 'struck oil'. Jones wrote that he would not attempt to describe their present living quarters, because 'some may misunderstand and think we are in Paradise instead of the opposite – London'.

He was, in fact, in paradise. He could take his pick of interesting lectures at various hospitals and at the Royal College of Physicians. He heard the great Joseph Lister (by then Lord Lister), the father of antiseptic surgery. He indulged in the medical-student sport of smuggling friends in to watch operations. (Half a century later, Sylvia Plath recounted in *The Bell Jar* how she was invited by her boyfriend, a Boston medical student, to watch dissections on cadavers and a delivery.) Entirely against the rules, Jones brought his other Cardiff mate, Bertie Ward, camouflaged in the white coat of a 'dresser' or surgeon's assistant, into the UCH outpatient surgical clinic to watch an operation on a pretty young actress. The fun did not stop there. The following Sunday the two rogues attired themselves in the silk hats and frock coats appropriate to a consultant and paid a call on the actress at her home and dressed the wound. It was the first realization of Jones's boyish fantasy, inspired by the family lodger, of a doctor's easy access to women.

The trio thought of themselves as the 'Cardiff Medicals'. Jennings and Ward were witty raconteurs, and all three were regulars at Speakers' Corner at Marble Arch, where the crowd knew them as 'the Holy Trinity' for their spirited debating, shouting facts and figures at angry anti-vaccinationists and anti-vivisectionists.

Jones's autobiography paints a merry picture of nights out – taking nurses home to Ealing in horse-drawn cabs, with the girls sitting on their laps, then walking six miles back to central London. There was 'some embracing', but no more. The sophistication and availability of young women (none of them fellow students from UCH, where women were not admitted to the medical school until 1918), combined with the glamour of the theatres and of dining out in restaurants from Soho to the Café Royal in Regent Street, made the three Welsh buddies fall in love with London. They took a vow never to leave it.

Their self-indulgent behaviour was in keeping with the international medical-school tradition that allows those acquiring power of life and death to be ribald and raucous about the body. Such levity, as Jones later put it, may be 'a reaction against the grim aspects of life with which they are brought into contact at an age when they are emotionally unprepared for it'.

London's medical students would mass together for special occasions, word being circulated in advance. Twice these pranks landed Jones in trouble with the law. The first instance was in May 1899, when the city was exhilarated by the leaving of the first London regiment for the Boer War. Medical students from Bart's and UCH gathered in the gallery of Daly's Theatre, off Leicester Square, and began singing along with the players, heckling the stars, and loudly cheering the minor actors. Afterwards, according to *Free Associations*, Jones and Ward shinned up a drainpipe to greet actresses in the green room. Out on the street, joining a larger gang, they tried to storm the Café de Paris, but were halted by police and were among those marched to the Vine Street police station.

When a friend tried to argue for the release at least of 'the little fellow', saying that his health was delicate, the police sergeant retorted with a gibe that Jones treasured all his life: 'Yes, bloody delicate. It took three of us to hold him.' Jones and Ward spent the night in a police cell, being discharged the next morning with a caution from the Great Marlborough Street magistrates' court.

Once caught did not make Jones twice shy. On 17 May 1900 he joined the wild crowds celebrating the relief of Mafeking after a 217-day siege. In street revels whose like was not seen again in London until VE Day in 1945, Jones spent three nights in the open as he threw himself into stunts such as hauling carriages backwards up Regent Street. When two friends were wrongly arrested for knocking a policeman's hat off, Jones and Ward went to the Vine Street police station to protest. Their reward was to be locked up themselves. Thus Jones, at twenty-one, spent a second night in the cells.

★   ★   ★

Despite his increasing worldliness, Jones was always proud of his ancestry and kept alive his Welsh links. The programme for the Old Cardiff Medicals' Dinner on 15 December 1899 shows that A. E. Jones performed a recitation from Kipling. More than that, exercising what would become a lifelong zeal for founding organizations, he helped establish the Swansea Society. Its name was soon changed to the more inclusive Glamorgan Society, and as such it was dedicated to 'Glamorganites who wander to London'. The society's stated purpose – grandiloquent with pity and Nonconformist apprehension of the dangers of the wicked capital – appeared in the Swansea-published *South Walian* magazine of January–February 1903:

> Nobody knows but those who have gone through it, what it means for young men – and young women as far as that goes – to leave their native homes and seek new ones in such a human-hive as London is: surrounded by countless human beings they soon taste the bitterness of that loneliness that is born of the knowledge that among all these thousands not a single eye brightens at their approach, not a single hand is held out to meet theirs in the grasp of friendship, or a single voice gives them friendly greetings . . .
>
> This longing breeds heart-sickness and loneliness; having no one to confide in, too diffident or too shy to mix with strangers, [the young provincial] becomes weary and discouraged, and then, as the days pass by, out of sheer desperation, he either seeks companionship that is fatal to his well being, or becomes but an atom amongst thousands – uncared for, unthought of, and unnoticed. The cruel monotony of all this – the soul-crushing effect of the unsatisfied hunger for the companionship of someone from home – may to some extent pass away, may become deadened by time or circumstances, but it never passes entirely away, and it is to satisfy this craving that such societies as that of the Glamorgan Society is [*sic*] brought into existence.

In August 1899 Jones made a second trip abroad with his father, who was negotiating for his company to buy an iron-ore concession in Portugal. The pair travelled by train de luxe from Paris to Lisbon, but on the way back, as in old times, they got on each other's nerves. The breaking point came in Bilbao, in an argument over their bedroom window. Jones *père* wanted it shut; Jones *fils* wanted it open – as a medical man, he considered the common view that cold air causes colds to be unscientific. Thomas Jones went straight home the next day. Ernest made his way back slowly, seeing Bayonne, Bordeaux and Paris for the first time on the way.

★　　★　　★

At the hospital that was the centre of his life, he was favourably treated by his superiors. He was highly intelligent, energetic and eager for responsibility. In 1900 he was made resident house-physician under the eminent John Rose Bradford, with responsibility for pathology tests, treatment of casualties, and teaching junior students.

His confidence was matched by growing competence. In line with the public policy of free vaccination, in his second year at UCH Jones became a licensed 'public vaccinator'. He went on to master obstetrics. Medical students were expected to go out 'on the district' to help midwives with difficult deliveries. They were summoned by a buzzer by their bed; an unbroken night's sleep was a luxury. These duties showed Jones a Dickensian side of London – children being born in squalid tenements and cellars, with the family's other children watching and fetching the hot water.

Surgery was in its heyday. Only twenty-five years before Jones's arrival, UCH's chief surgeon had declared that 'the abdomen, the chest and the brain will be for ever shut from the intrusion of the wise and human surgeon'. Until the mid nineteenth century, surgery was used only as a last resort, because of the high mortality rate – almost half of patients died after an operation. And the only palliative for pain was speed.

The revolution began with the introduction of ether in 1846. When ether was found to have drawbacks (chiefly lung irritation and vomiting) it was displaced by chloroform: Queen Victoria let it be known that she received chloroform for the birth of Prince Leopold in 1853. Anaesthetics were followed by the adoption of antisepsis in surgery. In 1867 Joseph Lister, building on Louis Pasteur's discovery that infection was caused by living organisms in the air, realized that patients were dying not from their operations, but from the aftermath. Lister made surgery safe by introducing antiseptic routines in the operating room. Sterilized masks, gowns, and instruments, and carbolic sprays, reduced infection.

By the time that Jones began his medical training, surgery was now the procedure of choice for many medical conditions, rather than the last resort. Surgeons were the celebrities of the medical world. At UCH, operating day was a weekly show. Even the brain was no longer closed territory. Jones, in his autobiography, claims to have stood in attendance as Mr Victor Horsley, FRS (soon to become Sir Victor), the leading neurosurgeon of his day, dissected and lifted out brain tumours and cut through the skull with bone secateurs, the chips of bone noisily hitting the floor as he worked.

Some surgeons did not take the Lister doctrine over-seriously. Jones remembered a day when, washing his hands for ten minutes as he had been taught, he saw the man in charge simply rinse his in the basin. Seeing Jones's look of surprise, the surgeon explained, 'I gave them a good wash before leaving home.' Another senior surgeon disdained the white sterilized gowns, preferring to operate, as Jones recalled, in a 'an old frock-coat, turning green, which hung on a hook outside the theatre'.

Jones himself preferred observation to operation. Early on, he decided that he would specialize in neurology, the scientific study of the central nervous system and its relation to the skin and the muscles. From his philosophic reading at Cardiff and believing 'mind' to be a property of the brain, he wanted to learn how human impulses were controlled. He was imbued with a Darwinist certainty that the answer to social problems lay in understanding man's biological nature.

Jones set his sights on becoming house-surgeon to Horsley. He sat a competitive examination with three others, and won. This positioned him not only as an eyewitness to a great man in action but as the under-study who was allowed to perform whatever surgical tasks Horsley dis-liked. He was soon adept at performing a wide variety of operations.

In 1901 he took a holiday break in Switzerland, and boldly climbed an alp above Zermatt alone. He found himself trapped for a time on a narrow ledge over a precipitous drop, but rescued himself by keeping calm (observing his pulse rate) and edging himself sideways. It was the closest to death he had ever come. He returned to London to do the Bachelor of Medicine examination while he was still a house-surgeon.

Unusually for a student still without a degree, he secured a clinical assistantship at the National Hospital, or, to give it its unblinking Victorian name, the National Hospital for the Paralysed and Epileptic. At this renowned centre for neurology, in Queen Square, behind the Russell Hotel, Jones enjoyed what he called 'clerking for a full year' with the eminent neurologist Dr C. E. Beevor, who impressed him with his under-standing of the behaviour of nerves and muscles. He came also under the influence of the neurologist John Hughlings Jackson, a specialist on brain and spinal-cord disorders and their effect on the interaction of mind and body. Jones had already developed a particular interest in hemiplegia – a paralysis affecting one side of the body. Why, he wondered, in some cases was the hand more paralysed than the shoulder, while in others just the reverse? When working with John Rose Bradford, renowned as a teacher of clinical medicine, he observed that stimulating a minute spot on the frontal lobe caused the tongue to twist. This observation led to his debut, (with Bradford's permission to publish) in the medical journal *The Lancet*, in September 1901. Describing the twisting movement of the tongue in a case of hemiplegia, he ventured the cause as 'a lesion in or near the cortex, but as to the side of the lesion I do not think that one can at present dogmatise'.

He was then, perforce, a workaholic. Most working days began with nine hours on the wards, followed by tea and an hour's tutoring by the house-physicians, who, he considered, did the real teaching. After all that, Jones then did four or five hours' reading, taking in the classics of medicine, particularly of the French Jean-Martin Charcot, who was using hypnotism to study hysterical paralysis. Thriving on this regime, he learned to get by with very little sleep, and developed the superiority of those who boast of how much they accomplish while lesser mortals take their rest.

His chief mentor – 'the most inspiring teacher I have ever known' – was John Rose Bradford. Bradford, who later became president of the Royal College of Physicians and a fellow of the Royal Society, excelled as a clinical teacher. Following him on ward rounds, Jones so hung on Bradford's every word that over several years he accumulated copious notes recording the great man's utterances on everything from aphasia to sciatica. Jones took down a description of each disease, followed by the assessment of its cause, the method of diagnosis, the ensuing treatment and the prognosis. His meticulous notes give a clear picture of the confidence of the medical man at the dawn of the twentieth century – appallingly wrong by today's standards, but nevertheless derived from intelligent and conscientious observation. 'General Paralysis of the Insane', Jones noted, was the commonest form of insanity, being often linked with syphilis (which he abbreviated as 'S'), the intoxicated sufferers exhibiting symptoms of melancholia, mania and delusions of grandeur.

Jones headed his notebook 'Crumbs from the Life of John Rose Bradford'. One of the crumbs saved was 'A Clinical Classification is of more value than one based on aetiology or morbid anatomy.' For his part, Bradford was well pleased with Jones, whose efficiency and devotion to duty were matchless. Bradford later said he never expected to find a better house-physician.

But others, to whom Jones was less respectful, were not so admiring. Jones was a good pupil, but a poor colleague. Nurses disliked being ordered about. Junior students resented his know-it-all manner and his readiness to contradict. The sharp tongue was also an insulting one. To judge from his later correspondence, offensive phrases such as 'stupid' (referring to the American psychologist Morton Prince) and 'despicable race' (describing Canadians) fell as easily from his pen as from his tongue. Diagnosing his youthful self with decades of hindsight, he could see that he could have been correctly considered 'opinionated, tactless, conceited, or inconsiderate'.

Even so, Jones made one lasting friend on the wards – Wilfred Trotter, an erudite, wry, philosophical and calm young surgeon, seven years older than Jones, from Gloucestershire. Trotter's mother came from a Welsh line, and shared the same maiden name as Mary Ann Jones: Lewis.

The two men worked side by side when Jones was house-surgeon to Trotter's higher post of surgical registrar, and they chatted constantly. Jones looked up to Trotter. He laughed at his jokes, and immortalized one from the operating-room: 'Mr Anaesthetist, if the patient can keep awake, surely you can.'

Trotter, who had 'dressed' for Victor Horsley, also believed that science could save the world: that the answer to social problems must lie in understanding man's biological nature. What was more, Trotter too considered that scientific prose must be carefully composed, and that English literature was a good adjunct to medical knowledge. Jones looked to Trotter for advice, and ran to him with every setback.

> What are the signs by which you could determine approximately the length of time which has elapsed since death in a body found dead?
> Describe the Vagina of the adult virgin, its naked-eye and minute structure, its form, its dimensions and its relations.
> Give the treatment of a case of severe Summer Diarrhoea, with collapse, in a child aged twelve months.

For his answers to sixteen such questions, put in four papers set by two examining boards, in April 1900 Jones became a licensed doctor at the age of twenty-one. This medical qualification gave him the opportunity of holding hospital appointments in surgery, ophthalmology and gynaecology, as well as in medicine and children's diseases, and research in cerebral circulation.

From there he sprinted up the steps of the medical ladder. In his examination for the Bachelor of Medicine (MB) qualification in 1901 he won first-class honours, a university scholarship and two gold medals. One medal was for obstetrics ('Describe the three best methods of inducing labour prematurely'), the other for medicine ('What are the symptoms and treatment of belladonna poisoning?').

His parents were overjoyed. 'My darling Ernest,' his mother wrote in

December 1901, 'I cannot possibly tell you how proud we all feel today. I did not think it possible that you could bear so many honours.' But he felt the distinctions were no more than his due. What he later called 'my omnipotence complex' was growing stronger.

He secured two temporary residential appointments at UCH, one of them as obstetrical assistant, which positioned him to supervise hundreds of deliveries. In the other he acted as pathologist, charged with carrying out post-mortem examinations.

In the autumn of 1902 the time came to leave his alma mater. His career plan was, first, to secure a house appointment at the National Hospital, Queen Square, then to return to UCH as staff medical officer. Before that, to broaden his general medical experience, he took a post at Brompton Chest Hospital – home of the fresh-air treatment for tuberculosis – and found himself assigned a bedroom with unopenable windows (he broke a pane to get ventilation). His duties included performing emergency operations and operating the rudimentary X-ray equipment, X-rays having been discovered by Wilhelm Röntgen in 1895.

He was a young doctor with gold medals, prospects, and good looks. A formal photograph shows him with neat moustache, symmetrical features, nicely waved hair and luminous eyes (and also with a high stiff collar and a waistcoat and watch chain).

Jones, all five foot four of him, had a flair for rapid captivation of the opposite sex. With his sharp intelligence, penetrating gaze and knowing smile, he had the look of a man – and a doctor at that – who understands what a woman wants. One of his later analysands, the Bloomsbury intellectual Joan Riviere, who became smitten with him, gushed in a letter about his being 'irresistible to women, meeting them on their own ground'.

In the summer of 1902, when he was on holiday in Brussels, his charm touched a young woman trapped in an unwanted engagement. To escape marriage, according to Jones's arch autobiography, 'she made a dash at some happiness in my company.' For this conquest, he claims, he was challenged to a duel by the angry fiancé. After the girl's mother interceded, Jones met the girl in Bruges, and there ensued 'a love scene at the top of its famous belfry. We then parted and she returned to her fate.'

Just one week later, on a holiday with his family and his friend Bertie Ward on the Gower peninsula, he met a Welsh girl in a similar predicament. (Arranged marriages were common at the time.) Gallantly, he offered to help her out by marrying her himself, and Jones's autobiography suggests that he became engaged, at least for a short time.

As he worked, Jones began to appreciate that an embryonic neurologist ought to know something about insanity. Bertie Ward having joined the London County Council Asylum Service, Jones formed the habit of spending Sundays with him to observe mental patients and their symptoms. For him this was hardly the equivalent of the old London habit of going out to Bedlam for Sunday amusement: he was a nerve specialist in search of knowledge.

The ironic situation of the physician who is unable to heal himself was bitterly brought home to Jones in the autumn of 1902, when Ward was suddenly taken ill and died. An infection in a finger turned into blood poisoning, then became the meningitis that killed him. Jones, who had never before suffered the loss of any intimate friend or relative, was numb with shock. He received a moving letter of condolence from a distant acquaintance, who expressed his sympathy 'for the deep sorrow that has darkened your life' and added that 'the knowledge of the deep abiding friendship between you and your dead friend is one of life's brightest realities'.

As the New Year of 1903 marked his twenty-fourth birthday, he moved on to become resident medical officer – a full-time job – at the North–Eastern Hospital for Children, in Bethnal Green. His intention was to gain experience that would serve him well when eventually he came to apply for a similar job at his distinguished alma mater. Among his responsibilities in his new post was the diphtheria ward, which was always full. Although Joseph Lister, in another revolutionary step, had introduced diphtheria immunization from horse serum five years earlier and sharply reduced the death rate, the disease hung on for many years. It was a major killer of children, especially in large cities, and an unpleasant one – the bacterium produced a poison that lodged in the throat and made it leathery. The title of the paper Jones published the following year conveys the suffering of victims at that time: 'The Healing of the Tracheotomy Wound in Diphtheria'. It appeared in the first issue of the *British Journal of Children's Diseases*, a new journal, working with which gave Jones, his first experience of the art and politics of editing.

At North-Eastern Jones ran into difficulties, and after nearly a year in the job he was asked to resign. In his autobiography he attributed the dismissal to having been absent without permission to go to the sickbed of his Welsh girlfriend, who had had an appendectomy. He declared that he had had 'more serious enemies than I had known', one of whom he identified as the matron – a commanding figure whom he had several times defied. It was she, he said, who persuaded the hospital's governing committee to ask him to resign.

The hospital minutes tell a different story. Jones had been absent without leave twice before – an offence he must have known was serious. This third occasion proved the last straw. If his girlfriend's illness was a factor, it was not to be the last time an appendectomy would ruin his life. Whatever the circumstances, this forced resignation in November 1903 unquestionably brought ruin. He was never to hold a serious hospital appointment again.

He rewrote his curriculum vitae, attached refreshed recommendations, had his application formally printed, and submitted it in November 1903 for a post at Charing Cross Hospital. He did not get it.

Undaunted, he applied himself to studying for his next examination, that to become a Doctor of Medicine (MD), and in late 1903 he came first. He added to his success with another gold medal. 'My darling Boy,' his father wrote, 'I cannot tell you what joy you have brought to [illegible] Mother and me.' His friend Jennings, in a letter of congratulation, addressed him as 'My dear Genius' and made plans to celebrate with an evening at the Criterion Restaurant followed by the theatre. Jennings closed with 'Good luck at Queens Sq.'

But Jones had bad luck at 'Queens Sq'. In January 1904 he applied to the National Hospital, where he had served as a clinical assistant in neurology. When he went for his interviews, he felt he was effusively welcomed by the members of staff who had worked with him. He thought he was on his way. Two of the senior people who knew him well – C. E. Beevor and Victor Horsley – were on the selection board. With his two gold medals plus the first-class honours in the Doctor of Medicine examination, he felt that no other candidate came near his high credentials. His references were from men of high standing: John Rose Bradford testified to Jones being 'an exceedingly well read man' with 'much acumen in his medical work', while Theodore Dyke Acland, who had worked with Jones at the Brompton Hospital, wrote, 'In my opinion he is in *every* way highly qualified for the post for which he is a candidate.'

But when he called at Queen Square to learn the results, Jones was stunned to learn that he had not got the job. The selection board had given it to someone he believed had lower qualifications. Failure to get the expected appointment at the National Hospital told Jones that he was a marked man – marked as awkward and irascible. His shaken parents took it well. They grasped what the problem was. Even Jones's strong backer Sir Victor Horsley had apparently told Dr Charles Bolton, resident medical officer at UCH, 'that Jones did not get on with the other resident doctors at UCH'.

His father, writing on 26 February 1904 with practical advice, urged his son to try to find out in what way his behaviour had given offence:

> This is most important to you as you may possibly be guilty of some trifling thing that told against you & of which you may not have observed any deficiency on your part. It may further be only a small matter. You see this agrees with N.E. [North-Eastern Hospital] statement so you must worry it out & Bolton [Dr Charles Bolton] should act the 'candid friend' to you. I quite agree with him that your wisest course is to act on Sir Victor's advice and this cannot be done without an expenditure. I suppose that is where I come in & you may rely on my straining a point to help you through and I feel very grateful to Sir Victor for having taken so much interest in your case. I presume you have every confidence in Bolton. Excuse my casting any doubt on this but you know the envy & jealousy that exist even in 'high places' . . . almost makes one doubt his best friends – Now will you looking at the matter in the light of Sir Victor's advice let me have an estimate of what you think it will cost for the next year & also the following year . . .

Insensitively perhaps, Thomas Jones ended his letter with the news that he had had to put down their old dog Tommy, and signed it 'love Father'.

One of the hospital staff – possibly Horsley, who was taking a personal interest in Jones's predicament – advised Jones to set up in Cardiff. Back to the Principality? It did not enter Jones's thoughts. He went on to take the examination that would make him a member of the Royal College of Physicians. Admission to the college, founded in 1518 by Henry VIII to protect the public from quacks, was a mark of prestige, and one borne mainly by Oxford and Cambridge men. Jones passed and, at the earliest possible age (he had turned twenty-five on New Year's Day 1904), was entitled to append 'MRCP' to his name.

The initials did not help. He kept a tally of his job applications, which showed a dismal record: thirteen jobs applied for, four acceptances (of part-time posts), nine rejections. A brilliant future faded as time and again he was passed over in favour of someone he believed to have poorer qualifications. Something was seriously wrong. What was it? Arrogance? Overconfidence?

But, if his fellow residents did not like him, strangely enough, women did.

4

Record Incomplete
1904–1906

In what I have had to say about my sexual and love life I have been entirely truthful, but I should be less than candid if I did not confess that the record is incomplete.　　　　Ernest Jones, *Free Associations*

WITHOUT A HOSPITAL position, Jones wove a lattice of part-time jobs, criss-crossing London north-west to south-east, Ealing to Greenwich, to meet his various commitments. His fluency, spoken and written, served him well. He coached students for medical examinations, he lectured (at a guinea – one pound and one shilling – a time) to popular audiences on health and to the police on ambulance work, he contributed to the *Medical Press Circular*, his Pitman shorthand proving useful in reporting meetings of the Neurological and the Ophthalmological societies and other groups of which he was a member. A bonus to the guinea an evening paid by the *Circular* was getting to know many London consultants personally. Lacking the board and lodging that went with a hospital staff post, he took a room at 18 Ampthill Square in Camden Town.

Administering anaesthetics was part of his repertoire. As he had done this hundreds of times during his hospital training, he readily obliged, for a fee, doctor friends who had entered general practice and wished to perform minor operations.

He continued to apply for and to be refused places at second- and third-rate hospitals. A break in the monotonous pattern of failure came when he was made physician to the Farringdon General Dispensary and Lying-in Charity in Holborn – a modest post, for one afternoon a week, that meant his name was listed for the first time under 'Hospital Staff' in the *Post Office Trades Directory* for 1905. In January 1906 he picked up another creditable position: as assistant physician at the Dreadnought Seamen's Hospital in Greenwich, where he also lectured on practical medicine in its related medical school.

He earned most as a coach for medical examinations. A stimulating pupil was a doctor newly arrived from South America. Montague David Eder from 1906 ran a general practice in the restaurant district of Charlotte Street. Although London-born, Eder had taken his medical degree at the University of Bogotá. He was an ardent Zionist, and had spent much time in Latin America serving the Jewish Territorial Organization in a quest for a national homeland for the Jews. Eder became Jones's first close Jewish acquaintance. A socialist as well, he introduced Jones to the Fabian Society and to socialist intellectuals, notably George Bernard Shaw and H. G. Wells. While Jones remained a political sceptic, he became a staunch admirer of Shaw's plays.

By mid-1904, at the age of twenty-five, Jones was earning enough to make a serious proposal of marriage. His intended was Maude Hill of Edgbaston, Birmingham. Nothing is known of her apart from what Jones chose to divulge in *Free Associations* at the end of his life. She was the daughter of a well-known Birmingham family, and 'years older than myself'. If taken literally, his autobiographical claim that, after his childish introduction to sexual intercourse, he did not resume it till he was twenty-four means that the end of his abstinence would have come in 1903. Very likely his fiancée was his partner. What is certain is that by the middle of 1904 he was preparing to become engaged to Maude Hill, and that his parents very much approved. They were keeping close tabs on his job applications, and told him to carry on trying.

His mother wrote to him on 4 May to arrange plans for a visit to London on which Maude would join them: 'We shall stay with Maude at the Thackeray. Nice enough, isn't it? You will have to buy her railway ticket in London & send it her (we shall pay) when all is arranged I shall write her tomorrow.' As for his attempts to find a good post, she advised, 'It will be better to try for the one you think safest to get & hope you will be lucky enough to pick the right one.' There followed a maternal warning:

> I wish you wouldn't work too hard now & keep yourself indoors too much. In this delightful weather, you ought to get your bicycle up & take rides in the country . . . you would get fresh hopes of life for I am sure you have had enough to depress you lately.
>
> I had a letter from Maude last week. How she wishes she were a man to help you fight your battles.

His alleged difficulties in getting along with his colleagues had made Mary Ann Jones more aware than ever of her son's sharp tongue, and she warned him to be gentle with his fiancée:

She is a treasure Ernest & you must never be cross or speak unkindly (even unintentionally as you know you can) to her, all your life. She couldn't bear it. You must promise *me* that. Shall you write or see Mr Hill before giving her the ring? . . . Heaps of love for my boy

From Mother

Early in 1905 – financed by his father, who bought the lease, and assisted by his elder sister, Elizabeth, who joined them as housekeeper (a younger sister, Sybil remained in Wales) – Jones and Trotter audaciously took consulting rooms in Harley Street. Doctors had begun moving into the neat town houses north of Cavendish Square since 1870, and Harley Street in particular became the right address for London consultants and specialists. In their leased eighteenth-century house at number 13, the two young doctors subscribed to London's three-year-old telephone service: their letterhead boasted 'Telephone: 2243 Mayfair'. Trotter, who had suggested the move, had some status – demonstrator in anatomy at University College Hospital. Jones, on the other hand, did not: among the nearly 100 doctors with a Harley Street address he was a rarity in lacking a serious hospital affiliation. Even so, he was acquiring a number of private patients, who were referred to him by doctor friends and colleagues.

As a pair, Trotter and Jones sparked each other off. They were accustomed to working together. Twice at UCH, according to Jones's recollection, they had performed a double amputation (taking one thigh each) on a patient with crushed legs. Several times a week they dined together at Frascati's in Oxford Street. Otherwise, they waited up for each other at night and chatted as they did up their boots in the morning.

More significantly, together they subscribed to a great number of scientific journals – between 50 and 100, according to Jones. Jones was first to have a paper accepted, with his tracheotomy article. Many others soon followed, including two papers in *Brain* and two in the *British Journal of Children's Diseases*, while Trotter made *The Lancet* in 1906 with a note on abnormal pressure on the brain. Both doctors were fascinated by the biological aspects of the mind and by how the brain receives and interprets signals from the body. Trotter put his thoughts into two papers on the 'herd instinct', arguing that conscience derives from the gregarious instinct seen in animals. The science of psychology, if studied in relation to biology, he wrote in his later well-known book *Instincts of the Herd*, was 'capable of becoming a guide in the actual affairs of life', and might even 'foretell some of the course of human behaviour'. Impressed by their joint output, Trotter predicted they would both be made members of the Royal Society. Time would prove him half-right.

Jones recalled that it was Trotter who first mentioned the name of Sigmund Freud to him. He was also aware of a favourable review in *Brain* of *Studies in Hysteria*, a joint book by Freud and Josef Breuer, published in 1895, describing for the first time the cathartic method of having the patient talk aloud about sexual traumas. (The book was later described as marking 'the beginnings of psycho-analysis'.) Jones went on to read, in the *Monatsschrift für Psychiatrie und Neurologie*, Freud's case history of a patient whose anonymity was concealed under the pseudonym 'Dora'. He had finished writing it in early 1901, but, as Jones would later explain, 'for motives of professional discretion did not publish it until April 1905.' The case described the psychoanalysis (truncated after eleven weeks in late 1900) of an eighteen-year-old Viennese girl who suffered from migraines, a curious whisper and a nervous cough. Listening to her, Freud drew out facts and fantasies that allowed him to construct a picture of an adolescence traumatized by sexual advances made by a friend of her father. Freud's presentation of the case centred on the patient's dreams: one about a jewel case seemed a reference to female genitalia. Probing further, Freud learned that Dora's father was having an affair with the would-be seducer's wife, and that the girl had passionate feelings for all three: incest, lesbianism and sexual desire all combined.

Dora was an example of an affliction now virtually unknown. 'Hysteria' was a blanket term covering a range of disparate symptoms from facial tics and phobias to emotional convulsions and paralysis. The word, taken from the Greek for 'womb', suggested (wrongly) that women were especially prone to these aberrations. In 1893 Freud had decided that the basic cause of hysteria was the sexual seduction of a child by an adult, usually the father. Several years later, however, after having put himself through what he called his 'self-analysis', uncovering his childhood passion for his mother and jealousy of his father, he abandoned what is now known as his 'seduction theory' as an explanation of the origin of neurosis, replacing it with the concept of the Oedipus complex. In 1900 his *Die Traumdeutung* was published (it did not appear in English, as *The Interpretation of Dreams*, until 1913), announcing to the world that it was the universal fate of the human condition to 'direct our first sexual impulses towards our mother and our first hatred and our first murderous wish against our father'. (He was writing for a male-centred world. For females, Freud simply transposed the gender references and Oedipus became Elektra.)

At the time, the most noted exponent of the treatment of hysteria was the French neurologist and psychologist Pierre Janet. Freud had attended some of Janet's lectures while studying in Paris, in 1885–6. Janet excelled in clinical descriptions of hysteria, anorexia, amnesia and obsessions. He used psychological techniques such as hypnotism and suggestion in order to explore the fixed ideas and memories buried in what, by 1889, he was calling the 'unconsciousness' of his patients. Janet's ideas at that point resembled Freud's (although by 1896 Freud had condemned hypnotism as 'senseless and worthless') and their reception in Britain and the United States was helped by the appearance in 1901 of *The Mental State of Hystericals. A Study of Mental Stigmata and Mental Accidents*, a translation of Janet's *L'Etat mental des hystériques*, published in 1892.

Jones took pains later in life, notably in his autobiography, to make his practice of psychoanalysis antedate his first meeting with Freud in 1908: 'I began practising his method at the end of 1906 and well I remember my first patient, the sister of a colleague.' From an interview given by a Lancelot Whyte to his first biographer, Vincent Brome, from his correspondence with the patient named Tom Ellen, and also from a published study of a different case, it would appear that in 1905 and 1907 Jones was using hypnosis along the lines presented in Janet's writings. The patient was asked to lie down. Jones would then invite him to close his eyes, think of sleep, and empty his mind. He would then ask the patient to open his eyes and stare into his own eyes, whereupon he would, in his confident voice, intone a stream of suggestions prompting the patient to release his thoughts and memories. What is clear is that very early in his career Jones knew how to wield the power of his intense gaze.

The treatment, whatever its theoretical underpinning, caused the patient to form a close attachment to his doctor, very like what in psychoanalysis Freud called the 'transference'. Tom Ellen, a postal worker, who had been injured in a train accident, had consulted Jones for blindness and allochiria – referral of a sensation from one side of the body to the other. Ellen was humbly grateful for the relief he received through Jones's talking and listening, and five years later he wrote to thank him for bringing 'tranquility to a mind that had nearly lost all hope of human aid . . . I never think of you', he continued, 'without a feeling of deep love and intense gratitude for all the love, respect and brotherliness you have shown me.'

Reading the case of Dora, Jones maintained, turned him in the direction of Freud and Freud's scientific interest in the workings of the mind. 'I came away', he pronounced in his autobiography, 'with a deep impression of there being a man in Vienna who actually listened with attention to every word his patients said to him. *I was trying to do so myself but I had never heard* of anyone else doing it.'

His interest in Freud was further stimulated by the arrival from the United States of the new *Journal of Abnormal Psychology*. In the inaugural issue, published in April 1906, was the first paper in English on psychoanalysis. It described the use of Freud's method of treatment with cases of hysteria at the Massachusetts General Hospital. The author was James Jackson Putnam, head of neurology at the hospital and professor of nervous diseases at the Harvard Medical School. Putnam's article was open-minded but sceptical, as well as being, as Putnam described Freud's own prose, 'written in a fluent style and with an abundance of illustration, which give evidence of wide reading, general cultivation, and imaginative ability'.

The second issue of this ground-breaking journal carried a clear summary of Freud's dream theory by one of its assistant editors. In a review of Freud's book *The Psychopathology of Everyday Life* (*Zür Psychopathologie des Alltagslebens*) the Russian-born Boris Sidis, a Harvard psychologist, explained Freud's view of the dream: 'a manifestation of motives and desires, temporarily suppressed and submerged in the subconscious'. 'Upon careful analysis – a task not always easy,' added Sidis – 'each element of the dream can be traced to co-existing subconscious states.'

Jones and Trotter, given their interest in psychopathology, realized they needed to master German. They hired a tutor, who left Jones with a working knowledge of the language and a Berlin accent. As for Jones's Welsh accent, it was disappearing. Conscious that his accent was no advantage in scaling the hierarchy of London medicine, Jones altered his voice so that, in time, he almost completely removed the rolled 'r's, over-enunciations and up-and-down cadences that stood in the way of the received pronunciation of the Harley Street medical man. He persisted in his Welsh connections, even so. The programme for the Third Annual Dinner of the Glamorgan Society, London, held at the Criterion Restaurant at Piccadilly Circus on 25 February 1905, shows that, after the turbot, the *ris de veau*, the saddle of lamb and the loyal toasts, Dr A. E. Jones rose to his feet and proposed the health of 'The Forces: Spiritual and Temporal'. It was not long, however, before he felt that he had almost ceased to be a Welshman.

In the summer of 1905 one of his better-paying part-time jobs came

Jones's way. He accepted an appointment as medical examiner of 'mentally defective children' for the medical service of the London County Council's Education Department. He was interested in speech development – an aspect of the brain–mind interaction – and the LCC paid well: he would receive £150 a year for three half-days a week.

At the end of March 1906 Jones's glittering qualifications made the national press, although not in a context he would have wished. The Sunday *News of the World* reported, 'From the point of view of medical knowledge he held almost every degree with honours which it was possible for a gentleman in his position to attain.' Jones was a man, the same paper had said of him the week before, who occupied 'a very considerable position' and 'who had had ample opportunities to flee if he had wanted to avoid the charge made against him'.

The charge was that he had indecently exposed himself when examining two girls – Dorothy Freeman and Fanny Harrigan – during a speech test at a school for retarded children, the Edward Street School in Deptford, south-east London, on Friday 2 March. The news hit the press on the afternoon of 20 March. Jones was in his consulting rooms when two police officers called at 13 Harley Street with a warrant. He knew why they had come. 'Is it in connection with the Edward Street affair?' he asked. Told that it was, Jones protested, 'It only rests on the statement of those two girls.' Detective Inspector Belcher, the senior of the two officers, corrected him. He said, according to local press reports, 'The table-cover has been examined and certain marks have been found upon it.'

Belcher knew the gravity of the alleged offence. 'Doctor,' he said, in Jones's recollection, 'Doctor, there are two ways out of this room, the door and the window; I hope you will choose the door.'

Jones chose the telephone. With permission, he called his father in South Wales with the news of this latest, and possibly fatal, blow to his career. Then, putting on his consultant's top hat and frock coat, he accompanied the policemen to Blackheath police station, where he was locked overnight in a cell with a stone bench.

The next morning, in the Greenwich Police Court, he was charged with two counts of indecent assault and was remanded on bail, which was posted in the form of two sureties of £200 each, one supplied by his father, the other by a Dr Bardsley. Jones said, 'I have nothing to say except that I am innocent.' At his side as his defence counsel was one of the leading criminal lawyers in London, Archibald Bodkin, swiftly hired at some cost to Jones's father. (Bodkin later became famous as the Director of Public Prosecutions who banned James Joyce's *Ulysses*.) The crowd outside knew what the charges were. As he made his way through, Jones heard a workman shout, 'He can cut his bloody throat, he can.' The story made the press – local, national and Welsh. The phrase 'Harley-St Physician Arrested For Alleged Serious Offence' was eye-catching in a deferential age.

Despite coded Edwardian language, press reports later made it possible for the poet and historian Philip Kuhn to reconstruct the case against Jones as it was presented, first in the LCC's own investigation held at the school, then in four court hearings stretching between 23 March and 1 May 1906.

The principal narrator of events was the Edward Street School's headmistress, Mrs Amelia Hall. According to her, Jones saw the children, twenty-eight in all, in the teachers' room, starting just after two o'clock on the Friday in question. He had repositioned the furniture so that his chair, at the end of a table, was only six or seven inches away from the chair where the children were to sit.

The children had gone into the room one by one. When someone brought him a cup of tea at 3.10, the doctor was examining a girl named Elizabeth Overton. At 3.30 he saw Dorothy Freeman. At 3.45 a boy named Walter Johnson, who had also been examined, protested to the headmistress about a question he had been asked – or, in one version of the events, Walter complained to another boy, who then relayed the story to the headmistress. Either way, Mrs Hall reprimanded Walter for making a groundless complaint. Just after four o'clock, when Dr Jones left the school, Dorothy Freeman and another girl, Fanny Harrigan, both complained to her about the doctor's conduct.

Dorothy told Mrs Hall that the doctor had interfered with her clothing, asked her an improper question, and subsequently 'acted in a grossly indecent manner'. To what he next suggested, Dorothy replied (according to Mrs Hall) that 'if she complied with his request her mother would beat her and put her to bed.' The nature of the objectionable request was reported neither in the school hearing nor in court.

As she had with Walter Johnson, the headmistress scolded the complainant. Why had she not resisted the doctor? The answer was that 'she tried to do so but [the] defendant pulled her away.' When Fanny Harrigan, aged about twelve, made a similar complaint Mrs Hall told both girls to go home; there must have been a mistake. However, when Elizabeth Overton appeared and made a similar allegation, Mrs Hall knew she had to act.

Four in a day? Mrs Hall had never heard any such charge in all her career. She went to her superior, the superintendent for special schools, who contacted Dr James Kerr, the medical officer for the LCC. He contacted Jones (whom he knew very well), and the two doctors went together to Edward Street the following Monday.

At a hearing in the school hall, the children were brought in, one by one. Under pressure of the occasion, Walter Johnson would say virtually nothing except that Dr Jones had asked him what certain things, including his trousers, were made of. Elizabeth Overton was not so timid: she recalled that Dr Jones had first asked her questions in sums and reading, then an objectionable question. (The school's notes did not record what the question was.) Next called was Fanny Harrigan, brought from the laundry where she worked; she said that, after asking her questions in arithmetic, 'Dr Jones spoke and acted in a grossly indecent manner.'

The last to be interviewed, Dorothy Freeman, was accompanied by her mother. The girl said that Jones had requested her to act in the (undescribed) way of which Fanny Harrigan had complained. To his next request, she repeated what she had previously told Mrs Hall: that if she complied, her mother would beat her and put her to bed.

When Dorothy had left the room, Mrs Freeman burst out. What Jones had done was 'shameful, disgraceful and disgusting'. Jones, never at a loss for words, replied, 'My good woman, if I did that, I would deserve to be horsewhipped and put in an asylum.' At that point the LCC's Dr Kerr intervened and told the irate mother to be reasonable: 'I am afraid the girls have made this up between themselves.' He told her to go home and rest easy: 'I feel sure this has never occurred.' Mrs Freeman shot back, 'If you try to quieten me, you cannot quieten my husband.'

There the matter might have ended. The LCC authorities accepted Dr Kerr's conclusion that the story was a schoolgirl invention, and nothing further would have been done had not Dorothy Freeman's father made a formal complaint at Blackheath police station on Monday 12 March.

The police then interviewed Fanny Harrigan. After hearing her description of the event, Detective Sergeant Beavis visited the school to examine the green-baize tablecloth that had been on the table in the room. Beavis then gave the cloth to the headmistress, who placed it under lock and key. He returned next day with the divisional police surgeon, who found what the *Kent Mail and Greenwich and Deptford Observer* reported as 'certain marks upon it which were regarded of great importance'. It was at that point that the police prepared papers for Jones's arrest.

All this came out in court, on hearings held on 23 March, 10 and 23 April, and 1 May. By special arrangement, the third hearing, on 23 April, took place at Tower Bridge Police Court, because the magistrate was determined to get the case finished and that court could sit all day. No attempt was made to protect the children's identities, or to spare them the ordeal of the witness box. It is not known whether anyone described the nature of the stains on the green cloth.

The word 'semen' was not acceptable in public discourse at the start of the twentieth century. In her memoirs, referring to the period between 1910 and 1914, Virginia Woolf describes how Lytton Strachey dared to utter the word in mixed company in a sophisticated Bloomsbury drawing room. 'Can one really say it? I thought and we burst out laughing. With that one word all barriers of reticence and reserve went down.' The barriers of reticence were not down in the police courts of 1906. When the time came to discuss the tablecloth evidence, the record shows that 'Ladies were asked to withdraw.' To the men-only audience, Dr Dudley Burney, the divisional surgeon, related how he had examined the cloth under suspicion and found three or four stains: 'In his opinion the stains were of such a character that they should not have been there.'

Jones was not asked to take the stand at any point. He sat there – according to the *Kent Mail and Greenwich and Deptford Observer* of 30 March 1906 – 'dapper and alert-looking . . . He frequently laughed and seemed quite unembarrassed.' During the headmistress's testimony, he took 'copious notes in shorthand'.

All the prejudices of the male Edwardian world were brought to bear in his defence. These were most apparent in the fourth and final hearing, back at the Greenwich Police Court, when Dr Kerr explained why, in his initial investigation at the school, he had formed the impression that the girls had made the story up between themselves. In his experience, defective children were often precocious and talked of sexual matters. The Cambrian *Daily Leader* reported the following exchange between the magistrate, Ernest Baggally, and the defence counsel, Archibald Bodkin:

THE MAGISTRATE: Are you sure they are both mentally defective?
WITNESS: Quite sure.
MR BODKIN: [for the defence]: Their family history proves that.

According to the *Daily Post*, the defence counsel then continued:

BODKIN: Romancing, with illustrative detail is not unknown, even in courts of justice. (Laughter)
MR BAGGALLY: Particularly by women. (More laughter)

That settled it. The case was literally laughed out of court. The magistrate knew that no jury would convict on the evidence of mentally unreliable children. After acquitting Jones and proclaiming his complete vindication, Baggally, according to Jones's autobiography, 'took the unusual step of sending me a friendly and sympathetic letter'.

Jones's friends and his profession rallied round. 'My dear old chap,' wrote 'Dyke' from Cardiff (probably the physician Sir Dyke Duckworth). 'I am quite unable to realize the appalling disaster which has happened to one of the best men on the face of the earth.' A doctor from Portland Place expressed his admiration for Jones's 'cheeky courage in a situation that any of us may find ourselves in during our careers. It is too bad that the ineptitude of the law should drag on the dismal farce for so long.' The secretary of the local branch of the British Medical Association (Wandsworth division) sent an invitation to its annual dinner, accompanied by the assurance that 'Many of your professional brethren have followed during the past few weeks the anxieties to which you have been put; & are rejoiced to hear that at last unwarranted accusations have been disproved.'

The Lancet rejoiced as well. In its issue following the conclusion of the case, the medical journal congratulated 'Dr Alfred Ernest Jones upon his complete exoneration from the infamous, and perfectly incredible, charges brought against him in connexion with his official visits at the schools for defective children.' It further carried a letter, under the heading 'The Infamous Accusation Against Dr A. E. Jones', in which four consultants connected with University College Hospital declared that 'Baseless charges of this kind are unfortunately only too well known to the profession . . . All are familiar with the class of persons by whom such false charges are usually brought.'

The *British Medical Journal* reported the case 'happily concluded' and dismissed it as 'nothing more than a case of imagination of a kind common in neurotics'. Jones's vindication made good news for Wales. The *South Wales Daily Press* announced 'Welsh Doctor Vindicated; A "Made-Up" Charge; Girls' Allegations Disproved', while the *Cambrian Daily Leader*'s story was headed 'Ex-Gowerton Doctor: Assault Charge Dismissed at Greenwich; Children Prone to Romance'.

At a party held at Sir Victor Horsley's house in Cavendish Square, the president of the Royal College of Surgeons of England formally presented Jones with the amount raised by subscription to pay his legal expenses. John Rose Bradford and Sir Victor each gave five guineas.

*　　*　　*

Was he guilty? Today the question could be swiftly answered by a DNA test. Lacking the green-baize tablecloth, all that can be assessed are contemporary press reports and the records of the LCC. Even so, from the perspective of a later century awake to the reality of paedophile priests and other abusers of vulnerable young people, it must be said that the evidence against Jones looks damning. Children's words are now taken seriously, whereas past generations routinely dismissed them as untrustworthy, if not malicious fabrication. Freud himself in 1897 abandoned the seduction theory as a direct cause of neurosis after deciding that what his patients were telling him were products of their own sexual fantasies.

The sheer number of children who complained of Jones's behaviour on the same day tells against him. So too does his misleading and inaccurate account of the episode in his autobiography. In *Free Associations*, published in 1959, he wrote that the charges against him had been made by 'two small children'. There were in fact four pupils who accused him on the same day, and they were not small. The youngest, Fanny Harrigan, was twelve; the rest were in their teens. Jones further clouds the record by saying that the LCC's education authority, after a delay of a couple of weeks, 'made the panicky decision of placing the matter in the hands of the police'. In fact it was a father's complaint to the police, followed by the discovery of the stained tablecloth, that forced the LCC itself to bring the case against Jones in the courts. There is little doubt also that in 1906 Jones was at the lowest ebb of his life. Could he have been so demoralized as to lose self-restraint and invite the schoolgirls to touch his swollen genitals?

On the other hand, if Jones had simply been asking pupils about their knowledge of the body or of reproduction, the question, in puritanical Edwardian England, would have been shocking in itself. Sex was not talked about. One of the words he was reported having put to them was innocent enough – 'baby'. It is less easy to explain how three separate girls would have misunderstood his explicit invitations.

What seems certain is that if Jones had not aired what he described, writing (according to his son Mervyn) in 1944, as the 'most disagreeable experience of my life', it would have been forgotten. The scandal was unremarked upon by the international circle who later knew him from his writings and from his long-time presidency of the International Psychoanalytic Association. His later publishing associates from the Bloomsbury Group gave no hint that they knew of it. Without his careful preservation of many newspaper cuttings of the event, the records of the

Edward Street scandal would not be easily available for historians of psychoanalysis to examine under the bright light of hindsight.

Among those who rallied round was Jones's friend and pupil whom he had coached for medical examinations, Dr David Eder. From his Charlotte Street office, even before the case was dismissed, Eder wrote to commiserate 'about the ridiculous charges that have been brought against you. I need not say that whatever was the nature of the evidence and however multiple the witnesses I should not believe a word against you – whatever you have been accused of.' (Eder contributed a guinea to the subscription for Jones's legal expenses.)

At some point before the summer of 1906, an abrupt change in Jones's life took place. Eder introduced him to Louise Dorothea Kann, a young Dutch-Jewish woman (perhaps a potential patient) who was as beautiful as she was rich. She lived not far away from Jones's rented room in Camden Town, but in a different world: the Edwardian elegance of a newly built large block of flats on St John's Wood High Street, north of Regent's Park. Her brother, Jacobus Kann, was active in London Jewish circles: he founded the *Jewish Chronicle* Trust to help those who wished to emigrate to Palestine. Loe, as Jones called her, was cosmopolitan and enjoyed a wide international circle, as was shown when he helped her entertain the delegation from the new Russian Duma on its visit to London in late July 1906.

What had happened to Maude Hill? It is one of the many unsolved mysteries of that period in Jones's life. His autobiography misrepresents the timing of the end of his commitment to Miss Hill, for it describes the engagement ending with his move to Harley Street in 1905 and blames the break on Maude's personal plea to John Rose Bradford to help Jones find a hospital appointment. In *Free Associations*, Jones says that he apologized to the great surgeon for 'this unwelcome petticoat influence'.

His archieves contradict this chronology. A letter from his former UCH house-physician, Ivor Tuckett, indicates that Jones remained engaged to Maude Hill until well into 1906, two months after the end of the Deptford scandal. In July of that year she appears to have been suffering from typhoid fever. Jones wrote to Tuckett that he was attempting to rearrange his schedule so as to spend as much time as possible with his fiancée in Birmingham. In reply, Tuckett, writing principally to ask Jones, as a neurologist with whom he had discussed his own emotional problems, to see a friend who had suffered repeated breakdowns, sent his 'best wishes for your fiancée's rapid restoration to active life'.

Jones, it would appear, had begun a new relationship before breaking off the old. Possibly the severance of his engagement to the well-to-do Birmingham woman was precipitated by his meeting the far more alluring Loe Kann. In any event, he began to share Loe's flat in the elegant new block called Hanover House. He introduced her to his parents in Wales, and in time he audaciously told them that he and Loe were married. Indeed, he now saw himself in fact, if not in law, as a man with a wife.

How he explained this change of partner to his parents and how he extricated himself from his engagement to Maude Hill are omitted from his autobiography. It is one of the episodes in his love life about which he was, in his words, 'less than candid' and about which he chose deliberately to leave the record incomplete.

5

Freud to the Rescue
September 1907–August 1908

E RNEST JONES LIKED travelling to the Continent. Crossing the Channel on Saturday evening and returning by seven o'clock on Monday morning in time to start work did not bother him. Sometimes he went with his beautiful Dutch consort to visit her family in an expensive residential district of The Hague, where the Kanns, Sephardic Jews, ran the family bank. At other times he went on his own for a brief exploration of Paris, Brussels, Ghent, Rouen or some other place within easy reach of the ferry.

It was in Amsterdam in early September 1907 that Jones met the rising star of psychiatric medicine, Carl Gustav Jung of Zurich. The occasion was the First International Congress of Psychiatry and Neurology. The principal speaker was the famed Pierre Janet from Paris. Jung, attending as assistant director of the Burghölzli sanatorium in Zurich, was in a state of almost religious exultation. Although he had been using and advocating Freud's theories of the unconscious for several years, he had met the great man himself only several months earlier.

Jung was thirty-two. Tall, square-jawed and handsome in a burly, bespectacled way, he was son of a Swiss-Protestant clergyman. At the Burghölzli, he worked in an atmosphere utterly unlike Freud's in Vienna. Freud was in private practice and saw his well-to-do, well-spoken patients in a flat on a lower floor of the block at Berggasse 19 where he and his family lived. Jung worked in a vast public institution holding hundreds of patients, many of them poor. With a doctorate in medicine from the University of Basle, he had made psychiatry his speciality, and pursued an experimental interest in spiritualism and religious belief.

The Burghölzli, sprawling long and low on a hillside above the city, served as a training clinic for the University of Zurich. It was known for its sympathetic and unorthodox treatment of *dementia praecox* – a disorder which in 1908 the Burghölzli's eminent director, Eugen Bleuler, was to rename 'schizophrenia'. Was the affliction a form of hysteria? Was it hereditary, or caused by trauma or chemical alteration in the brain? The

Burghölzli encouraged its staff to have friendly involvement with patients – to work and eat with them, and to participate with them in concerts. Bleuler supported Jung's innovation of word-association tests, in which patients' responses to stimulus words were timed with a stopwatch. This procedure echoed and expanded on Freud's innovative technique called 'free association' – as Jung acknowledged in a book on its use in diagnostic studies.

Jung had been drawn to Freud since reading *Die Traumdeutung* (*The Interpretation of Dreams*) in 1900, the year he arrived at the Burghölzli. This seminal text (later recognized as one of the most influential books of the twentieth century) established Freud as the founder of the theory of the unconscious. Bleuler had assigned Jung the task of explaining the book to the clinic's staff. For his part, Jung found Freud's theory of repression valuable in explaining the hesitations, silences and evasions he observed when asking patients to perform word associations. Their reactions proved to him that Freud's theory was true: that below the conscious mind existed an unaware self. In 1906 he had paid ample tribute to Freud's theories in an important monograph, *The Psychology of Dementia Praecox*.

In January 1907 Jung had been extremely upset when Bleuler had sent someone else from the Burghölzli, a young Russian-born medical student named Max Eitingon, to Vienna to meet Freud and see what their hospital could learn from him. In the process, Eitingon became the first non-Viennese to share Freud's ideas. Moreover, during long walks and long conversations, Eitingon told Freud all about himself, and received interpretations in return. 'Such', exclaimed Jones in his biography of Freud, 'was the first training analysis!'

Jung took himself to Vienna not long after, and felt rewarded with the high point of his life. Invited to lunch by Freud, he did not leave the Berggasse flat until two in the morning. Freud was equally moved by their discussions. He was delighted that a Christian – the son of a pastor, no less – had joined what Freud called *die Sache* – 'the Cause'. He had already congratulated Jung for converting Bleuler to what he felt was more than a cause – rather, a new science of psychology.

From the start, the older and the younger man recognized points of disagreement. Jung felt that Freud made too much of sexuality, while Freud warned Jung that his preoccupation with the mystical was an escape from sexuality. (Jung's doctoral dissertation at the University of Basle had been entitled 'On the Psychology and Pathology of So-Called Occult Phenomena'; as a doctor, he continued to attend seances to observe the manifestation of altered states of consciousness.) However, these differences did not impede the formation of a deep bond.

At the Amsterdam conference (which Freud did not attend) the following September, Jung was startled and delighted to hear Jones say that he too was practising the new Freudian method. (The paper Jones delivered there, however, had nothing to do with psychoanalysis; it dealt with the clinical significance of allochiria, the neurological affliction he had been studying.) Jung had had no inkling that Freud's ideas had reached Britain. He wasted no time in relaying the good news to Vienna. In a letter beginning 'I got back from Amsterdam yesterday evening', he announced to Freud, 'Now for a great surprise: among the English contingent there was a young man from London, Dr Jones (a Celt from Wales!), who knows your writings very well and does psychoanalytical work himself. He will probably visit you later. He is very intelligent and could do a lot of good.'

Freud shot back, 'The Celt who surprised you is certainly not the only one; before the year is out we shall hear of unexpected supporters, and you will acquire others at your flourishing school.' (Freud was apparently referring to Jung's plans for a 'Freud Society' in Zurich, the first to be formed outside Vienna.)

'The Cause' – psychoanalysis – had grown out of hypnotism. In late 1885 and early 1886 Freud, then thirty and a lecturer in neurology at the University of Vienna, where he had received his medical degree in 1881, went on a travelling fellowship to Paris, where he spent six months watching the famed Jean-Martin Charcot treat hysterics with hypnosis on the assumption that their physical symptoms arose from mental processes. Charcot's theatrical demonstrations were famous: he displayed his patients on a darkened stage, twirling and sleepwalking.

Charcot had the powerful effect on the young Freud that Freud himself was later to have on Jung. As Charcot induced and cured hysterical paralyses, he proved that the attacks were not faked, that they occurred in men as well as in women, and that they could be brought on by hypnotic suggestion. His most famous pupil, Pierre Janet, observed that it was a fact of Charcot's treatment that his patients fell in love with, or, as he put it, developed a 'magnetic passion' for, their hypnotist.

Freud had already been interested in the hypnotic state. On returning to Vienna he set up as a doctor of nervous diseases and wrote a book on aphasia – loss of speech. At the university, however, his drawing on what he had learned from Charcot in his presentation of a case, caused him to be excluded from the laboratory of cerebral anatomy. He thereupon withdrew from academic life and concentrated on making a living from private practice. He called the subsequent decade his years of 'splendid isolation'.

He developed his own singular method of treatment, derived from what he had learned from an older Viennese physician, Josef Breuer, his long-time mainstay and mentor. In 1880 Breuer had had a patient with bizarre difficulties: a squint, deafness, fear of water, nightmares of her father's head as a skull, fatigue, thoughts of suicide and, at one point, a loss of the German language so that she could speak only in English, French or Italian. When Breuer had listened to her thoughts about her problems over a long (and, he found, exhausting) period, the symptoms disappeared. The story of this patient, known as 'Anna O' (in reality a young Viennese named Bertha Pappenheim), became the first case history of what Fräulein Pappenheim herself dubbed 'the talking cure'. Freud was fascinated, and began using Breuer's cathartic method with his own patients.

In 1896, after the publication of their joint book *Studies in Hysteria* (composed of the case histories of five women), Freud broke with Breuer. Their dispute was fundamental. Freud was convinced that the origin of hysterical symptoms was sexual; Breuer was not. With his own patients, Freud found that, as they talked, their unconscious desires emerged, erotic and inappropriate. Similar feelings occurred in the dreams his patients recounted to him. Working alone, Freud saw himself developing a 'psychology for neurologists', and in 1896 he began calling it 'psychoanalysis'.

In 1897, abandoning his first deduction that his patients' symptoms were the products of actual acts of incest, mainly of parent against child, Freud reversed the chain of causation. Now he was convinced that incestuous wishes or fantasies originated with the child and were directed towards the parent; it was the repression of these taboo desires that produced the later symptoms. Freud grouped the passions aroused by the family triangle − child, father and mother − as 'the Oedipus complex', the concept that he first described in *The Interpretation of Dreams* and called by that name in 1910. In *Three Essays on the Theory of Sexuality* in 1905, he expanded and explained his theories of infantile sexuality: he declared that very small children experienced sexual pleasure and excitation. In his view, the mouth was a sexual orifice like the anus; sucking, stroking and inserting objects were erotically stimulating actions. The publication of these novel concepts, according to Jones's biographical account, 'brought the maximum of odium on Freud's name'.

★　　★　　★

Psychoanalysis may have been an outgrowth of hypnotism, but it was its very opposite: intent listening to wide-awake patients who were invited to speak their uncensored thoughts – in effect, to make their unconscious conscious through the method Freud called 'free association'. As the patient spoke, the analyst sat unseen behind the couch, silent until offering interpretations. Freud's first couch was his only couch. A gift from an early, grateful patient, the couch, with its inviting cover of oriental rugs, moved with him in 1891 from Rathhausstrasse to Berggasse 19, where he would live for the next forty-seven years. In 1938 it followed him to London.

Free association and drawing out buried memories were not the whole procedure of analysis. Sometimes patients would not talk at all. Freud labelled as 'resistance' the silences, arguments, latenesses and missed appointments of his patients. He interpreted these as part of the treatment, as he did the 'transference' – the emotional bond that the patient formed with the analyst out of psychological experiences from the past. In time, the transference came to be seen as the main instrument in psychoanalytic treatment.

Thus was born, simultaneous with the new twentieth century, the theory that constituted an annihilating assault on the faith in reason of the eighteenth and nineteenth centuries. The *Oxford History of the Twentieth Century* describes psychoanalysis as 'the somewhat estranged offspring of German philosophy – Nietzsche's vision of the amoral Superman whose project of self-exploration took precedence over all social duties and institutions'.

Jung provided Jones with his first close look at a psychoanalyst – and no ordinary one. Freud had already decided on the tall Swiss doctor as his 'successor and crown prince', or, in some recollections, his 'son and heir'. Particularly pleasing to Freud was that Jung was a Christian. Freud was unhappy that his 'Cause' was predominantly in the hands of Jews. All his followers, and many of his patients, in Vienna were Jews like himself.

There was one other Freudian non-Jew at the Amsterdam conference. An Austrian doctor, Otto Gross, was registered as a delegate, as was his wife, Frieda. Gross was a striking figure: tall, with intense blue eyes and tousled blond hair. Freud, ignoring what he knew of Gross's erratic behaviour, considered him, along with Jung, the only truly original mind among his followers.

Gross, then thirty, had trained as a neurologist and psychiatrist in Graz, the capital of the south-eastern Austrian region of Styria. By 1900 he had become a follower of Freud and a practitioner of the new cathartic treatment. However, by the spring of 1906 Gross had travelled far in the direction of Nietzschean reverence for the animal instincts. His motto, taken from Nietzsche, was 'Repress nothing.' Transposed to psychoanalysis, this motto had alarming implications, as Jung learned in Amsterdam. He quickly sent word back to Vienna:

> Dr Gross tells me he puts a quick stop to the transference by turning people into sexual immoralists. He says the transference to the analyst and its persistent fixation are mere monogamy symbols and as such symptomatic of repression. The truly healthy state for the neurotic is sexual immorality. Hence he associates you with Nietzsche.

For Jung, this was a polite way of saying that Gross was sleeping with his patients – a temptation to which he himself, though a husband and father, was not immune. At that time Jung was fighting his own conscience (unsuccessfully, according to her diary) to avoid becoming the lover of his attractive, intelligent patient Sabina Spielrein.

For Ernest Jones, the Amsterdam conference was a respite from a demanding routine. Thanks to his complete acquittal of the Deptford charges, his London schedule was full. And in early October 1907 he was made pathologist and honorary registrar at another of the Victorian charitable institutions with a full descriptive name: The West End Hospital for Diseases of the Nervous System, Paralysis, and Epilepsy, With Special Wards for Paralysed Children. At 73 Welbeck Street, the hospital was not far from his Harley Street rooms, and if his position there was second-rate, at least it was at a neurological hospital.

A month later, subsidized by his wealthy mistress, Jones went to Munich and enrolled for a month's postgraduate course at Emil Kraepelin's internationally known centre for clinical research. Kraepelin, dean of the faculty of medicine at Ludwig-Maximilians University, was famous for his systematic classification of psychiatric disorders by the behaviour they manifested. His system – clumsy in the light of a later age, when the diagnosis of disordered behaviour remains difficult – was an attempt to shift psychiatry away from such meaningless catch-alls as 'hysteria' and 'neurasthenia' (defined as 'depression due to exhausted nerve-energy') and into classifications on the basis of prognosis. Kraepelin divided insanity into two classes: manic depression, from which recovery was possible, and *dementia praecox*, from which there was a steady irreversible deterioration.

His *Nervenklinik* offered psychiatry with a strong academic cast. The lectures, in German, that Jones attended included those of Alois Alzheimer on 'Normal and pathological anatomy of the cortex' and of Kraepelin himself on 'Clinical diagnosis and forensic analysis'.

Psychoanalysis was for after-hours. Jones was pleased to re-encounter Otto Gross. Gross and his wife had moved from Graz to Munich, and Jones found him installed at his favourite café in the lively bohemian district of Schwabing. Gross had published highly original work on the sexual drive, symbolism, the harmfulness of repression, and the psychological differences between male and female, and in Jones he found an eager listener. As Jones later wrote to Freud about his Kraepelin period of 1907, 'In that autumn I was in Munich and learnt there more from Gross than I ever learnt from Jung.'

Jones took his lessons by sitting in the Café Stephanie, where Gross received his mail and his patients. Some, after their analytic hour over a café table, paid in cash which was immediately turned into drugs: Gross was a morphine addict. He seemed never to go home, hardly ever changed his clothes, and talked all the time – even, if his portrait in D. H. Lawrence's novel *Mr Noon* is accurate, during sexual intercourse.

Gross had been Kraepelin's assistant in psychiatry at the *Nervenklinik*, until Kraepelin sacked him for erratic behaviour (such as waking patients in the middle of the night for examination) and for drug-taking. Having become an addict as a ship's doctor after leaving medical school, Gross had twice been a patient at the Burghölzli, in 1902 and 1904, and managed to steal a quantity of drugs before he left. The fact that his father, Hans Gross, was Austria's foremost criminologist saved him time after time. It may have been to escape this overbearing father that Gross had moved to Munich in 1907. Jones considered Gross his first instructor in psychoanalysis.

In Munich, Jones was well placed to learn a bit about Gross's intricate private life. In November 1907 Gross not only made pregnant his wife's good friend Elsa von Richthofen Jaffe, but also began an affair with Elsa's sister (also named Frieda). (As Frieda von Richthofen she had married a Nottingham professor, Ernest Weekley, but later divorced him to become Mrs D. H. Lawrence.) None of this flamboyance disillusioned Jones. He saw in Gross an extraordinary 'penetrative power of divining the inner thoughts and feelings of others', and more: 'the nearest approach to the romantic idea of a genius I have ever met'.

Before returning to London, Jones stopped in Zurich to see Jung again. The two met for lunch at Zurich's finest hotel, the Bauer au Lac, for what Jung hoped would be the prelude to 'many interesting talks'. It was, and these talks continued for some days. Visiting the Burghölzli, Jones was introduced to A. (for Abraham) A. Brill from New York. Brill, an Austrian turned American, had taken a medical degree from Columbia University in 1903, and had remained to practise psychiatry in Manhattan. In Brill, Jones instantly spotted a rival. He was delighted, therefore, when Brill started patronizingly to explain to him psycho-galvanism – an electrical technique designed by the Swiss neurologist Otto Veraguth – to measure changes in the electrical resistance of the body in normal and insane people in terms of variations in breathing rate, pulse and perspiration. Jung interrupted Brill – charmingly, it seemed to Jones – to say, 'We didn't invite Dr Jones here to teach him, but to consult him.'

Jones's visit prompted another bulletin from Jung to the Master in Vienna:

> Dr Jones of London, an extremely gifted and active young man, was with me for the last 5 days, chiefly to talk about your researches. Because of his 'splendid isolation' [Jung is here borrowing, as Freud had, the nineteenth-century phrase for Britain's foreign policy of distancing itself from Europe] in London he has not yet penetrated very deeply into your problems but is convinced of the theoretical necessity of your views. He will be a staunch supporter of our cause, for besides his intellectual gifts he is full of enthusiasm.

Novitiate though he was, Jones swiftly suggested what should be the Cause's next move: an international gathering of Freud's followers. As Jung had heard a similar, if less specific, proposal from two analysts from Budapest, Sándor Ferenczi and Fülöp Stein, he took the advice and set about planning the first international congress of psychoanalysts for the following spring.

Freud needed no persuading of the merits either of a convocation or of Jones. He had already perceived Jones's potential usefulness, and told Jung that 'Your Englishman appeals to me because of his nationality; I believe that once the English have become acquainted with our ideas they will never let them go.'

It is hardly surprising that Freud had no concept of Wales as a place distinct from England. From the start, however, he perceived that Jones had one incomparable advantage over Jung: he spoke better English. And the English-speaking world was where Freud wanted the Cause to be carried.

The Englishing of Freud had, in fact, begun even before James Jackson Putnam's article 'on the use of the Freud method' had appeared in the first issue of the *Journal of Abnormal Psychology*. In 1904 Freud's researches were called 'fascinating and really important' by the British sexologist Havelock Ellis in the first volume of his influential *Studies in the Psychology of Sex*.

Freud's ideas had reached Britain even earlier. In April 1893, at a meeting in London of the Society for Psychical Research, the poet and essayist F. W. H. Myers had summarized Freud's and Breuer's paper, 'On the Psychical Mechanism of Hysterical Phenomena', then published the paper in June in the SPR's *Proceedings*.

At the end of the nineteenth century, psychics and physicists saw themselves not as separated by an unbridgeable gulf between the real and the paranormal but rather as allied investigators. Among the founders of the SPR (which still exists) were sober nineteenth-century physicists such as J. J. Thomson and Oliver Lodge, who believed there must be some connection between electromagnetic waves and thought waves. The propagating medium (until Einstein's theory of relativity made the concept obsolete) was thought to be the ether, an elastic substance permeating all space and through which electromagnetic waves were carried. Telepathy – electrical thought-transference – was therefore plausible. Alexander Graham Bell even considered that his invention the telephone might be a way of communicating with the dead. So entwined were physics and psychology that an early issue of the *Journal of Abnormal Psychology* carried an abstract of a paper by a British woman, Mrs A. W. Verrall of the SPR, on the phenomenon of 'automatic writing', in which the hand appears to be guided by a spirit.

Jones had begun to make his contribution to the literature on cathartic treatment. His name is prominent on the cover of the *Journal of Abnormal Psychology*'s December 1907– January 1908 issue: 'Dr Ernest Jones, M.D., M.R.C.P. (London)', contributor of the article 'Mechanism of Severe Briquet [Panic] Attack as Contrasted with that of Psychasthenic Fits'. ('Psychasthenia' at that time was defined as 'neurasthenia with marked psychic symptoms'.) In a dramatic narrative style, Jones described his treatment of an eighteen-year-old sailor at the Seamen's Hospital, Greenwich.

The illness had begun when the young man, after a period of alienation from his mother, could not get leave to attend her last illness, nor even her funeral. When at last allowed to return home, the sailor sat up late talking to his father. He then slept, dreamed of his mother, and woke up just before five in the morning in order to catch an early train. Jones's paper continued:

At this time dawn was just breaking and objects were dimly visible through the mist. As he left the front door, on his way down the garden path, he caught sight of an apparition of his mother standing some yards away at the gate . . . He observed every feature of her dress, including a shawl he had given her, her rings, earrings, etc. She looked fixedly at him, a little reproachfully, but did not move. He was intensely frightened and turned to run into the house. In the act of turning everything 'went red', and he fell unconscious on his face.

He was found hours later.

Jones, examining the patient twice in hospital and finding him 'trembling, dizzy and in severe pain', recognized 'a case of major hysteria in the making'. If not treated, it might lead to paraplegia, blindness or a hysteric coma.

The treatment then described sounds like hypnotism. Jones asked the patient to lie down and close his eyes. 'The young man's limbs relaxed and he began to talk in a quiet monotone.' Jones listened, then offered suggestions as to what the young man might remember in the future, then woke him up. 'He now felt completely well, was quite composed and clear, with a perfect memory of the recent events, and had no headache.'

Back in London, Jones began 1908 by adding still one more part-time job to his list, once against working for the London County Council, which had not turned its back on him. He delivered (for £1 each) fortnightly evening lectures on First Aid and Home Nursing at the LCC's Camden Evening School. He also continued his duties at the West End Hospital for Diseases of the Nervous System.

At the end of March, however, an old trouble reappeared. Jones's superior at the hospital, Harry Campbell, told Jones about a ten-year-old girl with a seemingly paralysed arm. Campbell challenged him, in the light of his enthusiasm for Freud's theories, to discover whether there was a sexual basis to the paralysis. Jones found one. Interviewing the girl, Rebecca Levi, in an operating room with the door open, he learned that she had been in the habit of going to school early in order to play with an older boy; one day the boy had made sexual advances, and she pushed him away.

That the arm subsequently went numb and weak was what Jones wanted to hear. What followed was not. Rebecca told other children on the ward that the doctor had been talking about sex with her. One of the parents learned of it, and notified the hospital authorities. The complaint was similar to (if, in the reported circumstances, far less grave than) the accusations made against Jones at the Edward Street School in Deptford two years earlier. But the consequence was worse.

In his autobiography, Jones's explanation for what happened appears straightforward. He had interviewed the girl in full view of nurses moving in and out of the room. But, at very least, he once again seems to have courted danger.

In the moral climate of the times, sex was a taboo subject. The body was a dark secret from which women and children had to be protected. Women's bodies were hidden from public view: their voluminous outdoor dress was the weight of three turkeys. A glimpse of stocking was something shocking. There had been no women's public lavatories until 1900. Brides were expected to approach their wedding night in a state of obedient apprehension. All children were presumed innocent even of curiosity about sex.

While Jones, after his liberating time in Munich, may have blinded himself to the reality of Edwardian Britain, when writing his autobiography fifty years later he also concealed the critical and damning fact that this incident in early March 1908 was his second offence at the West End Hospital. The hospital's chairman was in no doubt about this when he sent a curt, if well-phrased, letter on 23 March 1908:

> It has come to my knowledge that twice recently you have examined female patients in this Hospital without the presence of any third person in the room, and I am also informed that you had previously been told by the Matron that such procedure was contrary to the rule of this Hospital as well as of others.
>
> It is the fact that, after your examination of Rebecca Levi, the child asserted that certain questions had been asked her by you, which may have been misunderstood by your patient but which may form the basis for the subsequent investigation of a painful character.
>
> I must ask you therefore to discontinue from this date and for the present your visits to the Hospital, both for your own sake and for that of the Institution which I know you are anxious to serve.
> Yours faithfully
> Ian Malcolm.
> Chairman

There followed a meeting of the hospital committee, some members of which, if not all, must have been aware of the well-publicized charges against Jones two years earlier. In any event, the committee – which included the matron and a clergyman – were not well disposed towards Jones, for the girl in question was not his own patient, nor that of

Campbell, but rather was in the care of a Dr Savill. Four days later the chairman sent Jones a second letter:

> We have come to the conclusion that it will be in the best interest of this Hospital and of its staff that you should be asked to tender your resignation, and we therefore invite you to tender the same at your earliest convenience.

Jones's London career was finished. No one would hire him now.

Hope lay in the New World. He would not be the first to flee disgrace by crossing the Atlantic. Hearing that a Canadian professor of psychiatry and medical superintendent of the Toronto Hospital for the Insane was in Britain recruiting a director for a projected new clinic, Jones was quick off the mark. He took himself to call on the famed Canadian physician Sir William Osler, just made Regius Professor of Medicine at Oxford. The meeting was a success. Osler liked Jones and admired his credentials – so much so that he wrote, not once but twice, to the visiting Canadian, Dr Charles Clarke. The province of Ontario, Osler declared, would overlook 'a great opportunity if it did not avail itself of the services of this young man'.

Impressed, Clarke made an offer. It would be two years before he would set up a new psychiatric clinic in Toronto, he conceded, and there was no immediate prospect of a university appointment, but he could take on Jones to work on 'hysterical cases' at his asylum.

One door closed, another opened. The difficulty was that Loe Kann did not want to go. She had no inclination to leave her family or to transfer her social life and her health problems to Canada. It is a measure of the close attachment between the two in this largely unrecorded relationship that she finally said yes and agreed to accompany Jones to Toronto.

In April 1908, a month after the West End Hospital dismissal, the Swansea Valley met Austro-Hungary at last. It was at the Hotel Bristol in Salzburg at what was called the *Zusammenkunft für Freudsche Psychologie*, or 'Meeting for Freudian Psychology' (and turned out to be the first international congress of psychoanalysis). Forty-two of the world's few Freudians gathered for the first time with their founding father, then just short of fifty-two.

Jones liked what he saw: a well-shaped head; thick, dark, well-groomed hair with only a slight touch of grey; a handsome moustache and a full pointed beard. Conscious of height, Jones saw that Freud, at about five feet eight inches, was somewhat taller than himself.

Freud noticed Jones's head too. From its shape, he said (craniology was much in vogue) he deduced that Jones could not be English and must be Welsh. Jones was surprised, as he knew that Wales was virtually unheard of on the Continent. (Only later did he learn that Jung had already informed Freud that he was a Celt.) Freud spoke to him in German, slowly and clearly, and said, in Jones's recollection, 'What we most need is a book on dreams in English; won't you write one?'

The conference was a historic occasion: the first international public recognition of Freud's work, and the gathering of such later well-known names as Alfred Adler (from Vienna), Karl Abraham (from Berlin) and Sándor Ferenczi (from Budapest). Freud, conscious that he was emerging from his isolation, took a lot of care with the arrangements. He had overruled Jung, who had favoured Innsbruck. Salzburg was 'by far the more beautiful', Freud said, and promised that the Hotel Bristol would provide comfortable lodging and excellent fare.

The Salzburg conference was significant also for exposing the first signs of rivalry between the Viennese and the Swiss. Of the nearly four dozen participants from six countries, the majority were Viennese. Jones was accorded second place on the programme, at Freud's suggestion: he had told Jung they needed a foreigner in that prominent spot, otherwise 'my talkative Viennese' would drown the rest with their torrent of words. Jones's prominence was not inappropriate, as he was the author of many academic papers.

Speaking in English, Jones presented a paper on rationalization. He had not coined the term – the *Oxford English Dictionary* records the year of its first use as 1846 – but he was one of the first to use it in its contemporary meaning: 'an explanation, but a false one'. He delivered the paper with much tribute to Professor Freud's theory that 'human behaviour is driven by desires of which people are largely unaware': 'No one will admit that he ever deliberately performed an irrational act, and any act that might appear so is immediately justified by distorting the mental processes concerned and providing a false explanation that has a plausible ring of rationality.' His Salzburg audience cannot have appreciated how well this description fitted Jones himself.

Jones had a hard act to follow. His audience was still reeling from Freud's opening presentation of a case that would become known as 'the Rat Man'. Speaking without notes and in a conversational voice, Freud described his treatment of a Viennese lawyer, still in analysis, who had become obsessed with rats after hearing of an oriental punishment in which the victim had had clamped to his buttocks a pot of starving rats trying to eat their way out. Freud had begun at eight in the morning. When at eleven he suggested he should stop, his audience begged him to continue, which he did until nearly one o'clock. At the end, Otto Gross rose and enthusiastically compared Freud to Nietzsche, declaring him a scientific revolutionary and destroyer of old prejudices. Freud icily refused the compliment. 'We are doctors,' he declared, 'and doctors we intend to remain.'

One man in the audience who certainly intended to remain a doctor was Jones's friend Wilfred Trotter. Trotter sat through part of the Salzburg conference unimpressed, and apparently unbothered by the similarity of Jones's ideas of rationalization to those he himself would publish that same year on the herd instinct. Trotter had heard all he wanted to hear about psychoanalysis, and left early, apparently without listening to Freud. He and Jones followed different professional directions from then on.

One practical outcome of the first meeting was the decision to issue what Freud very much wanted – a periodical, the *Jahrbuch für psychoanalytische und psychopathologische Forschungen*, to which Freud would have free access for his publications. Jung was named editor.

From Salzburg, Jones and Brill at the beginning of May went to Vienna, where Freud received them. It was Jones's first sight of the city where Freud had lived since the age of four. Freud, born in Moravia (now the Czech Republic), had been brought to Vienna by his parents, escaping Czech nationalist resentment against Jews and Jewish textile merchants, of whom Freud's father was one.

Invited to lunch, Jones and Brill met Freud's German wife, Martha, and their youngest child, Anna. Freud gave the bilingual Brill the rights to translate his writings into English; the three men together struggled with what was to become a chronic problem: how to render into English the German technical terms that Freud had coined. Freud himself decided that *Verdrängung* would become 'repression'.

Freud invited the visitors to attend the weekly Wednesday meeting of what was to become the Vienna Psychoanalytic Society. Jones did not think much of the assembly: Adler, Fritz Wittels, Isidor Sadger, Maxim Steiner, Eduard Hitschmann and Wilhelm Stekel. (He later liberally dispensed derogatory adjectives such as 'morose, pathetic' (Sadger) and 'sulky, pathetically eager for recognition' (Adler)).

Jones and Freud had more in common than was apparent to either. Freud too was a Darwinist and a clinical neurologist with experience of brain anatomy and children's paralysis. He, like Jones, had been thwarted in the progress of his medical career, although his own frustrations derived in no small part from the fact of being Jewish in anti-Semitic Vienna. He had not been given the title of 'Professor' until 1902, long after his contemporaries had proposed it, and the book he thought would make his name – *The Interpretation of Dreams* – had not received the attention he expected.

While Jones was in Vienna, Freud wrote to Abraham in Berlin, forcefully spelling out his fears about Jewish domination of psychoanalysis. Having suffered from anti-Semitism, Freud was extremely concerned that psychoanalysis would be tainted by its Semitic associations. Having witnessed Abraham at Salzburg disagreeing with Jung on the nature of schizophrenia, Freud asked him to try to remain friendly with Jung, as he did not want any bad feeling among his followers: 'We are still so few.' He continued:

> It is easier for you than it is for Jung to follow my ideas, for in the first place you are completely independent, and then you are closer to my intellectual constitution because of racial kinship, while he, as a Christian and a pastor's son, found his way to me only against great inner resistances. His association with us is the more valuable for that. I nearly said that it was only by his appearance on the scene that psychoanalysis escaped the danger of becoming a Jewish national affair.

Whether Jones realized it or not, from that moment on he was Jung's understudy as Freud's Gentile.

On the same day, 3 May (the number of letters these analysts were able to write after a long day listening to patients is astonishing), Freud composed a letter to Jung, addressing the 'rift . . . in the making between you and Abraham'. He also addressed the Jones problem:

> Jones is undoubtedly a very interesting and worthy man, but he gives me a feeling of, I was almost going to say racial strangeness. He is a fanatic and doesn't eat enough. 'Let me have men about me that are fat,' says Caesar, etc. He almost reminds me of the lean and hungry Cassius. He denies all heredity; to his mind even I am a reactionary. How, with your moderation, were you able to get on with him?

Accompanied by Brill, Jones went on to Budapest. Ferenczi's hospitality and the warmth of the city moved him, especially as he was smarting from his rejection by London. He returned to Munich by mid-May. He wanted to work once more with Kraepelin, recognizing that Kraepelin's clinic and methods were what the Canadians wanted to replicate in Toronto. As he told Freud, 'It will be very important for me in Canada for they think the world of Kraepelin.' His thank-you letter for Freud's hospitality, written from Munich on 13 May, was the beginning of a long and revealing (on both sides) correspondence that would yield 671 surviving letters in all and continue to the end of Freud's life.

Jones in fact also had another motive for returning to Munich. Much of his first letter to Freud concerned the wife of Otto Gross. Frieda Gross, although no psychoanalyst, had attended the Salzburg conference, as she had that of the previous year in Amsterdam, and was once more listed among the main participants. At the Salzburg meeting or shortly afterwards, Gross asked Jones, whom he now recognized as a practising psychoanalyst and someone who was going to be in Munich for a period, to take her into analysis. Jones, to judge from his letter, had discussed the possibility with Freud during his visit to Vienna and said he was reluctant because of the patent instability of both husband and wife. However, Gross was obsessed with the idea, and Jones feared an outright refusal would destabilize him further.

The matter was not so private as to stop Freud from immediately reporting it to Jung:

> Jones wants to go to Munich to help the Grosses. The little woman seems to be seriously smitten with him. He should not accede to Gross's insistence that he treat his wife, but try to gain influence over him. It looks as if this were going to end badly.

Continuing the story by letter, Jones relayed to Freud the information that Frieda Gross was 'deeply in love with another man' but was concealing it from Gross as the two men disliked each other. Ordinarily, Jones told Freud:

> Gross gets great delight in getting other men to love her – no doubt a perverse paranoiac development of his free love ideas. This she doesn't like, as she says it is her own business; in addition she has been very jealous about his relations with other women. All this I know you will treat as strictly private, but I thought you ought to know it. I should be grateful for any advice you may have time to send me.

'Little woman' was not fair to Frieda Gross. She was a sophisticated, intelligent, calm beauty. Freud himself found her attractive, and praised her to Jung as 'one of the few Teutonic women I have ever liked'.

In May 1908 she was alone in Munich. Gross had broken down again, and she had taken him to Zurich to be committed to the Burghölzli under Jung's care. Freud was on the case, and sent some sort of certificate, telling

Jung, 'Once you have him, don't let him out before October when I shall be able to take charge of him.'

That left Frieda Gross free for what, from Jones's words, sounds like an idyllic month in Munich. In his memoirs, he made oblique reference to this period, saying, 'I began to understand why Germany was the land of youth, of romanticism, of wine, women and song.'

However, the idyll was short-lived. On an unattended stroll around the gardens of the Burghölzli on the afternoon of 17 June, Gross leaped over the wall and returned to Munich (having sent a telegram to Jung asking for money to pay his hotel bill). Jones, seeing him, found him back on cocaine and much worse – 'quite paranoiac'. Gross wanted to start a lawsuit against Kraepelin to expose his ignorance of psychoanalysis to the world.

In his veiled memoirs, in another reference to that early summer in Munich in 1908, Jones wrote, 'I never was in a town with such unattractive females, though fortunately there were a few foreigners there; with one, a lady from Styria, I left a little volume of poems after my stay in Munich, appropriately inscribed: "And May and June." ' Only he and the lady from Styria knew what the arch inscription meant.

Exactly when Jones committed himself wholeheartedly to psychoanalysis is a matter of some debate. A Scottish psychiatrist, Charles Macfie Campbell, himself thinking of relocating to New York, met Jones in Munich and reported to the distinguished American psychiatrist Adolf Meyer, in Baltimore, that Jones was 'quite up to date in psychiatry, is very hot on psychoanalysis and is going out to Toronto to see if he can work out there'.

Where was Jones's 'wife', Loe Kann, during this drama? Not in Munich, it would seem. Jones, sitting in the Café Stephanie, showed one of her letters to the philosopher Ludwig Klages, who prided himself on being an expert at character analysis from handwriting. Klages took a look at the generous flowing script and said, 'Between ourselves, I find her very attractive.' Jones replied confidently, 'Between ourselves, she is my sweetheart.'

In the late summer of 1908, after brief trips to Zurich and London, Jones took himself to Paris to work at the Bicêtre Hospital with Professor Pierre Marie, a pupil of Charcot. It was an intensive six weeks and, continuing his neurological researches on partial paralysis, hemiplegia and tongue deviations, he felt he learned a lot.

His mistress seems to have been with him (according to a later remark to the psychiatrist Michael Balint), and she seems to have enjoyed the city more than he did. Despite rooms in the Latin Quarter, he felt his heart was still in Bavaria. He joined the German club and made a brief trip to the Rhine (to quote his autobiography again) 'to meet a friend from Munich'.

It could have been during this stay that Loe Kann underwent what Jones referred to as 'the Paris operation'. Several years later, describing to Freud how he and Loe were trying to iron out their relationship, Jones wrote:

> We had a good talk, and she brought this to the subject of our child. She insisted with the greatest vehemence (and quite unnecessarily, for I did not contradict her) that she had never resented its loss, or reproached me in any way about it . . . I have never told her of the tooth scene where she repeated in French the Paris operation, and I don't suppose she remembers this, as it was under chloroform that it happened.

Miscarriage? Abortion? All that is certain is that a pregnancy in 1908 would certainly have impeded their progress to Ontario.

Loe's medical problems were constant. Having suffered from kidney stones, she took doses of morphine twice a day to control the pain. An embarrassment to any medical man, her addiction was a constant worry to Jones, as was her obstinacy. He could not even get her to reduce her dose.

Meanwhile, Freud and Jung were worrying about Jones. In July, Jung confessed to Freud, 'Jones is an enigma to me. He is so incomprehensible that it's quite uncanny. Is there more in him than meets the eye, or nothing at all? At any rate he is far from simple; an intellectual liar (no moral judgment intended!) hammered by the vicissitudes of fate and circumstance into many facets. But the result? Too much adulation on one side, too much opportunism on the other?' Freud, after apologizing to Jung for the heavy burden Gross had placed on him, admitted he too was puzzled about Jones, but 'I tend to think he lies to the others, not to us.'

It was then that Freud unleashed his racial remark: 'I find the racial mixture in our group most interesting; he is a Celt and consequently not quite accessible to us, the Teuton and the Mediterranean man.'

Jones's plans to move to Toronto with Loe Kann went ahead. Jones's family in Gowerton had accepted Ernest's word that he and Loe were married. If none of them had been present at the wedding, theirs was not the only family to ask no questions about a marriage alleged to have been performed somewhere out of their sight. Loe had visited them in Gowerton, and they liked her very much – so much, indeed, that both Jones sisters decided to go to Canada and join the new household.

Back from Paris, Jones paid a hurried visit to Wales, then he and his younger sister, Sybil, headed for Liverpool to sail on the *Empress of Britain* on 28 August. The plan was that Loe would follow on a separate ship with Elizabeth ('Bessie'). Thomas Jones went to see his children off, but Mary Ann Jones could not face the ordeal of parting. She wrote instead:

> August 26 1908
> My darling Ernest,
>
> Just a few lines to wish you good [*sic*] speed & bon voyage, with the hope that you are feeling quite brave & fit to face the new life & the fresh start. Have no regrets, darling boy, for they will not help you & so hindrances must be set aside with a firm will . . .
>
> I am very delighted that there is such good news of Loe. It has cheered us immensely, for we were troubled to think that perhaps after all, she would not be able to go away, but now we hope that she will soon be fit. She has been so good & is such a strength to you, that I dare not think of her not being able to join you. It was a wise arrangement to leave Bessie with her, they understand each other so well & you will not be so anxious as if Loe was going alone & they will look after each other. We fully appreciate Loe's goodness of heart & I hope she will have all the loving care possible & that all will go well with her in the future, as a reward . . .
>
> With every good wish for a good voyage & good opportunities for your work at the new place & a blessing for my precious boy whom I have loved & loved & shall love to the end. Hug Sybil & kiss her for me & Father will bring you one each from
>
> Mother.

Did Jones's analytic eye spot the anxious foreboding in the maternal phrase '& shall love to the end'? Probably not. Full of anticipation, crossing the Atlantic for the first time, he stepped on to a continent where, outside a few small academic circles, the name of Freud had scarcely been uttered. Virgin territory was just what he needed.

6

Hamlet in Toronto
September 1908–1910

R EACHING TORONTO IN September 1908, Jones felt very far from Europe. Hotel staff were rude, 'London' meant London, Ontario, and he found a large group of English longing for home. He had to pass medical examinations all over again, because British and Canadian qualifications were not interchangeable. Even so, he was in an Anglophile culture where his degrees from the University of London stood him in good stead. His first letter to Freud was positive: 'Here I am landed in my new country which I like very much so far.'

He prepared to take up the interim work Dr Charles Clarke offered until the projected neurological clinic was ready. One post was as pathologist and neurologist at the Ontario Asylum for the Insane, in Toronto, for which he was to get $600 a year. As the Ontario government's permission was required for this position, Clarke wrote glowingly to the Hon. W. J. Hanna the provincial secretary: Ernest Jones was 'young, quiet, unobtrusive and a devoted student', and bore a sheaf of recommendations from distinguished people such as Sir William Osler. Indeed, Clarke told Hanna (echoing Osler), 'The Government would overlook a great opportunity' if it did not avail itself of the services of this young man, who possessed special qualifications which no other man in Canada had. Clarke assured Hanna that Jones's presence would prove an inspiration to the other assistants; his experience was 'just what was required, as he was specially strong in the newer developments on the psychological side of medicine, and it was in that particular our people are so deficient'. In short, Toronto's acquisition of someone in touch with latest developments in psychiatry in Munich, Zurich and Vienna was almost too good to be true.

Clarke advised Jones to pay a courtesy call on the provincial secretary. Jones put on his Harley Street top hat and presented himself at the Parliament Buildings in Toronto, only to find the august figure in his shirtsleeves with his feet on the desk.

As in London, he collected a clutch of appointments. They included the junior academic post of 'demonstrator' in anatomy and physiology at the University of Toronto, and he contributed to the *Bulletin of the Ontario Hospitals for the Insane*. He also reviewed and abstracted articles for six neurological journals abroad. He became director of Canada's first out-patient psychiatric clinic – a modest two-storey clapboard dwelling with veranda, which could have passed for a boarding house. The cases were not boring, especially that of an unhappy wife who saw Holy Communion as a form of oral sex.

His domestic arrangements took some organizing. In early December he boasted to Freud, 'I am at present busy house hunting for my harem, which consists of a wife, two sisters and two servants.' The harem was eventually installed in a house at 407 Brunswick Avenue, and printed cards were dispatched: 'Dr Ernest Jones (late of London, England) begs to inform the profession that he has established himself at the above address and that he confines his practice exclusively to nervous diseases.' Psychoanalysis was not mentioned.

As Jones settled in, he realized that his first impressions had been misleading. He did not like the place. Freud, who had inquired about life in Canada, received a savage pen-portrait:

> Music is rare here, and there is not a picture gallery in the country. The people are 19 parts American, and one part Colonial ... They are a despicable race, exceedingly bourgeois, quite uncultured, very rude, very stupid and very narrow and pious. They are naive, childish and hold the simplest views of the problems of life. They care for nothing except money-making and sport, they chew gum instead of smoking or drinking, and their public meetings are monuments of sentimental platitudes. They are horror-struck with me because I don't know the date of the King's birthday, for they take their loyalty like everything else in dead seriousness and have no sense of humour.

His own speciality was equally neglected. No neurology was taught, 'for there is no one who even pretends to know anything about it'. As for hysteria, it was regarded as 'a discreditable form of imitating diseases'. Treatment consisted of telling the patients to snap out of it, that 'they have been found out'. Jones made it a point every month to travel eight hours each way to attend the meetings of the Detroit Neurological Society, as there was no such society in Canada.

In fact Canada was not quite the cultural desert he portrayed. The University of Toronto library was rich with books and journals in many languages, and Jones helped to reorganize its medical section. If he wanted to read *Geschichte der öffentlichen Sittlichkeit in Russland*, he could. In his spare hours he began writing the first of the dozens of papers he would see published during his four and a half years in Canada.

He was still very much a neurologist. His scientific articles of that time included 'The Pathology of Dyschiria' (loss of the power to tell which side of the body has been touched), 'Cerebrospinal Fluid in Relation to the Diagnosis of Metasyphilis of the Nervous System', and five papers on general paralysis. None of these disturbed his acceptance of Freud's discovery that human behaviour is driven by desires of which people are largely unaware.

Correspondence with Freud took high priority. Jones was humbly grateful that Freud wrote him so many letters. At the start Freud wrote in German, and Jones needed Loe Kann's help to translate his Gothic script. But soon Freud chose to write in English, and he continued to do so unless he was very busy. He also began to use, and Jones followed, the handy abbreviation ΨA or ψα – the Greek upper- or lower-case letters psi and alpha – for the cumbersome six syllables of 'psychoanalysis'.

After Christmas 1908, Jones made his way to Boston, the leading centre in the United States for the study and treatment of psychopathology. He stayed at the Beacon Street home of Morton Prince, founder and editor of the *Journal of Abnormal Psychology*. Prince, a Harvard-trained neurologist (and the son of a former mayor of Boston) was famous for his study of a case of multiple personality. A dramatization of this account of a young woman called Sally Beauchamp, who felt inhabited by several selves ('Miss Beauchamp', 'Chris' and 'the Idiot'), drew capacity crowds on Broadway.

Prince was at the heart of what was considered the Boston school of psychology – a small circle drawn from Harvard and the great teaching hospitals of the area. Its most notable member was the eminent Harvard philosopher William James (brother of Henry), whose *The Principles of Psychology* in 1890 valued human experience higher than logic. In the first decade of the twentieth century, the boundaries between psychology, philosophy and neurology remained to be drawn, as also did those between the natural world and the paranormal. James, as well as Prince, James Jackson Putnam and Josiah Royce, another eminent Harvard philosopher, all belonged to the American Society for Psychical Research – as did Jung: in 1907 the American SPR had made him an honorary fellow for 'services as an occultist'. Jung told Freud he had been 'dabbling in spookery again'.

Two decades after Krafft-Ebing's *Psychopathia Sexualis* had raised questions about the association of sexual aberrations and heredity, sexuality was an accepted subject of study. The old moral code was collapsing under the weight of its own unreality and the onrush of Darwinism. The existing rules – sex only within marriage and only for procreation – were unworkable and widely disregarded apart from rare men like ex-President Theodore Roosevelt, who had saved himself for marriage and was completely monogamous thereafter. A scientific investigation of the human animal was called for – collecting evidence, as Darwin had done, and drawing conclusions based on observation, description and induction.

Experiments in psychology were being performed at Clark University, a new, small and adventurous institution in Worcester, fifty miles from Boston. In 1904 Clark's president, G. (for Granville) Stanley Hall, produced a monumental treatise, *Adolescence*, in which he called attention to the crucial importance in a child's development of the years from eight to twelve. In his book, Hall paid tribute to Freud's writings in 1892 and with Breuer in 1895 about the importance of early sexual traumas.

The message of evolution, Hall argued, was progress. With evidence all around – plumbing, electric light, the motor car, the telephone – who could disagree? In this context the Boston psychologists were concerned to find new methods of treatment for disorders of the mind and personality. Mental breakdown, depression, alcoholism and related miseries were as widespread as they ever had been, yet there was hope that new forms of treatment in traditional sanatoriums and spas might bring relief (to families, if not to patients).

Advertisements in the *Journal of Abnormal Psychology* carried pictures of large Queen Anne houses renovated as care homes 'for Nervous People'. The Riverlawn Sanatorium 'For Nervous and Mild Mental Cases' in Paterson, New Jersey, offered 'two beautiful modern buildings . . . facing the picturesque waters of the Passaic', and promised (ominously) 'all approved forms of treatment used, including baths, massage and electricity'. The Dr C. O. Sahler Sanitarium in Kingston-on-Hudson, New York, suggested that 'Physicians and friends who have mental and nervous patients whom they desire to place in an institution having the principles of home and family life, non-restraint, and having tried all other methods of treatment without success, should inquire into the merits of this Sanitarium.' The advertisement added, '*No Insane Cases Received*'.

Jones was invited to Harvard as a representative of the avant-garde. Prince himself was wary of Freud. Freud had refused an invitation to contribute to the first issue of the *Journal of Abnormal Psychology* in 1906, and Prince had failed to turn up as expected at the Salzburg conference on psychoanalysis in 1908. Jones, in contrast, had heard Freud and had given a paper himself at Salzburg, and had gone on to meet Freud at his home in Vienna. He understood Freud's theories, and had, moreover, already contributed to the *Journal of Abnormal Psychology*. He felt that Freud would be happy if he were to proselytize by explaining Freud's theories in Prince's journal. Freud agreed: 'It might be the best way to introduce my teaching to your countrymen.'

Prince was an avuncular host, and saw to it that Jones met the right people. At one seminar at Harvard organized for Jones to expound Freud's theories, sixteen men turned up. Unfortunately, William James (then sixty-six) was unable to come. The discussion went on for four hours. Prince himself was very critical of Freud's narrow definition of the unconscious: to Prince, the phenomenon of inaccessible ideas could be explained by physiological changes in the cortex. Nor was Prince convinced of the accuracy of Freud's theory of the origin of neurosis. Prince's own view was that mental collapse was caused by a traumatic event – 'Psychical Shock', as he called it. How could Freud have overlooked it? he asked Jones.

As an illustration of psychical shock, Hugo Münsterberg, head of the Harvard Psychological Laboratory, described a case of hysterical vomiting supposedly induced by swallowing a hot potato. Jones, with European facetiousness, commented that 'we [presumably the sophisticated psychiatrists of London, Zurich and Vienna] did not regard the swallowing of hot potatoes as the kind of factor that was important in the pathogenesis of the psychoneuroses.' He drew a laugh.

This small Harvard group seemed to Jones the only people in America who were at all interested in psychotherapy, yet not one of them, he was shocked to learn, had read the still untranslated *Die Traumdeutung*, Freud's masterwork. Boris Sidis, associate editor of the *Journal of Abnormal Psychology*, told him he was 'going to'.

The most impressive person Jones met during his visit was James Jackson Putnam of the Massachusetts General Hospital and Harvard Medical School. Putnam, an elderly Bostonian of good family – his wife was a Cabot, and her father, his namesake (James Jackson), was one of the founders of Massachusetts General Hospital – was remarkably forward-looking and widely travelled in Europe. It was he who had invited Pierre Janet, the French neurologist and professor at the Collège de France, to open new buildings at the Harvard Medical School in 1906. Janet's Harvard lectures were dedicated to Putnam, and were published in 1907 as *The Major Symptoms of Hysteria*.

In the distinguished older medical man, Jones recognized a challenge. Jones appreciated that Putnam's article in the *Journal of Abnormal Psychology* in 1906 was the first explanation in English of Freud's method, but he also saw that it was on balance critical of psychoanalysis. Having tried Freud's techniques at his hospital, Putnam had concluded that Freud's claims were stimulating but exaggerated. The cathartic technique did not seem to Putnam to be as universally applicable as Freud maintained, and he was unhappy about the transference (although he did not use that term): 'It is an unfortunate feature of the Freud analytic method, as he [Freud] himself points out, that it makes necessary, as a result, the establishment of a relation of dependence of the patient upon the physician which it may, in the end, be difficult to get rid of.'

Meeting Jones, Putnam was taken aback. He had been expecting a tall man with a grey beard, but found himself facing a small, bright-eyed, 29-year-old Welshman. But he was deferential all the same to the man who had seen Freud face to face, and who had mastered the new literature on medical psychology. Jones, writing in retrospect, could only agree: 'I think his real interest in it in a positive sense dated from meeting me, Dec. 1908 – when he was 62!'

Back in Toronto, Jones poured out papers, mainly on neurological subjects. He explained to Freud that, considering the prevailing prudishness, he did not wish to be known as a sexual obsessive:

> A man who writes always on the same thing is apt to be regarded here as a crank, because to the superficial American every subject is easily exhausted except for cranks, and if the subject is sexual he is simply tabooed as a sexual neurasthenic. Hence I shall dilute my sex articles with articles on other subjects alternately.

In the next breath he disparaged the quality of American psychiatry and also of his New York colleague A. A. Brill. Brill, he said, was clever with patients but not 'a good scientific exponent'.

Shortly afterwards Prince tried to get Jones to tone down the sexual element in a paper for the *Journal of Abnormal Psychology*. The *Journal*, he wrote, had 'a large lay circulation of both sexes, and there is great danger of our losing our circulation if we shock unsympathetic readers'. He warned Jones himself to be wary: 'You are just starting in a new country. You may and probably will have opportunities offered you in the way of a professional chair in some one of our universities. I have something in mind for you myself.' Even if Jones's Freudian theory eventually became established, 'you will nevertheless not escape calumny. People resent theories which are distasteful even if true, and take it out on the author.' Jones could make his points 'without going into physiological details'.

Jones was not surprised. Freud had already relayed to him that Prince had told Karl Abraham he could not accept the term 'homosexual', because he had so many lay readers. Words such as 'anus' and 'penis' were not what readers of the *Journal of Abnormal Psychology* wanted thrust before their eyes.

Nervousness about sexuality was hardly confined to the United States and Canada. In Dublin in 1907, on the opening night of J. M. Synge's *Playboy of the Western World*, the mention of the word 'shifts', referring to female undergarments, caused the audience to stamp their feet, sing patriotic songs, and shout 'Kill the author!' The performance had to be abandoned in the second act. 'Shifts' had the same connotation as 'knickers', and was not to be uttered on a public stage.

Prurience was one thing; living in sin was another. Jones kept quiet about the fact that the 'wife' who accompanied him on some of his trips was not his wife. In one of his letters to Putnam, Jones wrote, 'My wife sends her kind regards, in which I heartily join.'

Back in the Old World, the king and crown prince of psychoanalysis saw Jones as an enigma. Was he on the side of psychoanalysis or on that of Kraepelin and clinical psychiatry? When Jones had been in Munich, Jung had feared that he was going to defect to Kraepelin. Freud, for his part, as much as he saw how he profited from Jones's diplomatic skills, disliked the way Jones disparaged Brill. Freud was impatient for Brill to bring out some of his writings in English translation, and rivalry between Jones and Brill could delay their appearance. He told Brill, 'I think [Jones] has an inborn tendency to intrigue and crooked diplomatic means which he playfully yields to'. And both Freud and Jung were aware of Jones's dalliance with Frieda Gross. Exchanging views of Jones's character, Jung replied:

> In any case he is a canny fellow. I don't understand him too well . . . He displays great affection not only for me but also for my family. To be sure, he is very nervous about the emphasis placed on sexuality in our propaganda, a point that plays a big role in our relations with Brill. By nature he is not a prophet, nor a herald of the truth, but a compromiser with occasional bendings of conscience that can put off his friends. Whether he is any worse than that I don't know but hardly think so, though the interior of Africa is better known to me than his sexuality.

There was nothing equivocal about the endorsement Jones gave to psychoanalysis in New Haven in May 1909 at a congress of the American Therapeutic Society. It was a gathering to explain the new Freudian treatment to general physicians. Jones presented analysis as a new method as radical as surgery for treating neuroses. He felt a shiver go through the audience when he said that Freud had sometimes treated a patient daily for as long as three years.

Putnam was there too. Showing how completely Jones had converted him, he said that Freud had shown how 'mental twists and habits' acquired in childhood could assert themselves in the adult character 'strangely altered and concealed'. He called for a change in the moral code, declaring that neurosis, psychosis and much misery were caused by 'the eternal, the fierce yet often needless conflict between natural instincts and an artificial social organization'.

In the late spring of 1909 Jones learned that his mother was dying. From Wales his father cabled the news of a cerebral haemorrhage, and asked whether one of his daughters could come home to help out. Sybil, the younger, obliged. (Jones had told Freud that he had never, until they came to Canada, been able to live with Sybil without quarrelling.) Mary Ann Jones died in Gowerton without ever seeing her 'darling boy' again. Nor he her. His mother's death may have helped steer Jones into the new dependent, adoring relation he was about to form with Freud.

By August Jones was free enough of his commitments in Toronto to recross the Atlantic, to attend the Sixth International Congress of Psychology in Geneva. From the Grand Hôtel de la Métropole, he wrote to Freud, 'Greetings from the right side of the Atlantic!' The paper he delivered at the conference – 'The Differences between the Sexes in the Development of Speech' – shows that, whatever else Jones had been thinking of on that troubled March afternoon in 1906 at the Edward Street School in Deptford, his interest in children's speech patterns was genuine.

How much this new life with its constant travel may have been financed by his wealthy mistress is unknown. It must be said, however, that of Jones's many chronicled personal failings – sexual licence, deviousness, arrogance, autocracy – miserliness was never one. He was not a Scrooge. He worked hard, liked earning money, and, when he had it, was generous with it. However, he considered himself married, and accepted that his 'wife' would keep herself in the style to which she was accustomed.

Certainly their two servants were hers. Probably Loe also bore the costs of their transatlantic travel. During the years that Jones was in Canada, he crossed to 'the right side of the Atlantic' every summer, usually to attend congresses, Loe undoubtedly accompanying him. She had a fear of being left alone, and was unlikely to forgo the opportunity to visit her family and get away from Canada.

'What am I to say to those people?' Freud asked Jung in June 1909.

'Those people' were the Americans who would attend the twentieth-anniversary celebrations of Clark University in Worcester, Massachusetts, in September. Jung and Freud, and Ferenczi too, had accepted invitations to attend and receive honorary doctorates of law. Freud, who had never been to America, thought it might be fun. At fifty-three, he felt despised in Europe, and now America was welcoming him. He was unconcerned that the tiny provincial institution, founded in 1889, was scarcely known.

The Clark conference was the decisive event for psychoanalysis in the United States. It brought Freud's ideas into the popular as well as the academic consciousness. Yet at the same time it left him with an undying loathing of America, with 'such a shifting variety of reasons', as the psychoanalytic historian Paul Roazen has written, 'that one can be certain only of the existence of the antipathy'. These reasons included over-rich American food, lack of public toilets, equality of the sexes, the fast pace of life and a preoccupation with money. Freud never swerved from his generalization: 'Yes, America is gigantic. A gigantic mistake.'

When the Clark invitation first arrived, in January, Freud wrote Jung that the travel expenses would not compensate him for the lost work. Besides, he said, 'I am inclined to agree with Jones. I also think that once they discover the sexual core of our psychological theories they will drop us. Their prudery and their material dependence on the public are too great.' Jung immediately shot back, 'I share Jones's pessimism absolutely. So far these people [the Americans] haven't a notion of what we're at. One of these days they will creep into a corner, prim and abashed.' However, when Clark raised the travel allowance to $750 and changed the date from July to September, Freud, Jung and Ferenczi all accepted.

Jones naturally planned to attend. He gave Freud explicit advice about his lectures: 'You absolutely must deliver them in English, for hardly anyone here understands German.' He also warned Freud to be prepared for a small audience.

The three foreign analysts travelled together on the *George Washington* from Bremen (and analysed each other's dreams on board ship). Brill got the first chance to show them Manhattan. He took them to Chinatown,

Coney Island and the Metropolitan Museum, where Freud admired the Greek antiquities. Freud found Central Park West, where Brill lived, the nicest part of the city (as psychoanalysts have found it ever since). When Jones turned up, he accompanied Freud, Jung and Ferenczi to their first film – 'with plenty of wild chasing', as he remembered it. The party then made its way to central Massachusetts by a tortuous route – night boat from New York to New Haven, train to Boston, followed by train to Worcester. Stanley Hall took Freud and Jung to stay with him; the rest were put up at the Standish Hotel. But Freud was already physically distressed, and on several occasions embarrassed. He blamed the rich American food for the trouble with his bowels.

Hall, as perhaps his book *Adolescence* indicated, was a hippy for his time – an enthusiast for walking barefoot and a critic of the Puritan suppression of pleasure in American life. He was also a good organizer. He had brought together an audience of interested academics, including sceptics such as the anthropologist Franz Boas and William James, who, despite failing health, came to Worcester 'to see what Freud was like'.

Morton Prince did not attend. He was keeping aloof from the Freudian movement. Not only was he put off by the sexual element, but he also objected to Freud's monopoly of the term 'psychoanalysis'. Any form of psychotherapeutics seemed to Prince to be 'psychoanalysis'.

Disregarding Jones's advice, Freud addressed the audience in German. He had found out that at Clark's tenth anniversary celebration none of the famous foreign scientists and psychiatrists invited had spoken in English. He improvised the lectures on morning walks with Ferenczi; even so, his charm and narrative style captivated his audience.

In his five lectures, Freud laid out the basics of what the *Boston Evening Transcript*, reporting on the conference, called 'psychic analysis'. Freud described the case of 'Anna O' and the success of her talking cure. He explained free association, dream analysis and the transference – the love and hostility patients feel towards their therapist. He spent some time on the sexual impulses of the child and the harmfulness of sexual taboos.

He devoted the fifth lecture to a denunciation of the social repression of sexuality. Repression caused neurosis; the neurotic was retreating from reality into the sexual gratifications of childhood or – worse – into fantasy. What an individual should strive for was conscious control over sexual impulses.

The Massachusetts press ignored the attack on sexual mores, but recognized an epochal event. 'Conference Brings Savants together: Long-Haired

Type Hard to Discover: Men with Bulging Brains have Time for Occasional Smiles', wrote the *Worcester Telegram* of 12 September 1909. The *Worcester Bulletin* watered down Freud's frank exposition of infantile sexuality by referring delicately to rocking, thumb-sucking 'and similar childish habits'. The *Boston Evening Transcript* also omitted mention of Freud's attack on unrealistic puritan morality. Its reporter, however, was also a translator, and he got a personal interview with Freud at Hall's house. Adelbert Albrecht saw a 'man of great refinement, of intellect and of many-sided education. His sharp, yet kind, clear eyes suggest at once the doctor.' Freud told Albrecht that psychotherapy was as old as illness, and that certain diseases, particularly those of a neurotic nature, are healed not by the drug but by the physician. He described how he had given up hypnotism as useless. The analytic therapy concerned itself with the psychic origin of the diseased idea it wished to destroy. The treatment was expensive and tedious, and unsuitable for those who did not want to be cured but were sent by their relatives.

Jones made good use of the occasion. From William James he elicited the prediction that the 'future of psychology' belonged to Jones's work; from Jung, the fact that Jung avoided 'unsavoury details' when talking with his patients — it was awkward when he met them at dinner parties later on. He approached Adolf Meyer, a Swiss neuropathologist resident in the United States since 1892 and editor of the *Psychological Bulletin*, and offered to write articles on Freud. Meyer accepted. (Then director of the New York state hospital system's Pathological Institute, Meyer was a good contact to have. He was soon to move to Johns Hopkins University in Baltimore as professor of psychiatry and director of an important clinic.)

The high point of Jones's visit came at the end, when Freud personally walked him the two miles between the university and the station. Freud's hope was aroused that there might be a future for psychoanalysis in the United States (Little did he know it would flourish there for many years as in no other country.) They talked frankly. Jones declared that from that time on he planned to devote his life to psychoanalysis. He said also — not shy of giving his idol an analytic interpretation — that Freud would find it difficult to give up his 'feeling for Jung'.

Jones had suggested that Freud come to visit him and Loe in Toronto. But Freud, with Ferenczi and Jung, had other plans. Leaving Worcester, they accepted Putnam's invitation to his camp in the Adirondacks.

What followed at the 'Putnam Shanty' was a classic and comic clash of cultures. One of the New England wives had decked the camp in German emblems, thinking to make the visitors from Switzerland, Austria and Hungary feel at home. The foreign trio did not. They found themselves addressed by their first names, housed in log cabins, and required to sit on the ground and watch steaks being grilled in front of their eyes and to play board games. Each cabin had a merry name; Freud, Jung and Ferenzi were assigned to one called 'Chatterbox'. A cabin called 'The Stoop' held a piano and card tables and a library with special instructions on how to use the primitive equipment, such as mixing bowls used as washbasins. Jung fell into the spirit of the occasion and sang German songs. Freud's strongest impression was the sight of a dead porcupine.

The effect on Putnam was more positive. Having seen the Freudians at close quarters, he found them to be far from sexual immoralists; rather, they were brave men who were 'kindly, unassuming, tolerant, earnest and sincere'. He became a regular correspondent of Freud's until his death seven years later.

In a letter to Freud, Jones explained his own conversion to psychoanalysis in Oedipal terms: 'Shortly put, my resistances have sprung not from any objections to your theories, but partly from an absurd jealous egotism and partly from the influences of a strong "Father complex".' He swore that he had determined not only to advance 'the Cause' by all the means in his power, 'but also to further it by whatever means you personally decided on, and to follow your recommendations as exactly as possible'.

Freud could not have prescribed that Jones be as eloquent and as entertaining as he was. His new missionary zeal took him, in November 1909, to the Niagara District Association at St Catharine's, Ontario, to give what can only be described as a sermon on 'The Psycho-Analytic Method of Treatment'. In a long, lively talk, he preached the wonderful advantages of Freud's new discovery: 'the fact that every psychoneurotic symptom is a distorted expression of a repressed wish-complex' – the wish, because unacceptable, having become 'buried in the unconscious'. The psychological mechanisms through which the repressed complex turned into manifest symptoms 'have been worked out with great accuracy by Freud'. When the process was reversed – that is, when the complexes were again made conscious – 'the abnormal manifestation, or symptom, ceases.'

Jones spelled out for his undoubtedly bewildered audience the rules of the treatment: the patient must hold back no thought from the physician, and must relate, in order of their appearance, the thoughts that spontaneously come to mind. He then described the importance of slips of the tongue, of remembering dreams, and of recognizing a 'compulsion

neurosis'. The morbid desire for cleanliness could have no better illustration than Lady Macbeth's hand-washing, to which Shakespeare had the
doctor say, 'This disease is beyond my practice.' 'And until the epoch-
making work of Freud fifteen years ago,' Jones declared triumphantly, 'no
doctor could but agree to the remark.'

He spelled out the conditions for successful treatment: intelligence, a
will for treatment, and relative youth. He addressed what was the main
American objection to psychoanalysis, even more than its sexual content:
the amount of time it required.

Treatment was limited to a few (as Freud had said at Worcester), but
so was surgical treatment of brain tumours. The result was educational 'in
the highest sense of the word', the reward 'a richer development of
will-power and self-mastery'. Jones then delivered a peroration that would
have done credit to a political convention:

> It is a matter of congratulation for our patients, for society, and for ourselves
> that we at last have in our hands a precise and formidable weapon to deal
> with the very maladies that up till now have been the despair of the
> profession and the triumph of the quack.

It was oratory born of absolute certainty. Jones was in no doubt that
Freud was on a plane with Darwin and Copernicus.

Conscious of native prudery, Jones nevertheless was unrestrained when
writing a paper on his nymphomaniac patient who (according to his case
history) was frustrated by her husband's inability to satisfy her or give her
a child, and took literally and viscerally the words she believed she had
heard from a minister at church – that oral sex was sacramental. 'The seed
was in this way to enter her body. Had not Christ', Jones reported, 'said
"Take and drink"?'

> When speaking of religious observances, particularly of Holy Communion,
> the patient broke off, and slowly and reverently, went through a perfect
> pantomime of the whole ceremony. This culminated in her taking a glass
> of water, which she had placed on a Bible, and gradually raising it to her
> lips, where she beatifically sucked the rim, slowly revolving the glass as she
> did so. During the latter part of the performance a complete and exhausting
> orgasm took place. I pointed to the glass, and asked her if it was the
> communion cup; she answered: 'Do you call it a cup? It has another name,'
> and later remarked: 'This is the Way, the Truth and the Life.'

Jones recounted this blasphemous scene from his consulting room in
detail and at length, as a man who loved narration as much he loved

exposition. He went from the specific to the general to discuss the equivalence, to some patients, of the sucking movements of the mouth and the vagina – 'clearly traced by Freud to the sucking movements of the infant at the nipple'. Jones might have rested content with publishing this paper ('Psycho-Analytic Notes on a Case of Hypomania') in the *American Journal of Insanity* in October 1909, but he went on to reprint it a few months later in the *Ontario Hospitals Bulletin*, of which he was co-editor.

This republication perhaps shows that Jones did not know when enough was enough. Was he spreading the word of Freud? Or had he taken another risk, verging on a sexual game, with a patient? Either way, the *Bulletin* considered the article unfit for a medical publication, and relieved him of further editorial duties.

With such evidence, by April 1910 his sponsor, Charles Clarke, now dean of the Faculty of Medicine at the University of Toronto, was beginning to have his doubts – about psychoanalysis and about Ernest Jones. From Freud's (now translated) Worcester lectures, Clarke judged that an ordinary reader would think Freud advocated 'free love, removal of all restraints, and a relapse to savagery'. Clarke seems also to have picked up rumours trickling across the Atlantic that Jones and 'Mrs Jones' were not legally married. Jones, asked to explain, did not deny it.

Jones was not rattled. He had grown used to being heckled. When he presented a paper to the Canadian Medical Association in Toronto in June 1910, two irate neurologists came from New York to taunt him because, after psychoanalysis, their wives had decided to leave them. Jones knew he was not the only target. He had seen a New York neurologist who was determined to stamp out 'Freudism' attack the dignified and august Putnam at a dinner in New York for reading a paper that was tantamount to 'pornographic stories about pure virgins'.

On New Year's Day 1910 (Jones's thirty-first birthday), Freud had written to Ferenczi in Budapest, 'Jones is now excelling in rueful and contrite letters; his resistance finally seems to be broken.' The next day he told Jung of a letter from Jones saying 'I'll be good from now on.' Freud had scolded Jones for his penchant for complicated plans, for his hostility to A. A. Brill and for his tendency towards evasion and circumlocution when talking about sexuality, and Jones had thanked him for the criticism.

A good Freudian's lot was constant censorship. When Jones submitted the promised article on Freud's psychology for Meyer's *Psychological Bulletin*, he found certain paragraphs deleted when the proofs arrived.

Meyer accepted the censorship as necessary. A former co-editor of that bulletin, a Johns Hopkins professor of philosophy and psychology, had been arrested in the summer of 1908 in a police raid on what was described as 'a negro house of prostitution'. The scandal cost the professor (James Mark Baldwin) his editorship and his professorship, even though he denied that he had gone to the house of ill-repute with immoral intent. The *Bulletin*, however, under a new editor and a new owner, felt it did not need any more sexual scandals.

Furious, Jones threatened to withdraw the whole article. Finally he accepted the argument that the journal went to many rural libraries and needed to take special care to avoid puritan susceptibilities. All the same, he allowed himself to sound off to Meyer: he deplored, he said, 'hateful pandering to the subscribing populace, and there is too much of it in America'. He passed this latest evidence of puritanism on to Freud, who told Jung. Jung was unsurprised: 'The so-called freedom of research in the land of the free has indeed been well guarded – the very word "sexual" is taboo.'

But Putnam was impressed with Jones's work, and, after a lecture to the American Psychological Association in Boston, considered him to be the clearest expositor in English of Freud's theories. In March 1910 he sought to get Jones an appointment at Harvard. The answer, from Hugo Münsterberg, head of Harvard's psychological laboratory, sums up the bind in which Jones found himself. Münsterberg entirely appreciated Jones's blend of 'medical experience and full neurological knowledge with psychological interest'. Indeed:

> among younger men I know hardly anyone who seems to fill the bill so well as Dr Jones. The only objection which troubles me is his inclination to put more emphasis on sexual factors than would be desirable in a course which is not intended for medical students and which is open to undergraduates. It might too easily degenerate into a sensational course by the loafers on account of its piquancy.

Münsterberg trusted that Jones would 'repress' his sexual explanations. Even so, Jones was not offered the job. (Perhaps Münsterberg had not forgotten the 'hot potato' jibe.) That was a moment when Jones's career might have taken a sharply different turn. That he was rejected shows that, in one case at least, his constant refrain that his Freudian attitude towards sexuality marred his advance was true. It cost him an appointment at the university whose anthem boasts it will be 'the herald of Light . . . Till the stock of the Puritans die'.

★   ★   ★

At the end of March 1910, committed to lectures in Toronto, Jones could not go to the Second Congress of the International Psychoanalytic Association, in Nuremberg, but Freud went. An International Psychoanalytic Association was formed (for accrediting Freudian psychoanalysts in any country), a new publication was created, the *Zentralblatt für Psychoanalyse*, to be the official journal of the International Association. It was to be quite distinct from Jung's *Jahrbuch*, which came out of Zurich twice a year. Jung was elected president of the association.

A triumph for Zurich over Vienna? The Viennese held a secret meeting of about twenty analysts to complain. Wilhelm Stekel, one of the four original members of Freud's Wednesday Psychological Society, and who had been analysed by Freud, reminded them that psychoanalysis had been founded in Vienna and that for a long time the Viennese group had been the only ones to fight for Freud. It would be preposterous if Vienna were deprived of the leadership.

Freud, however, broke into the meeting and tried to get them to accept Jung as lifetime president. He told them the truth as he saw it, Psychoanalysis was going to face strong opposition from orthodox science. Zurich, at the heart of Europe, was a more promising centre than Vienna, and the leader of the Cause must be an official psychiatrist and a Gentile. He continued, 'Most of you are Jews, and therefore you are incompetent to win friends for the new teaching. Jews must be content with the modest role of preparing the ground.'

Stekel claimed to have seen tears running down Freud's cheeks.

There were still too few psychoanalysts in America for a full Psychoanalytic Society, so an organization with a more inclusive title – the American Psychopathological Association – was formed in May 1910 in Washington, DC, for physicians and psychologists interested in psychopathology and psychotherapy. Morton Prince was named president, Putnam and Jones were officers, and the *Journal of Abnormal Psychology* became its official organ. Prince made Jones an associate editor of the *Journal*, and elevated his name to the masthead – not before time. Of the thirty-two contributors listed on the contents page for the April–May 1910 volume, most had one article on the inside pages; the prolific Jones was represented by eleven contributions. Putnam was full of admiration. He told Jones, a few months later, 'You are certainly the most energetic, precise and prompt and efficient individual I have ever met.'

Jones is often accused of exaggerating his own importance, but never of exaggerating the amount of work he produced. His staggering output is barely reconcilable with the positions he held in Toronto – none of them a sinecure. He blamed the cold weather and the unattractive environment for his productivity. Oddly, considering his earlier and later passion for skating, there is no mention of him enjoying Canada's abundant ice.

Prodigious output had been assisted by his position on the *Bulletin of the Ontario Hospitals for the Insane*. Until he was deposed, he filled the *Bulletin* with his work. Of the ten papers in the March 1909 issue, eight were by Ernest Jones. The following month, seven out of ten were his. He still wrote on allochiria and its transposition of sides in localization of a feeling, and hemiplegia, a paralysis of one side of the body. With his new point of view, he told Putnam that he traced 'my excessive interest in hemiplegia and allochiria' to an uncertainty whether one side of his body was male and the other female.

Freud enjoyed reading him. In April 1910 he wrote to Jones, 'Your letters prove a continuous source of satisfaction to me, I wonder indeed at your activity, at the size of your erudition and at the recent sincerity of your style.' The word 'recent' suggests that Freud had detected a change of heart. For his part, Freud was glad that he had refused to 'listen to the internal voices hinting at giving you up'. Now he trusted that 'we will walk and work a good bit together.'

Jones went to Europe every summer, and in 1910 his father went to Toronto to visit. Thomas Jones was soon followed back to Britain by his daughter Elizabeth, who immediately cabled Canada saying that, within the week, she was marrying Wilfred Trotter. She had returned with the intention of seeing another suitor, but Trotter met her boat train at the station and (having seen her virtues as a housekeeper during his and Jones's years in Harley Street) proposed. She accepted him on the spot. They married in early July 1910, and the marriage was an enduring and, from all accounts, happy one.

Whether either man analysed the meaning of Trotter marrying Jones's sister is unrecorded. Trotter distrusted psychoanalysis, but admitted that Jones wrote 'greatly about this business', and had urged him, as he was so committed, to come out in the open as a supporter of Freud's doctrines.

The International Congress of Medical Psychology in Brussels in August 1910 brought Jones in proximity to Freud, who was in Holland on a seaside holiday. Freud wrote to Jung, 'Tomorrow the geographically most distant of our friends is expected here in Noordwijk, where a relative of his owns a villa: Jones from Toronto. He has risen a good deal in my affections this past year.'

On that same holiday, Freud also managed to analyse the composer Gustav Mahler during a long afternoon. Mahler, at forty-nine, was having trouble with his young and beautiful wife, Alma, who was falling in love with other men; his neurologist in Vienna advised a consultation with Freud. Freud agreed, but told the acclaimed composer that their meeting would have to be in Holland. Mahler duly presented himself in Leiden, and the two men set out on foot together. Freud told Mahler not to worry about his age, because that was what had attracted Alma, who needed a replacement for her father, when, at twenty-one, she had married the famous composer in 1902. In the next breath Freud pointed out that Mahler had a mother fixation – 'Mutterbindung' – and identified Alma, young as she was, with his mother. He was impressed by Mahler's comprehension of psychoanalysis.

The walking cure worked. Mahler telegraphed Alma on his way back to Vienna: 'Feeling cheerful, interesting discussion', and on the train he wrote her a poem describing the dispelling of a nightmare by persuasion.

Jones did not think of himself as an immigrant in Canada. He dearly longed to go back to England. His status at the University of Toronto was improving nonetheless. He was promoted to 'associate in psychiatry', was assigned to give all the university's lectures on psychiatry, and was promised elevation to 'associate professor' the following year.

In a very long letter, he had more interesting news for Freud about his patients. One was a boy who was obsessed that Christ was sucking his penis all the time – 'a beautiful case', said Jones, 'as he was an excellent subject'. Another was a young man who, along with more erotic fantasies, believed not only that he could transfer his thoughts electrically over any distance, but also that sexual relations consisted in blowing flatus into the partner's anus.

Jones concluded this rich letter with a discussion of the 'Geld-complex' of an extravagant and generous woman whose generosity was a reaction against her miserly mother, whom she hated. Freud was as yet in no position to know, as Jones certainly did, that Loe Kann had hated the mother from whom she had inherited her wealth.

By mid-1910, having sent Freud a number of his publications, Jones felt ashamed to be taking up so much of his time. With uncharacteristic humility, he confessed to Freud that he was no theoretician. 'The original-ity-complex is not strong with me; my ambition is rather to know, to be "behind the scenes" and "in the know", rather than *to find out*. I realise that I have very little talent for originality; any talent I may have lies rather in the direction of being able to see perhaps quickly what others point out.'

Original is as original does. While Freud's other followers were constructing new theories of human behaviour – Adler was the first to break ranks, in 1911, with his proposition that the 'will to power' was a stronger drive than sex – Jones poured his gifts into exposition of Freud's ideas.

Toronto unleashed Jones's imagination. His essay on Hamlet was the first, and arguably remains the best, Freudian interpretation of a work of literature. A dubious distinction perhaps, yet the Oedipal theory fits the play like a glove. Hamlet could not kill the king, his uncle, for having done what he wished to do himself: kill his father and marry his mother.

'The Oedipus-Complex as an Explanation of Hamlet's Mystery: A Study in Motive' appeared in January 1910 in the *American Journal of Psychology*. The idea sprang from Freud's footnote to *The Interpretation of Dreams* that discussed Hamlet's feelings towards his mother, father, uncle and Ophelia, and commented that the play was very probably written after the deaths of Shakespeare's own father and his young son. Jones gave the play a sensitive and questioning reading, with scores of references ranging from Wordsworth and Bernard Shaw to Montaigne, Goethe and Otto Rank's *The Myth of the Birth of the Hero*. 'No disconnected and meaningless drama could have produced the effects on its audiences that Hamlet has continuously done for the past three centuries,' he declared.

Jones gave himself forty pages to raise and answer the question: if Hamlet is a man capable of action, why does he not execute his duty to avenge his father? The answer must lie in an internal conflict 'inaccessible to his introspection'.

By quoting an exchange from *Henry IV, Part 2*, Jones showed that, three centuries before Freud, Shakespeare was aware that the son has an unconscious wish to see his father dead. When Prince Henry says to his dying father, 'I never thought to hear you speak again,' the king replies, 'Thy wish was father, Harry, to that thought.'

As for *Hamlet*, it is a play about two crimes, said Jones, but 'there can be no question about which arouses in him the deeper loathing.' While the murder of his father evokes a plain recognition of his duty to avenge it, 'his mother's guilty conduct awakes in him the intensest horror'. Jones the diagnostician pointed out that Hamlet is depressed and thinking of suicide even before he learns of the murder. What appals him is his mother's second marriage and her patent sensuality; as her son, he is well aware of her own passionate fondness for him. As for Claudius, the uncle who has become his stepfather, 'The Queen his mother lives almost by his looks.'

Jones, speaking to an unaware age, defined 'the group of mental pro-cesses conspicuous in the Oedipus legend' as 'generally known under the name of the "Oedipus-complex"'. He quoted Freud's 'the mother is the first seductress of her boy', and spelled out that the 'long "repressed" desire to take his father's place in his mother's affection is stimulated to unconscious activity by the sight of some one usurping this place exactly as he himself once longed to do'. The intensity of Hamlet's repulsion against Ophelia is 'an index of the powerful "repression" to which his sexual feeling is being subjected'. Hamlet's indifferent courtship of her is, by Jones–Freud lights, only to be expected. How can he love a woman his own age when his mother is the more desirable?

Only when he has made the final sacrifice and brought himself to the door of death, said Jones, is Hamlet free to fulfil his duty, to avenge his father 'and to slay his other self – his uncle'.

Jones related Hamlet's conflict to the inner workings of Shakespeare's mind. He called attention to the facts that, long before he wrote *Hamlet*, Shakespeare had named his own son Hamnet, and that, just before he wrote the play in 1601 or 1602, his father had died – 'an event', said Jones, 'which might well have had the same awakening effect on old "repressed" memories that the death of Hamlet's father had with Hamlet'.

Jones concluded that Shakespeare's inspirations had their origin in the deepest and darkest regions of his mind:

> It is only fitting that the greatest work of the world-poet should have had to do with the deepest problem and the intensest conflict that have occupied the mind of man since the beginning of time – the revolt of youth[,] and [of] the impulse to love against the restraint imposed by the jealous eld.

The paper was published in German in the year it appeared, and 'Das Problem des Hamlet und der Oedipus-Komplex' found its way to James Joyce in Trieste, where he was a teacher at the Berlitz School. Joyce's biographer Richard Ellmann posits that it may have been given him by his friend and pupil Ettore Schmitz, whose nephew Dr Edoardo Weiss had introduced psychoanalysis into Italy in 1910.

Jones's argument and even its words are echoed in Joyce's *Ulysses*, published in 1922, in the scene in the National Library of Ireland where Stephen Dedalus debates Hamlet in the light of Shakespeare's relations with his son Hamnet. ('*Amor matris*, subject and objective genitive, may be the only true thing in life. Paternity may be a legal fiction.') Stephen follows Jones's diagnosis (and Freud's) in making the point that Shakespeare wrote *Hamlet* in the months that followed his father's death.

Nearly three decades later Jones's *Hamlet* influenced the Shakespearean actor Laurence Olivier. In 1937 Olivier, about to play Hamlet for his first season at the Old Vic, called on Jones in London and came away convinced, in his words, that

> Hamlet was a prime sufferer from the Oedipus complex – quite unconsciously, of course, as the professor was anxious to stress. He offered an impressive array of symptoms: spectacular mood-swings, cruel treatment of his love, and above all a hopeless inability to pursue the course required of him. The Oedipus complex, therefore, can claim responsibility for a formidable share of all that is wrong with him. There is great pathos in his determined efforts to bring himself to the required boiling point, and in the excuses he finds to shed this responsibility.

The highly Oedipal interpretation of Hamlet found its way into Olivier's film of the play in 1948, which won him two Academy Awards (for best actor and best picture) and which was startling in its aggressively sensual embraces between Hamlet and his mother.

'On the Nightmare', another of Jones's essays from the period 1909–10, has also endured. It was expanded into a book in 1926, with a terrifying illustration by the Swiss-born British Romantic painter Henry Fuseli. Jones wrote it as a psychiatrist who had had considerable experience of listening to patients. Unlike clinical doctors, who tend to have short attention spans, Jones was accustomed to spending an hour hearing the random thoughts and dreams of those who consulted him, and they did not always talk about sex. That he understood what fear feels like is apparent from this essay: 'No malady that causes mortal distress to the sufferer, not even seasickness, is viewed by medical science with such complacent indifference as is the one which is the subject of this book.'

His wide reading was displayed in a review of myths and legends of fiends, hags and monsters: 'The modifications which nightmare assumes are infinite; but one passion is almost never absent – that of utter and incomprehensible dread . . . In every instance, there is a sense of oppression and helplessness.' The victim 'can neither breathe, nor walk, nor run'. The three cardinal features of the 'malady', in his clinical summary, were '(1) agonizing dread; (2) sense of oppression or weight at the chest which alarmingly interferes with respiration; (3) conviction of helpless paralysis'.

In mid-century the power of his prose reached someone no stranger to terror. In 1956 Sylvia Plath gave Jones's *On the Nightmare* to her new husband, Ted Hughes, as a present for their first Christmas together. She boldly underlined passages about sadism and sexual curiosity, and also Jones's definition of the essential characteristics of a vampire: 'his origin in a dead person' and 'his habit of sucking blood from a living one'. She starred (less than seven years before her suicide) his pronouncement that 'the interest of the living in the dead, whether in the body or in the spirit, is an inexhaustible theme'.

Without acknowledging these essays, Freud accepted Jones's apology for lack of originality. He thanked him all the same for subordinating his personal ambition to the interests of the Cause, and paid him an extravagant compliment:

> Let me express again my conviction, that you are the most skilful, powerful and devote[d] helper, Psychoanalysis could have found in the New World. I trust your longing to go back to England will meet with no satisfaction for a long while.

It would, in fact, be just two years before Jones returned to England. He would continue as productive as he had begun, while running into turbulence of a kind with which he was all too familiar.

7

Perils of the Trade
January 1911–Summer 1912

W ITH THE PUBLICATION in English of Freud's Worcester lectures
in 1910, psychoanalysis entered American awareness. As respected
medical academics such as James Jackson Putnam of Harvard and Hugh
Patrick of the Bellevue Hospital Medical College in New York became
converted, the *New York Times* could report that the 'conclusion that all
the psychological life of human beings is based on the sex drive has gained
considerable hold on American physicians'. In Toronto, as his reputation
grew, Jones's work as a psychoanalyst increased, and he began to enjoy a
comfortable income. Among his patients was a University of Toronto
professor of romance languages. Another was the daughter of the university's chancellor, William Meredith, a distinguished Canadian lawyer and
politician. Jones also continued to pour out a stream of papers, including
a reworking, for a German translation, of the nightmare essay, now 'Der
Alptraum'.

But old problems re-emerged. In early 1911, while he was preparing a
paper on the criticisms of psychoanalytic treatment, to be delivered before
the Chicago Neurological and Medical societies, Jones was interrupted
by 'very serious personal trouble'. To the understanding Putnam, he wrote
in his usual graphic detail, 'A woman whom I saw four times last September (medically) has accused me of having had sexual intercourse with
her then, has gone to the President of the University to denounce me, is
threatening legal proceedings, and has attempted to shoot me. At present
I am being guarded by an armed detective.'

He described the woman as 'a severe hysteric' and 'pronouncedly
homosexual'. He had, he assured Putnam, been treating the woman not
by psychoanalysis, but rather by talking and trying to calm her down.

> Unfortunately she had an acute fit of *Übertrangung* [transference] . . . and
> made unmistakeable overtures. The aggrieved woman broke off treatment
> and nothing was heard of her for four months. In the meantime, however,
> she got into the hands of some doctors of doubtful reputation, as well as
> of a woman doctor of very severely strict views [Dr Emma Gordon, a

member of the Women's Christian Temperance Union]; the latter fell in love with her and it was reciprocated. They were people who had cooked up rumours about my 'lax' views and harmful treatment (stupid stories about my prescribing adultery, illicit intercourse, etc.) and a regular incubation of delusions took place all round.

Jones concluded his dramatic report by saying, 'I foolishly paid the woman $500 blackmail to prevent a scandal, which would be almost equally harmful either way.'

Five hundred dollars? Nearly his year's salary as pathologist at the Ontario Asylum for the Insane. And his costs did not stop there. He had engaged (shades of his Deptford legal battle) the best lawyer in Toronto, and did indeed have an armed guard standing outside his house. Loe Kann had demanded, and undoubtedly paid for, this personal protection. Her Geld-complex must have played a big part in getting Jones out of this imbroglio, which only confirmed her view that psychoanalysis was a dangerous profession.

Fortunately for Jones, the university's president, Sir Alexander Falconer, an ordained minister no less, was on his side. Falconer knew of the various rumours: that Jones recommended masturbation or going to prostitutes, that he showed patients obscene postcards, that he had made two patients pregnant. Nevertheless, he gave Jones a very sympathetic hearing, and dismissed the lurid stories as nonsense. When the patient's friend, Dr Emma Gordon, called on the president in his office and urged him to save the youth of Toronto by dismissing Jones, Falconer flatly advised her (according to Jones) to keep her mouth shut or be drawn into a serious legal action.

Jones, recounting the saga to Freud, said that the inflamed patient then attempted to shoot him, but her revolver was taken away and she was sent to a sanatorium. Telling Freud about the scandal a month after it occurred, Jones made no mention of the five hundred dollars.

The bribe indeed might have shocked Freud, but not the accusation. To Freud, the inappropriate love of patients was an occupational hazard of the psychoanalyst. When Jung, two years earlier, had complained about a woman who was introducing herself around Basle as his mistress, Freud expounded, 'To be slandered and scorched by the love with which we operate – such are the perils of our trade, which we are certainly not going to abandon on their account.'

In his letter of 8 February 1911 Jones had more interesting things to discuss than the attempt on his life. One was an article in Jung's *Jahrbuch* by the Burghölzli director, Eugen Bleuler, which showed him resisting

Freud's doctine that the function of dreams is to preserve sleep. Another was an account of his recent trip (accompanied by an armed detective) to Chicago. He judged the city 'the most hideous excrescence on God's earth', but found the community of doctors and neurologists well disposed towards psychoanalysis. So he judged from their warm reception of his paper on the criticisms of psychoanalytic treatment. Both Chicago and Baltimore, he told Freud, promised to be strongholds of 'ψα' in a short time. In particular, the psychiatrist Adolf Meyer from Johns Hopkins (the outstanding American medical school of the day) had 'behaved splendidly to us'. Jones concluded his very long letter (he was later pleased to have acquired 'the art of type-writing') with an account of his most interesting current case, that of a 40-year-old businessman who used commercial metaphors to describe his sexual difficulties: 'in coitus his wife took the upper position and "did all the work".'

In his relations with Freud, Jones himself often took the upper position: Freud was now addressing him with almost filial affection, closing letters with effusions such as 'I am with best love for you . . . Freud.' Thus Jones did not hesitate to rebuke Freud for having been flattered by an offer from the British Society for Psychical Research. 'Did you accept the corresp. membership?' he asked reprovingly. He hoped not. While he conceded that the society had done valuable work in the 1880s on hypnotism and automatic writing, 'for the past 15 years they have confined their attention to "spook-hunting", mediumism, and telepathy, the chief aim being to communicate with departed souls.' The SPR was not in good repute in scientific circles; Freud should not allow himself to be tarnished by association with spiritism – 'in spite of William James' ardent hope'. (James had died the previous year.) 'Poor James,' Jones joked. 'One hasn't even the consolation of thinking that he knows better by now.'

By the spring of 1911, Jones was having trouble not only with his patients, but with academics who had previously paid him respectful attention. From Harvard, Boris Sidis had attacked the 'mad epidemic of Freudianism now invading America', while the powerful Morton Prince was himself pulling back from Freud. In an article, 'The Mechanism and Interpretation of Dreams', in the October–November 1910 issue of his *Journal of Abnormal Psychology*, Prince disagreed with Freud that dreams express the fulfilment of repressed unacceptable wishes. To Prince, the symbols found in dreams were clear and open representations of simple ideas and fears. He could not accept Freud's distinction between the 'manifest' content of the dream (the remembered narrative) and the 'latent' content (the hidden meaning that only analysis could recover). To Prince, Freud was a poet, but not a scientist. Though all Freud's books held ideas 'which astonish by the intensity of their illumination . . . *when he attempts to demonstrate their validity, the facts often seem insufficient and the deductions unconvincing*'.

Jones was hardly going to let such insults slide by unchallenged. In the next issue of the journal, of which he was now an associate editor, he objected strongly. Prince had claimed to have psychoanalysed 'a dozen or more dreams' but Freud had analysed a thousand before writing *The Interpretation of Dreams*, and since then he and other analysts had investigated 'by the psychoanalytic method' fifty times as many, 'with uniformly consistent results'. Prince, by admitting to have encountered no resistance in his dream interpretations, showed clearly that he did not know what a symbol was. According to Jones, no one who had taken the trouble to acquire the psychoanalytic method had failed to confirm Freud's theory in all its essentials. Psychoanalysis, Jones insisted, was the only method of dream analysis that could give reliable results.

Prince used the following issue to reply to Dr Jones's 'very courteous criticism', but stuck to his argument that there were other methods than Freud's of investigating dreams. To maintain this view was not to belittle 'the distinguished Austrian author'.

Jones's private verdict on Prince, delivered to Freud, was 'too much the pet of Boston'. Yet Putnam, for his part, heard equally strong language from Prince. Prince warned Putnam (who, like himself, was a product of Boston Latin School as well as of Harvard) to steer clear of Ernest Jones: 'Jones is hopelessly lost, his judgement is gone. Jung ditto. You are raising a cult not a science.' Prince compared Freudian analysis to another new and popular cult, Christian Science. (Prince's personal letters to Putnam would read with even more force had he not written them under the pseudonym adapted from the Scottish poet William Sharp, 'Fiona Mac-prince'.)

There were other medical critics of the 'cult', and of Jones as its preacher. In a caustic attack before the Philadelphia Neurological Society, James Hendrie Lloyd mocked Jones's paper, in 'The So-called Oedipus-Complex in *Hamlet*', as an example of the new 'subterranean psychology', its sexual ideas 'highly characteristic of the whole Freudian school'. Lloyd expanded witheringly:

> According to Ernest Jones the whole mystery of Hamlet is to be explained by the theory of Freud's 'repressed emotions'. This is his thesis in a nutshell.

Hamlet is 'suffering from an internal conflict, the essential nature of which is inaccessible to his introspection'. In other words, the Prince did not know what it was that ailed him ... Shakespeare did not know; the audience has never known ... nobody knows what it was but Jones, and he has discovered it by the methods of psycho-analysis.

To Jones, the tenor of such criticism constituted evidence of the pressing need for an American Society of Psychoanalysis. He was not pleased when Brill raced ahead of him and in February 1911 founded the New York Psychoanalytic Society – 'without saying a word to Putnam and myself', Jones angrily complained to Freud. Jones and Putnam had gathered forces by May when, in Baltimore, they founded the American Psychoanalytic Association. For the meeting on 9 May at the Stafford Hotel on Vernon Square, nine East-Coast psychiatrists turned up. Putnam was named president, Jones, secretary. Coming away, Jones was able to give Freud the glad news that he had 'ardent supporters in towns so far apart as Chicago, Omaha, Louisville and Cincinnati, and . . . there is quite a colony in Baltimore'.

There was no danger of this organization being confused in its members' committed minds with the group of nearly the same name (the American Psychopathological Association) they themselves had formed in Washington in May 1910. Diplomatically, they promised to work with Brill's New York branch to train analysts, to prevent the work being 'damaged by amateurs and charlatans' and to unite against what Jones saw as the boycott of 'official science'.

By the summer of 1911 Loe Kann was growing more and more depressed in Toronto. Jones poured out his woes to Freud. His wife could not stand 'the anxiety and the suspense of the situation here'. If he stayed on, she might leave him for good. Or commit suicide. She still suffered from kidney stones and 'complicated abdominal trouble'. He had come to a definite decision: he would go with her back to Europe in September. Then, if he got his professorship from the university, he would return to Toronto for one term only, to lecture, and then leave. If he did not get his professorship he would not come back. In the meantime, he might try to get a position in the United States.

Perhaps to cheer her up, or perhaps because she could not bear to be alone, Jones had taken Loe with him to the meeting in Baltimore in May to found the American Psychoanalytic Association. It did his career no good.

It had crossed Jones's mind that he might be offered a position at Johns Hopkins Medical School. Indeed, Adolf Meyer, who had become professor of psychiatry as well as director of the new Phipps Clinic at Johns Hopkins, had been thinking of hiring him. However, one look at the pair from Toronto – particularly at the beautiful, earthy and addicted Loe Kann – killed the possibility. As Meyer explained in a letter to his brother:

> Mrs Jones and Ernest Jones, the best Freudian, expert scholar and earlier assistant to Horsley, came from Toronto and caused a minor storm; too much Bernard Shaw and lack of restraint; she in addition is a Dutch Jewess, very emancipated and also in bad health, and has to rely on morphines. I had often thought of bringing him here to B. But this just can't be done though he is pressing for it.

The morphine habit must have been conspicuous. By midsummer Loe was giving herself what Jones considered 'huge doses' for constant pain from what he now described to Freud as 'calculous pyelo-nephritis'. Lonelier than ever since Jones's sister Elizabeth had gone back to England, she took to spending most of the day in bed. Loe loathed, in equal measure, Canada and psychoanalysis. She feared for Jones's reputation, which took a dive when his patron Charles Clarke left his post at the Ontario Asylum for the Insane to become superintendent of the Toronto General Hospital and those whom Jones called 'my enemies' asked him to resign as pathologist. Another blow fell when the promised psychiatric clinic was delayed. (It was actually not until 1925, fourteen years later, that the long-awaited Toronto Psychiatric Hospital was opened.) The promised professorship also remained elusive. These discouragements hit Loe hard, as she had hung on in Toronto only to help Jones advance towards legitimate academic higher status. She was further upset by the illness of her little dog, and spent her time telegraphing Philadelphia for serum which had to be collected twice a day from the railway station.

Jones announced to Freud that their departure from Toronto was imminent: 'It would be inhuman of me to ask her to stay longer, and, I expect, fruitless.' His only options, he said, were to return with Loe to London 'or to separate, which is unthinkable'. He acknowledged that he had little chance of getting a hospital position in London, but thought he could probably count on the demand for his services as a psychoanalyst and 'should be able to do something for the movement there'.

Freud was disappointed: he wanted Jones to stay in Canada at least until he got the promised professorship. The title would enhance the Cause.

One month later Freud got his wish. Jones was made associate professor at last, and was also given responsibility for the neurology ward at Toronto General Hospital. The official change of heart was the result of intervention by Sir William Meredith, the university's chancellor, pleased with his daughter's successful treatment, and by Adolf Meyer, who wrote Dr Clarke a letter that Jones said did him 'much good', saying in effect that Toronto was wise to hold on to Jones even if he was unacceptable to staid Baltimore.

The rise to genuine academic status was, Jones told Freud, 'a definite triumph for our cause, since I am mainly known for my psycho-analytic work, and this was also the cause of the objections to me, which have now been defeated'. In consequence, the unhappy Loe had agreed to stay in Toronto until the following spring.

A photograph of Jones taken on board ship in 1911 shows him strolling jauntily around the deck as he crossed the Atlantic for the Third Congress of the International Psychoanalytic Association, at Weimar, in Prussia. Loe stayed behind. The conference gave Jones a chance to see Freud again, three months after he had poured his heart out about Loe's problems – and also after he had called Freud's attention to a deviation in Jung's thinking. (Jung, as Jones read in the proofs of Jung's two-part paper *Symbols of the Libido*, was beginning to equate the libido not with the sexual drive, but with general psychic energy.)

The new psychoanalysis was in fact proving to be a far more disputatious field than the natural science of which it claimed to be a part, because, unlike in 'hard' science, there were no facts, only theories and private observations of individual cases. In Vienna, not only Adler but Stekel had left – or been expelled – from the Psychoanalytic Society because Freud opposed their new ideas.

In private conversation, seeing Freud for the first time after a year of emotional correspondence, Jones unburdened himself and poured out his troubles with Loe – or, as he explained them, her troubles with her drug addiction and her unhappiness in Canada. Freud suggested that psychoanalysis might be able to help her. Indeed, to Jones's astonishment, he offered to conduct it himself.

Jones burst back to Toronto with the news and, to his equal surprise, Loe welcomed it. As he wrote back to Freud, 'Your opinion that there was a chance for her to get better carried very great weight . . . She was very definite on the point that she would rather be treated by you than by anyone else.' He said he found his wife 'distinctly better'.

Loe's abrupt decision was reinforced by a visit to Toronto from Meyer and his wife. The Meyers, putting aside any American prejudices about 'too much Bernard Shaw and lack of restraint', stayed as guests with Jones and Loe at their home on Brunswick Avenue. Meyer strongly supported Loe in her decision to go to Vienna as Freud's patient. In a following letter, Jones thanked Meyer for talking Loe out of her pessimism about her chances of recovery and so 'putting new life into her'; he was rewarded with Meyer's solemn repetition of his confidence: 'I am convinced that Mrs Jones will overcome some of the fundamental resistances and reach . . . a mastership over the disturbing dynamic factors.'

In his first letter since seeing Jones in Zurich, Freud wrote joyfully, 'My dear Professor Jones, I rejoice in giving you this new title, I did not make so much of it with myself in 1902, at least openly.' (Freud was being unduly modest. None of his followers, certainly not Jones, dreamed of addressing him as anything other than 'Professor'.) He was 'very glad at the disposition of your wife, let us hope her spirits will keep up until the time is come to do something for her in a serious way.'

As 1911 turned into 1912, Loe began to have her doubts. She refused to go alone to Vienna and leave Jones in Toronto. She had had 'a bad recrudescence of her hostility towards analysis', and was also 'sickly, tired, and weak' and obsessed with thoughts of death. But contrarily, Jones reported to Freud, she was getting along better with him: they had not been so happy together for a long time.

Freud did not reply for two months, and he did not (nor ever again) address Jones as 'Dear Professor'. Perhaps the long silence, he said, analysing himself in his letter to Jones of 14 January 1912, was the result of being too busy. Or perhaps he felt he needed more time to study the rewritten version of 'On the Nightmare' that had been sent him. Or perhaps it was dismay. 'I was sorry too', Freud admitted, 'having heard that you got yourself into fresh difficulties with a woman.'

Was the source of the 'fresh difficulties' the same woman who wrote to Brill in 1911 asking for a consultation to talk about her relationship with Jones? Her illegible signature – 'Mrs C. F. Blum Chouffett' – ends a letter revealing her so besotted that she longed 'for the melancholy pleasure of further discussion of Dr Jones with someone who knows him intimately . . . A sorry state of affairs, is it not?' She appears not to have been the woman who brandished a revolver.

Her letter does not suggest that Jones had sexual relations with her. However, the strength of her feeling testifies not only to Jones's attractiveness, but to the power of the transference: the special dependency of patient on doctor about which Freud had warned Jung and which James

Jackson Putnam had shrewdly spotted in his early paper as one of the drawbacks of the psychoanalytic method of treatment.

Jones acknowledged to Freud that he had often been conscious of a sexual attraction to his patients, and let slip that 'my wife was a patient of mine.' In truth, his increasing analytic practice brought him a succession of impassioned women. They tended to wish, and some to believe, that he had suggested a closer relationship, and they were loath to confine it to the consulting room.

At least Mrs Blum Chouffett had enough self-awarenesss to consider that her feelings might be the product of her imagination, for in her letter of 11 October 1911 she asked Brill to 'consider *unsaid*' everything she had told him about Jones. 'My vanity probably misled me into attaching undue significance to several ambiguous remarks of his,' she wrote. Jones, in fact, 'has been most kind to me, and is without doubt, the dearest fellow in the world'. She wanted to know whether Jones cared to continue to see her as a patient. 'Jones is not to see this letter,' she instructed Brill. The fact that the letter found its way into Jones's personal archive suggests that Brill placed professional fraternity over a patient's request for confidence. It was probably also Brill who passed the news about Jones's 'difficulties' on to Freud.

A more serious difficulty was the non-analytic relationship Jones had begun with Loe Kann's maid, a young woman called Lina. Exercising a kind of *droit du seigneur*, he had begun sleeping with Lina. It was an outlet for himself as well as a revenge on Loe for her long invalidism and what Jones and Freud referred to as her 'sexual anaesthesia'.

Jones did not inform Freud of this liaison until events forced a confession the following year, when he referred to it as 'an old affair'. Rather, replying in January 1912 to Freud's reference to his 'fresh difficulties with a woman', Jones was contrite, and fulsome in his praise for psychoanalysis. (He was not formally in analysis, but, like Freud, had analysed himself.) As he expressed it, 'One of the things for which I am most grateful to psycho-analysis for [*sic*] is that by the aid of it I have been able to get control of various wrong tendencies in myself, slowly and one after the other, and often after paying a high price for them, but in the end surely.' At last, he said, he was free from his 'terrible guilt-complex'. Even a few years before, if Freud had alluded 'to my difficulties' he would have been consumed with anxiety. Now he was not. Realistically, he knew he was perhaps being over-confident, but nonetheless, 'the tendency in question is I believe a matter of the past'.

★ ★ ★

He was basking in new recognition. From India an Englishman had sent him three hundred associations to interpret. Jones performed the task, and was congratulated on being right in every detail – such as the fact the lady in question was not neurotic but normal, that she was married to someone else but was having sexual relations with the man who wrote down her associations, and that she preferred *fellatio* to coitus. From Australia, another man came to Toronto to consult Jones, having read about him (so Jones told Freud) in the Australian papers.

Jones and Loe hoped to reach Vienna by mid-June. By late spring they had sold the house on Brunswick Avenue, and Jones had shipped their goods, including the library of 5,000 or so books he had acquired, to London. He intended in future to spend half the year in Europe and half in Canada.

Freud had congratulated him: 'You have, as it were, conquered America in no more than one or two years.' He expected Jones the conqueror to 'do the same for your mother-country'. England, Freud judged, was now 'better soil' for psychoanalysis than when Jones had left it. Only David Eder, and perhaps Jones's old colleague David Forsyth, were using its techniques.

America was conquered, up to a point. On 5 April 1912 the *New York Times* reported a speech at a meeting of the Academy of Medicine's neurology section by the eminent American neurologist and expert on brain surgery Dr Moses A. Starr, denouncing the growing popularity of Freud's ideas of sexuality. The theories were suspect for emanating from venal Vienna – or, as Starr put it, 'Vienna is not a particularly moral city.'

Vienna was where Loe and Jones were heading; they planned to get there by 13 or 15 June for her to meet Freud and discuss the arrangements for her analysis. Freud could not take her on a regular basis until October, however. There were a number of questions to be resolved. Should she go to a sanatorium until Freud was ready to work with her in October? Should she engage a suite of rooms in Vienna, with a nurse or a doctor to attend her as the morphine dose was reduced? Or could she reduce the dose in London – 'the home of her heart'? Brushing aside Freud's hint that perhaps she might be seen by another analyst, Jones conveyed Loe's determination to be treated by Freud and no one else. 'Perhaps I am influenced too much by her attitude in this,' he wrote to Freud, 'and also by the natural desire to get the best for one's wife.'

In any event, Jones would return to London, with or without Loe, and begin the task of establishing a psychoanalytic practice in the city he had left as a neurologist. He had at least two patients lined up.

8

Jung, Jones and Jones
June 1912–August 1914

～

THE RETURN TO the 'right side of the Atlantic' saw a dramatic change in Jones's life. Within little over a year he had shrugged off Toronto, founded the London Psycho-Analytical Society, published the first book in English on psychoanalysis, delivered Loe Kann to Freud in Vienna, supplanted Jung as Freud's second-in-command, and lost Loe to another man named Jones.

It was fortuitous that Jones reappeared on the European scene just as a rift opened between Freud and Jung. The king and crown prince of psychoanalysis had been increasingly estranged since May 1912, when Freud was in Switzerland and Jung had failed to travel a relatively short distance to visit him at Kreuzlingen on Lake Constance. Each blamed the other for the letters arranging the meeting failing to arrive on time.

Taking Loe to Vienna in June 1912 gave Jones the opportunity for long late evenings of conversation with Freud – sometimes not stopping until three o'clock in the morning, even though Jones was guiltily aware that the first patient was due at Berggasse 19 at 8 a.m. Jones and 'Frau Jones', as Freud referred to Loe, stayed in the Pension Washington in the City Hall quarter of the First District. She and Freud took to each other immediately, and it was agreed that she would return to Vienna in October to begin her analysis. Before she left, Loe wrote to Freud in German to thank him, signing herself 'Loe Kann Jones' and enclosing more money than he had expected because he had forgotten to include the first Sunday's consultation in his bill – a reminder to him, were any needed, of how well-heeled she was.

Jones returned to London and took rooms for himself and Loe in a lodging house in Princes Street, below Cavendish Square, near his old haunts of Harley Street. Freud wrote optimistically of the prospect that analysis might cure Loe's morphine addiction. 'Let us hope that the continuation will suit the beginning,' he said, 'and that we shall earn at least a good portion of recovery, although to be sure we will struggle for nothing less than the whole of it.' Freud looked forward to seeing them both again on his planned trip to London in September.

In his next breath, Freud reported receiving a letter from Jung that he could only read as 'a formal disavowal of our hitherto friendly relations'. That was just the hint that Jones needed. There was little doubt that Jung was heading off in a direction of his own. An extract from his new book, later translated as *Psychology of the Unconscious*, showed him downplaying Freud's theories of infantile sexuality and the Oedipus complex. What is more, in March that year Jung, president of the International Psychoanalytic Association, had cancelled its fourth congress, scheduled for September. Jung had something better to do just when he had been expected to preside over the congress: give lectures at Fordham University in New York. His action made clear that his own career took precedence over the cherished organisation that Freud called by the generic name for 'association', the *Verein*.

Jones then made a crucial move which has been seen as a deliberate manoeuvre to displace Jung in the Freudian power structure. 'Jung abdicates from his throne,' he declared to Freud. Knowing that Freud had already lost two other of his original stalwarts, Alfred Adler and Wilhelm Stekel, Jones proposed a way to forestall future defections. Building on a casual suggestion from Freud's close friend the Hungarian analyst Sándor Ferenczi, he raised the possibility 'that a small group of men could be thoroughly analysed by you, so that they could represent the pure theory unadultered [*sic*] by personal complexes'.

Freud loved the idea. He had once hoped that Jung would form an inner circle around himself, composed of the heads of the psychoanalytic associations in various cities. However, he now told Jones that he saw that any such union must exclude Jung and that it must be '*strictly secret*'. 'I dare say,' Freud wrote grandiloquently, 'it would make living and dying easier for me if I knew of such an association existing to watch over my creation.'

Jones was not easily outdone in grandiloquence. Dipping into his rich reading, he came up with the perfect phrase to delight Freud. The committee he envisaged would be 'a united small body, designed, like the Paladins of Charlemagne, to guard the kingdom and policy of their master'. He eagerly awaited Freud's visit to London, so that they could discuss it.

Freud's planned visit to London in 1912 never took place. In August that year, while he was in the Austrian Tyrol, taking his annual mountain holiday with his family, his married daughter, Mathilde, fell ill and and underwent an emergency operation that terminated her pregnancy. Freud, very upset, then fell ill himself, and the trip to England was cancelled. 'Assure your wife', he told Jones, 'that not seeing her at London is the most sensible [sensitive] loss of this affair.'

He took himself to his beloved Italy to recover. The restorative powers that Freud attributed to this country, especially its classical sites, would be remarkable was the belief not so widely shared at the time. From Rome, he wrote to Jones of being 'strengthened and relieved by the air and the impressions of this divine town'. There was, he added, 'no big danger of a separation between Jung and me'.

A few days earlier Jones, his own prose growing purpler, had written to Freud that Jung was wrapping himself 'in a divine and impenetrable shroud of mystery' to avoid too much contact with his followers – a mistake that Jung felt Freud had made. But, Jones told Freud, 'We cannot have a monarchy unless one man is strong enough to be king, and also willing.' More prosaic news was that he and Loe would soon leave for Holland and then move on to Vienna for her to begin treatment with Freud.

The group that Jones had proposed – what came to be called 'the Committee' – was set up with five members: Jones, Karl Abraham from Berlin, Sándor Ferenczi from Budapest, and Otto Rank and Hanns Sachs from Vienna. These five would write nothing contradictory to Freud's theories, would publish nothing without each other's approval, and would sniff out heresy wherever it might begin.

Loe's analysis was simultaneous with the birth of the Committee, and coincided with Freud's burst of gratitude towards Jones. (Freud was so pleased to hear that Jones was dedicating his first full-length book, *Papers on Psycho-Analysis*, to him that he signed his thank-you letter to Jones 'Yours in love Freud'.) For her new life in Vienna, Loe rented a small flat and moved in with her maid Lina and her dog Trottie (named, affectionately or sardonically, for Jones's old friend Wilfred Trotter). Once a day she presented herself to lie on Freud's couch for an hour of free association. It was not clear how she was expected to fill the rest of her time.

At Freud's request, Jones took himself away from Vienna to allow Loe's analysis free rein. As he was not required to return to the University of Toronto until the beginning of the new year, to deliver six weeks of lectures on psychiatry, he followed in Freud's footsteps and threw himself into a tour of the 'holy ground' of Italy. He saw himself, as he pictured for Freud, in the train of Milton, Wordsworth, Shelley, Keats, Byron, the

Brownings, Swinburne and Ruskin: 'They sing of Italy as of heaven.' But in reality he was lonely, and eagerly looked for letters from Vienna.

'Your wife shows, as I expected her to be, a precious creature of highest value.' Freud, sending this report on his new patient at the end of October, was not enough of a Freudian to catch the unconscious reference to Loe's great wealth. He may merely have been picking up Jones's earlier metaphorical description of Loe as a 'jewel'. (She was almost certainly paying for his Italian sojourn.)

That Freud should be captivated by Loe was not surprising. He liked beautiful women; he preferred Jewish to 'Teutonic' females; and he kept a practical eye out for wealthy patients – and this one showered him with gifts of gorgeous flowers. Loe Kann had the additional merit of being the partner of the increasingly indispensable Jones.

It was impossible, however, for Freud to keep an analytic distance from a patient with so many organic problems. One night Loe suffered an attack of pain, after which her maid Lina found blood in her urine. 'I eagerly wanted to see it and have it examined,' Freud the doctor wrote to Jones, but the specimen had been spilt, or thrown away, before he thought to ask for it.

So much for the secrets of the consulting room. Freud even sent word of Loe's symptoms to his good friend Ferenczi in Budapest: 'Mrs Jones is doing very well and has given up the first half of her dose of morphine without difficulty.'

Jones himself got a close look at the recalcitrant Jung in November, during a small meeting in Munich. Jung had called the group together to discuss the crisis caused by Stekel's quitting the International Psychoanalytic Association, and taking its monthly publication, the *Zentralblatt*, of which he was editor, with him.

Freud turned up from Vienna with a plan, which was adopted: to leave the *Zentralblatt* to Stekel and start a new publication (titled, unimaginatively, the *Zeitschrift* – the 'Periodical') in its place. To be published every other month by Hugo Heller in Vienna and Leipzig, its full name would be *Internazionale Zeitschrift für ärtzliche Psychoanalyse*. It would be the new official organ of the International Association, and would be edited jointly by Ferenczi, Jones and Rank. Jung would remain editor of the association's *Jahrbuch*.

On his travels, Jones had grown a thick black full beard with sideburns. Freud found him 'outwardly almost unrecognizable'. Jones himself was not in a good mood, having learned of the Munich meeting only through a chance message from Freud. Though Jung had invited him – in a manner of speaking – he had sent the notice of the meeting to Jones's address in Wales, and had given the wrong day as well.

The Munich meeting was memorable for Freud's fainting at the table in a restaurant. His companions, psychoanalysts all, noted that it was the second time that Freud had collapsed in Jung's presence (in 1909, while Freud, Jung and Ferenczi were in Bremen on their way to the United States, Freud had had a similar fainting spell in a restaurant), and they had little difficulty in diagnosing Freud's fear of Jung as the cause. Jones sent Freud his analysis of the incident, and Freud agreed: 'You are right in supposing that I had transferred to Jung homosex. feelings from another part but I am glad to find that I have no difficulty in removing them for free circulation.'

Jones went back to Rome, with plans to return to Vienna after Christmas. In early December Freud sent him a report on Loe's progress: 'Your wife is splendid, no trace of "kidney" pains since the first attack and no doubt, this first one was fabricated out of the monthly, which betrayed itself by definite somatic signs (no blood) at the right term and unaccompanied by pains these last days.' The morphia was down to one third, and Freud thought she was not so much 'maniacal', although in a good mood. The prognosis was for a permanent change 'though to be sure there is some doubt how far the chief point, the sexual anaesthesia can be gained'.

This letter is the first written acknowledgement between Freud and Jones that the sexual relations between Jones and Loe had run into difficulties. It also shows how Freud continued to pass on the confidences of his patient to her partner, who was coming to Vienna in a few weeks expecting to share her bed.

Freud was breaking the rules of psychoanalysis at the same time as making them. The mixture of friendship and an analytic relationship that would later be considered taboo was, in the early days of analysis, common practice. In the papers Freud published between 1911 and 1915 on psychoanalytic technique – on how to select patients, how to begin treatment, how to arrange the fee, and how to instruct the patient in the fundamental requirement of saying absolutely everything that comes to mind – he wrote that it was preferable that the analyst and patient should not have met socially. 'The physician should be opaque to the patient and, like a mirror, show nothing but what is shown to him.' Even so, Freud accepted that many of those who came to him were followers, potential analysts as well as patients. He found no difficulty in seeing them on social terms outside the analytic hour. Loe was no budding analyst, but Freud could not resist inviting her for an evening with his family before Christmas.

On the day after Christmas, Freud passed Jones a broad hint about his 'wife': 'I am under the impression that you do not realise completely how well she is.' Jones might easily find her in a different condition than she had been in. A lot of good had been done for her, but the future was hard to prophesy: 'it depends on her resistance against normal sexual relations, where I expect the citadel of resistance. Perhaps she will be eager to begin intercourse and feel highly disappointed when anaesthesia has not subsided, as will be the case.'

Freud in fact held something back when he told Jones that he thought Loe was 'enjoying her Vienna sojourn very much'. He knew that she was falling in love with a quietly handsome young American poet, who had brought his father, a Midwestern industrialist, to Vienna to be treated by Freud. The poet's name, as luck would have it, was Jones – Herbert Jones. Freud signed his letter 'your truthful friend'.

As he prepared to return to Vienna, wondering why Loe had let a whole month go by without writing to him, even though he believed one letter had been lost en route, Jones asked Freud's advice on making sexual advances to her. They might expose her to risks of pregnancy: 'She finds all kinds of precautionary measures very distasteful. On these grounds I do not think I will make any overtures myself . . . I anticipate she will desire intercourse.' Freud understood very well. He had curtailed, if not entirely abandoned, sexual relations with his wife, Martha, because, after six pregnancies in quick succession, they did not want any more children. He disapproved of contraception, and believed, according to his biographer Peter Gay, that using condoms was likely to produce 'neurotic malaise'. Indeed, as he would write to James Jackson Putnam of Harvard, he had made very little use of the freer sexual life he advocated for others.

Over the Christmas holidays of 1912, Loe's maid Lina developed pains remarkably similar to Loe's. Freud marvelled at the symbiotic relationship between employer and servant: 'The nicest case of "Übertragung" [transference] I ever saw. The girl takes upon her the kidney stones, which have left the mistress.'

That was not all that Lina took upon her. When Jones arrived from Italy, she took him – not for the first time, it seems – as a lover. The actual scenes behind the revelations in the Jones–Freud correspondence can easily be imagined: Loe learning about Jones's going to bed with Lina; Loe rushing to tell Freud, who was shocked but could not dispense with Jones, now that he regarded Jung as 'behaving quite crazy' (or, as he said to his fellow Jew Ferenczi, '*meschugge*'. But he knew, as Jones did not, that Loe was involved with Herbert Jones.

One relationship at least was clear. Freud wrote to Ferenczi of Jung, 'He can go jump in the lake; I don't need him and his friendship any more than I need his falsehoods.'

Open hostility had broken out when Jung, in a letter to Freud before Christmas, had reproached him for treating his pupils like patients, reducing everyone to the level of sons and daughters: 'Meanwhile you remain on top as the father, sitting pretty.' Jung could not have known that Freud now thought of Jones and Loe as 'my adopted children'.

It was left to Jones, from London on his way back to Toronto without Loe, at the end of January, to write a confessional letter to Freud about himself and Lina. It was 'an old affair', he said (implying that it had begun in Canada), and while in Italy he had determined to break it off. 'The continuation of it in Wien' was blamed on 'some devil of desire' and was 'dictated by a repressed spirit of hostility against my dear wife'. The guilt at hurting her 'whom I love so passionately' was 'almost beyond my endurance to bear'. If Lina (whose surname has not been recorded) was one of the two servants Loe had brought with her to Toronto in 1908, Jones's words about 'my harem' at the time were well chosen.

Freud glossed over the infidelity incident when he wrote to Ferenczi on 2 February, 'Jones left yesterday for Canada. There was transitory discord between him and his wife, in which the wife, especially, behaved charmingly. I am now altogether satisfied with my adopted children.'

He should have been satisfied with his adopted son. In November 1912 Ballière, Tindall and Cox in London had published Jones's *Papers on Psycho-Analysis*, with its dedication 'to Professor Freud as a token of the author's gratitude'. The book was the first full explication in English of Freud's ideas, for translations of his revolutionary seminal works *The Interpretation of Dreams* and *The Psychopathology of Everyday Life* had not yet appeared. It fell to Jones, therefore, to bring to the English-speaking world a description of the mechanisms, so obvious once pointed out but until then unrecognized, of such occurrences as slips of the tongue (*lapsus linguae*), mislaying objects and 'forgetting' which is far from accidental. Drawing on papers he himself had published or speeches given in North America, Jones explained the gospel according to Freud. Psychoanalysis showed that there was 'not only a definite psychical cause for the occurrence, but that this has always a logical meaning, and may strictly be called a motive'. He called attention to the importance that Freud attached to infantile mental processes, and to an individual's whole life being a continuity:

> He [Freud] regards the mental processes, and particularly the wishes, of early childhood life as the permanent basis for all later development. Unconscious mental life is indestructible, and the intensity of its wishes does not fade . . . A great number of the reactions of adult life owe their real force to the adjuvant impulses contributed by the unconscious. Freud, therefore, looks upon the whole of a subject's mental life as a continuity, as a series of associated trends . . . The main traits of character are permanently determined for good or ill before the fifth year of life.

Such was the appetite for Freud's new ideas that *Papers on Psycho-Analysis* was subsequently reissued, in revised and expanded form, four times.

Jones went back to Toronto alone, living at 321 Jarvis Street. The moral climate had not thawed. His murky reputation persisted, while in Boston police were threatening to prosecute Morton Prince for the 'obscene' material published in his *Journal of Abnormal Psychology*. Jones tried to imagine his re-entry into the London medical world. As he told Freud, who evidently knew of his troubled past, 'I have a black mark to my name in London, but I hope that by sitting tight and behaving well something will be accomplished in time, if not for myself, at least for ψα.'

Freud now wanted Jones in 'an influential and highly respected position in London and nowhere else!' But – he knew his man – 'you must promise formally never to spoil it when you have got it at last, *by no private motive*.' Other advice: 'Now make your heart easy for work, be careful with those bad women.' Even after learning that Jones's boast to have conquered certain bad tendencies in himself was false, Freud continued to close his letters effusively: 'write as soon as you can to your devoted Freud'.

Jones performed his North American duties, giving his lectures and attending the opening of the Phipps Psychiatric Clinic in Baltimore at Johns Hopkins Hospital in April 1913, when he gave an address on 'The Interrelations of the Biogenetic Psychoses'. He then returned to Vienna. Did he perceive the buried warning in the letter in which Freud had told him 'There is more going on now than I can make you know'?

Freud was beginning to appreciate how disruptive a psychoanalysis could be to other people in the analysand's life. He confided in Ferenczi that he did not know how Jones 'will bear finding out that his wife, as a consequence of the analysis, no longer wants to remain his wife'. In the same letter he told Ferenczi he was disturbed 'to expose one of my indispensable helpers to the danger of personal estrangement brought about by the analysis'. About a week later he considered the problem from the other point of view: 'Jones has had his wife for seven years, and she is actually a jewel. It is certainly not my fault that he has lost her, and hardly his own either, by the way. They were no longer together for a long time.'

By 24 May Freud could write to Ferenczi, 'Jones is here and is staying at the Pension Washington with his – former – wife.' For Jones, there was a compensation. The Committee had its first meeting the next day, and Freud gave each of the chosen five an antique Greek intaglio, which they each then had mounted on a gold ring; he himself was made chairman.

The next step was for Jones to be analysed himself, and the logical analyst was a fellow member of the Committee, Ferenczi, three hours away in Budapest. The analysis was to be conducted in German – Jones's German was just about adequate to the task – and, as it was to be an intensive treatment, would go on for two hours a day through June and July.

By the time that Jones took to the couch for the first time in June, he understood that Loe had given her '*full* love, which I had always dreamed of winning' to another man. Reporting back to Freud, he opened his heart:

> The idea of losing my wife has not yet penetrated fully into my mind. I have difficulty in 'taking it in'. She has meant so much to me for years, and I held so fast unconsciously on to the *Bedingungslosigkeit* [unconditionality] of her love, that it will cost me pretty severe depression before getting over the blow of seeing her love given to another, especially her *full love*, which I had always dreamed of winning. It is of course worse for me that I know how much I have contributed to the present situation.

Soon Ferenczi was matching Freud in bulletins about his most interesting patient. After initial resistance, with Jones trying to take control of the analysis, feeding Ferenczi with interpretations of what he himself knew about himself already, Ferenczi felt that Jones was making good progress. The hours were passing pleasantly, and the transference was established – in both directions. Ferenczi found Jones 'not only good and sensitive but also a very clever person, whose company stimulates one to one's best thoughts'.

Ferenczi ingenuously told Freud that Jones 'seems to fear that I will tell you everything that I experience in the analysis. For that reason I ask you not to mention anything about our correspondence in Frau Jones's presence. I now find Jones in some respects scientifically *much* more valuable to us than before our analytic acquaintance with him.' This increased value was *not*, Ferenczi modestly hastened to add, because the analysis had wrought changes: rather it was because he had somewhat underestimated Jones before.

Freud had advised Ferenczi to 'Be strict and tender with him. He is a very good person. Feed the pupa so that a queen can be made out of it.' He asked also that Ferenczi tell his patient that things are 'continuing to go well with Frau Jones'.

The analysis, not surprisingly, focused on Jones's small stature and what Ferenczi saw as his lowly social origins. Jones began by trying to overcome what he saw as his 'father-complex', and ended by transferring his hostility to his mother. He told Ferenczi that his mother had fed him 'quack' milk preparations as an infant. This denial of the breast had stunted his growth (according to the interpretation passed on by Ferenczi to Michael Balint, a Hungarian psychiatrist who later moved to London) and had left Jones with 'an omnipotence complex'. If so, Ferenczi cannot have claimed to have cured it.

Jones and his analyst met outside the analytic hour, even travelling to Vienna together, and had 'many interesting discussions' on such questions as the origin and significance of symbolism. Jones felt himself recovering from the break with Loe, who had gone to visit him in Budapest for a few days. It was 'the best thing' for both of them, he told Freud. 'We have both worked off our infantile sexuality at the expense of the other' . . . 'Now that I love her less, I can afford to feel more friendly and kindly towards her, and I will do all in my power to further her happiness.'

Jones's analysis was brief compared to the years-long analyses that would become the norm in the future, and by the end of July 1913 he told Freud that it 'was drawing towards a close'.

Jones left Budapest on 1 August. He and his analyst parted on the warmest of terms. 'I miss him *very much*,' Ferenczi told Freud early in August 1913. 'I grew to love and treasure him; it was a pleasure to have such an intelligent, fine, and respectable pupil . . . Let us hope he will succeed in mastering his neurotic tendencies from now on.'

Freud, for his part, was relieved. He confessed to Ferenczi that he felt 'less guilty of complicity in the outcome of the process with his wife since I see her blooming so, now that she is free'. He also admitted to what his profession would later call 'counter-transference', the analyst's attachment to the patient, but he had managed to stay free of sexual desire for her. As his letter to Ferenczi reads in translation, 'This Loe has become extraordinarily dear to me, and I have produced with her a very warm feeling with complete sexual inhibition (probably owing to my age).' But he was concerned that her feet were swelling; Jones was to know nothing of this possible thrombosis of her veins.

In August 1913 the freshly analysed Jones returned to London and wrote a report for the new *Zeitschrift* on the International Congress of Medicine which was held there. His identity card for the congress placed him at the University of Toronto. That was true, but not for much longer. He wrote to the president of the university asking to be allowed to practise in London and return to Toronto the following spring to give his lectures. His request was refused, and Jones resigned. Certainly the university's president, Sir Alexander Falconer, and Jones's original patron, Charles Clarke, were glad to see him go. He never returned, and the cloud over his reputation was to linger. 'Both by word and deed,' wrote a historian of Canadian medicine in 1981, 'Dr Ernest Jones had made himself something of a pariah to his Canadian colleagues.'

Uneasily he wondered how London would receive him, especially as he had installed himself in a flat in Portland Court, a block on Great Portland Street – a street filled with dealers in motor cars, tyres and spare parts. He knew he had put himself beyond the pale: 'In those days,' he wrote in his autobiography, 'no consultant could practise east of Portland Place or west of Welbeck Street.' His former friends received him, he said, 'with politeness, but without intimacy'. His old friend Harry Campbell told him he would be ostracized if he stayed in London – apparently as much for his association with things Freudian as for the incidents of the past. What hurt more was the aloofness of Wilfred Trotter, his former best friend, now his brother-in-law. To himself, Jones attributed the new barrier between them to Trotter's jealousy that Jones had replaced him with Freud as closest confidant. The coolness might also be explained by the difference in professional standing – Trotter was now on the staff of University College Hospital – and by Jones's highly irregular private life.

Jones began looking up former pupils. Bernard Hart, a friend of the late Bertie Ward, was medical superintendent of Northumberland House Asylum in London and the author of articles such as 'The Psychology of Freud and His School' (1910) that helped introduce psychoanalysis to the English-speaking world. Hart's view, as expressed to Jones, was that

'Freudism is strictly speaking, a religion; you can't *prove* it, but you have to accept it because "it works" '.

Another former pupil, David Eder, had become a practising analyst and was trying to spread the word. In 1911, speaking to the Neurological Section of the British Medical Association, Eder had read a paper on a case of obsession and hysteria 'treated by the Freud Psycho-Analytic Method'. When he described how he had released the patient's hidden memories of lying in bed naked at the age of three, stroking his sister, the audience of eight walked out without a word. (This incident would seem to reinforce Freud's statement in his foreword to a biography of Eder, which was later to infuriate Jones, that Eder was the first to practise psychoanalysis in Britain.)

Eder, who had introduced Jones to Loe, had in fact turned up in Vienna early that year, wanting three weeks of analysis with Freud, but found himself passed on to one of Freud's acolytes, Victor Tausk. With Jones back in London, Eder asked to be taken on as a patient 'for a few symptoms', as Jones explained to Freud, and 'so that he may get further into the work'.

Jones knew quite a bit about Eder, whose first wife (a former patient of Jones's) had committed suicide after he left her for another woman. Jones found Eder happily remarried to the other woman, and he pronounced Edith Eder 'especially intelligent and well-educated'. She was intensely interested in psychoanalysis, and had recently been treated by Jung.

With the Eders and six others, before October was out Jones had founded the London Psycho-Analytical Society and had applied to Jung for its membership in the International Association. He was president; Douglas Bryan, a general practitioner from Leicester, was vice-president; Eder was secretary. Another member was Jones's old acquaintance the paediatrician Dr David Forsyth, one of the few people in Britain to be practising psychoanalysis. Forsyth, according to Jones's autobiography, did not attend many meetings: 'his personal jealousy of myself was already beginning to manifest itself.' Havelock Ellis and William McDougall, head of the psychological laboratory at Oxford, declined to join.

The new Jones was on friendly terms with Loe Kann, who also was back in London, having left her maid and her dog in Vienna during a break in her analysis. She 'generously offered', Jones told Freud, to pay Jones's expenses for three years, to help him get re-established in London. But he thought it might not be necessary. (Possibly she paid for the lease on the flat in Portland Court. In any case, she supervised its redecoration.)

Herbert Jones was hovering in the background. 'Jones II', as Ernest Jones referred to him (with echoes of his old school rosters), was accompanied by his father and other members of his family, who knew nothing about his new love. The American Jones was managing to see Loe once a day, and told Freud (adding his letter to hers), 'I feel more certain every day of my love for Loe. I don't expect that we'll have a perfectly easy life . . . but if love and hard work can make it a happy one, I think it will be so.'

Loe intended to resume her analysis once the redecoration of Jones's new flat was completed. She was cross with Freud for having kept no hours for her in his autumn schedule, because he had not known whether to expect her or not. With the confidence of the rich, she scolded him: she knew that he always welcomed free time, and he surely understood that 'the money-side was all right.' She would pay, of course, for the missed appointments.

Loe's difficulties were not helped by 'Davy' (as she called him) Jones's need to return to America for some months and her uncertainty about whether they had a future together or not. Ernest Jones was well positioned to witness her continuing use of morphine, and told Freud about it, while asking him to keep the information to himself. But Freud did not.

Freud wrote Loe an angry letter, accusing her of hiding the fact that she had returned to morphine and of being ashamed of her addiction. Davy Jones, by then in the United States, consoled her by cable: 'He must be under some misunderstanding. Don't be too hard on him. Thousands of love − Dave.' But she was hard on Freud. Just finishing her work on Jones's flat, she answered back in a letter that shows her fiery and articulate:

> I have never been ashamed in my life, thank God, and am far from it now. I have taken morphine and never tried to hide it from anyone, least of all from you. I have done all I could without it and taken the minimum dose I required. I am sorry to say that the smallest doses had no effect whatever.
>
> Don't worry about my marriage . . . As far as I'm concerned − you know that I would rather die than make Davy unhappy − in which case I would choose a quicker and surer way than morphine.

She would not return to Vienna yet, but would arrive later, 'since no treatment awaits me now'.

In January 1914 psychoanalysis was flourishing. Loe eventually made her way back to Vienna, 'Davy' had joined her, and it now seemed that they would marry. Jones asked Freud what the couple were going to do about his long cohabitation with Loe. 'Is Herbert going to consult the lawyer about the marriage fiction?' he wondered.

His own appointment book was full. Of the thirty or forty psychoanalytic patients in London, he had eight, and he had to send a further applicant to Eder. Patients meant money – especially if they could pay his full fee of two guineas an hour. 'If things go on this way . . .' he told Freud, 'I shall be able to marry.'

Freud was aghast. He pleaded with Jones: 'Do me the personal favour of not making marriage the *next step* in your life', but to take some time in choosing.

The Jung saga played itself out. On 20 April 1914 Jung resigned the presidency of the International Psychoanalytic Association, withdrawing from the association as well and declaring that no Swiss analyst would attend its next congress, the fifth, planned for Dresden in September. The Committee agreed that, once that congress was over, Jones would take over as official president. Jung's defection was hailed by Jones's supposed friend David Eder in the *British Medical Journal* 'as a return to a saner way of life', and Jung was praised – 'in certain quarters', according to Jones's somewhat sardonic words – as 'the man who purged Freud's doctrines of their obscene preoccupation with sexual topics'. The New York Academy of Medicine, for example, heard Jung say that 'A purely sexual etiology of neurosis strikes me as much too narrow.'

Lina was now Jones's lover. She had left Vienna, leaving Trottie with Loe, and moved into the London flat that Loe had furnished and decorated. She was enough of a fixture in Jones's life for him to take her to Swansea and introduce her to his father and his new stepmother. (Jones found his father's new wife, Edith May Howard, 'a vulgar person'; he quarrelled with her, as did both his sisters.) Thomas Jones appraised his son's new consort and told him that he hoped his intentions towards her were honourable.

Freud's plea to Jones to postpone marrying for some time went beyond avuncular concern. Loe had alerted him that Jones had cast his eyes on eighteen-year-old Anna Freud. Someone else who spotted Jones's intention to become Freud's son-in-law was Edith Eder.

Edith and Jones had become close (or, according to Sonu Shamdasani in the *New Oxford Dictionary of National Biography*, rather more than close), to judge from her fevered letters to him. There was certainly a professional rapport between them. At a March 1914 meeting of the London Psycho-

Analytical Society, Mrs Eder read a translation of Freud's paper on the dynamics of the transference, and a lively discussion followed.

In a letter to Jones apparently written in the spring of 1914, Edith Eder wrote of what she saw as his aspiration to woo Anna Freud, and scolded him because of his open and continuing liaison with Lina:

Dear Ernest,

There are some things I want to say to you. I don't want an answer . . . First as to your lady in Vienna: I think it is because of t. way yr. relationship to Lina has developed that I have begun to doubt yr getting her. Speaking with 't. frankness that becomes our craft' I have found myself feeling there must be in you some v. deep unanalysed feeling that either holds you to Lina (for all t. admitted motives together seem quite inadequate, considering t. stakes at issue) or – as indeed seems to me more probable – that puts a barrier between you & Freud's daughter. I cannot otherwise account for such a man as you allowing such an obstacle to grow up, permitting himself to devote so much emotion, time and energy to 1 girl when he must know that his only hope of winning t. other lies in his letting the whole tide of his being sweep him towards her unresisted.

Against this backdrop, when Anna Freud planned a trip to England in July 1914, after passing her teacher's examinations, Freud the father went on active alert. But first he helped Loe Kann become legally Mrs Jones at last. He and Otto Rank went from Vienna to Budapest and served, with Ferenczi, as witnesses at her marriage to Herbert Jones. It was one of only three weddings that Freud would ever attend outside his family circle. Sending the news to Ernest Jones, Freud marvelled at 'a most remarkable chain of changes between persons and feelings . . . and the most striking points seem to me, that our relations have not been spoiled and that I have learned even to like the other man'. He trusted the couple would 'enjoy as much happiness as her health will permit'.

Then Freud turned his attention to his daughter. Without mentioning Loe Kann Jones by name, he sent Anna a warning: 'I know from the most reliable source that Doctor Jones has serious intentions of wooing you.' To his friend Ferenczi he confided that he didn't want 'to lose the dear child to an obvious act of revenge' – that is, marrying Anna would be Jones's retaliation against Freud for steering Loe Kann into marrying Herbert Jones. In any event, Freud thought, 'Loe will keep watch like a dragon.' Loe, whom Anna liked enormously and who was back in London, served at least part-time as Anna's chaperone during her English visit.

Forewarned is forearmed, but in Anna's case armour was unnecessary.

Above left: Willingly to
school: young Ernest
was good at his books

Above right: Jones with
sisters Elizabeth (left)
and Sybil

Right: 'Representative
Welsh types' as they
appeared in *The Life
of David Lloyd George
with a Short History
of the Welsh People,* by
J. Hugh Edwards, MP,
1917

Left: The Jones family home in Gowerton, South Wales, now bears a blue plaque

Below: Llandovery College at the turn of the century

The young doctor who never had to ask, 'What does Woman want?'

Loe Kann – Jones's common-law wife from *c.*1907 to 1913

In 1909 Jones ran Canada's first outpatient psychiatric clinic from this house on the corner of Chestnut Street and Christopher Street, Toronto

Otto Gross, the Austrian renegade, described by Jones as 'my first instructor in the technique of psychoanalysis'

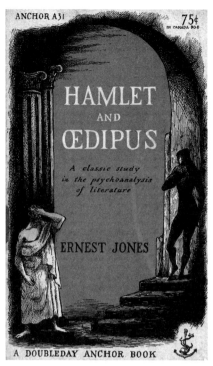

Above left: The jacket of the 1949 edition of Jones's *Hamlet and Oedipus*, written in 1910. It influenced James Joyce and Laurence Olivier

Above right: Jones, here *c.*1911, crossed from Canada to 'the right side of the Atlantic' whenever he could

Right: Herbert Jones, aka 'Davy' or 'Jones II', the American poet who stole Loe Kann away from Jones

Left: 'Men with Bulging Brains have Time for Occasional Smiles,' said the *Worcester Telegram* of 12 September 1909. Left to right (front row): Sigmund Freud, G. Stanley Clark, Carl Gustav Jung; (back row): A. A. Brill, Ernest Jones, Sándor Ferenczi

Portrait of Morfydd Owen, the first Mrs Ernest Jones – but only for
a year

Morfydd Owen (left) at the National Eisteddfod, Aberystwyth, 1916, with her friend Elizabeth Lloyd (Beti Bwt), flanking three Oxford poets: Eric Dickinson (standing left), Mansell Jones (seated) and Wilfred Rowland Childe

Passport photos of Ernest Jones and Kitty Jones at the time of their marriage in Zurich, October 1919

Left: Disciple and master: Jones and Freud, *c.*1918

Below: Anna and Sigmund Freud in The Hague 1920 at the Sixth Congress of the International Psychoanalytic Association

At eighteen, she was (as she would remain throughout her life) uninterested in marrying.

It was, in retrospect, not a good time to travel. The heir to the Austrian Imperial throne, the Archduke Franz Ferdinand, and his wife had been assassinated in Sarajevo on 28 June. Freud acknowledged to Ferenczi that the consequences to the 'surprising murder . . . cannot be foreseen'.

On 15 July Anna sailed for England from Hamburg, where her mother's family lived; she landed two days later at Southampton, where Jones was waiting to meet her, with a large bunch of flowers. He was on his best behaviour. Over the next fortnight he guided her to places he loved, took her on a boat trip up the Thames, and constantly corrected her English.

Freud, hearing about the pleasant sightseeing trips from Anna, wrote to thank Jones, but took the opportunity to warn him of her youth and inexperience:

> She is the most gifted and accomplished of my children . . . She does not claim to be treated as a woman, being still far away from sexual longings and rather refusing man. There is an outspoken [sic] understanding between me and her that she should not consider marriage or the preliminaries before she gets 2 or 3 years older. I dont [sic] think she will break the treaty.

When, on 27 July, Jones had the premature news that Austria had declared on war Serbia, he volunteered his services to escort Anna home if needed. Reassuring Freud of his respect for her innocence, he tucked in a barb: 'She has a beautiful character and will surely be a remarkable woman later on, provided that her sexual repression does not injure her. She is of course tremendously bound to you, and it is one of those rare cases where the actual father corresponds to the father-imago.'

At the end of July, Jones was steering clear of Jung, who was in England, and he chose not to go in person to the British Medical Association annual meeting in Aberdeen at the end of July, where Jung was to speak. Eder went, and read 'The Unconscious and its Significance for Psychopathology' on his behalf. Jones had told Freud that he was not having regular holidays that year, but it seems possible that he wanted to make time for Anna. To his regret, Jung was having a warm reception, and Jones was all the more mocking of his approach. From Edith Eder, who had just had a month's analysis with Jung, he had gleaned Jung's way of dealing with the patient–doctor transference. He described it sarcastically to Freud: 'The patient overcomes it by learning that she is not really in love with the analyst but that she is for the first time struggling to comprehend a Universal Idea (with capitals) in Plato's sense.'

Britain's declaration of war with Germany on 4 August 1914 made it urgent for Anna to leave England. Herbert and Loe Jones helped to organize Anna's departure by negotiating with the secretary of the Austrian Embassy in London to enable her to leave, with a woman escort, and return to Vienna by a circuitous route via Gibraltar and Genoa.

Even so, Anna stayed on in England for nearly a fortnight more. Jones's diary for 1914 spells out: 'Aug 12 Anna dined here, went to see Kismet; Aug 13 spent evening at Loe's, Anna; Sat Aug 15 Anna to Kensington Gardens; 16 goodbye to Anna.'

Any hope of making Anna 'Mrs Ernest Jones' had vanished. And so had another hope. The outbreak of war had forced the cancellation of the International Psychoanalytic Association congress scheduled for Dresden in September, and with the cancellation died the Committee's promise to make Jones the next president of the *Verein*.

9

Comforts of War
September 1914–December 1916

T HE WAR SPLIT the small world of psychoanalysis into enemy camps, divided by more than Freud v. Jung. English Freudians were cut off by post as well as by rail from their master in Vienna, while Jungians remained in direct touch with theirs in Zurich, growing stronger as a result.

Of Freud's trusted secret Committee, only Ernest Jones was on the Allied side. The four other Paladins were either Austrian (Hanns Sachs and Otto Rank), Hungarian (Sándor Ferenczi) or German (Karl Abraham). Such letters as Jones and Freud managed to exchange passed through neutral territory – mainly Holland, where the leading Dutch psychoanalyst, J. E. G. van Emden, acted as intermediary. One uncensored letter from Freud, reaching Jones via Italy a month into the war, allowed Freud to tell him, after a visit to Abraham in Berlin, 'It has generally been decided not to regard you as an enemy!'

Two of Freud's sons, Martin and Ernst, were in the Austrian army; Freud himself had little doubt that the Central Powers would win. To Ferenczi, he ascribed Jones's optimism to the contrary as 'the narrow-minded outlook of the English'. In the United States, untouched by the foreign war and enjoying uninterrupted communications, one American psychoanalyst, A. A. Brill in New York, sided with the land of his birth, Austria, while another, James Jackson Putnam in Boston, strongly supported the Allies. Putnam could nonetheless sympathize with Freud: 'How much must it mean for you, with your sons actually engaged and all your interests so intimately involved!' Putnam could only wish 'that each person engaged might be "analysed", as part of his preparation for the war'.

Neither side anticipated a long war. While few believed the Kaiser's promise that the troops would be home 'before the leaves have fallen from the trees', British expectations of a swift victory were boosted in early September 1914 when the British Expeditionary Force in France forced in France the Germans to retreat in the Battle of the Marne. The high cost in casualties was accepted as a fair price for success.

Jones took a detached, psychoanalytic view of the conflict. He could not see any point in it, he told Freud, other than 'rather a boyish one of wanting to see which side is the stronger'. In any case, he wrote, there was no animosity in Britain against Austria, 'the view being that she has been exploited by Germany'. He was pained that scientific men on both sides had shown so little objectivity in inquiring into the causes and conduct of the war. Indeed, he told Freud, 'The only people who have a real opportunity to display their superiority in this respect are psychoanalysts'. The only reason he wanted England to win, he continued, was that 'on the whole the average Englishman is nearer and more sympathetic to me than the average German, especially the average Prussian'. But his principal allegiance was to their Cause, as he said in words foreshadowing E. M. Forster's famous dismissal of patriotism decades later:

> If there is ever to be any salvation of the world from these nightmares it will surely be psycho-analysis that will point the way. That is why I feel that if the future of psycho-analysis had to be weighed with the future of my own country I should side with the former.

On Christmas Day 1914 Freud set down for Jones his bleak thoughts about the future of his movement – that is, he said, what Jung and Adler had left intact of it. (Jung, having resigned as president of the *Verein*, the International Psychoanalytic Association, in April, had pulled the Zurich Society out in July.) 'The Verein is as doomed as everything else that is called international,' Freud said to 'Dear Dr Jones' in a letter sent through van Emden. He saw his journals, *Imago*, the *Zeitschrift* and the *Jahrbuch*, heading for discontinuation. His tone to Jones was almost valedictory:

> Of course I have no fears about the final outcome of the cause, to which you are so touchingly dedicated, but the near future, which can only be of interest to me, seems to me hopelessly eclipsed, and I would not blame any rat I see leaving the sinking ship.

That was the last letter between them for six months.

The First World War was in fact good for the Cause. As the war progressed, psychoanalysis gained credibility, even admiration, for its demonstrable success in the treatment of shell shock. As soldiers with conspicuous symptoms, such as blindness, deafness and paralysis with no apparent physical basis, reached military hospitals, some suffering without ever having been in battle, doctors were less ready to accuse them of malingering and to send them back to the front. Freud's idea that such disabilities were the hysterical manifestation of unconscious mental states had taken root. The new therapeutic approach did not save many unfortunates from being shot as cowards or deserters, yet it did bring a widespread change of attitude towards what is now called post-traumatic stress disorder. In 1917 W. H. R. Rivers, psychiatrist and member of the Society for Psychical Research, after achieving cures with the new treatment, wrote of seeing destiny at work: 'Fate would seem to have presented us at the present time with an unexampled opportunity to test the truth of Freud's theory of the unconscious, in so far as it is concerned with the production of mental and functional nervous disorders.'

For Jones, the reward was more immediate, and took the form of an accelerated growth of his practice. Even before the horrors of the trenches began, he found himself consulted by men for whom the threat of military service released bizarre anxieties. One feared he could not command a battleship because of a crick in his neck; another imagined he would explode if someone stepped on his big toe. By January 1915 (when he turned thirty-six), Jones's daily roster of patients had nearly doubled from the previous year, rising from six in February 1914 to ten or eleven, with two or three on his waiting list. The first patient arrived at seven o'clock in the morning.

Jones had grasped the economic fact that the income of a psychoanalyst derives from a small number of patients seen very often over a considerable period. It did not take him long to build up a practice that paid all his living expenses and, by 1916, much more than that. When he was twice rejected for military service (on solid medical grounds, chiefly arthritis), he cannot have been sorry. He saw his personal war duty as defending the cause of psychoanalysis. Making money was one way to do it. He told Freud he might be able to help some of the Committee, such as Rank, who were in financial difficulties because of the war. He would have preferred, so he told Freud, to see no more than seven patients a day, but he needed the money and fees were lower in wartime.

Lower, perhaps, but not very low. One patient reported sending 'full fees this month – fifty-two guineas'. Even if Jones's other patients paid only half that sum – perhaps a guinea for an hour, his monthly income would have been above £100 at a time when a train driver was paid £2. 0s. 6d., the young actor Noël Coward £1.11s. 6d. a week, a pound of cheese cost 1s. 6d., and a return rail ticket from London to Manchester was £1.10s. 11d.

Analysis was not for the poor. Fees were no lower in New York, where, in 1915, patients were paying from $200 to $500 a month to their analysts. The treatment appealed not only to the well-heeled but also to the well-read, and the avant-garde with radical leanings and social concerns – a type epitomized by David Eder. A tall, lanky, cosmopolitan intellectual, Eder was a socialist, a Zionist, author of pamphlets on maternal health, and editor of a magazine, *School Hygiene*, through which he could try to bring about the improvement in social conditions he believed would change society.

Eder was a frequent contributor to the influential periodical the *New Age*, which preached a social Darwinism through which society would evolve and progress. Among the magazine's causes were divorce reform, abolition of the House of Lords, unemployment insurance, and a national health service. The *New Age*'s philosophy (like Freud's, some would argue) grew out of the teachings of the nineteenth-century German philosopher Friedrich Nietzsche, whose work it carried in translation. Its articles alerted its readers to the danger of prudery and of overestimating the conscious components of the human personality at the expense of the instincts.

Psychoanalysis was also sought by those who considered becoming analysts themselves. In 1915 one of Jones's patients was the secretary of the British Psychological Society, a lecturer at University College London, who presented himself for treatment saying that he was so impressed with the general importance of psychoanalysis that he wished to acquire the technique by being analysed himself. (At that early stage, there were no training committees or rules for admission to the profession of psychoanalyst. Jones and Eder had agreed, when founding the London Psycho-Analytical Society in 1913, that applicants for membership would be vetted personally by the society's president and vice-president (i.e. themselves).

Summing up his situation for Freud on 27 March 1916, Jones painted a rosy picture:

> The War Office decided I was of more use to the Army at my present work than doing hospital duty in France. I have 10–11 analyses a day (nearly all men), with 3 patients waiting, and besides that many consultations, society and committee meetings, lectures, etc. There is no doubt that I am now solidly established in London, *fest im Sattel* [firmly in the saddle].

He added that Loe and Herbert Jones were well, and also 'Lina is still with me, and I am as happy and contented as anyone can be in war time.'

He was solidly established – but only as a psychoanalyst. As a physician, he was still unacceptable. When he applied to join the staff of the hospital for shell shock at Palace Green, in Kensington, he was rejected. His forced resignation in 1908 from the West End Hospital had not been forgotten.

Having once been declared unsuitable for a staff appointment, he remained unsuitable – ostracized, as his former hospital colleague Harry Campbell had foreseen. He was left, as before, with his private practice of psycho-analysis.

He was all the more pleased therefore, later in the war, when the India Office sent him a case to test the value of psychoanalysis for the treatment of shell shock. The patient, C. D. Daly, was 'a valuable officer, whom they consider incurable'. Jones was pleased to see that, after five months, the treatment looked promising; its success would be important for the movement.

One man who consulted Jones was the writer D. H. Lawrence. In August 1915 Lawrence was living in the Vale of Health, on Hampstead Heath, with his German wife, Frieda (who had divorced her Nottingham pro-fessor-husband to run off with Lawrence). He had met Jones through David and Edith Eder, who were living in Hampstead Garden Suburb.

Lawrence, at twenty-nine, was thin and pale, but had formally been diagnosed not with consumption, but rather with a tendency towards it. He was physically and emotionally unfit for military service. When he was called to report to Battersea Town Hall for examination on 11 December 1915, Jones issued him with a medical certificate, apparently attesting to his poor health. On the day, Lawrence seems to have managed without the aid of the document: as he later explained, 'I said the doctors said I had had consumption.' The scene was repeated a year later when Lawrence, then living in Cornwall, was again called for examination and was again rejected. He told Barbara Low, Eder's sister-in-law and a pioneer of psychoanalysis in Britain, 'I didn't produce any certificate. I didn't think it fair to Jones.' Lawrence seems to have believed that Jones had bent the rules to help a friend, but failed to acknowledge that both to Jones's eye and to the examining doctors he was visibly unfit for military service.

It was a time when Lawrence needed friends. In November 1915 his new novel, *The Rainbow*, the successor to *Sons and Lovers*, had been not only withdrawn but confiscated. The publisher, Methuen & Co., when charged, had pleaded guilty to obscenity. Scenes of lesbianism, nudity and open-air lovemaking were unacceptable to a British society more prudish than ever owing to the widespread fear of the sexual temptations of wartime. The *Rainbow* scandal did not deter Jones, the following autumn, from becoming one of the first ten subscribers to Lawrence's new maga-zine, *The Signature*, a fortnightly launched to carry the reformist ideas 'on social and personal freedom' of Lawrence and John Middleton Murry.

Lawrence wanted his periodical to be read by 'just a few passionate, vital, constructive people'.

'Passionate, vital, constructive' was exactly how Jones saw himself. Even so, he declined to become one of the group Lawrence was trying to recruit for a post-war utopian community in Florida. Not only was Jones uninterested in utopias other than the one which he had created for himself; he had observed, over Hampstead dinner tables, Lawrence dominating every company 'with his eager assertive manner, his vital – all too vital – personality and his penetrating intelligence', expounding 'on every subject under the sun'. He judged that Lawrence wanted only disciples, and was the last person with whom anyone could co-operate for very long.

Having observed the Lawrences at close hand, Jones was hardly surprised when one night, following the couple's expulsion from Cornwall (in October 1916), Frieda burst into his consulting rooms, weeping that her husband was trying to murder her. 'From the way you treat him,' said Jones the analyst, 'I wonder he has not done so long ago.'

Jones was perhaps the only person in London who knew of Frieda's colourful past in Munich and her affair with Otto Gross, although their Hampstead circle were aware, as were the military authorities who had forced the couple out of strategically vulnerable Cornwall in October 1916, that the German baroness was the cousin of Baron von Richthofen, the 'Red Baron', who was almost admired for his success in bringing down Allied airplanes.

In his memoirs, Jones claims to have offered Mrs Lawrence a brief analysis of 'the dark forces that drove them into such tempestuous situations'. After all, he judged, 'she lived with him and survived him, so some elements of wisdom and self-control must have played their part. And she was a charming as well as an intelligent woman.'

Jones may not have appreciated the extent to which Lawrence owed his absorption of Freudian theory to his wife, who had acquired it from Otto Gross. The influence of psychoanalysis on Lawrence's fiction was overwhelming to those tuned to spot it. Ivy Low, the niece of Barbara Low and Edith Eder (who were sisters), read Lawrence's 1913 novel *Sons and Lovers* at one sitting – straight through to the very end, where Paul Morel thrusts away grief for his dead mother and chooses life:

'Mother!' he whispered – 'mother!'
She was the only thing that held him up, himself, amid all this. And she was gone, intermingled herself. He wanted her to touch him, have him alongside with her.

But no, he would not give in. Turning sharply, he walked towards the city's gold phosphorescence.

Ivy was so excited that she sent postcards to all her friends: 'Be sure to read *Sons and Lovers!*'; 'This is a book about the Oedipus complex!' She was right.

With plenty of money, free weekends, and no possibility of jaunts to the Continent, Jones began to explore the countryside south of London. When he was offered the use of a beach cottage made from a converted railway car near Shoreham, in Sussex, he bought himself 'an auto-cycle with side-car' and 'after five minutes teaching' (as he boasted in his autobiography) took off Saturday afternoons to spend the night in the country and have a weekly dip in the sea.

It was not long before he spotted, and bought, a lovely two-storey stone-and-brick Jacobean farmhouse nestled under the South Downs in West Sussex. An L-shaped structure, built in 1627 with low red-tiled roofs and a spacious fireplace, it stood about fifty-five miles from London and about fifteen miles from the Channel coast. The property included spacious grounds on all sides, with a large expanse at the front facing the tiny village of Elsted. Jones offered £400 in response to the asking price of £800, but when the demand dropped to £600 the deal was done. Jones wanted the place too much to quibble. He would say later that the landscape reminded him of the Gower; but there the comparison ended. His new piece of wilderness was within easy reach of London and of the many other rustic retreats of the British intelligentsia, for whom natural beauty, low rents and privacy were more important than dry walls and indoor plumbing. Moving from motorcycle to motor car, he formed the habit of going down to Sussex for Saturday and Sunday.

Jones named the property The Plat, borrowing the local Sussex word for the paddock which was attached. He gave the news of his acquisition to Freud, along with more personal details of the couple with whom Freud was still fascinated. 'Herbert Jones is better,' Jones wrote; also, 'Loe has had *all* her teeth taken out, which is an affair of many months, so I have not seen her lately, but hear by telephone.'

Freud, who had scarcely any patients, summed up the picture wryly for Ferenczi: 'Jones has eleven analytic hours, is working on nothing original, reads much, bought himself a little car and a cottage 90 km. from London, in order to spend Saturday and Sunday there. Still happy England. That doesn't look like an end to the war.'

New car-owner as well as new home-owner, Jones was well clear of the mud and misery of the trenches. In the summer of 1916, when 20,000 British soldiers died in a single July day during the Battle of the Somme, he took a three-week motoring holiday around and up the Welsh mountains. Thanks to the restrictions of the war, he had never seen so much of Wales, or England. Having been in England for three years, he told Freud, he was 'glad to be able to reassure you finally about any fears you may have had concerning my sexual life. I am a "reformed character", as they say. *Hoch die* ψα [Here's to psychoanalysis].'

The early war years and his affiliation with the British Psychological Society drew out of Jones one of his finest papers, 'The Theory of Symbolism'. Drawing on his vast reading in anthropology, history, philology, poetry and folklore, he related the symbols that appeared in dreams to the emblems, totems, talismans, metaphors and rituals used in various religions, societies and stories, and found them to be a short, condensed representation of an idea 'that is more or less hidden, secret, or kept in reserve'. An important characteristic was the evoking of a reaction of surprise.

As a graphic illustration for his hearers (a shorter version of the paper was originally read before a meeting of the British Psychological Society on 29 January 1916), he presented the idea of the 'funny little man' – as in Punch or Rumpelstiltskin – as a comic view of the male organ, as distinct from the powerful patriarchal symbols of the eagle and the bull. Symbols of the body, birth, love and death retain their unconscious power throughout life, and express the most repressed part of the mind.

He moved on to the symbolic power of money, especially in the form of gold coins, which he called 'unconscious symbols for excrement, the material from which most of our sense of possession, in infantile times, was derived'. Then, prophetically, he said, 'This superstitious attitude will cost England in particular many sacrifices after the war, when efforts will probably be made at all costs to reintroduce a gold currency.' This prescience, seen from 1929, drew high praise from the economist John Maynard Keynes. Writing to his Bloomsbury friend, the psychoanalyst and translator of Freud, James Strachey, Keynes said, 'Jones's forecast, written in 1916, as to the troubles in which the passion to return to gold would involve this country must be reckoned one of the triumphs of psychoanalysis.'

The war had spurred Jones's brother-in-law, Wilfred Trotter, to turn his old papers on the herd instinct into a book. In *Instincts of the Herd in Peace and War*, Trotter argued for a biological psychology, based on the whole range of animal life. Each herd had a type. The Germans, with their warlike songs and hatred of England, displayed the aggressive character-istics of the wolf, while England was like the bee: 'the most complete example of a socialized herd . . . living in unbroken security in the hive with no obvious means of government'.

Trotter went on – to Jones's dismay – to criticize Freud: not for his emphasis on sexuality, but rather for his concentration on the human animal. Unlike Freud, for whom the child's internal mental conflict over deflected gratification was central, Trotter was interested in 'the repressing forces' that came from outside. Not unlike Morton Prince in Boston, Trotter identified 'a certain harshness in Freud's grasp of the facts and even a trace of narrowness in his outlook'. While he conceded that the general validity of Freud's main propositions would be increasingly accepted, he regretted Freud's tendency to state 'his least acceptable pro-positions with the heaviest emphasis'. Indeed, 'his methods of exposition have not always tended to disguise the nauseousness of the dose he attempts to administer'.

Jones asked Loe to send the book to Freud via Holland (whence her brother, Jacobus Kann, the banker, was dispatching food parcels to Freud). 'You will I am sure be amused', Jones told Freud in advance, 'by the evidences of subjectivity in it (e.g. the sadism he projects on to you, etc.)'. Freud, however, when he read *Instincts of the Herd*, was neither amused nor angry, saying simply, on 14 July 1916: 'ΨA stands rather isolated in the book.'

However, the public seemed more interested in Trotter's views on the Germans, and the book went into three printings by mid-1917, and continued selling for decades after.

One of the first uses Jones made of his country house was to lend it to an analysand. While he went on his motor tour of Wales, Joan Verrall Riviere, thirty-three, lived at The Plat. She had been his patient for five months, and she too was a subscriber to Lawrence's *The Signature*. Wife of a barrister, mother of an eight-year-old daughter, social reformer, worker for divorce reform and women's suffrage, Riviere came from an established Sussex family with literary connections. Like many well-born girls, she did not go to university. After boarding school at Wycombe Abbey, she had spent a year at Gotha in Germany, becoming fluent in German.

She had found her way to Jones via the Society for Psychical Research, the SPR, in which her uncle, the Cambridge classical scholar A. W. Verrall, was heavily involved. She had suffered a nervous breakdown after her father's death in 1910, and had been in at least one sanatorium. By 1916 she felt she needed more help with her emotional problems. Her diary for February records the swift progression of her commitment to psychoanalysis: '12 S.P.R. borrowed Freud and Ernest Jones books; 19 consulted E.J.; 21 Begin psa. 12.30 daily with E.J.' (Incidentally, an entry for the following month is '22 read *The Rainbow.*')

Riviere liked her surname to be pronounced 'Rivere' (as in Paul Revere): her father-in-law, like many Victorians, thought it vulgar to use foreign pronunciations in English, and, to quote her biographer Athol Hughes, 'Joan Riviere could not in any way be considered "lower class"!' Tall, strikingly handsome, with superb carriage and elegant dress sense, she must have towered over Jones. In every other sense, she seems to have looked up to him.

Analysis struck her as just what she needed; she felt that Jones had uncanny insight into the workings of her mind. He and she were soon on good terms, so much so that he loaned her his Sussex house not once but twice: from 29 July to 8 August 1916, and for a longer period, from 18 December 1916 to 22 January 1917. Riviere was happy there. She enjoyed the walks in the bracing air, she invited friends to stay, and she offered Jones suggestions for altering and decorating the place, as if to remind him that a home needed a woman's touch. She was falling in love with him, and felt, as she would express in increasingly passionate letters, that she had the right to comment on his personal life.

Jones had told Freud his patients were 'nearly all men'. Perhaps so, but in 1916 at least two of them were women who fell desperately in love with him and were uninhibited about putting pen to paper. As well as Joan Riviere, there was also an eminent woman doctor, Dr Ethel Vaughan-Sawyer, of 131 Harley Street, the patient who paid him fifty-two guineas a month. Her inflamed letters show that Jones's capacity for stirring the passions of the women who lay on his couch was undiminished. What such correspondence reveals is a quality that does not come through in his cocky letters to Freud – the sympathy and insight that his patients, women particularly, felt that Jones had into the workings of their minds and hearts. With his penetrating observations, he swiftly made them feel that he understood them better than they understood themselves, and that they could rely on him to pull them through.

The postmark on one Vaughan-Sawyer letter – '4 Dec 1916 2.25 a.m.' – suggests, as do its handwritten contents, sleeplessness, frenzied composition and a midnight dash to a Harley Street letterbox. Under the superb postal system of the time, the first of five daily collections was made at quarter to one in the morning. Letters posted shortly after midnight would be on the addressee's breakfast table the same morning.

The letter's breathless opening, with echoes of Browning – 'Domine well-beloved' – gives a picture of a woman mesmerized by her analyst:

> I have travelled many miles since I first came across you, & I've many more to go; so many, to me, wholly unexpected things have happend in this quaint wonderland in which I find myself that I suppose it is only natural that I should feel a little dazed & bewildered & uncertain about my bearings, but I know that all will come right & straight in the end. I had to trust myself entirely to your strong arms & make a leap with you into the dark; & I did so with considerable trepidation, not knowing how strong & skilled they were nor how trustworthy. However I shall never regret it & I hug myself for having found you, for [illegible] you have landed me safely on a bit of bedrock; I now have the intimate & unshakeable conviction that not only have you found a key, as you once told me, but that you can use it with perfect & consummate art.

And so on, for the six closely packed pages that comprise just one of the surviving letters of the same tenor from the same correspondent. Dr Vaughan-Sawyer was a feminist, a war widow, a surgeon who had been working at the Royal Free Hospital since 1904, and a regular speaker at Fabian Society women's groups. Her progressive views, as presented in a Fabian pamphlet, included the belief that 'artificial' (that is, bottle) feeding was just as good as breastfeeding after the first two or three months.

For impassioned letters, however, few could match Edith Eder. By 1914 Jones had broken with Eder over his support for Jung's anti-libidinal views of child development. At the same time, Jones seems to have become increasingly close to Eder's intelligent, psychoanalytically sophisticated wife, Edith. Her letters to him are exceedingly personal. The earliest, from July 1914, in which she had warned him that his affair with Lina would ruin his chances with Anna Freud, shows her fighting her impulse to become his lover herself. Five years Jones's senior, Edith Eder accused him of treating her like a mother, which was not what she wanted. (Jones presumably grew accustomed to her abbreviating the article 'the' to 't'.)

> It's you yourself who have pointed out that a habit doesn't endure unless t. strong underlying desire (or fear) endures – Lina has become so strong a habit . . . You're wrong in supposing I don't realise you as a successful lover & accordingly my criticism is invalidated . . . You're altog. wrong in saying I regard you 'as a son' & am 'sorry' for you. Partly you don't understand

t. way a woman like me (I belong to a v. large class) loves a man at all, & partly you haven't seen my special position. I'm going to be equally frank abt. myself, so suppose a woman of pretty vigorous sexuality pretty strongly attracts to a man . . . Suppose she cares too much for her husband to be able to hurt him . . .

Mrs Eder ranted over six pages about the sleepless night and wretched day Jones gave her by telling her what he thought her motives were:

You were t. first *new* person I came across at all intimately after my Analysis & I approached you with it with t. first vigorous & honesty of that moment telling myself that if I could make you a friend t. relationship shouldn't be spoilt by t. old devouringness & exactingness.

She concluded her effusion with 'My dear Ernest, you've given me t. [most] valuable thing of all – you've opened doors to me, you've given me certain seeds that can grow. I'm grateful,' and also with a request for a favour. Would he interpret a dream she was sending him under separate cover?

Weekends at The Plat became part of Jones's life. He took Lina with him, and on at least one occasion invited his father to stay at the same time. If the visit took place over Christmas 1916, Joan Riviere may even have been in residence too.

It was at that point, as he approached his thirty-eighth birthday on New Year's Day 1917, that he told Lina she had to go. He broke the news by letter. Her sad and moving reply, dated 28 December 1916, was a fitting addition to the love letters to Ernest Jones, all the more so for, unlike the others, having been written from genuine feeling.

Lina blamed the break-up on what she felt was Thomas Jones's displeasure at seeing his son openly cohabiting with a mistress:

I felt in my heart he would not approve of our relations; no father would. But you assured me so firmly that it would be quite alright and I have felt that this caused the final break and oh! how my heart bleeds at the thought of it . . .

Oh but I have loved you my dearest Ernest in spite of the unhappiness I have caused you and but for that love that is still so deep for you my life would certainly end with the parting. Perhaps if I had not loved you so much we could have been happier together but in my heart I wanted you and only you and all of you. I see my mistake and you really have been a loving sweetheart to me.

News of this change in his domestic arrangements was dispatched to Freud in the third week of January 1917. 'I have recently parted with

Lina,' Jones wrote, 'and set her up in a little flat and found work for her. She has been with me for over three years . . . I feel I have paid heavily for my sin against her and Loe.' He had now, he told Freud, a respectable housekeeper of fifty.

In fact he had more than a housekeeper. He held back from Freud the most important news of his life: he had a fiancée. In a matter of days at the end of 1916, Jones had fallen in love and was about to propose to a young, brilliant, hauntingly beautiful musician from Wales.

10

A Druid Bride
1917–1918

WHEN MORFYDD (pronounced 'Morveth') Owen came to London from South Wales in September 1912, she used her Welshness as a shield. She would speak loudly in Welsh amid the silent crowd in the lift at the Tottenham Court Road Underground station. 'You,' she would announce in her native tongue, 'the man in the bowler hat, with the hard blue eyes . . . the woman with the dreadful hat and the miserable eyes . . . the awful little boy in the corner with the running eyes. The only one I love of the whole bunch of you is Beti Bwt ["Little Betty" – her nickname for her companion, Elizabeth Lloyd].'

Morfydd, born in Treforest, a Glamorgan industrial village north of Cardiff, had an irreverent wit, an extraordinary beauty, and a remarkable musical gift inherited from both parents. With her cloud of black hair, wide-spaced smouldering eyes and full pouting lips, she was said to have received twenty proposals of marriage by the time she came to London at the age of twenty-one. In Treforest her deeply religious father, a well-to-do accountant and leader of singing at the chapel, took a dim view of suitors for his only daughter. Anyway, Morfydd was not interested in early marriage. A musical prodigy, she was tutored from the age of sixteen by a professor at the University of Wales at Cardiff, and had performed the Grieg piano concerto in public before entering the university on a scholarship in 1909. She was already known as a singer as well, and, unusually for a woman, as a composer, particularly of choral works – many of the songs she sang on concert platforms were her own.

After taking her bachelor's degree in music from Cardiff in 1912, Morfydd moved to London to study advanced composition at the Royal Academy of Music. She was persuaded to this course by the Liberal Member of Parliament for Leicester, Eliot Crawshay-Williams. Crawshay-Williams was not only parliamentary private secretary to the Chancellor of the Exchequer, David Lloyd George, but also a poet. He met Morfydd when she set some of his poems to music; the two became fast friends.

Her parents, staid chapel-goers, were uneasy about her departure for the capital, but her receipt of the Royal Academy four-year Goring Thomas scholarship caused them to relent. Her subsequent record at the academy was one of glittering success: she won almost every prize and medal in her fields. When she was only twenty-two, her Nocturne in D flat major for orchestra won the Charles Lucas Silver Medal for original composition and was performed at London's Queen's Hall. Earlier, a Royal Academy concert at which she sang four of her songs drew good reviews in the national press, the *Morning Post*'s critic praising 'Miss Morfydd Owen, a young Welsh girl with a good soprano voice and all the command of expression typical of her race . . . Her powers as an interpreter are considerable. As a composer, they are still greater.'

At first her parents' anxiety about her welfare in the capital was justifed. Morfydd epitomized the lonely Welsh exile lost in the 'human-hive' of London whom Ernest Jones's Glamorgan Society had been formed to help. For a time she lived in cold and cheerless digs in Maida Vale; then, on doctor's orders, she moved to the higher, healthier ground of Hampstead. There in 1915 she shared rooms with her friend Elizabeth Lloyd.

Apart from the Royal Academy of Music, Morfydd's London life centred around the Charing Cross Welsh Presbyterian Chapel. She was an enthusiastic attender of Sunday services and, deeply religious, composed many hymns. The finest and most enduring of these, 'To Our Lady of Sorrows', suggests a depressive cast of personality. Singing it could leave her weeping. She often felt lonely. On Sundays, with nowhere to go between the ending of the morning service and the beginning of the afternoon Sunday school (religious discussions followed by tea), she sometimes took herself to lunch at the Strand Palace Hotel, but felt conspicuous; women dining on their own were looked upon with suspicion.

Her Sundays brightened when, at the Charing Cross chapel, she met, and was virtually adopted by, Sir Herbert Lewis, Liberal Member of Parliament for Flintshire, in North Wales, and his wife. The Lewises made themselves a refuge for Welsh people in London, and after Sunday service they would lead a lively group on a walk back to lunch at their home in Grosvenor Road, Victoria. When Morfydd learned that Lady (Ruth) Lewis collected Welsh folk songs, and was active in the Welsh Folk-Song Society, the Lewises' home became all the more enticing. As she later wrote to the Lewises' daughter Kitty, 'I simply *love* going there . . . *indeed* I don't know what I should have done without it since I have come to London – for I came very sheepish and timid although I was nearly 20, and I didn't like it at all until your mother came and took me under her wing.'

This undated letter reveals Morfydd shaving two years off her age, as she would continue to do. She was nearly twenty-two when she came to London in 1912, having been born, not in 1893 as she would claim on her wedding certificate, but in 1891. Her wish to conceal her true age may have stemmed from embarrassment at her single state. In 1916 she turned twenty-five – an age at which, in those days, an unmarried woman was an old maid.

Yet Morfydd was far from drab and nunlike. She liked jokes. She dubbed the literary critic William Hughes Jones 'Bili Museum' because he spent so much time in the British Museum. Her letters to friends were dashed off in an exuberant hand, full of exclamation marks. She had also a fondness for flamboyant dress. From her mother, a milliner (also a fine pianist), she acquired a love of big hats, and she was adept at adorning the wide brims with fruit and flowers.

She liked to wrap herself in feather boas and fake furs, or in large shawls of cloth she had dyed in bright colours for a bold, theatrical effect. At one point Lady Lewis got her to wear an elegant frock by a French dressmaker at a recital for an influential audience that included Mrs Lloyd George, but Morfydd soon reverted to her self-dramatizing style.

The more recognized Morfydd became in the capital, the more Welsh she got. Every August she went to the Welsh National Eisteddfod, the annual festival celebrating Wales's ancient tradition of music, drama and dance. A sign of her growing reputation was her admission in 1912 to the Eisteddfod's Gorsedd, its sacred inner circle, which gathers in an enclosure of high stones with the bards and Druids wearing long ceremonial robes. The rites suited very well Morfydd's taste for ceremony, fancy dress and extravagant belief – each participant in the Gorsedd was a member of the British Druid Order. The Druids saw no conflict with Christianity, as they too believed in the immortality of the soul.

Members of the Gorsedd chose bardic names, usually in three parts. For hers, Morfydd added the name of her father's birthplace in Montgomeryshire to become 'Morfydd Llwyn-Owen'. Some of her published compositions appeared under this ritual name.

The Eisteddfod of August 1912, held at Wrexham, admitted Morfydd also to the circle of people who could claim that they knew Lloyd George. It was there she met the then Chancellor of the Exchequer, and also got to know his wife, whose hair and hats she helped to fix. In 1916 at the so-called 'Great War' Eisteddfod, in Aberystwyth, she and Elizabeth struck up a friendship with three Oxford poets: Mansell Jones, Eric Dickinson and Wilfred Rowland Childe. They dined with the men, and later visited them at their Oxford colleges. Morfydd set to music a poem of Childe's from his published collection *The Escaped Princess*. Mansell Jones recalled meeting a 'shy, enigmatic little person' with 'dark, quizzical eyes'. He wondered 'was she a child, a girl or a fairy'? She 'approached gently; there was laughter and a touch of mockery in her gaze.'

When Morfydd moved to Heath Street in Hampstead with Elizabeth Lloyd, Lady Lewis was concerned that their flat lay above a shop bearing the dubious name of the Dress Reform Society. Lady Lewis asked the Hampstead Watch Committee to investigate whether the premises were respectable. They were. Even so, Hampstead's reputation for bohemianism and political radicalism was well deserved, and Morfydd soon made friends of whom the Lewises would not approve, including D. H. Lawrence, who (the rumours vary) was either invited to supper at Morfydd's flat in 1915 or joined her for a picnic on the Heath. Ezra Pound was another acquaintance. The Charing Cross chapel, in any event, was partly responsible for leading young people into the temptation of Hampstead, with its organized parties at the tennis club on the Heath at weekends.

In 1916, when her flatmate returned to Wales, Morfydd was invited by the Lewises to live with them at their fashionable Thameside address in Grosvenor Road. She assured them that she would not practise the piano at home, but did do a quarter of an hour's singing four times a day.

Had it not been for the war, Morfydd would not have been in London in 1916 at all. She had been awarded a grant from the University of Wales to study folk music in Russia and Scandinavia, but, as travel was out of the question, she instead used the money to extend her studies in London. Her compositions by this time numbered more than 150, including *Jubilate Deo* for chorus, organ and brass and *Pro Patria*, a cantata for soprano, baritone, chorus and orchestra (with lyrics by 'Bili Museum'). She stayed on at the Royal Academy of Music, which made her a sub-professor. She continued to attract admirers, and is known to have had a romance with a Russian émigré, Alexis Chodak; arrangements of Russian melodies in her work are all that survives of the relationship. A romance with Eliot Crawshay-Williams cannot be ruled out.

★   ★   ★

CHAPTER 10

As 1916 turned into 1917, the Lewises noticed that Morfydd was coming home very late. She had her own latchkey, but the vigilant Lady Lewis seems to have stayed awake until she heard their lodger come in. Making some enquiries, Lady Lewis found out that Morfydd was visiting the flat of Dr Ernest Jones, a psychoanalyst, a man well known as a follower of Sigmund Freud. She asked her brother-in-law, a Harley Street doctor, to explain what this meant. The answer was that the medical profession considered Freud's teaching to be of doubtful value, if not positively dangerous. The word 'hypnotism' entered their discussions.

Lady Lewis sent Morfydd home to Wales to consult her parents, and she herself wrote to her daughter on 4 February, 'She is a little monkey but that's no reason to let her get into a mess.'

It was too late. 'Proposed to Morfydd' is Ernest Jones's diary entry for 18 January 1917. Jones had met Morfydd late in December at a small party given by Eric Hiller, one of his analysands (present or past is not known). At the time, Jones was looking for a wife. He had his newly acquired country home in mind. As he said in his autobiography, 'A home needs a mistress and I was in the mood to find one.' But he was convinced that he was not attracted to Englishwomen.

An atheist in want of a homemaker and a professional musician dedicated to composing music and worshipping God: a mismatch from the start – or a match that might have been made by a Welsh marriage broker? The similarity in backgrounds is striking. Both Jones and Morfydd came from comfortable, middle-class Glamorgan families which had prospered from Welsh industrial expansion: Morfydd's maternal grandfather (whose name was Jones) had built the steelworks at Treforest. Moreover, the pair had graduated from the same university, Cardiff, and their abilities had brought each of them recognition in a wider world. And Jones was no philistine. He was a cultured man and, although not musical himself, held a season ticket to orchestral concerts and was a regular theatregoer, fond of Shakespeare and Shaw. 'To *Figaro* with M.' is one of his diary entries. The divide between them was religious and temperamental: he was a rationalist, she a romantic.

How far the worldly Jones succeeded in seducing his prey during their whirlwind courtship cannot be known. He did record 'Morfydd to tea' at his flat on 14 January. And a sensuous woman in need of awakening was not the kind of challenge that he would ignore.

Beyond a doubt he admired and applauded Morfydd's success. He was present on 10 January when she made her professional debut at a concert at the Aeolian Hall in New Bond Street (stall seats 7s. 6d.), and heard her sing songs by, among others, Scarlatti and herself. He heard her perform again on 16 January at a private recital given at the home of the music publisher Winthrop Rogers in Cheyne Walk, where the programme listed that 'Miss Morfydd Owen' was to sing ten songs, including three of her own and two Welsh and two Russian folk songs.

Within hours of his proposal, Jones told his patients he was getting married. It was unnecessary and perhaps unwise for a psychoanalyst to announce major changes in his private life to his patients. But Jones still had his consulting room in his flat, and alterations – such as the appearance of Morfydd's piano – were bound to be noticed.

The unstoppable Ethel Vaughan-Sawyer congratulated him immediately. On 19 January 1917, in another of her screeds, addressed to 'Beautiful & beloved Domine', she rejoiced 'from the bottom of my heart that you are in love again' (implying she knew something of his past entanglements). She trusted his instinct and knew she would like his fiancée, whom she would like to tell 'what a lucky girl she is in being chosen by a great man as his helpmeet, with a big career in front of him. I know you pretty well by now, though it is I who am being analyzed & not you & you have one of the most beautiful, straightest, sincerest, strongest personalities I have ever struck.' Her letter ended with a paean to the psychoanalysis of which Jones was a pioneer against great opposition: 'You will surely win, for it is firmly & truly based, & is as epoch making an advance in knowledge as the theory of evolution or the discovery of anaesthetics.'

Joan Riviere was less charitable. After two periods in Jones's country house in 1916, she declared her love for him and was furious when he rejected her advances. Having had a number of affairs, she was (as Jones later told Freud) 'broken-hearted' when he spurned her. She had never been rejected before, she said. Now, learning of his impending marriage, she saw his wife as an 'absolutely unquestionable' substitute for herself, and was all the more angry when Jones coolly told her that the woman he had chosen was her 'direct opposite'. Enraged, Riviere broke off the analysis and left London for six months.

The 'little monkey' married the dangerous psychoanalyst on 6 February 1917 – barely six weeks after their first meeting and one day earlier than the wedding had been scheduled to take place. Jones had dutifully gone to Treforest and met the Owens, who planned to come to London for the event. The Owens must have been deeply upset at the venue – the

Marylebone Register Office, rather than the Charing Cross chapel – and the choice of a civil ceremony shows that in the couple's first contest, over religion, the uncompromisingly secular Jones had won.

Morfydd must have been startled when Jones brought forward the marriage by one day. She had gone to Wales for the weekend preceding the event, and when she returned to London, on Monday, 5 February, Jones announced that he wanted the marriage to be the very next day, rather than on the Wednesday as planned. The abrupt advance of the date by a day deprived the Owens of seeing their daughter married – an extra blow at a time of stress: the Owens' twin sons, their only other children, were serving in France.

The wedding went ahead on Tuesday 6 February, with Jones's sister Elizabeth Trotter and David Eder as witnesses. For all the disagreements between them, Jones clearly still counted Eder as a close friend. The wedding certificate described the groom as 'Alfred Ernest Jones', thirty-eight, and his profession as 'Physician, M.D.'; his father's profession was given as 'colliery proprietor'. The bride's profession was left blank; her father's was given as 'accountant'. Her age was given, wrongly, as twenty-three, and her address as the Lewises' home, 23 Grosvenor Road, London.

The *Western Mail* in Cardiff carried the news 'From Our London Correspondent'. Morfydd Owen was described as the daughter of a Tre-forest resident and 'admittedly the cleverest student at the Royal Academy', while Ernest Jones, 'who hails from the Mumbles', was 'the neurosis specialist of Harley-street'. The haste of the event was noted: 'The wedding took place most quietly, and few even of their intimate friends knew of it.'

They left immediately for Cornwall. (Jones's diary for Tuesday 6 February 1917 said 'Married 12.15. Caught 4.0 to Exeter.) In a breezy letter from their honeymoon hotel, the Riviera Palace Hotel, Penzance, ten days later Morfydd broke the news to Eliot Crawshay-Williams:

Dear Eliot,
    Thanks awfully for the poems which your secretary sent to me at 23 and which I hope to set – they are real good. – I like When First We Met – it's a good joke – didn't you mention it at Porthcawl on the Links when I tried seriously and hard to uplift more moral sense! – Some days!
    Well, I'm married at last – rather incredible, isn't it? – true nevertheless. People in the Army seem to acquire an extraordinary ability in this direction, but in civil life, it's rarer . . .
    I hope life isn't troublesome. You seem to be very prolific in bed! – all your letters to me have been written there – *do* write me soon, and say

you're glad I'm married or something of the sort. I'm quite happy –
enormously so – and I'm convinced it's the right thing to do!

My town address & new name are: –

Mrs Ernest Jones

69, Portland Court

W.—

With my love to you – Morfydd

Not until they returned to London did Jones send the news to Freud:

I got married last week . . . She is Welsh, young (23), very pretty, intelligent
and musical. After taking her degree in music she studied four years at the
Academy and sang at her first and last public concert the week I captured
her; she has also composed some promising works.

The news pleased Freud. 'He regards himself as a reformed character,' he
told Karl Abraham in Berlin, echoing what Jones had indeed already told
him in October – two months before he met Morfydd.

The newly-weds moved into the flat at 69 Portland Court, Great
Portland Street, which Loe Kann had decorated and from which Lina had
just moved out. Jones gave Morfydd money to have the bedroom cleaned
and to buy a new carpet, curtains for the drawing room, pictures and an
armchair. To Kitty Lewis, Morfydd wrote that she wished Lady Lewis
would come and see how happy she was: 'exceedingly happy, without
doubt, much happier than I've ever been, and perhaps when she sees,
she'll come'.

But Lady Lewis would not come. She did not care to meet the notorious disciple of Sigmund Freud.

The year passed; the United States had entered the war in April 1917.
Jones and his wife struggled to remain productive. She published only
two songs under her bardic name, and appeared at Steinway Hall at the
piano in a concert on 19 April. He wrote two papers (published in 1918):
'War Shock and Freud's Theory of the Neuroses' for the *Proceedings of the
Royal Society of Medicine* and, for the *Journal of Abnormal Psychology*, of
which he remained an associate editor, 'Anal-Erotic Character Traits'.
The latter paper codified these characteristics in an understandable way –
orderliness, parsimony and obstinacy – that put the anal personality type
into popular parlance. Building on an earlier paper of Freud's, Jones began
his argument with a long exposition on the importance to the individual
of attitudes towards excretion and retention. He pointed out that frustra-
tion in these fundamental processes of 'giving out' or 'keeping back' could

result in qualities such as pedantry, hoarding or stubborn persistence that 'may make the person exceedingly unfitted for social relations'. He allowed as well that the syndrome might also express itself more creatively, in a fondness for moulding and manipulating, and a capacity for giving love. The essay was one of his classic papers; Anna Freud translated it for the *Zeitschrift*.

Jones moved his practice to 111 Harley Street. He was a professional man with a full day of appointments. What he needed was a secretary to handle his voluminous correspondence and a hostess for his country home. What he had instead was a wife who was now an associate at the Royal Academy of Music and who wanted to stay in London and spend her weekends at her chapel and with her Welsh friends.

But to the country she went, and found herself responsible for organizing breakfast, lunch, tea and dinner, plus a supply of clean linen, for an indeterminate number of psychoanalysts. Although a grand piano stood in a corner of The Plat's drawing room, Morfydd had stopped composing and curtailed her lecturing and singing engagements. She did learn, perhaps in compensation, to tinker with the Jones motorcycle and sidecar.

In August 1917, as usual, she went to the Eisteddfod, held that year in Birkenhead. From London, via Oxford, Jones drove her as far as Llandrindod Wells in mid-Wales, then motored home through Hereford and Tewkesbury: '500 miles' boasts his diary.

Jones claimed in his autobiography that he believed he was succeeding in drawing Morfydd away from her simple-minded religious beliefs and her irrational fear of deserting her father for someone else. Documents tell a different story. The chapel records Morfydd Jones as a paid-up member in the summer of 1917. Jones's own diary is even more revealing: the entry for Monday 24 September 1917 says, 'Married M, Charing X? Her parents came.' It would seem that, after six months of civil marriage, Morfydd won the battle for a chapel wedding in the presence of her mother and father.

Perhaps the second wedding was her birthday present. On 1 October, she celebrated the birthday which he thought was her twenty-fourth, with a celebration at Rumpelmeyer's restaurant. On 8 February 1918, just after the first anniversary of their wedding, she gave a celebratory concert at their Portland Court flat. With harp and piano, Morfydd's friends and contemporaries from the Royal Academy of Music performed six pieces, including works by the French composers Debussy, Fauré, Saint-Saëns and Gounod. The typed programme describes her contribution as 'Voice: Morfydd Owen Jones'.

April 1918 was difficult. Jones was ill, with ulcerated piles and neuritis, and on 6 April Morfydd's mother, Sara Jane Owen, was found dead in bed at her home in Treforest. It was a severe blow for Morfydd, who wrote to Kitty Lewis, 'I feel I have lost half of myself in losing her, and it has made me much less afraid of death.' At least Mrs Owen died with the satisfaction of having seen her daughter married in church.

Jones was not having an easy time with Joan Riviere, who had resumed her analysis. She sent him a barrage of letters, threatening on successive days to break off the analysis, to take her own life, or to continue to make him the centre of her life:

> Of course I know that you have done a great deal for me & put up with a great deal – but of course I have expected that from you, just as I have expected all other perfections in you – & perhaps your not having failed me more in this way is the reason that I still cling unconsciously to the hope of finding everything I seek in you.

By 1918 Morfydd, who had been made associate professor at the Royal Academy of Music, seems to have accepted the ritual of weekends at The Plat; their guestbook shows the Eders, the Trotters and his colleagues and former patients J. C. Flügels and his wife among their visitors. Surviving photographs portray the English intelligentsia at their most bohemian, with no regard for what the neighbours might see or think. Some of the men sit in the sunny garden in silk dressing gowns. Jones – tieless but natty – wears a white shirt, white trousers and his customary white Panama hat, while the women, including Morfydd, have braided their hair into long, rustic-looking single plaits.

Morfydd seems defiantly depressed, looking like a woman who knows how to sulk. In many of the group poses she is an outsider; in one, while the others sit smiling, she lies prostrate on the grass with her head under a hedge. Her friends considered the marriage a mistake, as she herself may have done. She would occasionally disappear for a day or two, leaving Jones frantic with worry until she returned.

Jones himself longed to take his wife abroad, where she had never been, but, with the war still on, for their 1918 holiday he chose to take her to the Gower peninsula, which she had never explored. Before leaving for South Wales at the end of August, the Joneses had the Trotters to stay at The Plat. By then Morfydd was fed up with housekeeping. On 23 August she wrote to Crawshay-Williams, who understood very well that she had other uses for her energies, 'I'm cleaning windows! – or was. Can't get anybody to do them, & we've been in the country so long that unless I do we shan't be able to see out . . . Oh dear! What it is to be married & have to run a household establishment. Oh dear! I'd love to live at an Hotel & have done with it.'

Two weeks later Morfydd had done with everything. She was dead.

She and Ernest had gone to stay with Jones's father and stepmother at their home in Oystermouth, a village to the west of Swansea. Thomas Jones had retired as a board member for various coal companies in Cardiff and London and was living at Craig-y-môr ('Rock by the Sea'), a substantial Victorian dwelling that had belonged to his former boss.

As Ernest and Morfydd arrived at Oystermouth towards the end of August 1918, she felt unwell, but recovered. They spent a vigorous few days walking on the Gower along the cliffs. One day they went to Caswell Bay, the next bay to Langland Bay. They lunched at the Kardomah restaurant, and dined with Ernest's sister Sybil and her husband, Christopher Blundell, at their home in Mumbles. On 30 August at Craig-y-môr the family sat and listened while Morfydd sang.

The following day, 31 August, upon returning from a visit to the nearby village of Sketty, Morfydd was struck by renewed pain and fever and took to her bed. As her temperature soared to 103 degrees, Jones suspected an abscessed appendix and tried to telephone his trusted friend Trotter – a brilliant surgeon – in London. It took him more than four hours to get through. When reached, Trotter agreed with Jones's diagnosis, but advised him to get a local surgeon as he himself could not get there quickly to operate.

The operation appears to have been performed at Craig-y-môr, even though Swansea Hospital was little more than four miles away. Morfydd's condition worsened. Despite doses of veronal and paraldehyde (according to Jones's diary), she became delirious and went into a coma. On 7 September at two o'clock in the morning, with her family at her bedside, she died.

When Trotter arrived, he blamed the anaesthetic: Morfydd was the victim of delayed chloroform poisoning. Her youth, suppuration (pus) in the appendix and sugar deficiency (common in wartime) were, he said, indicators for ether and against chloroform. (The relative merits of ether and chloroform were the subject of much medical debate at the time.)

Morfydd's stricken father, William Owen, who had lost his wife only a few months before, came from Treforest for the burial at Oystermouth Cemetery on 11 September, as did the minister who had known Morfydd as a child. Messages went out in all directions. Joan Riviere, in her diary, noted 'Telegram Mrs Jones Dead.' In a moving letter of condolence, Frederick Corder, professor at the Royal Academy of Music, wrote to Mr Owen, 'Your telegram came as a thunderbolt to me. Can it be possible that this glorious and beautiful creature whom I looked upon as a child of my own and was so very, very proud of, is taken away from us?' From the music department at Cardiff University, Professor David Evans wrote, 'My heart goes out to you and Dr Jones in your terrible trial. Oh, the lovely, darling girl. What a tragedy! . . . My wife and I are almost prostrate with grief.'

The Oxford poet Mansell Jones dedicated a poem, 'A Wreath of Rondeaux', to Morfydd. It included the lines:

> Land of her dream, she had come to wander o'er,
> Most ancient Gower! that now the sea-wind sweeps
> With hopeless moan, here at thy fatal door,
> She sleeps.

The Welsh press recorded the loss of a well-known musician. 'Brilliant Artiste's Death at Mumbles,' said the *South Wales Daily Post* on Monday 9 September. 'She was only 25 years of age.' Over a lovely photograph, the *Western Mail* in Cardiff noted the passing of 'a soprano singer of note and a promising composer'.

A red sandstone column was erected over the grave. Its inscription says, 'Morfydd, Wife of Ernest Jones' and includes three dates. The first, with an inaccurate year of birth, is 1 October 1893. The second, giving unusual information for a gravestone, is the date of her marriage: 6 February 1917. The third, the date of her death, is 7 September 1918.

On the base of the small monument Jones ordered to be engraved a quotation from the mystical chorus ending of Goethe's *Faust*: 'Das Unbeschreibliche, hier ist's getan' – 'Here the indescribable is done.' The words in German cannot have meant much to most visitors to Oystermouth Cemetery. They are still quoted, however, by some who make the pilgrimage to the grave of a woman who came to be mythologized as the finest composer Wales ever produced.

The death certificate was issued more than two weeks later, on 25 September. As the witness 'present at the death' it named the person least affected by the loss, 'May Jones Step Mother-in-Law'. The cause of death was given as 'Appendicitis Abscess and Operation Acidosis', certified by F. de Beverly Veale, M.D.

Jones was shattered. He could not bear to go back to their London flat. He cancelled all his patients for three weeks and spent the time wandering from friend to friend – to the Trotters, to Bernard Hart at his shell-shock hospital near Liverpool, and to the Flügels at their remote farm in Yorkshire. He wrote to Freud, 'My darling wife died last month, in very tragic circumstances. She was only 25, and a most rare and wonderful being.' It was 'a staggering blow' and, although he was trying to resume work, he was 'quite overwhelmed inside'.

Freud had heard the news already from van Emden. 'I do not want to console you! I had hoped that you had found lasting happiness; I am terribly sorry that it has turned out differently, for the years of separation have done little to change my feelings for you.'

A cloud of mystery continues to hang over the death of Morfydd Owen, and over Jones's reputation. As Freud's biographer Paul Ferris wrote, 'Despite the innocent nature of the medical findings, and Jones's evident grief, traces of gossip have persisted ever since.'

Did Jones in any way contribute to his wife's sudden death? Had he postponed the operation too long? Had he perhaps himself served as anaesthetist? After all, he had done so hundreds of times in his days at University College Hospital, and, in a time when rules of professional conduct about treating family members were less strict, he may easily have felt that his skill and experience surpassed any obtainable in Swansea.

Morfydd's friends were deeply suspicious – especially Elizabeth Lloyd, who could not understand the long delay in having the death certified. Even Jones's old mistress Loe Kann Jones sensed something amiss. Almost jokingly (some months later), she wrote to Freud that she was anxious to know 'how much you have guessed (psycho-analytically) about Jones's marriage and the consequent death of his wife. We'll tell you all about it someday.' If 'we' – herself and Herbert Jones – ever did, there is no record of it.

The lack of an autopsy or inquest leaves the precise cause of death unclear. Unease was not dispelled by Jones's facile account in *Free Associations*, published in 1959. There he claimed, unconvincingly, that a war-time diet low in sugar had made his wife susceptible to chloroform poisoning, and suggested that her life might have been spared if she had accepted the box of chocolates he had offered to buy for her.

From Vienna, even Freud sensed a mystery. Writing in English just before Christmas, he said, 'There seems to have been something particularly poignant about your loss, which I cannot make out by your hints. Life is harsh you know already. Good bye, dear Jones! Yours affectionately.'

One possible answer to the mystery may lie in the first line of Jones's letter to Freud announcing his wife's death. His sorrowful letter of

4 October opens with the statement 'I hope you got my cheerful letter sent on July 5, with the best personal news.'

That July letter is missing, but there is only one possible interpretation of the phrase 'best personal news': that Morfydd was pregnant. If true, Jones's hesitation about operating becomes more understandable; Freud's daughter Mathilde had lost a baby through an appendectomy. It would have been natural for Jones to delay the operation until he had spoken to Trotter on the telephone.

It is even possible that Morfydd's pain was caused by an ectopic pregnancy, a condition whose symptoms can be confused with those of appendicitis. An autopsy would have revealed a pregnancy, healthy or ectopic, adding to the distress of both Jones and Morfydd's father, and may have been avoided for that reason.

Nevertheless, the lack of an autopsy is puzzling. So is the relatively late issuing of the death certificate – two weeks after the death. However, it is a fact that the Britain of September 1918 was in a painful stage of a still-unfinished war – a time when record-keeping and public services were not at their most efficient.

It will never be known why, or whether, Morfydd Owen Jones was laid on the kitchen table for her fatal operation, rather than being sent to Swansea Hospital a mere four miles away. Or whether Jones himself administered the chloroform.

Whatever the truth, Jones clearly felt acutely that Morfydd's life ought not to have been lost. As a psychoanalyst, he also understood very well both the guilt and the relief that can accompany a death. With the stroke of a knife, he had been released from a troubled marriage.

When he resumed seeing his patients, Jones had to deal with their anger at the unexpected break. Joan Riviere, with a sharp analysand's eye, thought his grief was excessive, and told him so. As Jones wrote in his autobiography, 'Patients naturally expressed their resentment at the interruption by finding opportunities to flick my still unbearable raw wound; psycho-analytic treatment does not bring out the most charming aspects of human nature.'

The world had not stood still while the Joneses were on their ill-fated holiday. An assassination attempt on the Bolshevik leader Lenin in Russia had failed; another, on the Russian royal family, had succeeded. And the American government had recognized Czechoslovakia as a nation. The long war was drawing to a close without what Jones had been hoping for – a triumphal march on Berlin.

By December, with the war over and communications restored between England and Austria, Jones was able to look forward to meeting Freud again. He told him that he had read Freud's paper 'Mourning and Melancholia' and found it a great consolation after his 'terrible experience, signifying even more than a tremendous loss – owing to my inner psychical situation and the poignant circumstances of my wife's death'. He began to make plans for the coming year. It was time to begin planning for an autumn congress of psychoanalysts, and perhaps, he suggested to Freud, the time was ripe for a journal of psychoanalysis in the English language: 'You see I can look forward in life, although I have been through hell itself these last three months.'

His roster of patients was still full, and his income still healthy. His records show that he made £1,245,3s. 0d. in 1918, the year in which he lost three weeks' fees through tragedy.

11

Third Time Lucky
January 1919–December 1920

I N 1918 FREUD BELIEVED that the post-war centre of his movement
would lie in Budapest. The Hungarian government, impressed by the
success of psychoanalytic treatments for shell shock, planned a Psychoanalytical Institute in Budapest, where the university proposed to introduce
lectures on psychoanalysis. Accordingly, Freud chose the Hungarian capital to be the venue in September 1918 for the Fifth Congress of the
International Psychoanalytic Association, the first such congress to be held
since 1914. As the majority of Europe's psychoanalysts came from within
the Central Powers, a fair number turned up in late September: thirty-
seven from Austro-Hungary, three from Germany, and two from neutral
Holland. Freud was gratified that representatives of the Austrian, Hungarian and German governments attended as well – an expression of
interest in creating psychoanalytic clinics: Freud's tenet that flight into
illness is a way of escaping an intolerable situation appeared clearly applicable to military training. The warm official welcome extended to giving
delegates a fine banquet and a river trip along the Danube.

As the war still raged on the western front, analysts from Britain, France
and the United States were unable to attend the congress. Had Ernest
Jones been there, he could have heard Freud give a stern sermon
(delivered, unusually for Freud, from a written text) warning of the
dangers of the transference relationship. With their patients, Freud
declared, analysts must avoid affection, friendship, pity – even sharing
simple news like holiday plans. If a patient professes love, the analyst 'has
no grounds whatever for being proud of such a "conquest"'. None of
Freud's hearers except perhaps Sándor Ferenczi, his closest friend on the
inner Committee, knew that Freud at the time was analysing his own
daughter Anna.

Fittingly, the congress elected the Hungarian Ferenczi as the new
president of the International Psychoanalytic Association. Freud left
Budapest satisfied that his life's work, his Cause, was in the hands of those
who would carry it forward. His contentment was bolstered by the gift

of a sum of about £100,000 from a Hungarian brewer, Anton von Freund, who was grateful for what psychoanalysis had done for him and his wife. Freud intended to use the money to found a psychoanalytic publishing house, which would give him control over his published work, as well as to award prizes for significant writings on the subject.

There was a minor flurry at the congress when Hanns Sachs, a Viennese member of the secret Committee, collapsed with a haemorrhage of the lung and was found to have tuberculosis. It was decided that Sachs should go to Switzerland to seek a cure. At Ferenczi's suggestion, Freud used some of the von Freund fund to help pay Sachs's expenses.

Within months Freud realized that the 'centre of gravity' of psychoanalysis would have to shift westward. As the Austro-Hungarian empire disintegrated, it was scarcely possible to get letters or trains, let alone currency, between Vienna and Budapest, where a short-lived Bolshevik revolution was in train. Austria itself changed from the imperial centre of a vast region stretching from Czechoslovakia to Italy into a small truncated country: 'More or less the whole world', Freud moaned to Ferenczi 'will become foreign territory.'

A shift westward would make English the new language of psychoanalysis. This suited Jones, who had already proposed to Freud that the International Association should publish an official journal in English for 'the many men who do not know German'. He might have added 'and who do not wish to learn it'. At that time the German language was despised in the Anglo-American world, which had banned dachshunds and Beethoven during the war and had seen the Battenbergs in the British royal family become Mountbattens and the Bechstein Hall in London become the Wigmore.

Jones himself had vetoed Karl Abraham's proposal that the next congress be held in Berlin. Not that he had any personal animosity towards Berlin, he assured Freud, but he feared that their movement's reputation in England would be harmed by the German association – 'by reinforcing the view of ψα as a German decadent science, and not an International movement which we want it to be'.

But psychoanalysis had escaped the stigma of its geographic origins. There was a widespread and growing belief that, by revealing the nature of the primitive depths of the mind, it could help solve the moral and social problems of humanity so cruelly exposed by the war. This hope of transforming human nature was not unlike that of the Marxists, with their very different philosophy, or that of the Bauhaus architects of the 1920s, who firmly believed that the clean, open lines of their new buildings would guide people into happier, more harmonious lives.

Jones saw this optimism around him in London, and compared it to what he had seen in America in 1913:

> The *Aufschwung* [upsurge] in England is extraordinary; ψα stands in the forefront of medical, literary, and psychological interest. The 'Shell-shock' hospitals have ψα societies, lectures are given at medical schools, etc., etc. I have 10 patients daily, and this month 16 more have applied for my next vacant hour.

If work is a cure for grief, Jones was cured. Five months after Morfydd's death, he had thrown himself into new publishing enterprises as well as the reorganization of British psychoanalysis. Like a supreme pontiff, he called a meeting at his Portland Court flat on 20 February 1919 to inaugurate the new British Psycho-Analytical Society. Its name, to the outsider barely distinguishable from that of the organization it supplanted, was a matter of supreme importance to its members. Like the founders of a new church or political party, they never confused the new with the old.

The case, as he laid it out, was that the pre-war London Psycho-Analytic Society had to be disbanded because certain of its members had adopted views 'which were in contradiction to the principles of Psycho-Analysis'. The renamed organization, with a broader outlook, would supplant it and, as Britain's representative, apply for affiliation with the International Association.

Thus was David Eder, Jones's friend, a witness at his wedding and co-founder of the original London Society, ejected from the heart of British psychoanalysis. The 'Jung "rump"' that Jones had vowed to get rid of was epitomized by Eder, who had sidled too far towards Freud's rival. In any case, Jones felt he had seen off Jungianism with the second edition of his popular *Papers on Psycho-Analysis*. (The book was reissued in a new edition in 1918, its popularity spurred by the war.) In it he wrote that Jung had abandoned the principles of psychoanalysis for mysticism.

Not that Eder minded his expulsion at the time. He was not in Britain. Long a crusader for a Jewish national homeland, he had moved to Palestine in 1918 as a chief Zionist agent during the period when Britain, following the Balfour Declaration, was preparing to make Palestine a British protectorate after the collapse of the Ottoman Empire.

Jones was to be the president of the new British Psycho-Analytical Society, as he had been of the old London Society. He laid down stiff rules: all new members had to be proposed by someone who knew them;

all new members had to spend a year as associate members, during which time they would be required to give a paper. Those who remained associates rather than full members would have to be re-elected annually, and would have no vote on the society's business affairs. Ambiguous as this 'associate' status was, its effect was to draw in non-practitioners interested in the subject and to give British psychoanalysis a wider base than existed elsewhere.

The new society got off to a vigorous start. It resolved to apply for affiliation to the International Psychoanalytic Association. By the end of 1919 it had a total of thirty members and had met ten times to hear papers on such wide-ranging topics as the psychology of the newborn infant, 'street anxiety' and premature ejaculation.

Jones did not lack for female companionship. He loaned his Sussex country house to Eder's wife, Edith, who had remained in Britain with her sons by her first marriage. On at least one occasion he spent a weekend alone with her at The Plat. In this private interval, she poured out her heart to him. With Eder about to return to Britain for a visit, she was nervous about how to deal with her marital problems, not least of which was his impotence. Jones rewarded her confidences with stern and explicit advice, as well as with what she described as 'rankling & truthful epithets' about her own character. He told her she was oppressive in her vitality, oversimplistic and gushing. Like many of his patients, who felt Jones could see into their minds, for such a diagnosis she felt only gratitude:

Circumstances have brought us so close of late – they are not v. likely to again, but always, henceforth, you are *so much* in my life. Without that first week-end alone with you at Elsted, I don't think I *could* have pulled myself back from the sheer wall at whose edge I stood. And all that you said these last times has come home to me more & more as the real way out. The way you just indicated that I must take in regard to David – it *is* the way, I see, if only I can be firm enough to take – that's the difficulty, Ernest. I feel *intensely* towards you at the moment, yet cannot express it – t. joy that one has of t. *clean-cut* of your mind, t. courage & your spirit . . . how much you put aside yourself to help another struggling creature. I wonder if you know how dear you are to a woman like me. One simply sits at your feet in matters of mind, has to bow down & wonder at your grasp . . .

Is this rather like a love letter, Ernest? Well, of course I do love you – you know that . . . Neither in actual physical sex nor in affection can I see how or why one's to love only one person. My David's *more* to me than anything else in this world (save t. boys) – as you've seen, for him even so egoistic a creature as I will make a *great* sacrifice, but that doesn't exclude everyone else from love of any kind – It has been wonderfully good to have known you like this.

    Edith.

Jones's own struggle was to achieve a reunion with Freud. However, the ban persisted on British subjects travelling to a former enemy country before it had signed a peace treaty with Britain. For four months in 1919, as he later wrote, he 'haunted in vain various Ministries, of War, Health, Trade, etc., and only then succeeded in getting the Ministry of Education to vouch for my bona fides at least so far as Switzerland'.

Switzerland would do for a start. Hanns Sachs was still there, pursuing his tuberculosis cure, and their fellow Committee man Otto Rank arranged to come from Vienna to discuss the projected English-language psychoanalytic journal. Should it be a translated version of the existing German-language journal, the *Zeitschrift* (of which Jones was an editor), or a separate publication with editorial content of its own?

Over the Easter break in 1919, Jones set off for Basle, taking with him thirty pounds of luggage that Anna Freud had been forced to leave behind in her abrupt departure in 1914 and which she had been longing for, having been unable to buy new clothes in Vienna during the war and its aftermath. As part of the load that Rank would carry back to Vienna, Jones managed to include chocolates, tangerines and cigars. He managed also to send Freud's wife, Martha, a jacket, which she found absolutely beautiful and which also fitted Anna.

Seeing his fellow Committee members after a long absence, Jones was delighted to find both Rank and Sachs lively and sympathetic. Rank was wiry and tougher than before. The witty Sachs had, as always, an inexhaustible supply of Jewish jokes. Together the three went to Zurich and watched as guests as the new Swiss Psychoanalytic Society decided to join the International Association. All three addressed the group; Jones was glad that Freud was not there to hear his German. He himself was filled with admiration for (and reported to Freud) how Rank and Sachs 'turn these stupid and confused Swiss round their little finger. And you can imagine what jokes we all have together.'

The laughter did not relieve Jones's poor health. He was not well – full of aches and pains he ascribed to neuritis. He had a fall through dizziness, and was flooded with memories of Morfydd. He told Freud that he thought 'every minute of the day of my dear wife, who had never been abroad, with whom I planned all the details of this journey with such happiness'. Rank noticed, and reported back to their leader in Vienna,

'Jones is totally with us, very warm, unfortunately aged, depressed to the point of illness.'

For Jones there was no possibility of continuing on to Vienna; the Austrian treaty with Britain had not yet been signed. Perhaps it was just as well. Freud warned Jones that he had no idea how bad conditions were there: they were all, he said, 'hungry beggars', with no meat, bread, potatoes or, what was essential to Freud's well-being, cigars. Nor was there fuel. Freud worked in an unheated room, wearing a hat and overcoat as he listened to his patients. Worse for him, his son Martin was being held as a prisoner of war in Italy. When Austria signed a ceasefire in November 1918, the Italians responded by taking three hundred Austrian soldiers as prisoners. Freud sourly congratulated Jones on his correct prediction of the outcome of the war. In any case, Jones could not interrupt his analytic schedule with another trip abroad until the autumn break: 'You know how serious that is,' he told Freud.

He returned to London full of inspiration for what he saw as the great work ahead. He rejoiced to receive at last a letter direct and uncensored from Freud: 'The first window opening in our cage!' Jones thought he could handle the new *International Journal of Psycho-Analysis* by assembling sufficient financial support from America and Britain, without subsidy from the von Freund money. An editorial board of two English and three Americans was possible, but he stamped a fierce veto on one American – Samuel Tannenbaum, a charter member of the New York Psychoanalytic Society – dismissing him as a maverick unaffiliated with any neurological or psychiatric society, and associated with a questionable crowd. Jones himself tended to favour A. A. Brill's suggestion from New York that the *Journal* have no board at all, but instead be described as 'Edited for the International Psychoanalytic Association by Ernest Jones'.

He looked forward to the next international congress, to give the go-ahead for the publication. That would not take place for another year, however, as political conditions across Europe had made impossible the congress scheduled for Dresden in 1919.

The Englishing of Freud was well under way. Along with Jones's early papers, such as the Hamlet essay explaining Freud's work, there was Brill's translation of *The Interpretation of Dreams*, which appeared in 1913. The clumsy translation of Freud's seminal work had Jones, and not him alone, grimacing at its bad grammar and poor rendering of Freud's elegant prose. Jones's own explications of Freud had also continued, despite the war and the tribulations of his marriage. He produced eleven papers during the war years. Jones was pleased too with the excellent book on psychoanalysis written by his friend, and former patient, J. C. Flügels, a member of the British Psycho-Analytical Society. Flügel's *The Psychoanalytic Study of the Family*, written in 1919, was published in London in 1921 by the new International Psycho-Analytic Press, and deservedly became a classic.

Jones had set up the press on Weymouth Street in London, as well as a separate bookshop to sell books on psychoanalysis. He was full of unshakeable self-confidence, a trait he owed, he explained to Freud, to 'having been well loved by mother and wife'.

As he set about preparing the first edition of his *International Journal of Psycho-Analysis*, neither he nor Rank was yet clear about how different it was to be from the *Zeitschrift*. But the *Journal* would, in any case, be printed in Vienna, where costs were lower. Freud saw a compromise; the *Journal* would be built up 'partly on the work of your English staff and partly on good translations from out of the *Zeitschrift* . . . To be sure our expenses will grow higher, but there is no help, we want money – money – money –'.

What greater need had Jones in mid-1919 than a secretary fluent in English and in German? In Switzerland, Hanns Sachs, to whom Jones wrote asking for suggestions, knew that Jones was also in need of a wife. Sachs knew too that, for the good of the Cause, Jones needed cheering up. He did not look very far. He passed on to Jones the name of Kitty Jokl, the young and pretty sister of his mistress, the actress Gretl Ilm, a divorced woman with whom he had been living for at least a year.

Jones leaped at the idea. 'Dear Hanns,' he wrote on a postcard. 'Please send me at once Kitty's full name and present address.' Her qualifications were sound: a doctorate in economics from the University of Zurich, and good linguistic ability. She had worked at the Austrian consulate in Geneva and then at the Hôtel Bauer au Lac in Zurich, neither of which had suited her, and was looking for a new job.

Writing to 'Frl. Jokl' in May 1919, Jones offered her a post in London as his secretary at £150 a year. Going through the bureaucratic procedures for bringing a still-enemy alien to London, he managed to obtain and send to Zurich the necessary document:

> This is to certify that I am in *urgent* need, for scientific purposes, of Dr K Jokl's services as soon as possible, and that the Ministry of Labour in London, having considered the question, have granted me permission to employ her services specifically.

But no word came back. On 30 July he wrote again and asked if she had received the certificate. The next day brought a letter saying that she felt she had to return to Vienna to look after her mother. Shaken, addressing her as 'Dr Kitty', Jones wrote, 'Your letter was a great blow to me. I am anxious to have someone with a colloquial knowledge of German. Rack your brains and think of somebody suitable.' While he accepted her decision, he promised to look her up when he returned to Zurich at the end of August.

Preparing to set off for Switzerland, he left his dog with Joan Riviere to be cared for in the two months until he returned and she resumed her analysis with him. Hers was by now a training analysis. She had determined to become a practitioner herself, and had five patients already.

As August gave way to September, with his friend and former analysand Eric Hiller, Jones secured a Board of Trade permit to travel to an 'enemy occupied country'. Their destination was Austria, where they would at last see Freud. On their way, they stopped in Switzerland to collect Sachs, who was glad of their company, and went beyond the Alps to the lovely town of Locarno on Lake Maggiore. The sight was almost more than Jones could bear. In a letter to Freud, he confessed, 'The more beautiful are the things I see the more desolate and mournful do I feel, especially this week – the anniversary of the fatal illness of my wife, with whom I had so often planned this journey on the way to Vienna.'

Then the trio returned to Zurich. Fifteen days later Jones was in Vienna writing a letter which began 'My very own sweetheart Kitty'. He wondered 'if there is anyone else besides me in Switzerland in Europe who is quite completely happy'.

It was Sachs who played Cupid, but Jones was an eager victim. Always an elegant man even when he was not courting, he wore a white suit when he went to be presented to Dr Kitty Jokl at a lunch arranged by Sachs at the Café Terrasse in Zurich. She too was in white, as if arrayed for the bridal, and she brought her mother with her. When she had seen Jones's photograph on Sachs's wall, she had been unimpressed: he looked like an actor. However, in the man who strode towards her with outstretched hand and purposeful gaze she saw a scientist. He saw a small, curvaceous, merry-eyed young woman with a full head of brown hair, who, if not a great beauty in the Morfydd manner, was nonetheless desirable, intelligent and, he had been reliably informed, bilingual.

What followed was a Jonesian *tour de force*: dinner that evening in a large group; a telephone call next day, followed by a big basket of sweet peas with a card saying that sweet peas were an English flower; the following day a meeting that turned into a walk in the Dolder woods. As they strolled, Jones asked his companion if there was a part of Switzerland she did not know and would like to see. When she admitted 'The South! Lugano!' he replied, 'Let me take you there – I mean, as my wife, of course.' He opened his arms wide, she fell into them; they were engaged. Total time elapsed since meeting: under seventy-two hours.

In the next few days, the announcement of their betrothal was sent to the Vienna newspapers and they went to bed together for the first time. Jones the doctor gave his fiancée what she saw as 'preventative capsules', because they agreed they did not want children too soon. On 18 September he then left for Vienna. From there, the kind of impassioned love letters he had been accustomed to receiving were now his to write. In the first, written at 6.30 in the morning, he told her he would 'never forget the wonderful way in which you came straight to me to my heart in such complete confidence and faith and love at once that your heart had at last found its true resting place'. He appended an ornate compliment: 'Only Ernest has been vouchsafed the glorious sight of your locked-up treasure.'

Kitty could match him. 'Did I live before I knew you?' she wrote. People were surprised, she said, to see their names together in the newspaper, as, with good reason, no one knew they were courting.

Someone who was not surprised was Anna Freud. At the first intimation that Jones had found a bride in Zurich, she guessed that it was Kitty Jokl, who had attended school in Vienna with her and her sister Sophie. Freud himself must have been pleased. He knew Kitty's sister, Sachs's mistress, from a holiday in 1917, when she had joined his family in the Tatra Mountains, and he was accustomed to sending warm regards to 'Frau Grete' in his letters to Sachs. It would also not have escaped his notice that Jones had chosen someone from Freud's own background – Moravian Jewry.

Katharina Jokl, born in October 1892, was the youngest of eight children of a family of non-observant Jews in Brünn, Moravia (later Brno, Czechoslovakia), a town where the working classes spoke Czech. As a girl, she was called 'Kitty' to distinguish her from a cousin with the same name, who was called 'Kate'. The Jokls moved to Vienna, where her father was an insurance broker; they returned to Brünn for a time, and then went back to Vienna, where Kitty went to the school where the Freud girls studied. A clever girl but unconfident, overawed by her older brothers and sisters, she began university in Vienna. However, her subject, economics, was taught in the faculty of law, in which women were not allowed to take degrees. With some money from the savings account of a brother who had died, she shifted herself to the University of Zurich and got her degree with a thesis on the economic relations between England and Austria.

After several chaste infatuations and two unsatisfactory jobs, she was alarmed to find herself unmarried at twenty-seven. In fact Sachs had been eyeing Kitty himself before he sent her name to Jones.

With his private life settled, Jones went with Hiller to Vienna for the long-awaited reunion with Freud. They checked into the analysts' pre-war favourite hotel, the Regina, and had the pleasure of inviting the hungry Freuds and Ranks to lunch in a good restaurant outside Vienna. Jones found himself more enthralled than ever with Freud's presence – warm, wise, handsome (if thinner) – as with his intellect. The two men sat up late talking, Jones absorbing Freud's news, plans and ideas, and assuring Freud they would find fruitful soil in him. At their first meeting, they had not been speaking long when there was another joyful reunion: Ferenczi walked in the door and kissed them both on both cheeks. Jones had not seen his old analyst since 1914, and Freud had not seen him for a year.

During the visit, Freud proposed to Ferenczi that the presidency of the International Psychoanalytic Association, to which the Budapest congress had voted Ferenczi, be transferred to Jones. Ferenczi did not object. Freud's other suggestion was that Max Eitingon of Berlin be invited to join the inner Committee.

Meeting Anna Freud for the first time since 1914, Jones congratulated himself on the road not taken. From Vienna he wrote to Kitty how he had once thought of marrying Anna, but hearing again her 'strict hard voice only made me conscious of my defects, whereas with you it is easily the reverse'.

But time was marching on. He needed to get back to London to resume seeing his patients at the end of October. But it was no simple matter to negotiate the complicated manoeuvres involved in marrying an Austrian in Switzerland and taking her back to Britain. They needed to make the marriage valid in Austria, but the Austrians would not issue the required certificate if only one party was a Christian. Aha! said Jones triumphantly. His parents had been wise enough never to have him baptized, so he was not, and never had been, a Christian.

With Jones leaving Vienna, Freud thought it would be a good idea, to help finance the *Journal* publishing venture, to transfer half of the von Freund money that he held in Vienna. However, smuggling abroad a roll of notes worth about a quarter of a million Austrian crowns required some ingenuity. On crossing the Austrian-Swiss border, Jones and Hiller submitted to being stripped naked, but then waited to have their luggage inspected. Jones saw his chance. After his own suitcases had been examined, he 'calmly', as he boasted in his biography of Freud, 'fetched the roll of notes from Hiller's case and placed it in my own, which had now passed through the Customs'. Even so, both cases were due to be examined once more the next day (as his biography confusingly asserts) when the train left for Switzerland. Jones's solution was to hire a taxi to cross the bridge separating the two countries. Once on the other side, he and Hiller stated honestly that both cases had been examined. The fact that within another year or two, with the collapse of the Austrian currency, the notes were almost worthless hardly dimmed Jones's pleasure in telling the tale.

Jones married Kitty Jokl on 9 October 1919 at the register office in the Zurich town hall. A wedding breakfast followed at the Hôtel Eden, with her mother, Sachs and Hiller present. The couple then left for a week's honeymoon in the promised paradise of Lugano. Jones's letter to Freud of 12 October was euphoric: he had found 'great and unexpected happiness. Everything augurs perfectly for a most successful married life, which means for me a new life altogether in both happiness and inspiration to activity.'

The speed with which he achieved this second marriage suggests prior intention, even planning. In retrospect, his son Mervyn Jones concluded that, from the start, Jones sensed he was pursuing more than a secretary. Or was he? His reference not long after to 'my secretarial wife' shows that Kitty Jokl, from the beginning of her married life, did diligent service for the Cause.

On the way back to London, the couple spent twenty-four hours in Paris, where, Kitty confessed in her memoirs, 'I enjoyed sex for the first time.' A virgin, she had found it difficult to get accustomed to sexual intercourse. As they travelled towards her new life in an unknown country, Jones made it clear that one of her duties would be to carry his luggage; she did not mind, for 'the poor darling suffered severely from rheumatism then and after'. Even so, as they boarded the crowded train from Paris to Calais and spotted one compartment empty but locked, Jones climbed through an open window and opened the door from inside. A French onlooker said to Kitty, 'C'est pratique, Madame, avoir un mari acrobatique.'

As they arrived in London, the thick fog and absence of taxis made Jones afraid that Kitty would turn and go back home. Instead, they caught the last tube to Regent's Park station and walked to his mansion block in Great Portland Street, where they took the lift to the fourth floor and entered the flat where there was ample evidence of the two Mrs Joneses who had lived there before.

For Joan Riviere, Jones's marriage was the last straw. Two days after the wedding, she let loose a torrent of words that combined her growing insight as a psychoanalyst with the rage and pain of a spurned lover. As it was the last such florid letter Jones would receive from her, and as she would play an important role in the future of British psychoanalysis, it deserves to be quoted at length:

> 'Dear friend,' I want to say, 'I am glad you are happy' – This is what I feel – but it seems to have no meaning. Where is the *reality* in anything you feel? . . .
>
> A year ago I realized that your grief was inordinate . . . a madness . . . You seemed to me this year so much sobered and ennobled – dignified by it, at last 'grown up' . . . Since July though, I have realized that the old you is still there, the 'Celtic' quality, as I call it the unreliability . . . I don't condemn you – my judgement is this – one can't take you seriously.
>
> I have five patients now. I don't know how I am going on for I am horribly ill. I am frightened of what will happen of illness and exposure of every kind . . . My last hope of cure has gone . . . I must see you as soon as you get back. Chiefly I think for appearances – so many people know I know you well. I am afraid of being publicly thought to be in any way cut off from you by this. I must see and hear news of you as a friend . . .
>
> I *am glad* that you should be happy . . . what I so much love in you – you irresponsible Puck! irresistible to women, meeting them on their own ground, the emotions. May you always be proof against reality . . .
>
> God bless you & give you happiness – my dearly beloved one – my dear foolish one – my terrible one – weddings & funerals & weddings – how many more times will you kill me, Bluebeard? & shall I always love you? I want you to be happy, yes, with *her* – das Ewig Weibliche [the eternal feminine, also a quote from the last lines of Goethe's *Faust*].

Jones had not forgotten Morfydd Owen. As 1920 began, Freud was overwhelmed when his second daughter, Sophie Halberstadt, died in Hamburg in the great influenza epidemic, leaving two small sons. Jones wrote in condolence, 'She was just the same age as my first wife, who was as beautiful.' Kitty Jones also wrote to the Freuds: at school in Vienna she had been in the same class as Sophie. Her letter of condolence, Freud told Jones, was one of the most sympathetic he and his wife had received. Freud grieved also at the loss of his benefactor Anton von Freund, who had succumbed to cancer.

In February 1920 Jones's father, Thomas, died in Swansea. 'Can you remember a time so full of death as this present one?' Freud wrote after hearing the news. For Jones, Freud recalled that his own father's death had 'revolutioned my soul'.

Thomas Jones had been seriously ill with bowel and lung cancer during most of 1919. When, in November, Ernest brought his new wife to Swansea to meet him, Thomas had struggled painfully to get out of bed, but it had been worth the effort to see his son happy at last: 'This girl will manage him,' he pronounced. Three months later, on 4 February 1920, Jones was at the bedside when Thomas died at the age of sixty-six. There was no delay this time in notifying the authorities: the death was registered the next day. His son had no psychoanalytic advice for grief: 'About death I find there is nothing to say. Nature has omitted to provide us with any means of dealing with the idea.'

But the law does provide ways of dealing with it. Thomas Jones, described on his death certificate as 'Colliery Proprietor of Oystermouth near Mumbles, Swansea', left his son the substantial inheritance of £5,000. This good news coincided with the discovery that Kitty was pregnant. Jones shot off a telegram to Freud, and back came the sage response: 'The grandfather has to be reborn in the grandchild.'

Over the Easter break, in late March and early April, Jones and the expectant Kitty travelled to Vienna, where he introduced her to Freud and she, one assumes, presented him to her family. Once again awed in the presence of his mentor, Jones proposed to donate a quarter or a fifth of his inheritance to what he called the 'English Press', then in formation. From this sum, about £1,000, he suggested that £50 a year be given to Otto Rank, who was devoting much of his time to the slow job of putting together the *Journal*. Jones saw the gift 'as part of my donation to the Press'. Having seen at first hand the diminishing value of the Austrian crown, he was worried that Rank was not earning enough to cover the bare necessities of life.

Rank wanted to refuse, but Freud (perhaps using Jones's argument that it was better for money to come from within the Committee than from a meddlesome outside donor) persuaded him to accept the gift – but only for one year. Freud advised Jones against extravagance with his patrimony:

'You had only one father and [it] is not probable that you will get another inheritance of £1000 next year.'

Their regular correspondence resumed as before the war, but now their letters might have been written by accountants. Freud's income now derived almost entirely from patients whom Jones sent him from England and America, and who paid in their sound national currencies. There were also financial matters to sort out in connection with the new *Journal*, which was falling behind schedule. Who was to pay whom for what, out of what bank account?

Freud's practice was now conducted almost entirely in English, owing to his need for patients with hard currency. Americans paid ten dollars an hour, British two guineas. (The exchange rate of five dollars per pound sterling had remained steady during the war.) In the autumn of 1919 Freud was taking lessons to improve his English, but even so he found it exhausting to have to listen to a foreign language all day long.

Jones did not conceal his own appetite for patients who could pay in foreign currency. When a Dutch woman had arrived without warning and insisted on being treated at once, 'I took my revenge', he told Freud (whom he knew would understand), 'by charging her higher fees than I have ever been paid before (or after, I fear).' Still, he was unable to cure her problem: sexual anaesthesia with her husband, sexual satisfaction with a younger man, unwillingness to divorce. In the end Jones advised her to return to her husband. One wonders if she felt she got value for money.

To deal with their foreign income, Jones opened accounts for himself, Freud and the German Psychoanalytic Press (which between themselves they called the '*Verlag*') with Lippmann, Rosenthal & Co., a private banking house founded in 1859, with head offices in Amsterdam. Freud, happy at accumulating capital in Amsterdam, ordered himself a suit.

Both Freud and Jones were using Dutch accounts as a way of avoiding tax: income tax in Jones's case; inheritance tax in Freud's. Jones resented that a third of all the income paid into his London bank was, as he put it, 'deducted by the Government to help pay for its adventures in Mesopotamia and elsewhere'. When possible, he kept his money offshore – as he had a Dutch patient. For his part, Freud wanted a place where he could put money aside which 'does not come into the inheritance' and which his wife could draw on in the event of his prior death. What name went on the account did not matter: 'Any friend likely to survive me and sure not to rob my widow will do for this, my own name would not.' He suggested that either Jones or his wife should put their name on his account, and hoped that Jones could help him fill it. 'If you have got people willing to live in Vienna while they are treated I am glad to accept them', he said, 'but not at less than 2 guineas.'

All considered, it was no accident that the Sixth Congress of the International Psychoanalytic Association, in September 1920, was scheduled for The Hague. That Holland was the home of respected Dutch psychoanalysts, such as J. E. G. van Emden and J. H. W. van Ophuijsen was good reason enough. But there was also the influence of Loe Kann Jones, who longed to see the man she called 'Father Freud' once more. Loe had written to Freud the previous year, asking him to

> arrange a little Congress in Holland, and we'll meet. And all the other psycho-analysts (led by Ernest Jones) will do such a mighty lot of talking, to convince each other of their original ideas in inventing what you invented years ago, that nobody will miss you if we make a jolly little party of you, Anna, Rank & us two [i.e. herself and her husband Herbert Jones].

As plans for the congress took shape in 1920, Loe offered Freud a furnished house in The Hague and suggested that he might wish to move there permanently.

Loe was scathing about Jones's abrupt remarriage. From her home in Regent's Park she poured her venom into a letter to 'Dearest Professor Freud': 'Isn't it fun to see Ernest cast for the rôle of Henry VIIIth'. She questioned the circumstances of his first wife's death, and wondered why he was 'such an incorrigible fibber (to put it politely!)' – by which she meant that he had exaggerated Kitty's accomplishments and also her closeness at school to Anna and Sophie Freud.

With great gusto, Loe recounted the telephone conversation she had had with Jones when he returned from Switzerland with his bride. When she had asked him whether Hanns Sachs still had 'that mistress':

> Ernest began to stutter, pretended not to remember, then suddenly remembered & said 'Oh yes – quite so – I married the *sister* of that girl.' Of course, now everybody believes that Kitty was not the *sister*, but the ex-mistress of Sachs. It may be quite wrong, and if right there would be no harm anywhere, but he gives everything a 'louche' flavour by telling these unnecessary falsehoods. Everyone laughs about it, but it is a shame, since he has done so much better in controlling his indiscretions. I think that he did quite well (considering War-conditions) in his practice.

The last was perhaps the unkindest slur of all. During the war that had taken 750,000 British lives, Jones had turned himself into a man of means.

★ ★ ★

The transposition of Freud into English took a great step forward when, in 1920, the writer James Strachey contacted Jones, offering to do some Freud translation with a 'German collaborator' – that is, his wife, Alix. Jones liked the idea. To groom Strachey as a translator, he sent him to Freud for a period of analysis, describing Strachey as 'a man of 30, well educated and of a well-known literary family'.

That was putting it mildly. The Stracheys were the essence of Blooms-bury, the group of English intellectuals and artists centred around Gordon Square and the figures of Virginia and Leonard Woolf and the economist John Maynard Keynes. James's brother Lytton Strachey was celebrated for his open homosexuality, his outrageous wit, and his brisk, gossipy book *Eminent Victorians*, which had made a subject's emotional life fair territory for the biographer. In London, Jones tended to stay clear of the Bloomsberries: he felt they looked down on him as not of their class, while he considered them ignorant of the realities of industrial life. In time, however, he came to accept the attraction that psychoanalysis held for these unconventional intellectuals and social revolutionaries. Almost the only holdout was the sister of the psychoanalyst Adrian Stephen, Virginia Woolf, who disdained treatment for herself, but who built its ideas into her writings.

Jones is known to have analysed a woman lover of the Bloomsbury artist Dora Carrington. His patient was Henrietta Bingham, daughter of the American ambassador, who had come to England to be analysed. The Bloomsbury group knew about the affair and its break-up, which, according to James Strachey, left Carrington 'crushed'. Jones described the case within the British Psycho-Analytical Society, using a pseudonym which fooled no one. As James Strachey reported to his wife, 'Jones lectured about Henrietta, and explained that the real reason why she threw over Carrington was because she (Carrington) wasn't a virgin.' Jones himself used the case in a later paper on female sexuality, which attributed its genesis to 'the unusual experience, a couple of years ago, of having to analyse at the same time five cases of homosexuality in women'.

James Strachey suffered from recurrent periods of depression. Like Joan Riviere, he had come to psychoanalysis through the Society for Psychical Research. At Cambridge he had been actively homosexual and a member of the select secret group The Apostles, which pledged its allegiance to 'the higher sodomy'. James settled down into a heterosexuality of sorts after being pursued and caught by the crop-haired Alix Sargant-Florence, an American-born but otherwise entirely English intellectual, educated at Bedales and Newnham College, Cambridge. The pair married in 1920, after a five-year friendship sealed by their enthusiasm for what they saw as the new science.

Together they read Freud's *The Interpretation of Dreams*, and they capped their European honeymoon with an analysis for James with Freud in Vienna. Alix herself had not planned to be analysed, but after suffering from anxiety attacks during a performance of *Götterdämmerung* she too became Freud's patient. (Her analysis was interrupted by influenza and pleurisy, and convalescence in a sanatorium. Her full analysis would take place with the Committee's respected Karl Abraham in Berlin several years later.) Freud, in time, found the Stracheys 'exceptionally nice and cultured people though somewhat queer'.

Jones warned Freud that Strachey had only £300 to spend on fees, and therefore hoped to pay less than two guineas an hour in order to go on longer. Obligingly, Freud lowered his fee to one guinea per hour, but found Strachey's indistinct speech 'a torture to my attention'. For his part, Strachey left a vivid description of what it was like to lie on Freud's couch for six hours a week. On favourable occasions, after an encouraging hint from the Professor, 'a whole series of lights break in on you.' At other times, 'you lie for the whole hour with a ton weight on your stomach simply unable to get out a single word.' Either way, the session would end with the Professor rising and showing him out the door.

Jones got no such cut price for John Rickman, a young, tall Cambridge graduate and a Quaker. Jones had assisted in getting Rickman into analysis with Freud for two guineas an hour. Once in Vienna, Rickman was useful as an intermediary between Freud and Jones on the sometimes vexed matters of publications (and later became a leading British psychoanalyst).

The need of an acute English eye became apparent when the first volume of the *International Journal of Psycho-Analysis* appeared at last, in July 1920 – the first English-language periodical devoted to psychoanalysis. Freud hoped the Americans would consider it theirs too. However, the issue was full of foreign-looking errors and Germanic phrases – not the least of which was a reference to 'Frau' rather than 'Mrs' Riviere. All Jones could say in response to Freud's many complaints about the flaws he found was, 'When I am definitely appointed editor, I can set about collecting a permanent staff of reviewers, translators, etc.'

He was running into trouble, antagonizing his collaborators with his autocratic ways: Rank was rumbling in Vienna; David Forsyth, one of the members of the original London Psycho-Analytical Society – one of the first practising analysts in Britain, and the only one with a connection with the British medical establishment – strongly objected to Jones's handling of the start-up of the *Journal* and withdrew his support for it. Only one issue of the *Journal* had appeared. The psychoanalytic bookshops had failed, in Vienna and in London. But Jones denied that he was being autocratic; Forsyth's opposition was a reflection of his neurosis. Analysing himself, Jones could only conclude, 'I have rather laid myself open to the reproach of being too democratic, diplomatic and conciliatory.'

As the 1920 congress drew near, Jones took his heavily pregnant wife on a tour of parts of the English countryside – Warwickshire and Devonshire – which she had never seen. He then left her at The Plat, where he very much wished (vainly, as it turned out) that he could receive Freud after the congress in Holland.

The Sixth International Congress, held from 11 to 16 September, filled its role as the unifying event where the small and far-flung world community of psychoanalysts could meet and feel as one – a collegial spirit being encouraged by the generosity of the Dutch hosts. The Dutch analysts, as hosts, covered the travelling costs and housing arrangements for their colleagues from central Europe. Jones assumed the presidency, as Freud had arranged. Sixty-two members came, with the largest contingents – sixteen and fifteen – from Holland and Britain respectively. There were only two delegates from the United States – A. A. Brill did not come – but eleven from Germany, seven each from Austria and Switzerland, and the rest from Hungary and Poland. The Hungarian delegation included a woman analyst whom Ferenczi described to Freud as 'a Frau Dr Klein [not a physician], who recently made some very good observations on children, after she had several years of instruction with me'. There were also fifty-seven guests, including Anna Freud.

Together at last, the secret Committee reassembled. They were now six, as Eitingon from Berlin had been added, with the gift of a ring to seal his welcome. Jones remained the only non-Jew. Freud set out the rules for going on. The Committee would be co-ordinated but anonymous. Its existence must be kept secret. Because the members lived so far apart, they would write group letters to each other every week or so to keep abreast of developments. To Sachs, these *Rundbriefe* added to the aura of a schoolboys' secret society. For Freud the purpose was obvious: too much of their relations had been concerned with business in the previous months.

Freud, who would not consider moving from Vienna, had very much enjoyed the trip out of his 'cage', and every day he gave money to Anna to buy bananas and other luxuries unobtainable at home. At the end,

Freud was proud of the congress. With Abraham, Ferenczi, Jones and Rank able to take over the movement 'and ready to supplant me', Freud said he wanted to devote his time to making money to provide for his family.

One aftermath of the congress was that Jones opened up new bank accounts in The Hague, for himself, Freud and the *Verlag*, with Loe Kann's family bank of Lissa & Kann and transferred to these the funds that had been held in Amsterdam.

Back in London, three days before their first wedding anniversary, the Joneses' first child, a daughter, was born. The delivery took place in the Harley Street rooms of Dr Ethel Vaughan-Sawyer, who had risen from being Jones's devoted analysand to become a full member of the British Psycho-Analytical Society, while retaining her medical practice. (She remained a member until 1939.) Jones, inspired to return to his roots, undeterred by the adoring Kitty, chose the name 'Gwenith'. 'It had to be Welsh to go with Jones,' Jones explained to Freud, and 'Gwenith is Welsh for "wheat".' Freud congratulated him on becoming a father nearly at the same time as a president, and expressed his hope that the baby 'will soon be able to spell her own name, and so get the better of me'. Jones, he advised more seriously, based on considerable experience, was entering 'one of the queerest and most exalted situations in life, the beginning of infinite happiness and endless cares'.

The success of the Hague congress was a restorative to Freud after his daughter's death. He had seen his followers, or a good selection of them, en masse, and could see the way forward. In congratulating Jones, he let slip a reminder that he had not forgotten Jones's capacity for indiscretion. 'The centre of our activity has now shifted to the English affairs', Freud wrote to him, 'and we hope you will behave cautiously and lead us out of the stress we find ourselves in at the moment.'

Jones was all too willing:

> To me it is clear that I owe my career, my livelihood, my position, and my capacity of happiness in marriage – in short, everything – to you and the work you have done. Besides those outstanding facts all the small services I may be able to render must always weigh light in the balance, and I cannot hope to redress it.

But he could redress it. He was a changed man. His private life in order, he was ready to lead Freud's movement. No invitation was necessary. He was, at one and the same time, president of the International Psychoanalytic

Association, editor of its English-language journal and publishing house, and associate editor of its German-language publications. Not least, he was president of the British Psycho-Analytical Society, with absolute power over who could and who could not be a psychoanalyst in the United Kingdom. The reins were in his hands.

12

Name-Calling
1921–June 1925

It *is* curious what a disruptive effect Psycho-Analysis seems to have.

Alix Strachey to James Strachey, 1924

WITH HIS DAUGHTER eight months old, Jones reported to Freud, 'I am glad to say that wife and child are blooming like the spring. The child gives promise of being pretty, taking after my wife quite distinctly, and has a wonderful Jewish smile with twinkling eyes.'

Even more than marrying a Jewish woman, fathering a half-Jewish child validated Jones's status in his own eyes as an honorary Jew. His first contribution to the circular letters the secret Committee had agreed to write to each other opened, 'We are all good Jews.'

Not to the others he wasn't. To the other six, Jones was an outsider, a Gentile who spoke German like a foreigner and sat in distant London writing instructions to them all as if they were children. The *Rundbriefe* were the tie that bound the Committee. At the Hague congress in 1920 they had decided to write to each other every week or ten days – Jones in English, the rest in German: Karl Abraham, Max Eitingon and Hanns Sachs from Berlin, Freud and Otto Rank from Vienna, and Sándor Ferenczi from Budapest. Each letter carried the local psychoanalytic news; Jones reported, for example, that the University of London had arranged a series of lectures on five Jewish philosophers: Philo, Maimonides, Spinoza, Freud and Einstein. There was also information on training, press comments, and, not least, fees. Jones cautioned against any attempt to harmonize the cost of an analytic hour: their national economies and tax regimes were so different. Even within one country, a standard fee was impractical: 'If one charges a low fee the total makes it impossible to live, and if one charges a high one there are not enough rich patients.'

Before long, the circulars were more divisive than unifying. Members of the Committee used them to vent their anger against one to all the rest. A corollary temptation was the private letter, written sotto voce, from one member to another, and rarely failing to identify the infantile regression, sibling rivalry or other neurotic symptom of the colleague under attack.

In September 1921 the Committee met as a group to talk face to face; there was no international psychoanalytic congress that year. Freud chose the location – Hildesheim, a large medieval town in Lower Saxony – where he could stop on his way back from Hamburg, where he visited his grandsons, motherless since the death of his daughter Sophie. Walking in the Harz Mountains was on the agenda. Although Freud had turned sixty-five and felt he was 'really getting old', he led his troop on vigorous hikes and (according to Jones's biography), they all caught cold. Certainly Jones did, for he had arrived fresh from his sickbed in Sussex, where he had been laid low with an ear infection. Freud later expressed concern that Jones seemed easily tired and had disappeared once or twice a day without explanation.

For Jones, the Hildesheim evenings were even more arduous than the days, especially when Freud delivered a paper on telepathy. Freud still clung to his belief that there might be a scientific explanation for prophetic dreams and thought transference. To Jones, conscious of the strong opposition in Britain to psychoanalysis and quack therapists, any flirtation with occultism was to be avoided. He and Ferenczi managed to talk Freud out of his wish to read 'Psychoanalysis and Telepathy' at the next international congress, set for Berlin in 1922.

When Kitty Jones gave birth to her second child, a son, on 27 February 1922, Jones hoisted the Jewish banner once again. He sent to Vienna the news of 'an unmistakably male child, lusty and hearty. Typical *Judenbub* [Jewish lad], but with blond hair and blue eyes . . . My wife went through the ordeal splendidly, glowing with health and pride and feels very well.'

If Ernest Jones was an aspirant Jew, however, he remained an authentic Welshman. He told Freud, 'The name will probably be Merfyn (pronounced Merrvin), Ioan (pronounced as German Johann without the h, and with the same meaning) Gower Jones.' The birth of a male heir, however, confronted Jones once more with the 'Jones' problem. Within a few weeks, he was warning Freud that, 'unless you send me a hasty protest', he proposed

to amplify my own name to Ernest Beddoe-Jones, thus inserting one inherited by my father from his mother (analytically at the same time an affirmation and a repudiation of him). It seems to me a little unfair to expose one's children to the irksome task of gradually distinguishing themselves from the other half a million people called Jones (there are now even three psycho-analysts called Dr Ernest Jones).

Freud replied that he felt incompetent to give advice about the proposed 'amplification of your name':

> I only know that you will continue to be Dr Ernest Jones to us. What the effect with strangers may be I cannot imagine . . . So people will ask: Who is that Beddow-Jones? . . . Oh, it is the author of the papers on Psychoanalysis and president of the Inter. ψα Association. Now I know, it is a pity he did not introduce himself by this name from the very beginning.

Jones reluctantly accepted the good sense of Freud's advice. His *Papers on Psycho-Analysis* had indeed sold well, and was about to go into a third edition. Moreover, he lacked the energy for the legal formalities of changing his name, 'So I must continue to assimilate the pinpricks involved in being called Jones or E. Jones.'

The child was born in the Joneses' new home at 42 York Terrace, a narrow street backing on to Regent's Park. In late 1921 Jones paid £1,200 for a 21-year Crown lease on the small but elegant terrace house called Doric Villa. With a sizeable back garden facing the park, it was a far better place to raise children than was his old flat in Great Portland Street. The fashionable address was just a short walk across Marylebone Road from Jones's consulting rooms at 111 Harley Street, and was also a convenient place to see patients out of hours and to hold meetings with his fellow analysts.

The capital expenditure left Jones temporarily feeling less well off. Under England's post-war economic difficulties, his inheritance from his father had diminished in value, and he noticed (briefly) that fewer applicants presented themselves for analysis. He worried about bills – complaining, for instance, to 'Kittinka', as he called her, about having to paint the front of the house and its railings under orders from 'King George' (he was obviously pleased to have a Crown lease). But his situation righted itself. His income was holding up, as he was charging three guineas an hour and advising Freud (at the end of 1921) that analysts in London, 'even unqualified ones, get two to three guineas'. He himself charged some patients four.

He was a happy man. He and Kitty had a nanny for the children, and went to the theatre often and to Elsted every other weekend. He boasted to Freud that his wife's beauty was growing daily from 'radiant *Mutterglück* [mother happiness]'. Kitty, for her part, sent Freud a photograph of their little girl.

Judging, editing and negotiating the contents of the *International Journal of Psycho-Analysis* were not all Jones did in addition to seeing his patients. He devoted much energy to explaining and defending his profession to the British world around him. One of his main opponents was Lord Alfred Douglas, former lover of Oscar Wilde, now head of the Catholic Purity League, who wanted to uproot psychoanalysis from Britain.

With such enemies around, Jones sharply rebuked Barbara Low, a member of the British Psycho-Analytical Society, for an interview she gave to *Lloyd's Sunday News* which appeared on 5 February 1922 under the headline 'Psycho-Analysis Dangers. Need for Protection Against Quacks Who Exploit Hysterical Women'. The article carried a picture of Jones in profile, identifying him as the president of both the British Psycho-Analytical Society and the International Psychoanalytic Association.

Far from pleased with this publicity, Jones felt that Low had not made clear that there were no dangers in psychoanalysis when it was properly practised by someone trained in Freud's method. He was angry too at the prominence Low had given to David Eder, whom she had described as 'one of the first doctors to practise Psycho-analysis in England'. The question of primacy was a sore point with Jones. While Jones was still in Toronto, in 1911 Eder had given a talk on psychoanalysis before the British Medical Association, and he subsequently used this appearance to justify his claim to have been the first to introduce Freud's ideas to Britain. Jones could not accept this. He told Low that Eder, far from being the leader of psychoanalysis in Britain, had probably hindered the movement more than he had ever helped it.

This question was particularly touchy because by 1923 Eder had returned permanently to London from Palestine, to find Jones offering him mere associate membership in the new British Psycho-Analytical Society. In a hurt and angry letter from his office in Harley Place, Eder reminded Jones that the two of them together had founded the original society in London and that 'in my absence although my address was known I received no notifications of the new Sty.'

Drawing on his early experience of giving popular lectures around London, Jones enjoyed going out to the suburbs to talk on psychoanalysis. He was highly pleased to draw an audience of four hundred at the Croydon Natural History and Scientific Society. The audience for his speech to the Tooting Neurological Society included the staff of what Jones saw as 'the only remaining War Shock hospital'. He reported in a circular letter to the Committee that the doctors were 'all in various stages of assimilating Psa, the most advanced being Miller, of course a Jew'. ('Miller' was Dr Emanuel Miller, later founder of the East London Child Guidance Clinic and father of Sir Jonathan Miller, neurologist, satirist and opera director.)

Jones continued to be a prolific writer, especially as he now had his own *Journal* as an outlet. As an essayist, he always had a good eye for a news peg. In 1922, observing Ireland's final break with Britain and the formation of the Irish Free State, with the largely Protestant north of Ireland partitioned off from the overwhelmingly Catholic south, he proposed to write a paper on Ireland's fascination with the virgin birth. He would, he outlined in a circular letter, connect 'the political reactions of the Irish with their love for the Virgin Mother'.

It was Freud's turn to try to ward Jones away from a dangerous path: psychoanalysis in England 'has its personal foes and so have you'. But Jones would not be stopped. He got a legal opinion from the Society of Authors to say that his bold paper, 'The Island of Ireland', delivered in the quietness of the British Psycho-Analytical Society, did not offend against the blasphemy laws. He therefore included it in a new collection of his writings, *Essays in Applied Psycho-Analysis*, brought out by his International Psycho-Analytical Press in 1923.

Jones used the essay to ask why Ireland 'should differ so profoundly from both Scotland and Wales' in its reaction to British rule. He found the answer in the country's clinging to Catholicism and its tradition of personifying Ireland with a wide variety of feminine names such as 'Cathleen ni Houlihan' and 'Dark Rosaleen'. His most useful piece of evidence was the closing lines of Yeats's 1902 play *Cathleen ni Houlihan*, in which a young lad asked, 'Did you see an old woman going down the path?' answers, 'I did not, but I saw a young girl, and she had the walk of a Queen.' In these famous (and revolutionary) lines Jones saw the 'identification of maiden, old woman and queen . . . so characteristic of the unconscious conception of the mother'. This identification, to Jones, explained Ireland's refusal in the sixteenth century to relinquish the Catholic cult of the Virgin Mother, and made the settlement of Ulster by Protestants 'an abiding rape'.

The question of lay analysis was the psychoanalytic world's Ireland. The sides were absolutely divided, and no compromise seemed possible. Should a psychoanalyst be medically trained? The Americans said yes, the

Europeans no. Jones, despite his own high medical qualifications and belief that medical training was an asset, supported the right of non-doctors to be analytic practitioners. Well he might have done, as he was surrounded by able lay analysts, not least of whom was Joan Riviere. Riviere had offered to edit all the translations for the *Journal*, but Jones feared American criticism as Riviere was known to be a lay analyst.

There was another problem. Jones's increasing reliance on the tall aristocratic beauty with fluent German was inconsistent with listening to her free associations for an hour a day as she lay on his couch. The summer of 1921 saw her analysis with Jones finally break down. After five stormy years, she either walked out or was pushed.

The way forward, as Riviere saw it, was to go to Vienna and continue her analysis with Freud himself: the seal of approval for any analyst. Jones let her go, sending in advance a withering character analysis combined with a confession that she was his 'worst failure'. It was then that he acknowledged the mistake in loaning her his country cottage (in 1916) which had led to her declaration of love. He warned Freud:

> From that time on she devoted herself to torturing me without any intermission and with considerable success and ingenuity, being a fiendish sadist; my two marriages gave her considerable opportunity for this which she exploited to the full. The treatment finally broke down over my inability to master this negative transference.

As Jones summed up Riviere, she had far-reaching insight and was a valuable member of the British society. On the other hand, she had 'a strong complex about being a well-born lady (county family) and despises all the rest of us, especially the women'.

Within a month, Freud begged to disagree. Once more Jones had sent Freud a woman who spent a good portion of her analytic hours telling Freud what was wrong with Ernest Jones. Moreover, Jones had underestimated Freud's appreciation of good-looking, sophisticated women who were willing and able to pay his fees in hard currency. In Freud's eyes, Riviere did not appear 'half as black as you had painted her'. But on one score, Freud was relieved: 'I am very glad that you had no sexual relations with her as your hints made me suspect.'

Jones was astonished. How could Freud ever have thought that he had had sexual relations with Riviere, or indeed with any patient? Freud need have no fear about him in such respects, he declared: 'It is over twelve years since I experienced any temptation in such ways, and then in special circumstances.' Jones did not take the opportunity to enlighten Freud as to which of his controversial Toronto patients in 1910 had physically attracted him.

Freud plunged further into troubled waters. He declared that Riviere deserved the full title of 'translating editor' on the *Journal*, rather than, as Jones proposed, 'revising translator'. He judged that Jones owed Riviere some compensation for having aggravated her analysis by inappropriate behaviour. 'Agreeing to give her function and little of "translating editor" and then cutting it down to the part of a "revising translator" . . . leaves her no responsibility and no stimulus for spontaneous work'.

This rebuke worked. Riviere was listed as translation editor on the inside cover of the third volume of the *Journal*, which appeared in June 1922. Overall, Freud diagnosed the problem with both the *Journal* and the Press to be Jones himself: 'your personal interference in every little step of the process . . . Every Korrectur has to go to you.'

Freud seemed not to appreciate the difficulties inherent in editing across national boundaries. He complained that the *Journal*, and his translated works, were too slow to appear. But the reality was that all articles in English, even corrected proofs, had to go through Eric Hiller, Jones's assistant, who had arrived in Vienna in 1921 to help Rank with English-language matters at the *Verlag*. Naturally Jones wanted to see the corrected proofs and do the final editing himself. Rank complained that Jones was personally obstructing their work.

Freud could only conclude that Jones was incapable of delegating or organizing. Returning to the charge on 25 June 1922, he made a sweeping indictment: 'Accuracy and plainness is not in the character of your dealings with people.' Faced with what he saw as Jones's distortions, evasions, memory lapses and 'a certain predilection for sidetracks', Freud found that, whenever the evidence conflicted, he had to decide that Jones was wrong and 'that implacable woman', Riviere, was right.

Thus rebuked, the president of the International Psychoanalytic Association went to Sussex for his August holiday, and had the pleasure of taking his wife and little daughter to the seaside.

When it came to pressing patients into the service of the Cause, Freud himself still did not hesitate to overstep the boundaries of the consulting room. In 1920, only two weeks after accepting as patients the Bloomsbury intellectuals James and Alix Strachey, Freud acted on Jones's recommendation and gave them an assignment. He handed them a recent paper of his to translate, 'Ein Kind wird geschlagen' – 'A Child is Being Beaten' (which they had no reason to suspect was based in part on the fantasies of Freud's daughter Anna, as revealed in her analysis with him). Freud followed that assignment with a longer essay, *Massenpsychologie und Ich-Analyse* ('Group Psychology and the Analysis of the Ego'), and then rewarded the couple with a project that would take five years and lead them to their major life's work as Freud's English translators – translating his five principal case histories.

To Jones, Freud explained the advantage of the Stracheys' proximity, and told him he was wasting his time on translations rather than contributing to psychoanalytic theory. Jones disagreed. His own faith in the written word and his admiration for Freud's clear prose was supreme. Indeed, he declared to Freud that if he could bring out a collection of Freud's works in English he would feel his life had been worthwhile.

James Strachey himself was very pleased to have this new direction in his life. From Vienna he wrote to his mother, Lady Strachey, in London that he and Alix were translating 'a series of Freud's "clinical papers" . . . Our appearance as official translators of his work into English will give us a great advertisement in psychological circles in England.'

In the early 1920s the new world capital of psychoanalysis, as of the arts, was Berlin. The leading analysts Karl Abraham and Max Eitingon established the first psychiatric institute offering treatment, training and lectures. Their 'Polyclinic' attracted people interested in analysis from all over the world, including James and Edward Glover from London. Many who went there preferred Abraham's style of analysis to Freud's. The lure of Berlin had attracted Hanns Sachs away from Zurich and Vienna. Sachs had abandoned the law in 1918, become an analyst, and gone to Berlin to assist Abraham at the Polyclinic.

It was the Berlin Polyclinic that established the rule that no one could be an analyst who had not undergone an analysis. The institution was widely understood to be subsidised by the wealthy Eitingon, but he would not admit to being its benefactor. Jones, in his presidential address at the congress in Berlin in 1922, delicately acknowledged Eitingon's role by saying 'Charity will out.'

The psychoanalytic movement blended well with the modernist atmosphere of the Berlin of the Weimar Republic. The excitement of new ideas in architecture, music and film was fed by curiosity over what the liberating theories of Dr Freud might mean for artists and philosophers. Fittingly, Berlin – so unthinkable as a meeting place for psychoanalysts in 1920 – was easily the choice for the Seventh Congress of the International Psychoanalytic Association, held from 24 to 27 September 1922.

Joan Riviere came from London to attend the Berlin congress, on her way to Vienna to resume her analysis with Freud. Letters to her mother and sister give some flavour of the time (as well as of the snobbism and anti-Semitism fashionable in Bloomsbury). On her way from London, she wrote, she shared a sleeping car with the wife of 'a Maida Vale Jew travelling to Berlin to buy furs'. In Berlin she had lunch at a good hotel where the restaurant was 'full of Jews'. But Jewish wealth did have its advantages, as she recognized in the taste and modernity of the house of Max Eitingon, whom she saw as 'the material and social leader' of Berlin's analytic community.

During the congress, Freud stayed with the Eitingons, who lived at 22 Altensteinstrasse in the fashionable suburb of Dahlem, and when Riviere was asked to dinner she felt she 'owed the invitation to F.'. The house was impressive:

> a private house, so unusual looking into a garden at the back – with glassed-in balcony – but all very new and grand, in beautiful modern taste – wonderful paintings, panelling, Chinese wallpaper and influence on furniture, beautiful bookshelves, pictures, rugs, objets d'art – and marvellous *food*.

She also reported that Ernest Jones accompanied her on an evening visit to the Abrahams: 'They live still further out in a sort of Hampstead Heath.' In the small drawing room everyone was crammed together, and she was amused when a Dutch lady guest 'talked about her own dogs for nearly an hour and poor Jones' face got blacker and blacker – *he* likes to do the talking. The result was I did not get to know the Abrahams in the least and we drove away again rather bored.'

The 1922 congress was memorable for the Committee's first, and last, photograph together: the now-classic portrait of the Paladins surrounding their Charlemagne. It illustrates that, as Jones noted, 'none of the Committee was well-favoured in looks'. It was the last amicable meeting of the Committee.

The congress, however, was a success. There were seven papers every morning, and seven in the afternoon. Anna Freud delivered her first international paper, and a German analyst, Karen Horney, raised a theme that was to reverberate through the rest of the twentieth century: that psychoanalytic theory, developed by men and centred on male development, grew out of male narcissism and wrongly suggested that the female is no more than a disappointed male. Horney did not deny the existence of penis envy, but called it a metaphor for female resentment of male power. To assert 'that one half of the human race is discontented with the sex assigned to it and can overcome this discontent only in favourable circumstances – is decidedly unsatisfying, not only to feminine narcissism but also to biological science'.

At the congress, Jones was re-elected president of the International Association. In his presidential address, he reported that the numbers of analysts who belonged to the association had risen from 191 to 239, and that 112 analysts were among the 256 people attending the congress. The largest number of delegates came from Germany – ninety-one from Berlin alone. England had the second highest representation, with thirty-one. There were twenty-eight from Vienna, twenty from Switzerland, and eleven from the United States.

It was the last psychoanalytic congress that Freud would attend. He gave a paper previewing the new ideas to be published in *The Ego and the Id*, in which he paid more attention than before to the whole self (or, as Jones called it in his biography, 'the non-repressed ego'). The new emphasis moved psychoanalysis towards the everyday world and away from its initial preoccupation with the dark unconscious.

Early after the birth of Jones's son, Freud thanked Jones for his good letters, which showed him to be more kind and considerate 'owing perhaps to the happy turning of your family life'. But their letters in the rest of 1922 descended into bitterness and acrimony. Freud accused Jones of Chinese rigidity, bad management and inability to get along with people. All Freud could send him as New Year greetings was a wish for 'a complete restoration of faith and friendship in 1923'.

The past year, he said, as if in a schoolmaster's reprimand to the head boy, had brought 'a disappointment not easy to bear. I had to find out that you had less control of your moods and passions, were less consistent, sincere and reliable than I had a right to expect of you and than was required by your conspicuous position.' Jones himself had proposed the circular letters, and had then used them to score points against Rank, particularly on publishing matters. Freud blamed not only Jones but the English as a group: they were bad to collaborate with – even Mrs Riviere. She had impressed him, 'but she is a true Englishwoman and Hiller did not react differently'.

Freud was unhappy that the Press was taking too long to bring out its publications. Eric Hiller had annoyed him by failing to learn German and to integrate with Viennese society. When, in November 1922, Rank proposed to move the whole English-language publishing operation to

Berlin, where costs would be cheaper, Hiller resigned; he returned to London a few months later. The International Psycho-Analytical Press was separated once and for all, and to lasting effect, from its German cousins. Above all, Freud was fed up with dealing with Jones, who seemed oblivious to the offence he created with his autocratic manner.

Such a reproof from on high left Jones grovelling. Freud 'must know what part you play in my life', he said, and if he could alter himself he would. At the same time, he was optimistic that things would change for the better as his own spirit was always indomitable, and 'my domestic happiness is all that man could wish it to be.' He returned to his self-defence in January 1923 (he was now forty-four). He cowered under the lash, but would not apologize for his temperament. It was Welsh, or 'Keltic', he said, deliberately spelling the word in an esoteric form:

> It is doubtless true that the fact of my Keltic blood gives me a quick reaction and that I have not the phlegmatic Anglo-Saxon temperament, though I have tried to acquire some of it. It may also be true that I am unduly sensitive; of that I cannot judge. But when you say that I am insincere and not to be trusted, there, I am sure, with all respect, that your judgement is at fault.

In May 1923 he was laid low by an appendectomy operation complicated by influenza and rheumatism, and was in bed for the second half of the month. After a convalescent stay in Wales, he got back to work, trying to sort out questions of the *Journal* and preparations for the International Congress of Psychology, which was coming up at Oxford at the end of July, when he would deliver a paper on 'Classification of the Instincts'.

During a retreat at San Cristoforo in the Italian Dolomites in late summer 1923, the Committee turned on Jones *en masse*. (Freud was not there but nearby, on a mountain top at Lavarone, having his holiday rest in the hope that his little group of stalwarts would learn to get along without him.) The clash was precipitated by Jones's continuing difficulty with Rank as a business partner. Not only did Jones feel that the translations and editing from London had been botched at the Viennese end, but he could not get any clear figures from Rank on the numbers of subscribers. To be sure, the International Psycho-Analytical Press was now completely separated from the *Verlag*, and stood as an independent entity in London. However, there was much bad feeling, and each side thought the other owed it money. Rank and Ferenczi, who were allies and were writing a book together, wanted to throw Jones off the Committee. When the others refused – Abraham and Sachs remained friendly to Jones – Rank stormed out.

Even so, the Committee decided that Jones was in the wrong in the business wrangles and, moreover, that he was neurotic. Ferenczi went so far as to demand that Jones be reanalysed, because he seemed unaware of his unconscious motivation.

Something nastier underlay the bitterness – the charge that Jones was anti-Semitic. Ferenczi could barely speak to Jones because A. A. Brill, when visiting Budapest from New York, had told him that Jones had called Rank 'a swindling Jew'. In fact what Jones had written to Brill, complaining about the difficulty in extracting figures from Rank, was that Rank's 'general way of conducting business was distinctly Oriental'. Brill took it on himself to harden up 'distinctly Oriental' into a direct anti-Semitic slur: 'swindling Jew'. It was some months before Brill acknowledged to Jones having added the anti-Semitic phrase in passing the comment on to Ferenczi.

Jones apologized to the group for having given offence. He told his wife that the phrase attributed to him was grossly exaggerated. 'A Jewish family council sitting on one sinner must be a great affair, but picture it when the whole five insisting [sic] on analysing him on the spot and all together!'

Jones was easy in his conscience. He knew he had not used the offensive phrase. He wrote to Freud that, having looked up the letter (presumably a copy) on his return to London, he found that 'The word Semitic, for instance, never occurred in it.' Moreover, as he later wrote to Ferenczi, 'Anyone who is so happy in his love-life as I am and able to work so satisfactorily cannot be in any urgent need of further analysis.'

The 'swindling Jew' row at San Cristoforo at least had the merit of distracting the Committee from the ominous news that Freud had cancer of the upper palate. Anna Freud and Freud's doctor, Felix Deutsch, told them at dinner. How to persuade him to have the necessary operation? Jones wrote to Kitty that Freud had a real but slow-growing cancer that might last years: 'He doesn't know it and it is a most deadly secret.'

Much of the *Rundbriefe* correspondence moved on to consider Rank, who was tending to heresy. Rank had rushed out his book on the birth trauma (*Das Trauma der Geburt*, Vienna, 1924) – an open contradiction of Freud's theory that the Oedipus complex was the determining factor in development – even though Freud had asked him to wait. Hanns Sachs was very bitter about Rank deserting Freud 'practically on his death-bed, to pick up dollars in America'. He regarded Rank's book as an expression of the son's wish to kill the father. Jones agreed: he confided to Abraham that Rank, in contradicting Freud's Oedipus complex with his own birth-trauma theory, was showing signs of *Vaterablehnung* (rejection of the father).

The Committee was falling apart. Freud told Abraham that the *Rund-briefe* had splintered into private letters, and that 'the state of mind is lacking that would make a committee of this handful of people'. However, it clung to life in truncated form for several more years, picked up several new members such as Anna Freud, and continued the compulsive habit of circular letters.

Freud distanced himself from the disputes by announcing that he would not come to the international congress set for Salzburg in the autumn of 1924. His decision was surprising, because the location was the nearest to Vienna of any psychoanalytic congress since 1908. Jones ventured that Freud stayed away because, ill and old, he could not face another defection like Jung's. Indeed, Rank left for the United States the day before the congress ended (because, some thought, he could not bear to see Abraham elected president). His name soon disappeared from both the *Journal* and the *Zeitschrift*. Handing over the presidency to Abraham, Jones gave a farewell speech that sounded to Ferenczi like a premature funeral oration for Freud.

The tedious difficulties of publishing Freud in English were triumphantly resolved in the late spring of 1924. On the initiative of James Strachey, and after a good deal of bargaining, Jones's International Psycho-Analytical Press came to an agreement with the Hogarth Press, founded in 1917 by Leonard and Virginia Woolf. Hogarth – personified as 'the Woolves' by Strachey and others – undertook to buy all the existing stock of the six books already published by the Press. It also agreed to continue the series of monographs brought out under the name of the International Psycho-Analytical Library, with Jones as editor, and, further, to publish translations of Freud's *Collected Papers*. Jones and Joan Riviere, happy colleagues at last, sacrificed much of their holiday in 1924 to fulfilling the contract with Leonard Woolf to provide the required translations. Jones wrote the preface to the collection.

Freud continued to worry about the American rights to his work. Hogarth had not bought these, and the problem remained to plague Freud in part because he had casually given some of his American rights to his American nephew Edward Bernays. He could not understand the muddle, but asked Jones, 'What is the use of Americans, if they bring no money?' Even so, he was pleased by the Hogarth connection, and told Jones that 'the final success of the Press is a matter you may be proud of.'

Translating Freud was no easy matter. The English language had no words to convey Freud's German terms, many of them quite simple. Jones himself had already offered his own approximations in his *Papers on Psycho-Analysis*. But whether his neologisms should be continued or new ones adopted was a subject of constant debate.

With the Stracheys and Joan Riviere, Jones formed a Glossary Committee, to wrestle with the linguistic subtleties. Their work was complicated when Alix Strachey moved to Berlin to continue with Abraham the analysis she had begun earlier with Freud in Vienna. She went eagerly, even though the procedure meant a long and painful separation from her husband, James. Their closeness was reflected in frequent, highly personal letters. (These, later published, provide an entertaining and revealing record of the development of psychoanalysis in London.)

As often as not the Stracheys and Riviere accepted Jones's suggestions – aware, perhaps, of the literate, bilingual wife at his side. For example, when the Glossary Committee proposed to render Freud's 'Es wäre gewaltsam' as 'It would be a bold thing' and Jones responded with 'It would be very forced', the Stracheys agreed that Jones was right. Some of the terms, such as 'repression' for *Verdrängung*, meaning 'The keeping from consciousness of mental processes that would be painful to it', have entered non-specialist English. Others, notably 'cathexis' for *Besetzung*, literally 'occupation' but used to mean 'Investment (of an idea) with feeling and significance', have not.

One of the Glossary Committee's fiercest rows was over Freud's simple term 'der Es'. Literally translating it as 'the It' would not do. Like Riviere and her set, the Stracheys were as comfortable with their class superiority as with their anti-Semitism, and they sneered at the provincial Jones for ignorance of accepted slang. On 9 October 1924 James reported to Alix 'a very tiresome hour with Jones & Mrs Riviere. The little beast (if I may venture so to describe him) is really most irritating':

> They want to call 'das Es' 'the Id'. I said I thought everyone would say 'the Yid'. So Jones said there was no such word in English: 'There's "Yiddish", you know. And in German "Jude". But there is no such word as "Yidd".' – 'Pardon, me, doctor, Yidd is a current slang word for a Jew.' – 'Ah! A slang expression. It cannot be in very widespread use then.' – Simply because that l.b. hasn't ever heard it.

The net result, however, was good. Jones could tell Freud in July 1924 that four volumes, translated by Strachey and revised by himself, would be ready by Christmas. He accepted that Strachey now 'ranks as easily the best translator here or in America' – better even than Joan Riviere or himself.

Translations of Freud and notable papers on psychoanalysis were not all that Ernest Jones published in the early 1920s. In 1924 he brought out a book of songs composed by his late wife, Morfydd Owen. Her close friend Elizabeth Lloyd was very moved by the volume he sent her. Thanking Jones, she wrote, 'Each page brought fresh memories of our lost darling.' She signed her letter with Morfydd's pet name for her: 'Beti Bwt'.

Also in 1924, Jones followed the Berlin example and inaugurated an institute. The Institute of Psycho-Analysis (spelled with a hyphen since dropped) absorbed the Press, and took on the legal and financial status that allowed it to own a building, found a clinic and run training courses. In this consolidation Jones was helped by John Rickman, who had returned to London in 1922 after his analysis with Freud and became an influential member of the British Psycho-Analytical Society. At the first meeting of the institute, Jones was elected chairman and Rickman secretary.

Jones, with his family, had taken to spending some time in Wales. In the summer of 1924, perhaps with Morfydd in mind, he wrote to Freud, 'You will be most amused to hear that at the annual Druid festival in Wales – the National Eisteddfod – the chief bard received his prize for a poem dealing among other things with psycho-analysis. So you see your work is penetrating even into remote fastnesses.'

By December 1924 the place name of Llanmadoc appears on the list he kept of his holidays. Then or soon after, in that tiny Gower village he bought a small house that had served as the village bakery. It had just one room downstairs and one above, but boasted a large stone fireplace and panoramic views out over the Llanrhidian Sands and the Loughor estuary.

He was increasingly focused on his children and their development. When Gwenith, just under two, inserted some coins between her thighs and then drew them out, Jones interpreted this for Freud as the child presenting the coins as bodily products. However, he caught himself: 'One must perhaps remember that she is the child of an analyst and an economist.'

Jones was in a receptive mood, therefore, when he heard from Alix

Strachey of the pioneering work of a Berlin child analyst, Melanie Klein. Alix's German exile meant, among other things, that there was a shrewd London eye on the Berlin analytic scene. On 13 December 1924 she was impressed by Klein's presentation of two cases at the Berlin Polyclinic. According to Klein (who was the divorced mother of three), observing a child at play could reveal its inner feelings and fear of its parents. That fear, Klein said, originated from an internal, self-punishing guilty conscience that was projected outward on to the mother and father.

To Alix, this was how children really were. To her husband back in London, she sent a jokey but admiring sketch of Klein's technique. When a child refused to pay any attention at all, Klein would tell him:

'Do you know what you're really doing when you keep on breaking every toy you get, & can't play with them? You're breaking your brother's widdler because you're jealous', etc. etc., & the child suddenly became confidential & began to show interest . . . *If* die Klein reports correctly, her case seems to me to be quite overwhelming.

Alix reported further that Klein was off to Vienna, where she expected to be opposed by, among others, 'Anna Freud, that open or secret sentimentalist'.

Alix's letter so impressed James that he asked her to prepare a paper summarizing Klein's views on early analysis, which she swiftly did. Forty people attended the meeting of the British Psycho-Analytical Society on 7 January 1925 to hear an exposition of Klein's theory and methods of early analysis. James immediately reported back to his wife in Bloomsbury-speak: Jones's reaction was 'absolutely heart-and-soul whole-hoggin pro-Melanie'.

Jones was indeed converted. He had children of just the age Klein considered ripe for 'prophylactic', or preventative, early analysis, and his beloved wife was finding them hard to handle. The next step was obvious.

13

Importing Klein
June 1925–September 1927

THE NEXT STEP was obvious to Melanie Klein too. Her love affair with a *Berliner Tageblatt* journalist was coming to an end, and the Berlin Polyclinic was uninterested in her novel technique of child analysis. When she heard how well the British Psycho-Analytical Society had received the summary of her views in January 1925, she lobbied Alix Strachey to have Jones invite her to lecture in London.

Jones was easily persuaded. London was fertile ground for child analysis. In the British Psycho-Analytical Society (the largest such society in the world) there was more interest in the problems of childhood than anywhere, possibly because of a British sense of childhood as evidenced by J. M. Barrie, Lewis Carroll and many other writers, or an unusually large number of women analysts. These included Susan Isaacs, Barbara Low, Sylvia Payne and Joan Riviere. Their numbers testify to the improved status of women in Britain. In 1918 they had achieved the vote (those over thirty, that is) and were entering politics and advocating contraception.

But the child's psyche was not a woman-only subject. Had not Freud himself opened the way to child analysis with the publication in 1909 of his famous case of 'Little Hans' – 'Analysis of a Phobia in a Five-Year-Old Boy'? Little Hans was famous for ceasing, under treatment, to fear horses and regaining confidence in his father. In Britain, David Eder had long concerned himself with the psychology of schoolchildren, while, in May 1919, at the British Psycho-Analytical Society's second meeting, Jones's old medical friend David Forsyth had presented a paper on 'The Psychology of the Newborn Infant'. This British focus on the child accompanied the new trend in progressive education, and would continue to develop, producing in later decades such notable child analysts as John Bowlby and D. W. Winnicott.

Once Jones had invited Klein to London for a series of talks in the summer of 1925, the Stracheys began to worry. To Alix, still in Berlin, Klein's English seemed poor, and even in German she tended to ramble in unstoppable sentences. James advised Alix to write the lectures for her.

Klein, a former nursery-school teacher, had trained as an analyst in Budapest (with Ferenczi) and in Berlin (with Abraham), and had never had close contact with Freud. In her early forties, she was a good-looking woman with erect carriage and a flamboyant style, with a penchant for big hats and floppy cocktail pyjamas. To Alix Strachey, Klein looked like 'a sort of ultra-heterosexual Seminaris in slap-happy fancy dress'.

When Klein arrived in London early in July 1925, she felt immediately welcome. She stayed at a hotel off Bloomsbury Square. Virginia Woolf's brother, Dr Adrian Stephen, and his wife, Dr Karin Stephen – both analysts – opened their drawing room in the heart of Bloomsbury, at 50 Gordon Square, for the lectures. Klein, as enchanted with her audience as they were with her, later saw her visit as the happiest three weeks of her life.

Jones himself saw her on five successive days. At the conclusion of her series on *Frühanalyse* (early analysis), he sent to Vienna exuberant words that 'the Professor' was not happy to receive: 'She made an extraordinarily deep impression on all of us and won the deepest praise both by her personality and her work.' He added that he himself had 'from the beginning supported her views about early analysis'.

By 'early', Jones meant 'very early'. Klein believed in preventative analysis – bending the twig before it warped. She worked with children as young as two, and had analysed her youngest child, Erich, since he was three. She placed the crucial time of development as the first and second year of life. To her, the child's personality was shaped by the traumas of weaning and separating from its mother, and by the destructive impulses thus stirred up. The inescapable fact, as Klein saw it, was that the mother (or, in Kleinian terms, 'the breast') whom the child loves is also the figure that it hates, nurturing destructive fantasies, such as biting and destroying. By 1935 she had conceptualized this double-bind of love and hate as 'the depressive position'.

Klein had no difficulty in applying the adjective 'Oedipal' to this early internal battle. She thus placed the child's Oedipus complex about two years earlier than Freud had done with his theory about the jealousies stirred in a child at about the age of three.

Her pioneering technique was play analysis. She observed children's fantasy world as they played, offering her little clients a set of small toys (preserved today at the Institute of Psychoanalysis in London), rather than expecting them to talk as adults did in analysis. In play, she believed, the child reproduced its Oedipal feelings towards its parents: two cars banging together was the parental intercourse. As she saw it, the transference between child and analyst, corresponding to that created in adult analysis, was established immediately.

Klein's theory was clearly attractive to those of the avant-garde who were happy to see the mother placed at the centre of a child's development and the two sexes treated as developing along the same lines. As the concern to achieve sexual equality increased, Freud's 1920s theories which treated the female as a failed boy and the little girl as seeing the absence of a penis as castration looked as patriarchal and anachronistic as the Austro-Hungarian empire. (About his concept of 'penis envy', he wrote in 1925 in 'Some Psychical Consequences of the Anatomical Distinction Between the Sexes', 'After a woman has become aware of the wound to her narcissism, she develops, like a scar, a sense of inferiority.' In consequence, he reasoned, jealousy played a far larger part in the mental life of women than in that of men, bolstered by 'displaced penis-envy'.

Jones did not need to describe Kleinian theory for Freud, who knew it well and responded to Jones's enthusiasm with a splash of cold water. 'Melanie Klein's works', Freud wrote dismissively to Jones on 22 July 1925, 'have been received with much skepticism and opposition here in Vienna.'

But Jones was no longer listening to his master's voice. Both he and his wife were having difficulties with the squabbles, eating problems, sulks and tantrums of Gwenith and Mervyn. That an ounce of prevention was better than cure was obvious. That there was opposition to Klein in Vienna and Berlin was clear evidence of resistance stirred up by the reality of her conclusions on infantile life. 'Prophylactic child analysis', Jones asserted to Freud, 'appears to me to be the logical outcome of psychoanalysis.'

Within four days of Klein's talks, he was writing to Kitty in Wales, 'Shall we send the children to Melanie Klein or to Butterfield?' 'Butterfield' has not been identified, but Jones was clearly planning to seek professional help. He added to Kitty that he would be glad to see his family and the Gower again; he was lonely without them, and had gone to the Russian ballet to cheer himself up.

Between husband and wife there were no difficulties. Ernest and Katherine Jones grew closer as the years went by. Their brief separations, when she and the children were in Sussex or Wales and he was in London or on the Continent, were filled with loving letters that never failed to profess joy at hearing from the other and a longing to be together again. He would write to her as 'Kittinka' or 'Heart of hearts'. The tenor of their three decades of correspondence is conveyed in a letter from Kitty to Ernest written in 1923: 'Our love has become deeper but not less passionate.'

It is arguable that Ernest absorbed so much of his wife's love and time that the children got short shrift. Their son the novelist Mervyn Jones wrote in later life, 'My real mother was Nanny. It was left to Nanny, most of the time, to give me my bath and supper, to see that I was properly dressed, to watch over me when I was ill . . . to sooth me when I had nightmares, and to console me at times of distress' (distress such as the death of their dog Pat from lapping rat poison left in the stables at York Terrace).

Doubtless, as is shown by the complaining letters of Morfydd Owen Jones written in 1918, being Mrs Ernest Jones was a full-time job. As a busy analyst, editor and administrator, Jones relied on his wife constantly for translating, and often typing, his vast correspondence. At the same time, he expected her to keep two or three households running smoothly. There was much to organize in the refurbishment of 'our sweet, tiny place, Ty Gwyn' and their haven, 'our dear Plat'. Undoubtedly, his wardrobe also required some care. As his son Mervyn recalled, he always insisted on 'the correct turnout for the time and place'. Even for an excursion on the rocks of the Gower, he was always impeccable, in Panama hat and white trousers, shoes and socks. Kitty's wifely duties also included remaining sympathetic and unruffled when receiving news of the frequent 'smash ups', as Jones called them, as he drove his motor car around London, southern England and Wales.

Importing Klein to Britain took a little over a year during which time Abraham died, Max Eitingon became president of the International Psychoanalytic Association, and Freud turned seventy. Freud seems not to have sensed the imminence of a rival centre forming in London when Jones went to Vienna for the birthday celebrations on 6 May 1926. The survivors of the secret Committee were there – Eitingon, Sándor Ferenczi and Hanns Sachs – and, together with some of Freud's pupils, they made him a gift of 30,000 marks (£1,500) collected from the International Association. (Freud shared the money between the *Verlag* and the Vienna clinic known as the Ambulatorium, which offered psychoanalysis to those who could not otherwise afford it.) One guest at the party was Freud's favourite among the five patients to which he had reduced his schedule (at $25 per hour): an apprentice psychoanalyst with the eye-stopping name of Princess Marie Bonaparte. The title was genuine: she was the wife of

Prince George of Greece, as well as being a cousin of the king of Denmark and a descendant of Napoleon's brother Lucien. Intelligent, chic, sharp, 'the Princess', as Freud always called her, was the woman to whom Freud uttered his lyric cry '*Was will das Weib?*' – 'What does Woman want?'

Jones also brought Freud a cane and the good news that, with $10,000 from an American benefactor, the British Psycho-Analytical Society had bought the lease of a house at 36 Gloucester Place (later renumbered to 96) west of Baker Street, where patients could be treated for low fees or none at all. He, Jones, was honorary director. A clinic was set up to emulate the Berlin Polyclinic much admired by Barbara Low and Alix Strachey, and, not incidentally, to counter criticism that analysis was a luxury for the rich. Each member analyst volunteered to see one patient a day free.

By the time that Klein arrived to set up practice in London, in September 1926, Jones had spotted a double advantage: she could analyse his own children and establish London as a leading centre for child analysis, perhaps supplanting Berlin as a centre for training and innovation. He was quick off the mark. Four-year-old Mervyn Jones had his first appointment with Mrs Klein on 15 September; his sister, Gwenith, just short of her sixth birthday, started a fortnight later. In a matter of days, on 4 October, they were followed by their mother. Presenting herself for analysis, Kitty Jones was neither the first nor the last spouse of a psychoanalyst to undergo the procedure sustaining their family life.

Before the month was out, Klein wrote to Jones to tell him that she had decided to make London her new home. 'The great warmth with which you, dear Dr Jones, assure me of your assistance strengthens this confidence.' She had come to her decision after talking with Joan Riviere and also after sensing that London would be a good place to bring up her son, Erich, away from the damaging influence of his father – and also away from the anti-Semitism the boy had endured in Berlin. Pleased with her decision, Klein nonetheless suggested to Jones that he not mention it to his wife.

Clearly Kitty Jones was jealous of Mrs Klein. While in their married life there was never a whiff of a suspicion of infidelity (despite Jones's premarital habits), she nonetheless disliked seeing her husband utterly absorbed by the thought and personality of a new and powerful woman. Klein, of course, spotted the rivalry. No less ready than Freud to divulge the secrets of the consulting room, Klein sent Jones a very long letter reporting on the progress of his wife's first few analytic sessions, spent mainly discussing her relationship to her children. It was then that Klein advised Jones to leave her out of any conversations with his wife, and especially not to mention her permanent emigration: 'I believe the prospect of my staying here for good could, at present, have a very negative effect on her.'

Above all what she needed from Jones, Klein said, was the referral of patients. She agreed with Jones that analysis was essential for his wife: 'I have the same impression as you that her relationship with the children would have led later on to severe problems.'

As 1926 drew to a close, Jones received as moving a testimonial as any disciple could wish for from his master. Addressing him as 'Dear Jones' (in German), Freud enthused (in Jones's translation):

> Is it really twenty years since you have been in the cause? It has really become altogether your own, since you have achieved everything there was to be got from it: a Society, a Journal and an Institute.
>
> We may be well satisfied with each other. I have myself the impression that you sometimes overestimate the significance of the dissensions that have occurred between us. It is, it is true, hard to succeed in completely satisfying one another; one misses something in everyone and criticizes a little . . . Only the speeches at the grave-side deny these indications of reality.

When Freud wrote this warm letter on 20 November 1926 he was denying the reality of Mrs Klein's place in Jones's life.

For all involved in psychoanalysis, the practice of analysing children raised the inescapable question: did probing its darkest secrets hurt the child? An even larger issue was the question of lay analysis: should a psychoanalyst be medically trained?

This rumbling, unsolved question threatened to bring the secession of American analysts from the International Association. Freud and Jones were more or less at one on lay analysis, mainly because both, in their respective spheres, were so dependent on them: Freud on his daughter Anna above all, and Jones on a regiment of women, not least Joan Riviere. Jones, however, continued to maintain that some medical instruction for analysts was not a bad idea – a compromise position that left Freud uneasy.

In 1926 Freud summed up his thoughts in *The Question of Lay Analysis*. While he advised in this book that patients be medically examined before analysis, and that analysts should know something of medicine, the essentials were insight and a preparation in psychology. It was wasteful to require someone who wanted to treat phobias or obsessions to take the long detour of medical training. What was more, doctors tended to be preoccupied with the organic aspects of a case. He himself, although a trained doctor, recognized that 'After forty-one years of medical activity, my self-knowledge tells me that I have not really been a true physician.'

In September 1926 Jones thanked Freud for *The Question of Lay Analysis*, which he saw as settling 'beyond all doubt' that 'it would be very injurious to our movement to forbid lay analysis. There will be lay analysts, and there must be because we need them. The necessity for training is of course obvious.'

Across the Atlantic, views were hardening. In 1927 the New York Psychoanalytic Society passed a resolution condemning lay analysis and restricting the practice of therapeutic psychoanalysis to 'physicians (doctors of medicine) who are graduates of recognized medical schools' and who had had special training as well. The understandable fear was that a non-medical analyst would not recognize signs of somatic disease or psychosis in a patient. A corollary was the belief that only a trained paediatrician could treat children without doing harm. The issue was so divisive that only three Americans attended the Tenth Congress of the International Psychoanalytic Association, held at Innsbruck in 1927. The congress wrestled with the question of how an international body could make rules for training and practice in disparate countries – and dealt with it by postponing it until the next congress, set for Oxford in 1929.

In Britain, such was the growth of psychoanalysis that the British Medical Association decided that it ought to have a view on the phenomenon, and set up a committee. Was psychoanalysis therapeutic or harmful? Was there a distinction to be made between Freudian and Jungian treatment? Jones apprised Freud of the formation of the BMA committee. Attending his first meeting, he had 'received a not unfavourable impression'. 'In all probability', he assured Freud, 'the final report will contain nothing denunciatory, the only difficulty being to clear up the confusion with the so-called allied analytic methods [Jungian, etc.]'. Jones conceded that American secession from the International Association was possible, but he thought it unlikely.

By September 1927, however, open war had broken out between London and Vienna. Each side blamed the other. The opening shots were the publication of Anna Freud's first book, *Introduction to the Technique of Child Analysis*, and a paper she delivered in Berlin on 19 March, in which she criticized Melanie Klein by name. London countered with a symposium on child analysis in May. The difference between the two women's approaches was clear enough: they disagreed on the age of onset of the Oedipus complex, and also on whether a child could form a transference relationship with its analyst. Anna Freud's tenet was that Klein was wrong in thinking that transference was possible. The child, in the Anna Freudian view, was too immersed in its relations with its parents to permit a transference to develop.

Privately, Jones and his colleagues did not expect Freud to be open-minded about Klein's theories: they felt that he was too dependent on his thirty-one-year-old daughter, who, to them, was obviously in the grip of an unresolved Oedipus complex. Freud, for his part, believed (and wrote to Eitingon in Berlin) that Jones favoured Klein out of revenge for Anna's refusal to let him court her in 1914.

At the first meeting of the London symposium, on 4 May 1927, Barbara Low read a long review of Anna's book, after which, in an animated discussion, David Eder, Edward Glover, Riviere, Searl and Sharpe were unanimous that the relative novice Anna Freud was undermining the development of early analysis as pioneered by the experienced clinician Melanie Klein. So lively was the debate that it had to be continued at a further meeting later that month, on 18 May.

Joan Riviere was uncompromisingly anti-Anna and pro-Melanie. She said, and wrote:

> The analysis of a child, however small, is a process by which it learns, just like an adult, to tolerate the bitterness of frustrated and disappointed desires. Once disappointment can be endured, desire diminishes. Therefore it is of cardinal importance that the Oedipus conflict should be fully analysed in children, for on this all depends.

She continued:

> Psycho-analysis is Freud's discovery of what goes on in the imagination of a child . . . [It] is not concerned with the real world – simply and solely with the imaginings of the childish mind, the phantasied pleasures and the dreaded retributions . . . Morality is nothing but frustration under another guise.

Jones's own contribution was a summing-up, concluding on a note of victory: the fears of the critics – i.e. Anna Freud – that the superego (the internal self-censoring agency of the mind) of the young child was too weak and undeveloped to function independently of the parents were unsubstantiated. In his judgement, the evidence already accumulated justified 'the hope that we shall experience this last triumph of psycho-analytic theory and practice'.

Jones, one might say, had handed over his own children to be used as evidence. However, to a true believer such as he was, child analysis seemed no more problematic than baptism would be for a Christian parent.

The battle continued in the adversaries' respective publications. Jones boosted Melanie Klein by publishing the proceedings of the symposium in his *International Journal of Psycho-Analysis*, while at the same time refusing to allow his International Psychoanalytical Library to bring out an English edition of Anna Freud's book. In turn, Sándor Radó, the editor of the *Zeitschrift*, took revenge by refusing to translate the London symposium papers into German.

Such was the small world of psychoanalysis that many found themselves double-dealing. Sándor and Gisella Ferenczi, for example, enjoyed a happy visit to the Joneses at The Plat in Sussex on 18 and 19 June 1927. That did not prevent Ferenczi from writing to Freud to alert him to Melanie Klein's domineering influence over Jones, who was 'not only adopting Frau Klein's method but also her personal relationships with the Berlin group'. Nor did it stop Jones telling Freud of Ferenczi's great success in London – though 'his value', Jones said cuttingly, 'lies essentially in the inspiration of his personality rather than in his intellectual judgements.'

Two days before the end of his May symposium on child analysis, Jones wrote a letter of gratitude to Freud for the wonderful effects of psychoanalysis on his two children. He did not mention the name of their analyst.

> Though we had brought them up as wisely as we knew how, neither child escaped a neurosis, which analysis showed, as usual, to be much more serious than appeared. The symptoms of moodiness, difficulties with food, fears, outbursts, and extensive inhibitions seemed to make it worth while, and now I am extremely glad.
>
> The girl proved to have a severe castration complex, intense guilt and a definite obsessional neurosis. The boy was very introverted, lived in a babyish dream world, and had an almost complete sexual inversion. They have responded excellently to treatment, are in every way freer, and are constantly gay and happy.

The transformation in his children was so striking and so important, he said, 'as to fill me with thankfulness towards the one who made this possible, namely yourself'.

If Jones had stopped there, a schism might have been averted. However, changing the subject, he went on to say that he regretted that Anna had published her book 'so soon' (that is, before she had more clinical experience); he commented, 'It is a pain to me that I cannot agree with *some* of the tendencies in Anna's book, and I cannot help thinking that they must be due to some imperfectly analyzed resistances.'

'Imperfectly analyzed'? With this charge, Jones was criticizing not only Anna Freud, but also her analyst. Who did he think had analysed Anna?

Freud sprang at him like a man cornered.

14

'Who then has been sufficiently analysed?'
1927–1929

⁓

FREUD, HALF HIS palate removed, in constant pain from his ill-fitting prosthesis, was more dependent than ever on his youngest daughter. Anna was not only his trusted and indispensable nurse, but his intellectual heir. His previous intended successors had died, defected or, in the case of his friend Sándor Ferenczi, veered off on a curious path. Ferenczi was indulging in practices of which Freud strongly disapproved, such as kissing his patients. It was on Anna – a child analyst, a member of the Vienna Psychoanalytic Society and a developing theoretician – that Freud's hopes for the continuation of his cause rested.

A month after the London symposium on child analysis, Jones tried to draw the sting from the theoretical argument between Anna Freud and Melanie Klein. The only difference he could see, so he told Freud, was that Klein dated both the onset of the Oedipus conflict and the origin of the superego a year or two earlier than Anna and Freud had done. On the contrary, Freud replied politely: the difference was much greater than that. Mrs Klein presented the superego of children as being independent of their parents, while Anna – rightly, it seemed to him – held that the child's superego was so dominated by its parents that no transference relationship with an analyst was possible. But in his letter of 6 July 1927 Freud showed himself more worried by the far-reaching problem of the American stubborn opposition to lay analysis: he feared that Jones himself, as a doctor, was too sympathetic to the American insistence on 'medical analysis'.

Within weeks, Freud was the enraged father once again. The more he learned about child analysis, the more he was convinced that Klein was wrong and Anna right. During that summer, before the world's psycho-analytic community gathered at the congress in Innsbruck, Melanie Klein had repeated her charge that Anna Freud was avoiding the Oedipus complex in her analyses of children. Worse was the report of the London symposium that Freud read when his copy of the *International Journal of Psycho-Analysis* arrived. Jones, as editor, had included a full account of the London child-analysis symposium in which Anna had been criticized by six analysts – including Jones and Joan Riviere, for whom Freud retained affection.

It now seemed to Freud that Jones, from his powerful positions as editor of the *Journal* and president of the British Psycho-Analytical Society, was organizing in London 'a regular campaign against Anna's child analysis, accusing her of not having been analyzed deeply enough'. Such a criticism, he declared, was as dangerous as it was impermissible. He allowed himself to insult Jones: 'Are you pursuing a particular aim or are you yielding to your inclination to make yourself unpleasant?' He hurled at Jones a rhetorical shriek: 'Who, then, is really sufficiently analyzed?' He then gave his own answer: 'I can assure you that Anna has been analyzed longer and more thoroughly than, for example, you yourself.'*

Both men knew very well that Jones's analysis in 1913 with Ferenczi in Budapest had lasted only two months, even if the sessions had been two hours long. But who had analysed Anna with the thoroughness that Freud claimed? Who had listened to her masturbation fantasies, her resentment of her prettier sister, her reasons for clinging to virginity, and, not least, her sense of professional rivalry with her father?

That Freud was oblivious to curiosity about the identity of Anna's analyst seems odd. In the small world of psychoanalysis, most leading figures knew who had analysed whom. Anna, it was assumed, must have had an analysis in order to become an analyst. There were rumours that her analyst had been Lou Andreas-Salomé, the brilliant Russian-born analyst known to have been the mistress not only of Nietzsche but also of Rilke. 'Frau Lou', as Freud called her, had come to Vienna in 1921 as a guest of the Freuds and had remained, to become a member of the Vienna Society, an analyst and a close friend of Anna's. There were other members of the Vienna Psychoanalytic Society, such as Paul Federn or Helene Deutsch, who also might have taken on Freud's daughter as a patient. But the question was neither raised nor answered.

As later became known, Anna's three-and-a-half-year analysis with her father began in 1918 and was resumed in 1924. Freud did not consider it a dark secret. In 1935, for example, he revealed his analysis of Anna to the Italian analyst Edoardo Weiss, who wanted to analyse his own son and asked Freud's advice. Freud replied that what had worked well for him and his daughter might not work for the Weisses: 'I would not advise you to do it and have no right to forbid it.'

---

* His actual words were: 'Wer ist denn eigentlich genügend analysiert? Ich kann Ihnen versichern, Anna ist länger u. gründlicher analysiert worden als. z.B Sie selbst.'

Did Ernest Jones know the truth? In 1919 Anna Freud herself had told a young woman friend who was also in analysis that her father was her analyst. The friend often talked about her own therapy. Anna explained, 'I did not think it was fair that I knew about her and she not about me.'

Freud, defending his daughter, was determined to unearth the motives behind the London attack on her. 'Is this directed against me because Anna is my daughter?' he asked Jones, adding sourly, 'A nice motivation among analysts, who demand that others control their primitive impulses.' In reality, Freud said, Anna's views were independent of his own and independently developed. However, he said he did share them.

It took Jones ten pages to answer: five sheets, closely typed on both sides. He dealt with 'the American situation': countries should attempt to harmonize their conditions for accepting candidates for training, the strictest standards should apply, and the names of candidates should be exchanged internationally. But, regret though he might the American rigidity on lay analysis, he wanted to try to prevent the 'two sets of people' drifting apart in mutual misunderstanding.

On the more painful matter of his alleged campaign against Anna, Jones summed up the London position. For many years in London special attention had been paid to the problems of childhood, probably because of the number of women analysts. Their interest in Mrs Klein's new approach of deep child analysis was understandable, and was stirred by Anna's unexpected attack on Mrs Klein's work in her *Introduction to the Technique of Child Analysis*, which condemned the analysis of children below the latency period. It had been noticed in London that Mrs Klein had not been allowed to reply to Anna's book in the *Zeitschrift*.

The London view, summarized Jones, did not arise from any personal feelings about Freud or Anna: the mood was 'of entire devotion to your personality and fidelity to the principles of psycho-analysis'. To Anna he sent his greetings and assurance that he entertained the highest respect for her and looked forward to their future co-operation.

Did this lavish exercise in politeness work? Not at all, except that Freud allowed that he agreed with Jones's condemnation of the 'New York group'. Otherwise, he saw 'the English' operating as a pack:

> In the behavior of the English toward Anna, two points remain inexcusable: the reproach, which is not customary among us, and offends against all good practice, that she was not analyzed sufficiently – put forward by you publicly and in private – and Mrs Klein's remark that she believed Anna is

avoiding the Oedipus complex on principle. With more good will, this misunderstanding could easily have been avoided.

As a counterbalance to Jones, Freud had an epistolary confidant in Max Eitingon. Eitingon was a friend, and, as a wealthy Jewish émigré to Berlin, not only had subsidized the formation of the Berlin Polyclinic but also had loaned money to Freud and tried to persuade him to settle in Berlin. His elegant Berlin home impressed his condescending visitor Alix Strachey, much as it had Joan Riviere, with its unexpected good taste. ('It was heavenly', Alix wrote James, 'to lean back & look at rows & rows of bookshelves, & well-arranged furniture & thick carpets & 2 or 3 almost passable pictures.')

Eitingon was small – shorter even than Jones – bald, bespectacled and moustached, and had a stammer. Unlike Abraham, he was not a theoretical innovator. But he had warmth and charm, and his loyalty to Freud and the Cause was unshakeable. In his new role as president of the International Association, he rallied his troops at the Innsbruck congress in 1927, congratulating them on holding the tenth of such psychoanalytic gatherings, which he pictured as 'silent but ever-increasing milestones in a splendid progress, an unchecked march to the conquest of man, of humanity'.

It was to Eitingon that Freud confided his suspicion that Jones favoured Klein out of anger with Anna for having refused him as a suitor. Moreover, Freud now suspected Jones of fostering the Kleinian schism out of ambition 'to become independent from Europe and to establish his own Anglo-American realm, something which he cannot very well do before my demise, and he believes he has found a good opportunity in the partial contradiction between Anna and Mrs Klein'.

Freud's fury at 'the English' was inspired particularly by Joan Riviere's long paper in the child-analysis symposium. As published, it contained some strong language. Riviere called Anna's ideas 'superficial', 'not even logical' and 'contravened by the facts'. Freud, unaccustomed to English forthrightness, found phrases like these intolerant, and wrote to scold Riviere, explaining to Jones, 'I would like her to appreciate her blunder for herself.'

In reply, Jones told Freud that he had tried to get Riviere to moderate her arguments, but Freud knew very well what a determined woman she was. However, defending herself to Freud, Riviere said the very opposite. Stung to receive a rebuke from her old analyst, she placed the blame on Jones himself: he had pressured her to take an extreme position, but had then betrayed her by telling Freud he had tried unsuccessfully to tone her down.

There was no doubt in Freud's mind who was the villain. He let fly to Eitingon on 27 November 1927: 'I don't believe that Jones is consciously ill-intentioned; but he is a disagreeable person, who wants to display himself in ruling, angering and agitating, and for this his Welsh dishonesty ('the Liar from Wales') serves him well.'

At a time when casual anti-Semitism was common currency, Freud had no more hesitation about attributing racial characteristics to the Welsh than to 'the English' or 'the Americans'. In jibing at Jones's 'Welsh dishonesty', Freud, no lover of the Versailles Treaty, was echoing the popular doggerel aimed at one of its instigators, the British prime minister David Lloyd George:

> Lloyd George, no doubt,
> When his life ebbs out,
> Will ride in a fiery chariot,
> Sitting in state
> On a red hot plate
> Between Satan and Judas Iscariot.
>
> Ananias that day,
> To the Devil will say:
> 'My claim for precedence now fails.
> So move me up higher,
> Away from the fire
> To make room for the liar from Wales.'

Jones himself never shied away from racial generalizations. Long having recognized the idiosyncrasies of his countrymen, in early 1929 he dashed off a light essay for the *Welsh Outlook* called 'The Inferiority Complex of the Welsh'. The very fact of the assigned title, he wrote, showed that the magazine's editor 'shares the common opinion that this [inferiority] is a typical Welsh feeling'.

He then made short work of the syndrome. The feelings of inferiority arose from within, had nothing to do with reality, and always proceeded from a sense of moral inferiority deriving from past oppression. 'Misfortune and suffering often have the effect of evoking a sense of inferiority' – a quality which those possessing it tend to conceal 'beneath trumped-up boastings of their good qualities'. Then came his peroration: 'There are few nations to whom these remarks apply more strikingly than the Welsh and the Jews, two peoples who have a great deal in common in their psychology as well as notable differences.'

★   ★   ★

The tone of the Freud–Jones correspondence moderated early in 1928. Jones began to hint to Freud that efforts were being made to secure him the Nobel Prize (which would have solved Freud's financial worries). He also sent Freud a small book he had written, as he saw it, to place psychoanalysis in a setting of science. Freud was startled by Jones's audacity in the opening of *Psycho-Analysis*, in saying that psychoanalysis fell between two extremes. The practice could, on the one hand, seem common sense: 'nothing but the translation into high-sounding jargon of platitudes that are well known to every writer about human nature'. On the other hand it could sound obscene, consisting 'of a number of statements and conclusions that would be in the highest degree repellent were it not that the fantastic improbability of them prevents their being taken seriously'.

Freud would never have allowed himself to give such comfort to the enemy: the truth obviously lay in the middle of the two extremes that Jones had sketched. He found it hard to generalize on the field he had created. Ignorant it would seem of what outsiders could find repellent in his ideas, Freud told Jones that on the vexed question of early female development he saw only two points clearly: 'that the first representation of sexual intercourse is an oral one – sucking on the penis, as earlier, at the mother's breast; and giving up clitoral masturbation on account of the painful realization of the inferiority of this organ. On everything else I must reserve my judgement.'

Tactfully, Jones did not share these anatomically explicit absolutes with his fellow members of the British Medical Association committee that was investigating psychoanalysis.

By March 1928 what remained of the feud was ended by tragedy. After an eighteen-day illness, seven-year-old Gwenith Jones died. Taken ill with influenza in February, she developed double broncho-pneumonia. She clung on during Mervyn's sixth birthday, on 27 February, when he was taken into her room so that she could put a present into his hands. When the boy then came down with German measles, he was sent to his Uncle Trotter's house to be looked after.

The fight to save the girl went on for four more days. An illness that a decade or so later would have been easily cured cost the child her life and much suffering. For Jones, the bedside vigil revived the agony of his first wife's sudden end nearly ten years earlier. Once again medical skill was helpless against the approach of death.

The Joneses chose to bury Gwenith in a quiet churchyard on the Gower peninsula. The grave (which would later serve the two of them as well) was in the cemetery of the fourteenth-century church of St Cadoc in Cheriton, a village below Llanmadoc. Jones, still an unbeliever, chose the spot for its beauty and for its proximity to Llanmadoc and to the stream where Gwenith used to play.

Freud sent a telegram of condolence, showing Jones that despite their disputes, 'you retained some affection for me'. Never did Jones treat Freud more like a father than when he poured out the details of his daughter's last hours:

> For nine days she breathed at 70 to the minute, which is rarely possible for more than two days, and this went with an incessant hacking diaphragmatic cough that wore her out. For ten days she had no sleep, an active and most distressing insomnia that no drugs could influence. We had seven doctors and on three occasions they gave her only a few hours to live, but her vitality survived crisis after crisis. Transfusion of blood was tried twice and venesection [the opening of a vein] when her heart began to fail. At the end she was unconscious for two hours and the respiratory centre gave out. I cannot picture to you the agonies of alternating fear, despair and painful hope we experienced, but it left us little able to bear the final blow.

In a few bleak phrases in his letter to Freud, Jones linked their daughters' deaths: 'When you lost Sophie you wrote to me that you wished you could die too. At the time I only partly understood this, but now I do so fully. I am finding it hard, and as yet impossible, to discover enough motive to go on living and to endure the present and future suffering that this blow has brought.'

Strangely, he said, their boy was little consolation, in spite of their love for him. As for the other main interest in his life, the psychoanalytic work, it had brought more pain than pleasure 'and what else is there?'

> I thought I had tasted ten years ago all that the suffering of grief could bring, but life always knows some trump card with which to destroy such illusions. To lose one's first-born, one's only daughter, when one is nearly fifty and cannot begin again, is in itself a fearful blow, but two other features have here combined to make it a crushing one.

He then mentioned Gwenith's rare sweetness and vitality – she had astonished the Swiss at Andermatt the previous winter with her endurance in an Alpine snowstorm – and her premonition that she would die when she was seven, 'as she did'.

Freud and his wife were deeply touched. Having lost their daughter Sophie in 1920, they had been shattered when three years later Sophie's little son Heinerle, Freud's favourite grandson, died of tuberculosis. That child too, Freud told Jones, was of superior intelligence, incredible grace and premonition: 'How do these children know?' Freud wondered.

Freud's wife, Martha, wrote to Kitty Jones:

> Only a mother who has herself had to give up a loved child can feel with you as much as I. We were already, at the first news of the illness of your sweet little girl, quite disturbed, and since the evil news came we feel the loss you have suffered almost as our own. For it is now already eight years since the death of our Sopherl but yet I am always agitated when something similar occurs in our circle of friends.

In fact Jones was disappointed with Freud's own response, for, rather than offering him words of wisdom, Freud urged him to begin a new project on Shakespeare to help him through his grief.

Grief, guilt, depression: Jones had to deal not only with his own but with his wife's. He feared for her stability: she seemed unable to face the future, and found herself conversing with the dead child. Contrary to Mervyn's memory of being the troublesome one, Kitty had found Gwenith the more difficult to handle (perhaps the reason for her seeking treatment by Klein for herself), and in her own memoir she described the girl as 'peculiarly his own child'.

As Freud's seventy-second birthday approached, he found some words of wisdom to offer: ' "Young" and "old" now seem to me the most significant opposites that the human soul can harbor.' He told Jones that he and his wife were young enough to overcome the cruel blow they had suffered.

In the end, time did its work. Kitty went to stay with her mother in Vienna, and in the summer she also visited the Freuds at Semmering in the Styrian mountains. She worried, as she wrote to 'My darling husband', whether she would be able to make him happy when she was so unhappy herself. She thanked him for his 'great and enduring love. Only you in the whole world can understand me and I understand you.' And in little more than a year, at thirty-six, she was expecting another child.

Recovering, Jones had to force himself into a taxi to resume attending the meetings of the British Medical Association's 'Psycho-Analysis Committee'. Set up in 1927, prompted by fears about the possible dangers of the psychoanalytic emphasis on sex and its influence on education, the committee devoted two years and over twenty meetings to its task: 'to investigate the subject of Psycho-Analysis and report on the same'. Jones relished the opportunity to combine his didacticism with his caustic wit, and also to recognize that the committee had read his own published work on psychoanalysis. Their questions, for example, suggested a knowledge of his important 1916 paper, 'The Theory of Symbolism'.

He cautioned the committee against over-literalism in interpreting Freudian symbols. A Zeppelin was indeed a common symbol for the penis, as a house or a room might stand for a woman, but while 'all these objects may function in this way . . . that is a totally different thing from saying that they always do function in that way – fundamentally different'. Such associations, in any case, could be interpreted only in an analytic session, and were not to be taken out of context.

At the BMA meeting on 20 December 1928, Jones jousted with Dr L. A. Parry, consulting surgeon of the Royal Alexandra Hospital for Sick Children in Brighton. Dr Parry had been instrumental in the committee's formation, alarmed by what he had heard of psychoanalysis from his patients. He offered in evidence the experience of a woman who had visited a school 'run on psycho-analytical lines'. The BMA's transcript recorded the exchange:

> DR PARRY: She visited the school taking with her a daughter aged 13. She pointed out to the headmaster certain things to which she objected. One of these was that all the scholars, boys and girls, whatever their age, had their baths together, totally nude. She took her boy out for a walk, leaving the girl of 13 meanwhile at the school. What was her indignation when she returned to find that this girl had been compelled or induced to have a bath stark naked before the master. She went to her doctor, by whom the school had been recommended. After being kept waiting, all the satisfaction she could get was to be told that she was not educated up to these things.
>
> DR JONES: I share Dr Parry's views straight away. I think that would be a very unwise proceeding for the young. I should deprecate it myself, and I should take my child away from a school of that kind. But why should psycho-analysis be burdened with this discredit?
>
> DR PARRY: This was a school run on psycho-analytic lines.
>
> DR JONES: There is no school in England run on psycho-analytic lines.

Jones was being disingenuous. The BMA's committee had already been told about schools 'infected with Freudism'. Moreover, the 'new schools movement', with its relaxed attitudes to discipline and nudity, was well known from pioneering institutions such as Bedales, Dartingon Hall and Beacon Hill, a new school started in September 1927 by the philosopher Bertrand Russell. Russell, having become a father for the first time at the age of forty-nine, was determined that his children should be educated according to his views. Not least of these was a belief in the importance of regular bowel movements. To encourage his pupils in this daily rite, Russell himself would sit on the lavatory, trousers round his ankles, surrounded by children on their pots. As for sex, he adamantly opposed any form of repression, maintaining (according to Caroline Moorehead's fine biography) that 'no other evil in our society is so potent a source of human misery.' For bravura, this statement was easily matched by A. S. Neill, headmaster of the archetypal progressive school, Summerhill, who declared, 'A child is nearer to God in masturbation than in repenting.'

But progressive education was none of Jones's concern. His sacred patch was psychoanalysis, and he defended it by swamping the BMA committee with statistics, clinical evidence and historical information it could get from no other source. He reported that there were about 400 members of the International Psychoanalytic Association, who met in a congress every second year. The British Psycho-Analytical Society was one of ten national societies around the world. In London there were no more than twenty analysts. Training was extensive, and took at least three years. But psychoanalysis was not a treatment only for the rich: while he himself charged three guineas an hour and the average analysis took about three years at 240 sessions a year, there were clinics where patients could be treated free. In any event, psychoanalysts earned less than other doctors.

Jones wangled, probably with little difficulty, the task of writing much of the BMA's report himself. Drawing on his new book, *Psycho-Analysis*, he stated the fundamentals of Freudian theory in language aimed at the intelligent, uninstructed and slightly sceptical reader: that beyond the conscious mind there is a mental territory (the unconscious mind) which is extremely foreign to our conscious perceptions; that the sexual instinct is present from infancy, with the child passing through a series of developmental phases by the age of four, and that the repression of the conflicts aroused by infantile sexuality is the kernel of every neurosis.

Rather than ducking the common criticisms of psychoanalysis, Jones dealt with them one by one, including the supposed danger posed by psychoanalytic treatment. He had never heard of any moral harm being done to a patient by psychoanalysis, he wrote (using the first person), but he had 'ample experience of changes in exactly the opposite direction'. There was no danger, as often alleged, in 'thinking too much about yourself'; the risk was rather in suppressing troublesome thoughts.

When it appeared, the BMA report was hardly a resounding endorsement of psychoanalysis – more a shrug of the shoulders. It concluded that 'the Committee has had no opportunity of testing psycho-analysis as a therapeutic method. It is therefore not in a position to express any collective opinion either in favour of the practice or in opposition.'

Its real significance was in avoiding outright condemnation of Freudianism and analytic treatment. And the BMA accepted that the term 'psychoanalysis' should not be used for any other technique than Freud's (so much for the Jungians) and reserved the term 'psychoanalyst' for members of the International Psychoanalytic Association.

For Jones, the BMA report represented a personal victory over what he told Freud had seemed 'an invincible opposition'. It was, in effect, his revenge against the medical establishment which had ruined his promising career twenty years earlier. With his forceful prose and wide experience, he had raised psychoanalysis, and himself, to respectability

The BMA's small neat pamphlet, *Report of the Psycho-Analysis Committee*, priced at threepence, was published in August 1929 – in time for the Eleventh Congress of the International Psychoanalytic Association in Oxford that month, the first to be held in an English-speaking country.

Freud's praise for Jones had long been double-edged. 'Jones makes trouble all the time, but we know his worth,' he had told Ferenczi in 1925. At the start of 1929, to Eitingon, he had used an Oedipal metaphor to belittle Jones's achievements:

> Since his very first work about rationalization, he has not had any original ideas, and his application of my ideas has stayed on a schoolboy level. Therefore his sensitivity. I am a piece of his superego, which is dissatisfied with his ego. He fears to discover this dissatisfaction in me, and, as a by-product of his pathological displacement, he has to take care that I have reason to be dissatisfied.

Freud remained dismissive when Anna left Vienna for the congress. Although he sent along a fiftieth-birthday present for Jones, he advised his daughter to treat Oxford 'as an interesting adventure, and be glad that you did not marry Jones'.

In contradiction, Freud sent to the Oxford congress the most unequivocal public statement of praise and thanks for what Jones had contributed to the Cause. Jones had

> worked tirelessly for psycho-analysis, making its current findings generally known by means of lectures, defending it against the attacks and misunderstandings of its opponents by means of brilliant, severe but fair criticisms, maintaining its difficult position in England against the demands of the

'profession' with tact and moderation, and, alongside of all these externally directed activities, accomplishing, in loyal co-operation with the development of psycho-analysis on the Continent, the scientific achievement to which, among other works, his *Papers on Psycho-Analysis* and *Essays in Applied Psycho-Analysis* bear witness.

Jones, said Freud, was 'not only indisputably the leading figure among English-speaking analysts, but also recognized as one of the foremost representatives of psycho-analysis as a whole'. Freud would continue to think of him, even beyond fifty, as 'zealous and energetic, combative and devoted to the cause'.

By the end of September 1929 Freud was mocking no longer. He was, he told Jones, very happy with the outcome of the Oxford congress. The New York analysts had moved closer to the Europeans on lay analysis, and, owing in no small part to Jones's efforts, the danger of a split had receded. As for the BMA report, Freud could see that parts were 'easily recognizable as your work, with its precision and correctness'. He praised Jones's 'extraordinary capacity for work' and acknowledged 'how indebted we are to you'.

As the decade closed, the worsening political climate in Germany and Austria would ensure that Freud's appreciation of his fluent (if Welsh) English-language exponent would grow.

15

Skating to the Top
December 1929–September 1932

<hr>

AGILITY, ENERGY, SPEED: essentials for anyone determined to hold a commanding position in psychoanalysis, national and international. But only Ernest Jones was attempting such a feat. By the early 1930s he was crossing the Channel by air, flying from Lympne, a small airport on the Kent coast. While having no alternative to crossing the Atlantic by sea, in 1929 he went to New York for three days, returning to Britain on the same ship.

With his multiple roles as editor, writer and psychoanalytic diplomat, Jones's reputation grew, particularly through his books, *Papers on Psycho-Analysis* and *Essays in Applied Psycho-Analysis*, and he was much in demand as a speaker. In New York he delivered the inaugural address at Columbia University's Psychiatric Institute, where he praised the American treatment of psychoanalysis as a psychiatric discipline, saying that America had 'created a new profession of psychiatry such as exists nowhere else in the world'. In Paris, he spoke, in French, at the Sorbonne on 'La Jalousie'.

His short book *Psycho-Analysis*, written in 1928 for Benn's Sixpenny Library, went into three printings within three months, and by 1932 was in its sixth, as well as having been translated into several languages. The book exuded the authority that was Jones's stock in trade. 'Psycho-analysis attempts to answer questions that had previously not even been raised,' he wrote. 'It deals almost entirely with a field of knowledge, the unconscious mind, the existence of which is both unknown and denied.' Knowledge of the unconscious might prove useful, for it was 'certain that man's power over his material environment . . . has far outstripped his control over himself'.

In 1932 Jones was invited to broadcast on the BBC. Before then he and the philosopher Bertrand Russell had been considered too immoral to be allowed on the airwaves, as was the subject of psychoanalysis. But the BBC reversed its view, and planned a course of lectures on psychology, the second of which was to be given by Jones. He had the pleasure of describing the BBC to Freud: 'The Radio in this country is a Government institution with great prestige.'

Much of Jones's energy in London went into synchronizing the activities of the British Psycho-Analytical Society, its clinic and its institute. One practical, cost-saving step was to abolish the barriers between the three. This relaxation made it possible for all lay members of the society to work at the clinic, performing what would now be called psychoanalytic psychotherapy. All staff would treat one patient daily without a fee, or perform some equivalent service. Jones called this 'revolutionary'. Everything was going smoothly except for a bitter dispute with John Rickman about Jones's handling of the society that he, Rickman, felt he had worked hard to create. The dispute was all the bitterer for being conducted over long distance. Rickman was in Budapest, being analysed by Ferenczi, and felt that Jones was endangering the London clinic and institute 'by carelessness or indifference'.

Jones's days were filled with patients, his after-lunch break with answering correspondence through his secretary, his evenings with committees, and his weekends with travelling back and forth to Sussex to get a breath of clear air away from the smoke of millions of London coal fires. It was only a short respite, as he worked on Saturday morning and had to be back by Sunday evening. After some accidents, he decided not to drive in town and let his wife take the wheel for much of the journey.

Somehow in such a schedule Jones found time to go skating. Not just gliding around to relax, but figure skating to precise international standards. Skating had been part of his life since Llandovery College, and he had taken lessons on family holidays in Switzerland, often joined by his wife. The rheumatism from which he suffered was in his hands but not in his legs. In 1931 he joined the National Ice Skating Association, and earned its bronze medal for his proficiency in performing such required figures as changes-of-edge and threes-to-a-centre.

Skating allowed him also to practise the art of making friends in high places. Many people in high society skated at that time. At a gala at the exclusive Grosvenor Skating Club at the Grosvenor House hotel in Park Lane, the Prince of Wales attended to watch about a hundred people, champions and socialites, take to the ice. Among notables to hold the bronze medal were the Admiral of the Fleet Earl Jellicoe, Captain the Hon. Tom Mitford (brother of Nancy, Jessica et al.) and the Duchess of Bedford.

Through skating, Jones became friendly with Sir Samuel Hoare, Conservative MP for Chelsea and (from 1929 to 1931) secretary of state for

India in the National, or coalition, government under the Labour prime minister Ramsay MacDonald. Hoare matched Jones almost exactly in age, size and fastidious appearance, although his background could scarcely have been more different. From the Anglo-Irish branch of an old Quaker family converted to Anglo-Catholicism, Hoare had gone to Harrow and Oxford, and had turned to skating to bolster his delicate physique. He became an excellent skater. As Indian secretary, he was a strong advocate of independence for India, and was known to get on very well with Mahatma Gandhi.

Jones's diplomatic associations led him to meet, at a reception at the Austrian Embassy, 'an entrancingly beautiful damsel'. Introduced and asked to look after her, he invited her to join him at his skating club. However, his boyish dreams of waltzing on ice with a Viennese beauty were dashed when she announced that she could do only modern dances on skates and was unable to waltz.

Never one to waste a resource, in 1931 Jones published an entertaining and authoritative book called *The Elements of Figure Skating*. Brought out by the commercial firm of Methuen rather than by the International Psycho-Analytical Press, and dedicated to 'My Partner Katherine', it described the experience of skating in terms that hint at the author's sensual *savoir faire*. The aim of the art, he said, was to acquire 'control over every fibre of the body' so that 'the whole body responds with perfect harmony to the lightest expression of the will'.

> The nature of the promised pleasure, already contemplated in imagination, is the exhilarating sensation of gliding without effort or resistance while one feels that all the while the motion is under one's sure control . . . It combines and surpasses the joys of flying and dancing; only in a certain type of dream do we ever else attain a higher degree of the same ravishing experience of exultantly skiing the earth.

Strong imagery, coming from a psychoanalyst. The book went on to address the lack of confidence (never a Jones problem) that hampers many beginners. 'Fear', Jones pronounced magisterially, 'has many degrees and forms: apprehensiveness, timidity, anxiety, bewilderment, panic.' It was a state of mind which could be remedied by psychological treatment, but precise knowledge was preferable.

Before going on to elucidate the ways of tracing on ice the required patterns, such as the twenty-four different forms of the figure eight, Jones gave a lesson on 'the art of falling'. The place to learn was the bedroom, 'with an ample supply of cushions and eiderdowns'. Then, fall with relaxed muscles, and try to fall on your side – best of all on the shoulder and upper arm – and above all not on the head: 'to learn to slither is really the art of falling on the ice'. This advice might have served Jones as his life's motto. Having overcome his early catastrophic falls, he was now in sure control over his every move.

Skating was not the only hobby to be turned into a readable narrative. Jones was a keen chess player: he studied the history of chess, and engaged in games by correspondence. He also wrote, again in 1931, 'The Problem of Paul Morphy', the story of a chess prodigy born in New Orleans in 1837. Having been taught chess by his father at the age of ten, by the time he was twelve the boy had gone on to defeat international masters, often playing them blindfolded. Some pronounced him the greatest chess player of all time. At the age of twenty, after a European tour and being lavishly feted in America, he declared that his career was over. He first became a lawyer like his father, then lapsed 'into a state of seclusion and introversion' and died suddenly at the age of forty-seven of apoplexy, as had his father before him.

What was the connection between Morphy's brilliance and his neurosis? Jones had little difficulty in detecting the unconscious motive behind a fascination for chess, from William the Conqueror to Napoleon on down: 'father murder'. 'Check-mate', he reminded the reader, means literally 'The king is dead.' He observed also that 'in attacking the father the most potent assistance is afforded by the mother (= queen).'

Jones diagnosed that Morphy's problem was not that excessive preoccupation with chess had addled his brain. Rather, as the game was a substitute for the act of killing his father, anything that impugned his motives (as when someone suggested that his chess was a means of making money) exposed his hidden motive and left him with a strong revulsion against chess.

As usual, Jones discerned a wider Oedipal meaning in the story of one unhappy man. The well-recognized association between genius and mental instability, he declared, came from the capacity to apply unusual gifts with intense concentration. In Morphy's case, achieving such concentration meant holding unconscious guilt in complete abeyance. When this restraint was broken, as it was by challenges to his motives, his unconscious parricidal impulses were released and his ability to use his genius collapsed.

Jones's life at 42 York Terrace was well ordered. Doric Villa, a Nash house divided vertically to make homes for two families, gave them three floors, a basement and a good-sized garden facing Regent's Park. The new baby, Nesta, born on 2 May 1930, was thriving, and Mervyn was a satisfying child – a bright boy, who got top marks for writing at Arnold House in St John's Wood. He played his father at chess, and observed his parents shrewdly. His father, he said later in his autobiography, *Chances*, was the most important person in his life. He felt his mother to be in awe of his father, thirteen years her senior and her instructor in how things were done in England. He noticed also that his father was very busy and liked to think of himself as a mediator – a role that was difficult because of his conviction that he was always right.

When Jones turned fifty, Freud wrote a special birthday letter to congratulate him. 'I have always counted you as one of my closer family members, and will continue to do so, which indicates – beyond all the discords that are seldom lacking within a family and have also not been lacking between us – a fund of tenderness that one can draw on time and again.'

Any thought that Jones was a sycophantic follower of Freud disappears in the light of his persistent efforts to dissuade Freud from his Lamarckian belief in the inheritance of acquired characteristics. Jones had always savoured the idea that Freud was the Darwin of the mind and that he himself was T. H. Huxley, the hero of his youth, who was known as 'Darwin's Bulldog'. But, like Huxley, Jones dared to contradict his Darwin. Like most reputable biologists, Jones knew that Lamarckism, a pre-Darwinian theory, was nonsense: the giraffe's neck does *not* get longer over the generations by repeated stretching for high leaves. Nor, as Julian Huxley pointed out, did centuries of circumcision produce Jewish male babies born without foreskins. Jones tried to convince Freud that Lamarck's ideas had been discredited by August Weismann, an important biologist, who showed that behaviour and life experience did not enter, let alone alter, the germ plasm and could not be transmitted by biological inheritance.

The 'death drive' – the *Todestriebe* – was another concept on which Jones disagreed with Freud. In 1920 Freud had proposed in his *Beyond the Pleasure Principle* that beyond life (or pleasure) is death, a return to the condition before life. This drive leads, according to his argument, to a compulsion, or instinct, towards the disintegration of life into inorganic lifelessness. This theory appears to draw a psychic analogy with entropy, as defined in the Second Law of Thermodynamics by Rudolf Clausius in 1850, as the natural disintegration of order into disorder unless another force intervenes. Freud developed this death-drive concept in the wake of the world war which had demonstrated human aggressiveness and zeal for destruction unimagined in his earlier philosophy. In a later booklet, *Civilization and its Discontents*, he allied this instinct to the tendency to repeat painful experiences over and over again. (The title of this booklet called for some creative ingenuity on the part of Joan Riviere. Freud's original title had been *Das Unglück und Kultur*, but *Unglück* – 'unhappiness' – was then altered to *Unbehagen* which had no obvious English equivalent. Jones mused that the old English word 'dis-ease' would be ideal; he suggested also 'unease' and 'malaise'. ' "Discomfort" ', he told Freud, 'seems to be hardly strong enough; "discontent" seems too conscious.' But Riviere finally prevailed with *Civilization and its Discontents*.)

For his part, Jones could recognize the impulses towards hostility and aggression as the 'essential obstacle to civilisation', but he argued with Freud that these impulses to kill and destroy served the function of trying to remove obstacles to pleasure. They did not express a wish for non-existence.

Then there was the matter of the clitoris. Was it an inferior penis, a sign to the female of her innate castration? Or was it an equivalent organ, playing the same part in a girl's emotional growth as the penis did in a boy's? Jones was in the feminist avant-garde, contradicting and scolding Freud for his phallocentric attitude of woman as a disappointed man. In 1929 Riviere, now Jones's close colleague, opened her paper on female sexuality (written for Jones's *International Journal of Psycho-Analysis*) with a fulsome compliment to the editor: 'Every direction in which psycho-analytic research has pointed seems in its turn to have attracted the interest of Ernest Jones.' She referred to his 1927 paper on 'The Early Development of Female Sexuality', in which he declared that male analysts had underestimated the importance of the female organs. It was an error to interpret 'castration' too literally: the concept could be applied to both sexes, but it obscured the deeper and common fear – 'the permanent extinction of the capacity (including opportunity) for sexual enjoyment'.

Jones restated the phallocentric charge to Freud in 1932, saying, 'Hitherto you have laid such stress on the father and male side (owing to the obscurity of the mother).' However, Freud and Jones were at one in believing that homosexuality in both sexes was a developmental phenomenon, caused by young children's fantasies about their own and their parents' sexual organs. In females, Jones told Freud (after analysing many homosexual women), 'the phantasy of the father (especially of his penis in her womb)' played a part of some importance.

*　　*　　*

By 1932 Freud had much to be discontented about. He was desperate for new patients. The stock-market crash of 1929 and the resulting Great Depression had stopped the flow of Americans and Britons to his couch; he had only four patients, and soon would have only three. He moaned to Jones that 'there is very little analytic work to do'.

All of Europe and the United States suffered from rapidly rising unemployment, bank failures and bankruptcies, and all watched the rise of the National Socialists in Germany, where, in the faltering Weimar Republic, Adolf Hitler's party became the second largest party in the Reichstag, winning 107 seats.

Psychoanalysis is a deferrable expense, and the economic depression hit it hard. The international congress planned for 1931 had to be cancelled, as few analysts had the money to travel. (Psychoanalysis was now truly international: a new society had been recognized in Japan, and there were others in India, Russia, Sweden, Holland, Hungary, France and Switzerland, as well as in Britain and, in America, in Chicago, Baltimore– Washington and New York.) One consequence of the postponement was that there was no new president. Eitingon, the interim president since Karl Abraham's death, was now in difficulties as his wealth had been wiped out by the collapse of a family fur company in New York, and was determined to step down at the next congress. Freud wrote to his close friend Sándor Ferenczi in Budapest to say that they all agreed that he should be the next president. Ferenczi liked the idea, but told Eitingon that, even so, they all would have to come to terms with Jones. 'I can't help looking at the despotism and maliciousness of his character and actions as anything but harmful for psychoanalysis.'

Ferenczi had a grievance against his old analysand. Jones, he felt, had manoeuvred him out of the presidency at the Oxford congress of 1929. That was not entirely true. While Freud himself had wanted Ferenczi for president that year, he was a realist and a passionate defender of his cause. He recognised that the Central European Ferenczi lacked the flair or organizational skill, let alone the mastery of English, to reach the kind of compromise with the Americans on lay analysis that Jones had brought about. It had seemed easier to leave Eitingon in the post temporarily and replace him with Ferenczi at the next congress.

This plan was fine with Jones. In December 1930 he met Eitingon in Paris, and together they agreed that Ferenczi would be named at the next congress – whenever and wherever it might be. Freud was delighted that peace had broken out. He wrote Jones that, while he was sorry that Jones had paid for the fleeting Paris trip with another of his ear infections, 'Your relationship with Eitingon pleased me very much. You, he, and Ferenczi are indeed the crucial individuals at the I.P.V. [that is, the international *Verein* or association], whose future will depend mainly on unanimity among you.'

Over the next two years, the fierce negotiations about the presidency would have done credit to a political party. But few politicians have the kind of publishing worries carried by the leaders of psychoanalysis. Their *Verlag*, the German psychoanalytic publishing house, was failing and, as he was now a poor man, Eitingon could not bail it out. Jones took himself to Berlin on 21 May 1932, leaving on the same day he had arrived back in London after a week in the Lake District. The intention was to rescue the *Verlag*, and the solution that was reached was highly pleasing to Jones. It was that the International Association would take over the *Verlag* and tax each of its several hundred members the equivalent of fifteen shillings each to pay its debts. Freud was pleased. His son Martin had taken over as the *Verlag*'s managing director, and that job was now secure. While in Berlin, Jones heard rumours that Jewish analysts there might not be safe, but he saw no evidence of danger.

Jones had publishing worries of his own. A rival English-language publication, the *Psychoanalytic Quarterly*, had appeared in New York, and he had not been told about it – not even by Freud, who had contributed a paper. The *Quarterly* threatened to siphon off the American subscribers who kept Jones's *Journal* solvent, providing half its income, and its existence spoiled Jones's claim for the *Journal* as being the official organ of psychoanalysis in North America. He had fondly hoped that his own publication had catered for Americans '(in spite of Mrs Riviere's stern veto on American contributions)', he told Freud, and he would have been willing to appoint an American co-editor or reserve a special section for them. For the unwanted competition, Jones blamed a young Russian-born analyst, Gregory Zilboorg, calling him 'a completely wild Russian' (even though Zilboorg had taken his medical degree at Columbia). In the event, both publications survived.

But the main worry was Ferenczi. Jones, Freud and Eitingon felt he had been behaving erratically. Freud was puzzled why his closest friend in the inner circle – a man whom he would have welcomed as a son-in-law and a fellow Jew, with whom he had exchanged far more letters (1,246) even than he had with Jones (671) – had now lapsed into long silence. In any event, Freud was disposed to interpret any disagreement between himself and a close follower as the son's rebellion against the father; he now interpreted what seemed Ferenczi's growing hostility as a death wish against himself.

Moreover, Freud was bristling with apprehension, having heard from an American analyst, Dr Clara Thompson, that Ferenczi was indeed kissing his patients (of whom she was one). That Ferenczi defended his tactic as a new technique only upset Freud more, for new techniques were, as Freud told him, 'an expression of inner dissatisfaction'. Freud did not, and could not, appreciate that Ferenczi's technique – to act the part of a loving parent in order to neutralize the early unhappiness of his patients – was based on a new philosophy. Ferenczi believed (so he wrote in his diary) that letting his analysands analyse him – 'mutual analysis' was the term used – and merge their emotional lives with his was a step towards his utopia: 'elimination of impulses of hatred', which could have 'a humanizing effect on the whole universe'.

The dispute intensified as the 1932 congress, planned for Wiesbaden in September, grew near. In April, Freud wrote to Eitingon, 'Isn't Ferenczi a tribulation? He is offended because one is not delighted to hear how he plays mother and child with his female patients.'

By the end of 1931, Freud had let fly at Ferenczi. 'Lieber Freund,' he began, before asking where such a technique, forbidden by all the rules of psychoanalysis, might not lead: to petting parties and worse.

> Now, picture to yourself what will be the consequence of making your technique public . . . So-and-so many independent thinkers in technique will say to themselves, Why stop with a kiss? Certainly, one will achieve still more if one adds 'pawing', which, after all, doesn't make babies. And then bolder ones will come along who will take the further step of peeping and showing, and soon we will have accepted into the technique of psychoanalysis the whole repertoire of demiviergerie and petting parties.

As the controversy boiled on, Ferenczi made the surprise announcement, in mid-August 1932, that 'after long tormented hesitation' he had decided to withdraw his candidacy for the presidency, because his own thinking was so much in conflict with classical psychoanalytical principles that it would be dangerous for him to accept it.

Freud ought to have been pleased, but his reaction was quite the reverse. He wrote and asked Ferenczi to assume the presidency, because the responsibilities of office might bring him back into the mainstream of the movement. Ferenczi replied merely that he would come to Vienna before the congress to talk it over. But Eitingon had had enough. He wrote to Jones to ask him to stand.

Ferenczi did appear at Berggasse 19 and, in a scene made famous by Jones's biography of Freud, he entered the room without a word of greeting and announced that he would read aloud the paper he had prepared for the congress. Just as he began to read, A. A. Brill from New York walked in and sat down to listen. Ferenczi was bitterly resentful that Freud had violated their long friendship by bringing in a third person as a witness.

What Freud heard sent him into shock. Ferenczi was proclaiming an idea that he himself had discarded before the turn of the century: that children were often raped, seduced or sexually interfered with by adults, and this abuse was a common cause of neurosis. Afterwards, Freud sent a telegram to Eitingon in Berlin: Ferenczi's paper was 'Harmless, stupid, also inadequate. Impression unpleasant.'

In a long letter to Anna, Freud used stronger language about Ferenczi: 'He has completely regressed to etiological views I believed in, and gave up, 35 years ago: that the regular cause of neuroses is sexual traumas of childhood, said it in virtually the same words as I had used then.' Freud was now convinced that Ferenczi was another defector in the making. Sick with his cancer, conscious of his advancing age, he saw that he had lost all of his crown princes. (Did he foresee that he would be left with a crown princess, Anna?)

Freud never denied the reality of child abuse, but he did not accept his own earlier theory that it was a necessary precondition of adult neurosis. And what offended Freud just as much in the paper were Ferenczi's observations on mutual analysis – the need of the analyst to accept analysands' criticism of the analyst and 'to acknowledge one's mistakes *before* them'.

He was struck also by Ferenczi's deteriorating physical and psychological condition. Ferenczi's letters had been getting more and more erratic, while as early as 1927 Eitingon, having been visited by Ferenczi in Berlin, had told Freud, 'I have been, and am, fairly alarmed.'

Eitingon forbade Ferenczi to read his paper at the congress, but Jones thought it too vague to do any harm, so Ferenczi delivered it anyway. With Jones in the chair, his was the first paper on the programme, and the reaction of the audience was mild indifference. Not so later in the century. In 1984 the psychoanalytic historian Jeffrey Masson, in a shrill book, *The Assault on Truth*, accused Freud and Jones of suppressing the truth of child abuse that Freud had abandoned when he gave up his 'seduction theory' and decided that children's reports of mistreatment were products of their own imaginations.

At the Wiesbaden congress, despite such conference treats as a boat trip up the Rhine to see the Lorelei, the delegates sensed trouble. As Jones wrote to Kitty, 'Here a great crisis. Eitingon and Brill announced this week (to Anna) that Ferenczi's new ideas (consisting chiefly of negations of the Oedipus Complex) were so incompatible with psycho-analysis that Eitingon thought he should not be President . . . They all insisted that I must take the Presidency.'

Thus on 5 September 1932, to warm applause from the delegates, Jones slid into the presidency of the International Psychoanalytic Association. Neither he nor his enemies could have dreamed how long he would hold the post, nor what heavy responsibilities it would place on him.

16

Goodbye to Berlin
1933–1937

SÁNDOR FERENCZI WAS dying. On 29 March 1933, in the next to last
letter he would ever write to Freud, from the city James Joyce put
into *Finnegans Wake* as 'Judapest', Ferenczi scrawled a plea to his close
friend and fellow Jew to get out of Austria.

Freud would not be moved. When the National Socialists came to
power in Germany and swiftly began a campaign against enemies of the
Fatherland – Jews in particular – Ernest Jones wrote to Freud, 'You must
be glad that Austria is not a part of Germany.' In reply, Freud stated that
he expected 'the Hitler movement' to spread to Austria, and that Jews
would then not find life pleasant. He had faith, even so, in the Treaty of
Versailles's guarantee of the rights of minorities, and he did not expect his
country to annex itself to Germany. Besides, Austrians were 'not inclined
to the German brutality'.

In Germany, however, for psychoanalysts the world had collapsed. In
1932 Berlin remained an international centre for psychoanalytic training
and treatment. The Berlin Psychoanalytic Institute on Potsdamerstrasse,
with its spare modernist furniture and well-known names such as Max
Eitingon, Karen Horney, Ernst Simmel and Otto Fenichel, had thirty-six
members and a teaching staff of twelve. They met every week to hear
papers on such topics as the prognosis for neuroses of long-standing. Their
main concern at the fourth-quarter general meeting in October 1932 was
the pressure of work. A proposal from Eitingon – the institute's president
and, with Karl Abraham, its founder – that future meetings be restricted
to two a month was warmly welcomed. No one seems to have cared that
most of the membership was Jewish, nor that of the institute's five-
man governing council only two – Felix Boehm and Carl Müller-
Braunschweig – were Aryan. Eitingon, Simmel and Fenichel were not.

Three months later the rush to leave had begun. Under the dictatorial
powers given to Hitler by the Reichstag on 23 March 1933, all organizations, from universities to the press and professional groups, had to be
absorbed into the Nazi cause under the banner of *Gleichschaltung*, co-

ordination. Anti-Semitism became government policy. Many professions saw their Jewish members join the general exodus: scientists, architects, artists and writers were among those driven out in what has been called 'Hitler's gift' to the countries which took them in. What hit psychoanalysts directly was a decree that no non-Aryan doctor could participate in any state or private health-insurance schemes. This move effectively deprived Jewish doctors and psychoanalysts of their incomes. Eitingon announced his intention to emigrate to Palestine.

He resigned as head of the institute even before the spectacular burning of banned books in May, during which much of the psychoanalytic canon – classified as 'Jewish' – was thrown into the flames. Fuel for the fire included the works not only of Freud but also of Melanie Klein, Anna Freud, Erich Fromm and Bronislaw Malinowski.

The analysts were leaving Germany, Freud and Anna were at pains to stress, not because they were analysts, but because they were Jews. But how to tell the two apart? The Nazis lost little time equating psychoanalysis with Jewishness. An article, 'The Psychoanalysis of the Jew Sigmund Freud', in the August/September 1933 issue of the magazine *Deutsche Volksgesundheit aus Blut und Boden* spelled it out:

> Psychoanalysis is an impressive example of the fact that nothing good for us Germans can ever come from a Jew, even when he produces 'scientific achievements'. Even if he [Freud] gave us 5% that was novel and apparently good, 95% of his doctrine is destructive and annihilating *for us*. His own fellow-Jews and other races may derive advantage from Jewish ideas, we Germans and all peoples with Nordic blood always find it turns out badly for us if we eat anything out of the Jew's hand.

From London, Jones, in his capacity as president of the International Psychoanalytic Association, was in constant contact with Anna Freud, the association's secretary, about organizing help for those analysts who wished to emigrate. They saw it as their common obligation to members in difficulties. By 5 April, having heard from the Dutch psychoanalyst J. H. W. van Ophuijsen, who had visited Berlin, that 'Germany is at the present a hell for the German Jews' and having been warned that his letters to Eitingon were being opened, Jones dipped into his personal savings and personally financed the departure and resettlement of Abraham's widow and their daughter, who wished to come to study medicine in London. Their problems in Berlin, he wrote to Freud, seemed the most urgent – 'With the exception of personal ones: my wife has two sisters and a brother in Berlin!'

The Times carried daily reports from Berlin of the effects of the policy of discrimination against German Jews – shops boycotted; beards of Jews being cut in the street; the drive to remove Jews from the professions. The large London Jewish community was passionately concerned. It was also reported that, at a meeting of the Jewish Board of Deputies, Neville Laski, KC, said that the campaign of discrimination against the Jews had made it impossible for any Jewish member of the professional class to pursue his occupation and earn his livelihood in Germany. A refugee reception committee had been formed, and had raised at least £10,000.

The wish to help was aired in the House of Lords. The Marquess of Reading (Rufus Isaacs) declared that, 'as a member of the Jewish community and a member of their lordships' House', he appealed to His Majesty's Government to use whatever legitimate means were in its power to let Germany know what was felt by the British people. He was greeted with cheers. The Earl of Iddesleigh agreed, speaking not only for himself but as a member of the Roman Catholic Church. The Archbishop of Canterbury then rose to associate himself entirely with what Lord Reading had said in a way which had touched their hearts.

'Not so fast' was the essence of the reply from the Secretary of State for War, Lord Hailsham. Speaking as a member of the National government (headed by Ramsay MacDonald, who, expelled from the Labour Party he had founded, had drawn the Conservatives and Liberals into a ruling coalition), Hailsham said that there were limits to what it could do. After enquiries, the government had found no evidence that any British citizen of Jewish descent had been arrested or ill-treated in Germany. The government had no right to make representations to the German government in regard to the treatment of its own citizens. The situation called for tact.

By 2 May Jones could alert Brill in New York to the terrible situation: no Jews were allowed to hold any official position, such as in the German Psychoanalytic Society. (Its new president was a Gentile, Felix Boehm, of the Berlin Institute.) Jones wrote to Smith Ely Jeliffe, an analyst in New York, in April 1933:

> We are having a hectic time over here with political refugees. Some seventy thousand got away from Germany as the blow was falling. Among them are most of the German Psycho-Analytical Society; I only know of four or five members still left in Berlin. The persecution has been much worse than you seem to think and has really quite lived up to the Middle Ages in reputation. It is a very Hunnish affair.

Refugees apart, London was far removed from the turmoil. In March *The Times* gave prominent coverage to the opening of the redesigned Derry and Toms department store on Kensington High Street, where, once the green and gold ribbon was cut, crowds thronged in. The new building was spacious and beautiful, 'a meeting of modern and traditional ideas in architecture', with a rooftop restaurant, a feeling of lightness and airiness throughout, and new and attractive merchandise chosen to appeal to 'women of taste'.

It was a peaceful time for the Jones family too. A fourth child, a son, was born on 3 May 1933, after a surprise but welcome late pregnancy for Katherine, now forty-one. Jones, as was his custom, was present at the birth, and helped make a decision at midnight to induce labour because of an acetonaemia (presence of acetone in the blood). The news of the arrival of Lewis Ernest Jones coincided with Jones's annual birthday greetings to Freud on 6 May.

With his psychoanalytic world in upheaval and his hours filled with correspondence, with visits to the Home Office and even with costly international telephone calls, Jones paused for reflection when he received the news of the death on 24 May 1933 of his old analyst Ferenczi, the founder of the International Association of Psychoanalysis. It left Jones as the only surviving member of the original secret Committee, the Blood Brotherhood, the Order of the Ring, whose Wagnerian overtones now rang hollow.

He and Freud exchanged condolences. 'Ferenczi takes a part of the old era with him,' Freud pronounced, adding, 'To be sure, the loss was not a new one; for years Ferenczi has no longer been with us, indeed, not even with himself.'

Freud described Ferenczi's decline: 'In his last weeks he could no longer walk or stand at all. Simultaneously a mental degeneration in the form of paranoia developed with uncanny logical consistency. Central to this was the conviction that I did not love him enough.' To Freud, Ferenczi's 'technical innovations' were connected with this disappointment: 'he wanted to show me how lovingly one has to treat one's patients in order to help them.' Ferenczi was convinced that his mother had not loved him enough, Freud continued, so that he turned himself into the mother of his patients and even persuaded himself that one of these, an American woman, was influencing him by sending thought waves across the Atlantic. Thus a 'once so brillliant intelligence was extinguished. But let us keep his sad end a secret between us.'

As one neurologist to another, Jones answered that presumably there had been 'degeneration of the spinal cord which sometimes accompanies pernicious anaemia'. He assured Freud that he would 'of course keep secret what you told me about the American lady, but I am afraid the paranoia is public news.'

By 'public news' Jones meant that anyone who had heard Ferenczi's last congress paper would have been aware of his deterioration. As for the paper, now that Ferenczi was gone, Jones was thinking of not publishing it in English, although he had promised Ferenczi that he would do so. Joan Riviere suggested holding it back from the *Journal*, even though the paper had been translated, edited and set in type. When Brill from New York supported the decision not to publish, Jones told Freud it was a *fait accompli*, saying to Brill, 'It would certainly not have done his reputation any good.'

In the century following, Ferenczi's perceptive criticisms of psychoanalysis would not be so easily dismissed. In *Secrets of the Soul*, Eli Zaretsky in 2004 wrote that, like many analysts of the time, Ferenczi had returned to the actual and the social as opposed to the psychical. In his last, disputed, paper Ferenczi argued that, because of its emphasis on abstinence and privation, the analytic situation reproduced the infant experience of deprivation and trauma. He also criticized analysts for their indifference to the length of the analysis, and for 'the tendency to prolong it for purely financial reasons; if one wants to, one turns the patients into taxpayers for life.'

In September 1933 Jones travelled to Holland so that he and van Ophuijsen could meet Boehm and Müller-Braunschweig from Berlin and hear at first hand how the German Psychoanalytic Society was being harassed by the police about its ethnic composition and the possible Marxist leanings of controversial figures such as Wilhelm Reich. (Reich, transferred from the Vienna Society, had been admitted as a full member of the German Society in 1931, only to give a paper in June 1932 arguing that the National Socialist movement illustrated that the German lower middle classes, because of their family environment, were more inclined to be political reactionaries than revolutionaries. Reich later emigrated to America and got into trouble with the Federal Authorities with his 'Orgone Box' (a supposed sexual-energy accumulator). For their part, Boehm and Müller-Braunschweig clung to the hope that the Nazis might accommodate psychoanalysis in its purged form.

The problem of the refugee analysts was worsened by the economic slump, the Great Depression, that had helped precipitate Germany into fascism. It was hard enough for refugees to get out of Germany: the Nazis demanded an exit visa and an emigration permit, and all money and jewellery were to be left behind. But they were also faced by demands from their recipient countries for financial guarantors or assurance of a job waiting. Not only were these difficult to obtain, the analysts themselves were unsure whether their skills, tuned to the speech and milieu of their patients, could be transposed into a foreign language.

Where should the German analysts go? In most of the major cities with psychoanalytic societies – London, Copenhagen, Stockholm, New York – the existing analytic community was already hard hit by the slump, while the provinces were, by and large, uninterested in the Freudian couch. Jones reported to van Ophuijsen that, while Britain was proud of its reputation in welcoming people fleeing political persecution, the high British unemployment rate was provoking a reaction against admitting foreigners. 'Fear', Jones expostulated, 'can easily arise at the idea of immigrant hordes.' In England, he said, there was also still 'some prejudice against German-speaking people and a vague association with Communism'. And he told Eitingon, who had not yet left Berlin, 'We cannot recommend anyone to come here because even if all the great difficulties are overcome, there is not enough work for our own people and the prospects of making a living are at present very poor indeed.' Those who came first would have the best chance of settling in. Any intending to come should learn English as fast as possible.

America presented a special problem – New York, particularly, where most of the foreign analysts wanted to go. Indeed, despite the Depression, America remained the promised land, with the Statue of Liberty waiting to greet the tired, poor and huddled masses – as long as they came from northern Europe, not from southern or eastern Europe, nor Asia, regions whose ethnic groups the stringent 1920s quotas on immigration were designed to exclude. Yet the American Psychoanalytic Association was the most faction-ridden and the most uneasy in its relation to the International Association.

Jones saw the phenomenon psychoanalytically. He interpreted it for Brill, who was struggling to keep control over the fractious elements: 'As you know, new arrivals in America develop a peculiarly rebellious psychology. It simply means that the son–father complex is still unresolved and keeps being imparted into all sorts of unnecessary situations.'

Brill, although eager to help, wanted the refugees to go anywhere but

New York. He told Jones in May 1933, 'New York really has enough analysts. In fact I believe we are beginning to be overcrowded.' Wherever they ended up, the influx of German and later Viennese and Hungarian analysts had a great impact on the American scene. The membership of the American Psychoanalytic Association rose from 92 in 1932 to 157 in 1938. By 1945 it was 247, triggering the post-war explosion of psychoanalysis in the United States.

Quite apart from the problem of the American distrust of lay analysis, the absorption of Jewish psychoanalysts was made more difficult by the professional barriers that faced American Jews. At the time, many – perhaps most – American medical schools imposed Jewish quotas, to deal with the fact that a large proportion of their qualified applicants were Jews. (Such quotas were not dropped until the mid-1960s.)

Jones, however, recognized that the 'gravest of all' obstacles in placing refugees was the 'quarrelling and internal dissension in so many Societies'. In September 1933 Jones put to Freud a question that many outside the field have asked before and since: why were psychoanalysts so neurotic? Or, as he worded it, why had psychoanalysis 'not been more successful among analysts themselves'?

Never at a loss, Jones had his answers ready. Many analysts were neurotic to start with: that is why they had chosen the field. Second, they were overworked, and under constant strain. Third, so few of them had been adequately analysed. He suggested that analysts be required to take a refresher analysis course, to give them a fresh look at their inner workings. He quite ignored that he himself had fiercely rejected suggestions in 1923 that he submit to more analysis.

Even Freud's sanctuary, the Vienna Psychoanalytic Society, was not immune to rows. Jones was drawn into one of these in October 1933, when the Vienna Society was upset about a book written by one of its older members, Isidor Sadger. The book, *Recollecting Freud*, was highly anecdotal and highly critical of Freud, drawing on his early lectures, and the society was thinking of going to law to stop publication. Jones advised against legal action. With exasperated sarcasm, he ended a letter to Paul Federn, one of Freud's earliest followers, by saying that the only practical solution was to put Sadger in a concentration camp unless he agreed to rewrite the book.

Irony does not age well. This sour comment, read decades after the Holocaust, has been interpreted literally by the historian of psychoanalysis Paul Roazen as a 'request'. E. James Lieberman in his 1985 biography of

Otto Rank also took it literally: 'Jones was so upset by the Sadger manu-script that in order to suppress it, he suggested Sadger be put in a concen-tration camp.'

The facts argue in Jones's favour. He had no power to put anyone in a 'concentration camp' – a phrase which, in 1933, suggested Lord Kitchener and the internment camps of the Boer War, not the death camps that were to come. What he did have, and was using to its utmost, was the power to persuade the British Home Office to admit refugees and give them permission to work.

By October 1933, four German psychoanalysts had arrived in England, including, from Berlin, Walter Schmideberg (Melanie Klein's son-in-law – her daughter, Melitta Schmideberg, was already in England) and Paula Heimann. Two more were expected. The tumultuous year ended with Eitingon leaving Berlin for ever.

On 9 January 1934 the president announced that Dr Eitingon had made a gift to the Berlin institute of the furniture and equipment of its premises at 10 Wichmannstrasse in the Tiergarten district. As well he might. Eitin-gon was already in Cap Ferrat on his way to settle in Palestine, where, on an earlier visit, he had founded the Palestinian Psycho-Analytical Society. The new president, replacing Eitingon, was Felix Boehm. The hope was still that the new German regime might accommodate psychoanalysis, if it seemed less alien.

With the 1934 congress of psychoanalysis coming up – the first he would address as elected president of the International Association – Jones wondered how to discuss the refugee crisis while keeping to his firmly held convictions that psychoanalysis must stay out of politics and that a medical science had nothing to do with ideology. This high-minded tactic would be difficult, as one of the main problems facing the fleeing analysts was, as he put it in a letter to Boehm in Berlin (referring to the German Psychoanalytic Society), 'the storm of indignation and opposition which is at present agitating certain circles, especially among the exiles from Germany'. What he wanted to avoid at all costs was a congress decision to expel the German society from the International Association. He explained in his letter – marked 'strictly confidential except to Müller-Braunschweig':

> You will know that I myself regard these emotions and ultra-Jewish attitudes very unsympathetically, and it is plain to me that you and your colleagues are being made a dumping-ground for much emotion and resentment

which belongs elsewhere and has been displaced in your direction. My
only concern is for the good of Psycho-Analysis itself.

At the Thirteenth Congress of the International Psychoanalytic Association, held at Lucerne from 26 to 31 August 1934, Jones accepted the
proposal of Eitingon (who had come from Palestine for the event) that
the central executive would grant 'direct' membership of the International
Association to analysts forced to leave their country for political reasons.
Direct membership would allow them to subscribe to the official psychoanalytic journals and to attend the scientific meetings of any other
psychoanalytic society in the countries where they found themselves.
Jones saw it as membership 'on the lines of the Nansen passport', which
the League of Nations was just then issuing to stateless refugeees. (Named
for Fridtjof Nansen, the Norwegian head of the League of Nation's
High Commission for Refugees, the passport acted as an international
identification document, and was eventually recognized by fifty-two
governments.) The congress also agreed that the International Association
would set up an emigration office in London to keep a record of what
was happening in the international movement of analysts.

Analysts from Berlin were one thing; those from Vienna quite another. It
is to Anna Freud's lasting credit that she assisted Jones in the campaign to
get refugees into England at a time when she was in deep dispute with
Melanie Klein, whose stronghold London had become. (Klein was not
without her critics in London, however. These included her daughter,
Melitta Schmideberg, who had been in England since 1928. She had
begun to distance herself from her mother's views, and when her husband,
Walter Schmideberg, arrived from Berlin he took her side against his
mother-in-law.)

By 1935 it began to look as if Austria would go the way of Germany,
and that London would therefore be invaded by analysts from Vienna,
all of the Freudian, anti-Kleinian persuasion. Apprehensive, Klein in
May accused Jones of harming British psychoanalysis by bringing in the
Viennese contingent. Freud, for his part, was also on the alert. That same
month he reminded Jones of the theoretical gulf that separated the two
schools of thought, and declared his belief that the British Psycho-
Analytical Society, under Jones's leadership, had followed Mrs Klein down
a wrong path. He was forgiving, nonetheless, because of Jones's kindness
to the refugees.

To a war-threatened Europe, female sexuality was hardly an issue of prime concern, but it remained so to psychoanalysts. Perhaps as a preventative measure, foreseeing the arrival in London of many Viennese analysts, Jones arranged an exchange of lectures to clarify the differences between the two groups. The areas of dispute, apart from the sexual development of the female, also included the death drive, the origin of the superego and the practice of child analysis.

Giving his own lecture on the subject to the Vienna Psychoanalytic Society in May 1935, he declared that the gulf between the two schools had existed for years. He then delivered the pure Kleinian line, clarified by his own eloquence. He spoke from some experience. As a man who had never had to ask 'What does Woman want?', he delivered his views that, for example, the young girl 'is more concerned with the inside of her body than the outside'. He agreed, he said, with Klein's conclusion that 'the girl's repression of femininity springs more from her hatred and fear of her mother than from her own masculine attitude.' He sided with the Kleinian view that the Oedipus complex begins very early, and has more to do with dissatisfaction with the breast than with the child's rivalry with the parent of the same sex. Femininity, in sum, does not develop from the shock of viewing a penis, but rather from 'the promptings of an instinctual constitution.' In short, unlike the Freudians, he did not see a woman as '*un homme manqué*, a permanently disappointed creature struggling to console herself with secondary substitutes alien to her true nature'.

With him in Vienna were his wife and their two oldest children, brought along to see Kitty's mother, who was dying. On Easter Sunday he took them to see Freud. He was proud of his children. Mervyn, then a bright thirteen, had won a scholarship to Abbotsholme, a Derbyshire boarding school, and Nesta was an engaging five-year-old. When Freud pinched the girl's nose with two fingers, Jones wondered if the child had noticed the castrating symbolism. Apparently she had not, for she offered to let Freud hold her doll. Respecting Mervyn's intellectual abilities, Freud presented him with a small Etruscan statue from his collection of antiquities. Later, Freud wrote to Jones that he had seldom seen two such delightful children.

But they were not problem-free. By early 1937 Nesta was in analysis with Donald Winnicott, 'our only man [child] analyst', Jones told Freud, the reason being her 'pathological jealousy of her little brother'. Four years earlier Mervyn, then nearly eleven, had been returned to Klein for treatment, as he suffered from nightmares.

★   ★   ★

Theoretical arguments evaporated in late October 1935 when Edith Jacobsohn, a Jewish analyst on the teaching staff of the Berlin Institute, was arrested and thrown into jail. An active left-winger, she was accused of high treason for allegedly treating, rather than denouncing to the authorities, patients who were Communist. One of her patients, taken into custody, had been killed. Jones felt that the International Psychoanalytic Association should try to get her released. He was encouraged by Jacobsohn's lawyer, who thought that outside intervention might help her case.

To be associated with a left-wing suspected traitor was not what Felix Boehm, now president, wished for the German Psychoanalytic Society (henceforth the DPG, for *Deutsche Psychoanalytische Gesellschaft*). Boehm was terribly afraid that the society as a whole would be tarnished by the political charges against one of its members, and that the Nazis would take the opportunity to dissolve the DPG, and with it the source of livelihood for all German analysts. Dramatically, he telephoned Jones in London and asked him to come to Berlin.

Jones said he would be right over. His own fear was that the DPG might disband or resign as a group from his International Association. Accordingly, he boarded a ship and after a rough sea crossing arrived in Berlin late in the afternoon of Friday 30 November. All weekend, over lunch and dinner and far into the night, he sat through heated discussions with all concerned. Jacobsohn was just the presenting symptom. The DPG needed to plan its future moves so as to ward off Nazi attention. He did not have time to visit Jacobsohn in jail, but after seeing her lawyer he agreed to hold back any intervention until her case came to trial.

The debate ranged over three questions. Should the DPG, as the society representing psychoanalysis in Germany, resign from the International Association altogether and try to exist on its own? Should it disband and leave its members to practise psychoanalysis in secret? And should the Jewish members be expelled? Jones reiterated that psychoanalysis was purely a medical matter and had nothing to do with ideology.

The Jews, by and large, thought of resigning but held back, reasoning that to resign would be tantamount to an admission of guilt. After one late meeting, however, Therese Benedek, one of the Jews concerned, told Jones they had decided that they probably would do so.

On returning home on Monday morning, Jones immediately reported the encounter to Anna Freud, prefacing his letter with 'I got back this morning after a terrible sea-crossing both ways ... Sleep the first night two hours, second night four hours, third night nil.' He said that the German Society had reached two conclusions: that the DPG would not be dissolved, and nor would it break its connection with the International Psychoanalytic Association. The question of the Jewish members was stalled. The Jews themselves felt that a group resignation would suggest that they agreed that psychoanalysis was tainted by its Jews.

Back home, Jones made up his mind. He sent a telegram to Benedek: 'Urgently advise voluntary resignation.' He then wrote to Anna, saying 'I suppose most of the Jews will now emigrate,' then to Brill asking him to raise money to help their flight.

Jones felt he had saved psychoanalysis in Germany. With hindsight, it can be seen as an act of wishful thinking, at best, or, at worst, of appeasement. Among his many later critics, for example, Paul Roazen said, 'I do hope that if I had to face such a choice, I would have decided that the game was not worth the candle.'

Indeed, it was not. Jones had correctly judged Boehm as a weak unconfident type, and Müller-Braunschweig to be an anti-Semite and loyal Nazi. The pair remained at the head of the DPG until May 1936, when the Berlin Institute was absorbed into the new (now notorious) German Institute for Psychological Research and Psychotherapy, the *Deutsche Institut für Psychologische Forschung und Psychotherapie*), headed by a man with a fearsome surname. M. H. Göring was a cousin of the deputy Führer, Reichsmarschall Hermann Göring, and routinely closed his business letters (but not those he wrote to Jones) with 'Heil Hitler!' As part of the amalgamation of organizations, the Berlin Institute's library was confiscated, and the books and assets of the psychoanalytic publishing house, Internationaler Psychoanalytischer Verlag, which had been operating from Leipzig, were seized. The DPG clung on as a member of the International Association for two more years.

As for Jacobsohn, she remained in prison for two years, but managed to escape during medical treatment and made her way to Prague and then to New York, where, with her name anglicised to Jacobson, she practised successfully as an analyst until her death in 1978.

Jones was in a position personally to help one of Freud's sons, Ernst, an architect, who had left Berlin for Paris, then settled in London (with his children, including Lucian and Clement, each later famous in his own right). Jones gave Ernst a commission to design an extension for his Sussex house, The Plat. As he described the project to Freud, 'Although it is a small matter it is surprisingly complicated and that gives me an opportunity for the highest admiration of his extraordinary ingenuity and masterly efficiency.' Freud was glad to hear it: 'Your recognition of Ernst's capacity for work is balm to my paternal heart.'

Jones was delighted with the completed structure. With brick chimneys, a tiled roof, and stonework matching the original, it doubled the size of the seventeenth-century house without in any way spoiling its character or charm. Jones found it 'so attractive that it would tempt me to go there to live if only I had the means – an unlikely contingency'. One of the new features was a small conservatory with a separate entrance that allowed the new wing to be used as a consulting room which patients could enter without going through the main house.

On 6 May 1936 Freud turned eighty. Jones went to Vienna for the celebrations. These included the opening, at Berggasse 7, a few doors from Freud's home, of new quarters to bring together under one roof the *Verlag* (whose premises and stock in Berlin had been confiscated), the Vienna Psychoanalytic Institute and its free clinic, the Ambulatorium, and the Vienna Psychoanalytic Society's library. Freud was delighted that Jones, president of the International Association, with his flair for ceremonial speech, would open these new premises, as he did, with an address on the future of psychoanalysis.

As part of the exchange lectures organized by Jones to explore the growing differences between the London and Viennese psychoanalytic schools, one of Freud's young disciples, Robert Wälder, had come to London the previous November to talk on 'Problems in Ego-Psychology'. Now Joan Riviere appeared in Vienna, and gave a paper – 'On the Genesis of Psychical Conflict in Earliest Infancy' – that went straight to the heart of the battle. In Kleinian terms, Riviere described the oral-sadistic and cannibalistic impulses relating to 'unmistakable Oedipus situations'. At the same time, she gracefully acknowledged that 'no psychoanalytic facts and laws can be proved in any written form.'

Reaching his ninth decade, Freud received several awards that greatly pleased him. The first, the previous year, was honorary membership of the Royal Society of Medicine. He said he knew it had not come 'because of my beautiful eyes'; he liked to think that it was a sign of respect for psychoanalysis in England. More impressive was Freud's election in June 1936 as a foreign member of the Royal Society. Jones welcomed the news as formal recognition that psychoanalysis was 'a branch of pure science'. He reminded Freud that 'membership of this Society (with the letters

Natty as ever, Jones sits with his family on the Gower rocks, *c.*1927. Left to right: Gwenith, Mervyn, Ernest and Kitty Jones

Ty Gwyn, the Joneses' holiday home – the former village bakery in Llanmadoc

Spot the Gentile: The 'Committee' in Berlin, 1922 – their first and only photograph together. Left to right (front row): Freud, Sándor Ferenczi, Hanns Sachs; (back row): Otto Rank, Karl Abraham, Max Eitingon, Ernest Jones

The Plat, built in 1627, with a new wing (left) added in 1935 by Freud's architect son, Ernst Freud

Bloomsbury Freudians: Alix and James Strachey, stalwarts of the Glossary Committee which determined the English equivalents for Freud's German terminology

'Is that what you think or what you think you ought to think?'

How to do it: illustration on performing the figure 'Left Forward Outside', from Jones's *The Elements of Figure Skating*, 1931

Left: Dropped waists: Joan Riviere (left) and Melanie Klein show off their 1920s fashion sense at the Congress of the International Psychoanalytic Association at Innsbruck, 1927 – Klein with more success

Below: Jones, Mervyn and Kitty, with baby Nesta, born April 1930

"Oh, doctor, I'm having such terrible headaches."

"So, please lie down on the couch and say whatever comes into your mind."

"Roast . . . medicinal waters . . . blotter . . . handkerchief . . . knife . . ."

"Stop! Knife! That's it! The thought 'knife' manifests your sexual desires. Your headaches thus arise from the fact that you find no sexual gratification in your marriage. Hence it follows automatically how you can be cured . . ."

Above: The Nazis saw psychoanalysis as the black art of 'the Jew Sigmund Freud', as shown by this cartoon from the *Deutsch Volksgesundheit aus Blut und Boden*, August/September 1933

Left: Hitler reached Vienna on 15 March 1938, the day before Jones flew in to rescue Freud

Above: Journey's end: Freud reaches London, 6 June 1938, flanked by his daughter Mathilde Hollitscher, Jones, and his daughter-in-law Lucie Freud

Left: The odd couple: Jones and Anna Freud, *c.*1956, their lives entwined once more as he wrote her father's biography

Right: Jones and Kitty in old age – still at 'our lovely haven, The Plat'

Below: Last congress: Marie Bonaparte (left), Ernest Jones, and Anna Freud at the International Psychoanalytic Congress in Paris in 1957

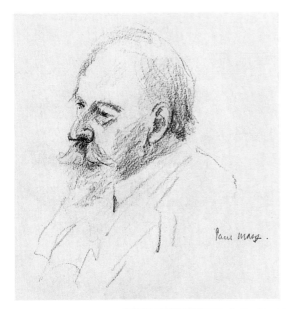

Left: Jones *c.*1957, sketched by his good friend, and neighbour, the artist Paul Maze

Below: The churchyard of St Cadoc, Cheriton, Gower, South Wales, where Jones' grave lies (*lower left corner*)

F.R.S. after one's name) is by far the highest honour that any scientific man can attain.'

Freud's name had been put forward, Jones knew, by one of his own former analysands, Sir Harold Jeffreys, a Cambridge geophysicist and mathematician. He omitted to say that his close friend and brother-in-law Wilfred Trotter was a member of the Royal Society (elected for his neurological research into sensation) and, as a member of the society's council, must have been influential in securing Freud's election. That the Royal Society had accepted psychoanalysis as a science is doubtful. No psychoanalyst before Freud had been made an FRS, and none has been since. It was an honour that Jones himself would dearly have loved to have had for himself, and might have done had he followed a more conventional academic path.

The award that Freud really coveted eluded him: a lucrative Nobel Prize. Long rumoured, it never arrived.

Another honour Freud might have appreciated but never got was an honorary degree from Harvard. When, in June 1936, as part of its tercentenary celebrations, Harvard bestowed an honorary Doctorate of Science on 'a philosopher who has examined the unconscious mind', the recipient was not Freud but Jung. Freud is thought to have been ruled out because of his great age: Harvard rules require the recipient of an honorary degree to attend in person. (At the Harvard ceremonies, Jung took second place to the principal speaker, President Franklin Delano Roosevelt. To the *New York Times* Jung praised Roosevelt as a great man, but in a private letter he called him 'an American edition of a dictator'.)

According to Jung's biographer Deirdre Bair, Jung had been invited to Harvard in the face of some opposition because of his alleged Nazi sympathies. In fact Jung's Nazi links are still the subject of debate. In 1936 he accepted the presidency of the International General Medical Society for Psychotherapy, reorganized by the Nazis, and also assumed the editorship of the psychotherapists' periodical, the *Zentralblatt für Psychoanalyse*. Jung defended himself against charges of Nazi collaboration by insisting that he was working on behalf of dismissed or persecuted psychotherapists. However, his denunciation in 1934 of Freud's deleterious influence on psychoanalysis remains on the record. Jung said then that psychoanalysis was 'unremittingly Jewish', and that Freud did not know 'that most precious secret of the Germanic people – the creatively prophetic depth of the soul'.

Jones's sharp eye took in the British system of government. Upon the death of King George V in January 1936, he was quick off the mark with an article for the *New Statesman* on 'the psychology of constitutional monarchy', which appeared on 1 February 1936, four days after the late king's funeral at Windsor. After deftly sketching the human need for government – an ordered society must balance the need for freedom with the need for order – Jones praised the British constitutional monarchy for preventing 'the murderous potentialities in the son–father (i.e. governed–governing) relationship from ever coming to grim expression'. To split the monarch's role into two persons – one symbolic and untouchable, the other functional and replaceable – gave 'a safe outlet for parricidal tendencies'. He concluded smartly, 'We have thus learned how to prevent monarchy from degenerating into tyranny.'

Firm in this belief, Jones was shocked in December 1936 by the abdication of the supposedly irreplaceable king, Edward VIII, who stepped down in order to marry the woman he loved. Indignant, Jones wrote to *The Times* to ask that future heirs to the throne should be tested for psychological stability. The letter was not printed.

With himself unshakeable as president, the Fourteenth Congress of the International Psychoanalytic Association was held in September 1936 at Marienbad in Czechoslovakia. The location was chosen so that Anna Freud could get home quickly if her ill father needed her. (Freud was in great pain from the radium treatments for his jaw.) In his presidential address, Jones, keeping to his resolve not to mention Hitler or Nazism, told his fellow analysts, 'Last Christmas the Jewish members of the German Society found it necessary to resign their membership. Availing myself of the privilege bestowed on me by the Lucerne Congress, I have granted direct membership of the International Association to all those who asked for it.'

When the next volume of the *International Journal of Psycho-Analysis* appeared, with its long-standing custom of listing names and addresses of members of the Internal Association around the world, it recorded twenty-three 'direct' members, all formerly from Germany, whose new addresses told the story. These included Dr Therese Benedek, Los Angeles; Erich Fromm, the International Institute for Social Research, New York City; Dr Bernd Kamm, Menninger Clinic, Topeka, Kansas; Dr Adelheid Koch, São Paulo, Brazil; and Dr Lotte Liebeck-Kirschner, Oslo.

In 1937, while the political outlook was darkening, Jones had the pleasure of taking Kitty on her first trip to Italy. In Vienna, Freud was beginning to give way to gloom. He saw that Mussolini, now reliant on German support for the war in Ethiopia, would no longer be able to protect Austria and that his hope that Austria would be spared 'Hitlerism' was unrealistic. As he conceded to Jones, 'the consequences are disastrous for analysis as well.' He stated openly, 'I should like to live in England like Ernst, and travel to Rome like you.'

The wish did not fall on deaf ears.

17

Into an English Garden
1938–1939

❦

OR JONES, MANOEUVRING his flight into occupied Vienna in March
1938 and persuading Freud to leave would be the easy part. The *Anschluss* had changed everything. After Jones returned to London on 22 March,
he pulled out all the stops to get the necessary papers for Freud and his
entourage – not only to enter Britain, but also to work. Admission was
granted under strict conditions. Refugees had to be able to provide for themselves or show that they would not be a drain on the public purse. The
Jewish Chronicle and the personal columns of *The Times* were full of pleading
messages from desperate Jews seeking jobs as domestics, private secretaries
or dressmakers – anything so that they could get entrance visas.

With people panicky and depressed in Vienna, Anna Freud began to
shower Jones with names of analysts, of training candidates and even of
their relatives who wanted to come to England with them. He cautioned
her, 'It is important that no one travels to England without giving me some
days' previous notice (if possible, also port of entry).' Ideally, he would deal
with Freud's list all at once, but everyone did not have to come at the same
time. As far as the analysts among them were concerned, it was impossible
for them all to come to London, which could not support more than eight.
Four provincial cities – Edinburgh, Glasgow, Manchester and Bristol –
were possible destinations, along with Oxford and Cambridge.

Jones put his skating connections to good use. Sir Samuel Hoare, now
Home Secretary (in Neville Chamberlain's Conservative government),
gave him blanket permission to fill in as many permits as he wished for
the large retinue Freud wished to bring to London with him. In any
event, the Home Office had routinely consulted Jones about applications
from analysts from central Europe as the trickle turned into a flood.

Permits to exit Austria were another matter. Jones pulled strings here
too. Calling on his personal friend Earl de la Warr, the Lord Privy Seal,
he reminded him (according to a Foreign Office minute) that President
Roosevelt 'had sent a message to Herr Hitler, asking for leave to be given
to Dr Freud to leave Germany'. ('Germany' now included Austria.)

Jones turned to the scientific establishment as well. Securing from Wilfred Trotter a letter of introduction to the president of the Royal Society, he used it the very next day. Visiting Sir William Bragg at the Royal Society's offices in Burlington House, he found Bragg somewhat uninformed. 'Do you really think the Germans are unkind to the Jews?' Bragg asked him.

Bragg nonetheless was swift to take action. He took up the case of Freud along with that of another distinguished Austrian, the physicist and Nobel laureate Erwin Schrödinger. (Schrödinger, although not Jewish, had left Berlin in 1933 out of revulsion for the new regime; after a brief stay in Oxford, he had returned to the University of Graz, undoubtedly fooling himself, like Freud, that Austria would not go the way of Germany.) On behalf of both Freud and Schrödinger, Bragg wrote a nicely understated plea to Lord Halifax, the Foreign Secretary, asking that Sir Nevile Henderson, British ambassador in Berlin, call the attention of the German authorities to 'the harm that could be done to friendly relations between scientific people in the two countries by the anxiety which is felt here for our colleagues in Austria – of whom these are outstanding instances'. Perhaps it could be suggested to the Germans that 'they might prefer to be less harsh'.

The plea worked, for Freud. The Germans authorized his departure to live abroad, but refused it for Schrödinger. Joachim von Ribbentrop, the German foreign minister, told the British ambassador that Schrödinger would not be allowed to return to Oxford because he would there take up once more his anti-German activities. (Schrödinger managed to flee to Italy. In 1940 he was invited to Dublin by the Irish premier, Eamon de Valera, to work at the Institute of Advanced Studies, and there he wrote the treatise *What is Life?* that contributed to the 1950s revolution in biology.) Sir Nevile Henderson on 8 April was asked to associate himself with the American ambassador in Berlin on Dr Freud's behalf, and was then informed by his American colleague that Dr Freud had been authorized to leave 'Germany'.

An assiduous letter-writer, Jones wrote to thank Lord Halifax for the British Embassy's assistance during his own visit to Vienna the previous month. He also wrote another of his letters to the editor of *The Times*, who on this occasion printed it:

> To reassure the many friends of Professor Freud in this country who might well get an alarmist idea of his condition from the description given by Commander Locker-Lampson in the House of Commons yesterday, I would like to say that it is an exaggeration to speak of Professor Freud 'as

a dying man who has been denied liberty'. Having visited him not many days ago I can testify that he was in fairly good health for his age and still at work. As for his being deprived of liberty, he is under no police detention or surveillance, though he would, of course, like other Jews, have to fulfill various formalities if he wished to leave the country.

Yours faithfully,
Ernest Jones
81, Harley St, W.1, April 13.

With this letter Jones publicly positioned himself as Freud's chief protector in England and downgraded Locker-Lampson, who had given hospitality at his Norfolk cottage to one distinguished refugee, Albert Einstein, who had left Germany in 1933, and clearly hoped to do the same for Freud.

'Various formalities' was a mild description of the Nazi requirements for leaving Vienna. Freud was confident that he would eventually arrive at Victoria station, but he cautioned Jones to be patient. Waiting for exit applications to be processed and settling financial and tax affairs was no small matter. From Berlin, Reichsmarschall Göring had declared that all Jewish holdings over 5,000 marks (about £250 at the then rate of exchange) must be declared, 'to ensure', as *The Times* put it, 'that the capital so declared is used in accordance with the requirements of German business and industry'. This declaration applied to Austria as well as Germany, and to assets at home and abroad. All Jewish assets were assumed, as the official party organ, *Der Angriff*, reported, 'to have been improperly acquired'. There would be severe penalties against any Jews trying to transfer their property into Aryan hands to escape confiscation.

This was a formidable barrier for Freud. For years he had kept money in his Dutch bank accounts – accounts to which his will referred. When Martin Freud wanted to tear up the will, he was stopped by the Nazi official superintending Freud's financial affairs. As luck had it, the official, a Dr Sauerwald, turned out to have studied chemistry at the University of Vienna with a Jewish friend of Freud's. Out of respect for his old professor, Sauerwald turned a brave blind eye to the will and undertook to see that its existence, and its disclosure of foreign assets, was not discovered until after Freud had left the country.

Freud's principal benefactor at that point was Princess Marie Bonaparte. On an earlier visit to Vienna, she had taken his supply of gold to the Greek Embassy in Vienna, to be sent to the King of Greece, who transferred it to London. To help with the departure, the Princess returned to Vienna at the end of March and stayed three weeks, sorting out Freud's papers with Anna and mustering a large sum in Austrian schillings to meet the various Nazi demands for payments to avoid confiscation of the papers and Freud's collection of antiquities. The Princess had taken two pieces to Paris on an earlier visit, and had bought others for him in Athens, which she was also keeping for him.

The Princess is also credited with rescuing many of the papers that Freud wished to throw away or that he and Anna thought the Nazis might use to incriminate them. Bonaparte, with an eye to the future, snatched things back from the wastebaskets into which Freud had thrown them. Among the saved papers were Freud's letters from Jung, Jones, Abraham, Eitingon, Ferenczi and Lou Andreas-Salomé, and his courtship letters to and from his wife when she was his fiancée, Martha Bernays.

The well-used couch on which Freud's patients had stretched themselves for more than forty years was marked for storage and shipping to London, as was his now-ransomed collection of objects from ancient civilizations.

During the interval before departure, Müller-Braunschweig, representing German psychoanalysis, arrived in Vienna from Berlin for a hastily called meeting of the Vienna Psychoanalytic Society. The members – nearly all Jewish – voted to disband the society entirely, to flee the country, and to re-form wherever Freud settled. (In the end, most went to the United States. Of the twenty-six who came to Britain, nearly half had moved on to the States by 1941.)

Freud had hoped to leave by his eighty-second birthday, on 6 May, but was disappointed. He whiled away his time by spending an hour a day working on an essay on Moses and walking round the streets to say farewell to Vienna. The departures began in stages, as his family and friends piled their things into huge suitcases. First to go was Freud's sister-in-law, Minna Bernays, who left with Anna's constant companion Dorothy Burlingham. (To Anna's later associates and followers in London, any suggestion that there was a sexual relationship between her and Mrs Burlingham, devoted friends who shared their lives and homes for decades, is considered not so much improper as unrealistic.)

In the end, Freud took seventeen people to England with him. Among those he had to leave behind were his four elderly sisters. When the Nazis had burnt his works in May 1933, he had joked, 'In the Middle Ages they would have burnt me, nowadays they are content with burning my books.' He did not realize, as he left for the safety of England in 1938, that they would destroy his sisters. He and his brother Alexander (who had reached Switzerland) had left the sisters the equivalent of £8,000 – a sum that ought to have lasted them for the rest of their lives – but all four perished in concentration camps.

Hindsight is a self-deceiving exercise, and never more so than when looking back at the 1930s. Although Germany had built concentration camps, these were not yet extermination factories: the 'Final Solution' was not adopted until the Wannsee Conference in 1942. Ernest and Kitty Jones had their own bitter example of failure to anticipate the terrible turn of events. In 1938 and 1939, Kitty's niece and nephew, children of her sister Gina, who had married a Czech Jew and lived in Prague, came to visit the Jones family in London – Lily in 1938, and Felix in 1939. As Mervyn Jones recalled, 'Nobody suggested that it might be unwise to go back to Prague.' After the war Kitty made enquiries, but none of the four Pollaks could be traced.

Poised for exile, Freud saw that his health was worsening. His operation in January 1938 (the latest of perhaps two dozen procedures on his tortured mouth) seemed not to have been radical enough. 'I wish I could arrive in England in better condition,' he said. Although he would be travelling with his personal doctor, he would need to find an ear specialist and one for his jaw. Was the trouble worth it for such old people? He, his wife and his sister-in-law, Minna, were respectively eighty-two, seventy-seven and seventy-three. But the advantages to Anna of emigration outweighed all the bother. He thought she would do much for analysis in England, but would not 'obtrude herself'. (There was no question of her or him wishing to go to America. He did not like that country, while Anna, as a lay analyst, would have been unable to practise there.)

For the first time, Freud was writing more letters to Jones than Jones wrote to him. On 23 April he added yet another name to the list of those for whom Jones was to clear entry: Dr Maxim Steiner, a dermatologist who was a special friend of Freud's and one of the original members of the Vienna Psychoanalytic Society. Jones obligingly got him into Britain, and Steiner practised as an analyst within the British Psycho-Analytical Society. As the eve of his own departure in early June drew near, Freud added yet another doctor to his list. His personal physician, Max Schur, was stricken with appendicitis on the eve and had to travel later. In his place, to look after Freud on the journey, was put the name of Dr Josephine Stross, a friend of Anna's. Jones procured the necessary documents, and Stross duly made the trip – and remained in London, to become paediatrician to Anna's wartime Hampstead Nurseries.

★   ★   ★

At quarter to three in the morning of Saturday 4 June 1938 the Orient Express train carrying the Freud party left Germany, crossed the Rhine, and entered into France. 'After the Rhine Bridge', noted Freud in his diary, 'we were free!'

In Paris, Marie Bonaparte met them and took them to her elegant apartment on the rue Adolphe-Yvon in the 16th arrondissement, where they rested until leaving for the boat train to Calais. The American ambassador, William Bullitt (with whom in 1930 Freud had written an unpublished, critical book on Woodrow Wilson) came to see him, glad, undoubtedly, that Freud had chosen to take his large company to England, not to the United States. Freud's son Ernst arrived to escort them across the Channel.

Neither during the journey nor on their arrival at Victoria station was any of the party's luggage examined, thanks to another favour from Jones's friend the Lord Privy Seal, who also arranged for their train to arrive at an out-of-the-way platform, away from the press and curious onlookers.

Waiting at Victoria were Freud's eldest children, Mathilde and Martin (who had fled Vienna on 14 May, fearing arrest after the destruction of the *Verlag*), and Jones, back from his Whitsun holiday in Sussex. Jones took charge. He could overcome his aversion to driving in town when the occasion demanded, and he drove Freud and his wife past Buckingham Palace, down Piccadilly past Burlington House, and through Piccadilly Circus into Regent Street, before depositing them at the house Ernst had rented for them at 39 Elsworthy Road in Primrose Hill. It was Freud's first trip to England in thirty years, and only the third in his lifetime as an Anglophile. With Jones, he went into the house, stepped out into the garden with its view over Regent's Park and the City of London, threw up his arms, and said, 'Heil Hitler!'

The press was warm and receptive. Photographs next day of Freud, with his daughter Mathilde Hollitscher, Ernst's wife, Lucie Freud and Ernest Jones, shared the picture pages with scenes from Eton's Fourth of June regatta on the Thames. Ernst Freud was quoted in the *Manchester Guardian* as saying that he and his father's family had not been mistreated in Vienna, but that 'the general treatment of the Jews has been abomin-able.' The *British Medical Journal* declared that the British people were proud to have offered Professor Freud asylum, and were bringing him flowers and gifts of antiquities. However, the welcome did not exempt Freud from the strict British quarantine laws for pets. His chow, Lün, was placed in a kennel in Ladbroke Grove for six months, during which Freud managed only occasional visits.

The first weekend after their arrival, Jones invited Anna and Dorothy Burlingham down to The Plat, where he proudly showed off his roses. (He loved his garden, but not gardening. With two gardeners to tend to the spacious grounds and borders, he was never seen with secateurs or trowel in hand.)

Within days came an irrefutable sign that Freud's new country considered him an honoured guest, with the arrival of three scientists from the Royal Society. Knowing of his frail condition, they brought the hallowed Charter Book to Elsworthy Road so that he might add his signature to the list begun by King Charles II in 1660. He was, however, surprised that he was not allowed to sign himself simply 'Freud'. It was explained to him that in Britain only peers of the realm were entitled to designate themselves by surname alone.

Not all of the British reaction was favourable, however. On 19 June the *Sunday Express* warned of the 'influx of foreign Jews' overrunning the country and the medical profession. 'Worst of all', it noted, 'many of them are holding themselves out to the public as psychoanalysts,' with the dangers of gaining 'an ascendancy over the patient of which [the analyst] makes base use if he is a bad man'. Noting the undercurrent of anti-Semitism in Britain, the German–Jewish Aid Committee had published a pamphlet advising newcomers not to speak German or to be seen reading German newspapers, and not to wave their hands about or talk in a loud voice.

The Freuds stayed at Elsworthy Road for four months ('living vertically', Freud called it after a lifetime spent in flats). He had to be carried up the stairs to bed at night. The family then moved to a hotel in Maida Vale, run by Austrian émigrés, until a Hampstead house bought for about £6,000 and being renovated by his son Ernst was ready. In his unsettled, transient state, Freud found signs that the malignancy in the roof of his mouth had returned. His oral surgeon, Hans Pichler, was brought from Vienna. Operating at the private London Clinic, Pichler cut through Freud's cheek to reach the tumour. It was clear to all – Freud not least – that there would be no more operations. Pichler, not being Jewish, flew back to Vienna the next day.

On 27 September Freud moved into the Hampstead house that is now a museum bearing his name. He and Anna joined his wife and the maid, Paula, at 20 Maresfield Gardens, a spacious three-storey neo-Georgian house, with French windows opening out on to a large and secluded garden – and a new lift, added by Ernst. His couch, with its Turkish-rug cover, was waiting. So were his books and antiquities, and also his desk, arranged by Paula just as he had left it in Vienna. It was the prettiest place he had ever lived anywhere. Martha much enjoyed going down the steps at the end of Maresfield Gardens to the shops on Finchley Road. The *quartier* of London NW 3 was by then so full of German-speaking refugees that the bus conductors routinely called out 'Finchleystrasse'.

Like a king at court, Freud received his visitors. There were a great many, including his old favourite Loe Kann Jones – still living in London and still married to Herbert Jones – Max Eitingon from Palestine, Arthur Koestler, Bronislaw Malinowski, Salvador Dalí and, from New York, his publisher's wife, Mrs Alfred (Blanche) Knopf, who suggested changes in the 'Moses' manuscript that Freud would not accept.

His British publishers, Virginia and Leonard Woolf, were invited to tea on 28 January 1939. Freud's posthumous reward, in Leonard Woolf's autobiography, was the description of a courteous old man with great gentleness and strength and 'an aura, not of fame, but of greatness'. Mrs Woolf was less flattering. Resistant to psychoanalytic ideas, she saw 'a screwed up shrunk very old man: with a monkey's light eyes'.

Freud also kept working. Even though he could speak only with great difficulty, he took four patients in analysis and continued to write his book on Moses. Kitty Jones offered to translate it, and began immediately.

Freud's four analysands were almost as many as Jones had. Jones's patients had reduced to just six, but they filled the large part of his working day at Harley Street. It was in the evening that he used his godlike powers over the disposal of lives. From Hungary, he began to receive appeals from analysts wanting to flee. 'We need your help so much that without you we cannot move,' one Hungarian woman analyst wrote. Finding that she and her husband could not get into Britain but would be allowed into one of the British colonies, they had decided on Ceylon. Anna Freud had found two who might like to go to Honolulu.

Getting through the American maze of quotas, visas, visitors' visas and transit visas led some analysts to find themselves landing as far away as Australia, New Zealand and South America. The 'letters of transit' that form an important subplot in the film *Casablanca*, made in 1942, were not a fictional device.

Presiding over meetings of the British Psycho-Analytical Society, Jones was in a strong position to decide who came to Britain and who went elsewhere. The policy was to favour immigrants 'who we think can work harmoniously with our Society'. Thus the Lampls (Hans Lampl and his wife, Jeanne Lampl-de Groot), who had left Berlin for Vienna in 1933, were considered 'unfavourably on personal grounds' and directed to Holland – only an hour from England, Jones reminded Anna. There was widespread disapproval also of the Wälders, Robert and Jenny, who were deemed better suited to Boston or Belgium.

The British Society had welcomed the members of the former Viennese Psychoanalytic Society and given them full membership. Those who had been training analysts in Vienna were allowed to continue training in London. A hospitality committee for 'Colleagues from Austria', led by Barbara Low, was formed at a special meeting in March 1938 at which members considered what they could offer. Among the suggestions were hospitality in their own homes, escorts for unaccompanied children, introductions to friends, the sharing of consulting rooms, and perhaps meeting the new arrivals with a car at the port or at Victoria station.

However, the arrival of *echt* Freudians from Vienna boosted the weak forces of the anti-Kleinians within the British Society. Long a minority, they now found themselves becoming more courageous as upholders of 'Freudian analysis'. The incumbent Kleinians soon saw the Viennese as invaders. Any paper served to bring out the schism. There was no need to ask 'which side are you on?' as allegiance was obvious from the content.

When Melanie Klein twice read a paper putting forth her thesis of the 'depressive position' – the dilemma of the infant whose idea of the breast as 'a good internal object' must coexist with the sadism and hatred directed at it – the Freudians heard heresy on a grand scale. This theory was putting the mother, rather than the father, at the centre of the infant's development. The disagreement between the two schools was not simply theoretical: it affected how psychoanalyses were conducted, and how the technique of analysis was taught to candidates in training.

Jones was always seen to be on the side of the 'Melanieser'. An imperious chairman, he was disliked, and sometimes feared, for his autocratic manner. He liked to challenge opinions, saying, 'Is that what you think or what you think you ought to think?'

Tensions within the British Psycho-Analytical Society were nothing compared to those with the American analysts. Why should they belong to the International Psychoanalytic Association, an organization, run in Europe by Europeans, that forced them to subscribe to its *Journal* and embraced non-medical analysis of which the Americans disapproved? More fundamentally, the Americans were alarmed by the influx of refugee analysts, whose ambiguous status as 'direct' members of the International

Association created difficulties for the local American societies attempting to take them in despite the fact that American regulations prevented them from practising. In May 1938 the New York Psychoanalytic Society informed Jones that it would send no official delegation to the international congress scheduled for Paris in early August that year.

Freud, settling into his Hampstead home, expected the full withdrawal of the American analysts from the International Association. With his ebbing strength, he sent a sarcastic reply to a letter from California suggesting that he had changed his views on lay analysis and now believed that psychoanalysis should be practised only by medical doctors. He dismissed it as a 'silly rumour': he was consistent and constant in his opinion that analysts did not need to be medical doctors. 'I insist on them [his views] even more intensely than before, in the face of the obvious American tendency to turn psycho-analysis into a mere housemaid of psychiatry.'

The dispute came to a head at the Paris Congress of the International Psychoanalytic Association – the movement's fifteenth. The tepid compromise reached was the setting up of two committees, one on each side of the Atlantic, in search of a solution. However, the problem was suspended by the outbreak of war. It was not finally resolved until the late 1980s, when, according to Riccardo Steiner in 'It is a New Kind of Diaspora', the International Association accepted the American non-psychoanalytic societies in which many of the European lay analysts had come to play an important role.

As president of the International Association, Jones mustered his finest rhetoric for his opening address to the Paris congress in August 1938. He spoke of the blow that had fallen 'on the mother of all psycho-analytical societies, at the very birth-place of psycho-analysis. That there should no longer be psycho-analysis practised in Vienna, of all places in the world, is a thought that catches the breath.' Of the 102 analysts and candidates in Vienna, he said, only a half-dozen remained. However, 'we can with confidence maintain today of psycho-analysis that the time has passed when it can be annihilated: it will survive any opposition it will encounter.' He praised the British Home Secretary, Sir Samuel Hoare, and the special refugee committee in the United States, then continued in French. At the end of the congress he was duly re-elected president.

By November 1938 Jones fell into disagreement with Freud over Kitty's slow translation of Freud's *Moses and Monotheism*, a work with which he disagreed. She felt she was translating it in a hurry, working at one end of Jones's enormous desk.

When Jones told Freud that the translation would not be finished until February or March of the following year, Freud was irritated. He knew that his days were numbered – but also that Jones was up to his ears in refugee work and was often unwell. 'But I remember that you took on this new burden voluntarily, without my requesting you to do so,' Freud wrote. However, he clung to 'the understandable wish that I myself may see the book finished'. He had already accepted payment from his New York publisher, Alfred Knopf. If Jones could not complete the translation quickly, Freud said, he should give the job to someone who could. He had the grace, however, to sign off 'With kind regards to your wife whom up to now I regarded as the actual translator'.

Jones replied by return of post. With the sophistication of a published writer, he said that, as the autumn publishing season had already passed, there was no point finishing the work before the following February. If Freud for personal reasons wished to find an outside translator, he was free to do so. However, from Jones's experience, others would be slower.

Ten days later such worries were insignificant. After *Kristallnacht* on 10 November, when Jewish shops throughout Germany were smashed and Jews were transported to concentration camps, Freud asked Marie Bonaparte if she could bring his four old sisters to France. She tried, but could not. (In fact, when the Nazis wanted their apartments in Vienna, the sisters were removed to camps and died in 1942: Mitzi Freud in Theresienstadt, Rosa Graf in Auschwitz, Dolfi Freud and Paula Winternitz in Treblinka.)

In February 1939 the faithful Wilfred Trotter, now bearing the grand title of Serjeant Surgeon to the King, as well as being director of the surgical unit at University College Hospital, called on Freud to examine a swelling. Trotter in turn called in an expert from the Curie Institute in Paris. A malignant, inaccessible recurrence of the cancer was detected. There was nothing to be done apart from a daily painful trip to Harley Street for radiation. Freud wrote to his friend the Austrian writer Arnold Zweig that he had 'a new recurrence of my dear old cancer with which I have been sharing my existence for sixteen years'. There was no question of him attending the twenty-fifth anniversary banquet of the British Psycho-Analytical Society at the Savoy on 8 March. He marked the occasion by writing to Jones that he could not have imagined, in 1914, when Jones told him he was about to found a society for psychoanalysis in London, twenty-five years later, he would be living 'so near to it and you'. Freud then gave Jones just the compliment he would wish: 'The events of recent years have so ordained that London has become chief venue and centre of the psychoanalytic movement.' It was his last letter to Jones.

Late in April 1939 Max Schur, Freud's doctor since 1929, torn between his responsibilities to Freud and to his own family, left his patient, to go to the United States for several months, as a preliminary to emigration with his wife and children. It was a wrench for Freud. Schur was part of the family; it was he who had given Anna and Martin the lethal dose of veronal they took with them in case they were tortured when the Gestapo summoned them in Vienna the previous spring. What must also have been on Freud's mind was the vow he had extracted from Schur on their first meeting, when he had broached the subject of assisted death: 'Promise me also: when the time comes, you won't let them torment me unnecessarily.' Schur's assent sealed their relationship.

Kitty was driving herself to finish translating *Moses* so that it would appear in English in Freud's lifetime, and she succeeded by 19 May 1939. *Moses and Monotheism* was published shortly thereafter. Freud sent copies to people he admired, and got letters of thanks from H. G. Wells and Albert Einstein. It got a less polite reception from the critics, who used adjectives such as 'regrettable' and 'unscientific'. Jones himself deplored the book's reiteration of Freud's insistence that Jewish guilt was inherited from the unconscious memory of the slaying of the father of the Jewish race, Moses. He did not try to argue with Freud, however, asking only that Freud correct the glaring factual error of the statement that Egypt was free from earthquakes. Jones reminded Freud that one had been recorded in 27 BC and another reported on the BBC in November 1938.

It was time for the Joneses to rethink their lives. Jones was financially stretched. He had no more than three patients now, and wondered if he would ever get a new one. With war threatening and with the two younger children – Nesta, nine, and Lewis, five – to protect, he and Kitty decided to leave London and make their permanent home at The Plat.

Their older son, Mervyn, was about to enter university. Just as he was finishing school, Mervyn had been expelled from Abbotsholme – *not* for founding a branch of the progressive movement's Left Book Club, nor for joining the Young Communist League (both of which he had done) – but for being out of the dormitory after lights out. Jones was coldly angry at his son's refusal to accept the place Oxford had offered, as well as at his embrace (following the Spanish Civil War) of Communism. At the time Mervyn was, in his own recollection, a 'small and baby-faced' young man who wore double-breasted suits, smoked cigarettes and spoke confidently. Perhaps, he and his father agreed, he should think of going to university in America.

On 19 August 1939 Mervyn and his mother embarked on a trip across the Atlantic. His father, who planned to join them in New York, drove them to the docks at Southampton and, as Mervyn described the scene, 'waved his stick in farewell, looked at his watch, and walked off briskly to where he had left his car'.

Mother and son sailed despite the growing belief that war was imminent. If it broke out, Mervyn felt, as a Communist, that he must refuse to support either side. The expectation in Britain was that, if war came, it would start with air raids and gas attacks. That fear doubled the Joneses' resolve to live at The Plat.

During August, Jones stayed at their Welsh cottage, Ty Gwyn, with the two younger children. Writing to 'My Own Dearest', he hoped, with most people, that 'there will be no war again,' and he still planned to join her in New York.

All changed on 1 September, when the Germans invaded Poland. From their Sussex house, to which he had returned, Jones wrote to 'my sweetheart Kitty' (in letters he was not certain were getting through) that he had moved everything out of 42 York Terrace and was getting her jewellery out of the bank. He had cancelled his sailing, and urged her either to come back on an American ship – not on the French *Normandie* – or to consider flying.

He doubted that he would be able to meet her. He expected petrol soon to be rationed to twenty gallons a month. Trying to return from a quick trip up to London, he found all the bridges clogged; he could not cross the Thames until Kew. In the country at last, he had to drive with no lights because of the blackout – a task made harder by the rain and the failure of his windscreen wipers. But he arrived home safely, and he and the children started their own campaign against Mr Hitler by digging up the playground for a potato patch. He rather hoped that Mervyn would stay in the United States for university (which he did, enrolling at New York University with the assistance of A. A. Brill). On 6 September, writing that all the cinemas, theatres and street lights had closed down, he still thought of their Sussex home as a haven of peace: 'I can so well picture sitting with you in this lovely September weather (is it hot in N.Y.?) in our beautiful garden. Fondest love, from Ernest.'

On the day that Britain and France declared war, Jones wrote a valedictory letter to Freud: 'This critical moment seems an appropriate one for me to express once more my personal devotion to you, my gratitude for all you have brought into my life and my intense sympathy for the suffering you are enduring.' This new war, he said, unlike the last, saw Freud and himself 'united in our military sympathies'. Neither of them might see its end, 'but in any case it has been a very interesting life and we have both made a contribution to human existence – even if in very different measure'. He signed off, 'With my warmest and dearest regards, Yours always affectionately Ernest Jones.'

On 19 September Jones was called to Maresfield Gardens to say good-bye. He found Freud dozing in his study, gazing out at the garden. He called him by the name with which he always addressed him, 'Herr Professor'. According to Jones's account of the scene in his biography, Freud 'opened his eyes, recognized me and waved his hand, then dropping it with a highly expressive gesture that conveyed a wealth of meaning: greetings, farewell, resignation . . . In a second, he fell asleep again.'

Two days later Freud reminded Schur, his doctor, who had returned from America, of his promise to assist him to die. Freud said, according to Jones, who was quoting Schur, 'You promised me . . . you would help me when I could no longer carry on. It is only torture now and it has no longer any sense. Tell Anna about our talk.'

Schur obliged, and Anna, with some reluctance, let him administer a series of small doses of morphia over the next day and a half. Freud, says the Jones biography, 'sighed with relief and sank into a peaceful sleep'. He died just before midnight on 23 September 1939.

Kitty was safely back in England in time for Freud's funeral, on 26 September. From the country she and Ernest went up to London to attend the service at the Golders Green crematorium. The Freud family had asked Jones to speak, and he did not let them down.

It had been hard, Jones said, to wish Freud to live a day longer when his life had been reduced to a pinpoint of personal agony. He thought now of 'friends far away' – Brill, Sachs and Eitingon, and also 'of the shades of Abraham and Ferenczi'. He paid respect to 'what in others expresses itself as religious feeling [but] did so in him [Freud] as a transcendent belief in the value of life and in the value of love'. Reaching back to a phrase from W. Kingdon Clifford that he had once copied into his schoolboy notebook at Llandovery College, Jones said, 'One can say of him that as never man loved life more, so never man feared death less.' Recalling Freud's 'vivid personality' and 'instinctive love of truth', he declared (with unwitting irony, unaware that Freud had once called him 'the Liar from Wales') that 'One feels that no one could ever have lied to him.' Freud had died 'in a land that had shown him more courtesy, more esteem and more honour than his own or any other land, a land which I think he himself esteemed beyond all others'. Jones ended his oration with an alliterative flourish: 'And so we take leave of a man whose like we shall not know again. From our hearts we thank him for having lived; for having done; and for having loved.'

Kitty, deeply moved, recorded in her diary, 'Ernest makes a most beautiful speech and delivers it perfectly.' Martha Freud herself wrote to him to thank him for it, and said that all the sympathy she had received had made her forget that she was in a strange country.

'But what of ourselves?' Jones had asked in his funeral oration, after bleakly picturing 'A world without Freud!' It was a self-addressed question. Having devoted thirty-one years of his life to serving Freud and, not least, to developing his own ideas in correspondence with him, what was he to do now?

It could seem that he was shutting down his London life to coincide with the end of Freud's. That was not the case. At sixty, Jones was not so much retiring as short of work.

18

War within a War
1940–1949

'I'VE ALWAYS HAD a hell of a superego,' Jones told his son Mervyn. No one would deny it. When war broke out, he was ruling in virtual perpetuity as president of the British Psycho-Analytical Society, for no limit of tenure had been set in the constitution when he inaugurated it in 1919. However, he surrendered the editorship of his beloved creation the *International Journal of Psycho-Analysis* to James Strachey, yet ensured that each subsequent edition carried 'Founded by Ernest Jones' above the editor's name on the masthead.

As for the British Society itself, Jones thought it should suspend meetings for the duration of the war. Practices were broken up as analysts and patients joined the armed forces or left London. The government was distributing gas masks and bomb shelters, urging all who could to move out of heavily populated areas. But the society kept on meeting at its headquarters at 96 Gloucester Place. The refugee analysts – stuck in London because they were enemy aliens and restricted from travel – needed their gatherings more than ever. They met on the first and third Wednesday of each month, just as they had in Vienna.

Jones came up from the country for the meetings, but asked that they be held in the afternoon. He was furious when he arrived on an April afternoon in 1940 and found that his ambitious deputy, the Scottish doctor Edward Glover, had rescheduled the meeting for the evening, when Jones had to get back to the country. It did not take a psychoanalyst to see a deliberate snub.

As a doctor, Jones found he had all the petrol he wanted and could drive himself up to London if he wished. Otherwise he caught a train at Petersfield and changed at Haslemere to reach Waterloo, returning the same day with the exclamation 'That's enough London for me!' (Kitty heard these words wistfully. She loved London – especially for the music – and longed to go to the capital more often.)

The hamlet above Elsted where The Plat stood was so small that there was no shop; the vicarage served as a post office. But Jones loved it, and

Kitty felt safer there. No one, least of all anyone working with refugees from Nazism, had any doubt what would happen to Britain's Jews if Hitler invaded the UK. The Joneses had managed to bring Kitty's sister Valerie to England, even though the two sisters did not get on well.

The war had done nothing to heal the growing schism within the British Psycho-Analytical Society, except to separate the opponents temporarily. During the Blitz on London, which began on 7 September 1940, Melanie Klein moved to Pitlochry in Scotland. Anna Freud stayed in London, where, with Dorothy Burlingham, she founded the Hampstead Nurseries for children whose homes had been disrupted by the war.

Within the British Society, forces were aligning for a war within a war. At a meeting on 17 December 1941, a paper by Barbara Low on 'The Psycho-Analytic Society and the Public' spurred John Rickman, a leading member, to lose his temper and to attack the officers – Jones and Glover – for rudeness and indifference to the wider community. Rickman, who was active in the Medical Peace Campaign and the Quaker Medical Society, was concerned with the widespread psychological problems created by war. He felt that the British Society should be more socially conscious, and he deplored its cool relations with the Tavistock Clinic, a psychotherapy clinic formed in 1920. 'The Tavvy', as it was known, followed mainly Freudian techniques, but it was less doctrinaire than the British Society and its staff included some Jungians. Jones had firmly forbidden students of psychoanalysis to work at the Tavistock.

Both the British Society and the Tavistock were separated by more than the River Thames from the Maudsley Hospital in south London. Opened in 1922, the Maudsley, and its subsequent Institute of Psychiatry, took a medical, neurological, approach to mental illness, and operated as a centre for training and research in psychiatric medicine. Under its influence, London's medical schools looked with suspicion on treatments associated with the name of Freud.

Over the next two years, Jones juggled the roles of country self and city self with an ease that Oscar Wilde's Ernest might have envied. In West Sussex he was the home warden, a member throughout the war of the West Sussex Civil Defence. Even after the threat of invasion receded, its members felt they shouldered a serious responsibility. The South Downs bordered the English Channel, through which German submarines patrolled. Nearby, on the coastal plains, British and Canadian troops rehearsed the landing they hoped to make in France.

When in London, Jones, as president of the British Society, took the chair at 'extraordinary business meetings', called to deal with discontents such as Rickman's, but also with the glaring differences in theory and practice between the Kleinians and the (Anna) Freudians.

As the meetings were about to begin, Jones's tactic was to tell each of the adversaries that he was on her side. On 21 January 1942 he wrote to Anna Freud to assure her that she was wrong to think he had no faith in her judgement. On the contrary, he said: although Mrs Klein had forcibly called attention to 'the existence of such mechanisms as introjection and projection at an earlier age than was generally believed possible . . . she has neither a scientific nor an orderly mind, and her presentations are lamentable.' He called Klein neurotic, with a tendency to be *'verrannt'* – that is, stubbornly attached to her views.

On the very same day, writing to Klein, who had returned from Pitlochry, Jones described Anna as 'an indigestible morsel'. He said, 'She has probably gone as far in analysis as she can and she has no pioneering originality.'

The first of the business meetings, held on 25 February 1942, was more than extraordinary: it was prickly. The society's members were full of grievances – not least that Jones and Glover were running the society as a personal fiefdom. There was bitterness too between those who had stayed in London during the Blitz and those who had spent the harrowing months from September 1940 to 11 May 1941 in rural beauty spots. To the embarrassment of all present, Melanie Klein's daughter, Melitta Schmideberg, began publicly to attack her mother's theories. At the next meeting, after another diatribe against the Kleinians by Schmideberg (née Klein), Jones observed, 'Dr Schmideberg has really admirably illustrated the difficulty of discussing these matters without personal attacks.'

Schmideberg's personal attack was not the only one. Barbara Low (a Freudian) complained that Joan Riviere (a Kleinian) would not refer patients to her. The fierce Glover (who all knew was Schmideberg's analyst and encouraging her rebellion) thundered against the Kleinians, whom he saw as trying to insinuate themselves into control of the British Society.

By the summer of 1942 a split in the society looked inevitable to Glover and Anna Freud. Jones, as ever, managed neutrality. He had little choice, having brought both Melanie Klein and Anna Freud to England. So unresolved was the bitterness within the society in the summer of 1942 that it was decided to devote one 'scientific' meeting every month to airing and exploring the differences between the two schools. The future direction of the training programme depended on it. Anna Freud declared that the two theories could not coexist.

Thus was born what came to be known as the 'Controversial Discussions'. Jones left the task of organizing the programme to Glover, Marjorie Brierley and James Strachey, and found that he had to spend more time in the country.

There was plenty to do in Sussex. Jones wrote to the Ministry of Information offering suggestions for its pamphlet on how to behave in an air raid. He still saw patients. Some travelled to Elsted for their appointments. One wealthy patient, according to Katherine Jones, even moved to Sussex to continue analysis. Others kept the tie alive through correspondence. Jones heard from former patients, such as one C. Eleanor Chilton, who seemed still to be in love with him and also to owe him money. One man wrote to discuss an unhappy love affair. Another, who signed himself 'J. T. M. Davies', sent his dreams, apparently expecting an interpretation by post. One old analysand, Joan Riviere, returned to familiar haunts when she came for a weekend at The Plat.

His younger children, Nesta and Lewis, went to school nearby. Because of the move away from London, Lewis became the only one of the Jones children to escape analysis. He took after his mother, and was a musical child. Nesta was obstreperous. The girl, Jones wrote to Kitty when she was in the United States, did not know what obedience meant. (Nesta's anatagonism towards her mother later led to her being cut out of Kitty's will.) In November 1941 Mervyn returned from his studies at New York University. With his left-wing sympathies, he had taken no real interest in the war until Germany invaded Russia (in June 1941), whereupon he came home. He worked as a mechanic while he volunteered for several regiments. Rejected at first (perhaps because he was only nineteen), he finally succeeded in joining the army.

Membership in the West Sussex Civil Defence led Jones into a new circle. He became a good friend of the fine Impressionist painter Paul Maze. Maze had been born in France, but had moved to England after the First World War. He lived in Treyford, just a village away from Elsted and English landscapes, including the Sussex hills, were among his subjects. His family recalls how he very much enjoyed talking with Jones. Maze became particularly reliant on Jones during a personal crisis, when his daughter from his first marriage committed suicide and Jones helped him talk through his depression. Jones often visited Maze at his home, as did another painter, Winston Churchill, who would come down from

London to escape the war. Another frequent visitor to Maze's home was the new commander-in-chief of Bomber Command, Sir Arthur 'Bomber' Harris.

In 1942, in one of the signs of recognition from the British medical establishment he so coveted, Jones was elected a fellow of the Royal College of Physicians. It was thirty-eight years since he had become a member of the RCP. Sadly, his brother-in-law and friend Wilfred Trotter was not there to congratulate him. Trotter had died in November 1939, not long after Freud, and not long after he had written a letter to *The Times* on 'The mind in war – democracy's chief advantage'. An obituary notice called Trotter 'one of the most contemplative minds that has ever been trained towards surgery'. Jones had the consolation of giving Trotter an obituary in his *Journal*, in which he credited Trotter for introducing him to Freud's works. The same issue contained Jones's magisterial valediction to Freud, as well as his obituaries of Eugen Bleuler, Havelock Ellis, Otto Rank, Monroe Meyer and Alice Balint. One of Jones's perquisites as the long-standing and long-lived editor was to write the history of the psychoanalytic movement and pass a last judgement in the form of obituaries of his contemporaries: Putnam, Ferenczi, Rank, Brill, Sachs – he did them all. (Rank fared little better than Ferenczi: after his death in New York in 1939 at the age of fifty-five, Jones wrote of 'the melancholia that was to cloud his later years . . . alternating between feverish endeavours to find some short and efficient form of psychotherapy, and moods of apathetic depression'.)

Trotter's place among the *Journal*'s obituaries was justified by two facts: his attendance in 1908 at the first congress of psychoanalysis, in Salzburg, and then, in 1938, his having provided medical care for Freud on his deathbed.

At the start of 1943 psychoanalysts braved the London blackout and the constant threat of air raids to debate what goes on in a child's mind during the first months of life. Glover had thrown down the gauntlet. It was for Melanie Klein, the challenger, to explain and defend her new theories in the 'Controversial Discussions', not for Anna Freud to support the traditional teaching of Freud. Glover himself chaired the meetings at the opening session on 27 January 1943. Jones left him to read to the group a bland peace-making statement that averred that nothing in Klein fundamentally diverged from Freud. Glover himself, thoroughly anti-Klein, found the Continental analysts with him – solidly behind Anna and suspicious of Melanie.

As the series of meetings progressed, papers laid out the essence of Klein's theory: that pre-verbal fantasy life exists and can be analysed in play; that the love–hate relationship of the infant to the breast leads to the 'depressive position' – the double bind of split feelings and guilt – and that the infant is flooded with envy of the good object, the breast.

The word 'bottle' was not mentioned. Did the Kleinians believe that the glass or plastic container of milk arouses in the suckling child the same cannibalistic fantasies of biting and tearing as the fleshy, unreliable breast? No one appears to have raised the question.

At the start, Anna Freud held back from the discussions, until on 7 April 1943 she set out her view of the difference between herself and Klein. While Klein felt that 'object relations' begin at birth, she herself saw a blank phase of several months during which the child just wants its own well-being and has no 'phantasies' (to use the favoured psychoanalytic spelling) of devouring the mother.

For the entire first year of the discussions, Klein sat mute. She conveyed her views in letters to her supporters, expounding ideas she thought they might present. Speaking at last on 16 February 1944, she distanced herself from Freud's link between the so-called 'death instinct' and aggression. What was important, she believed, was to understand the origins of aggression in the early weeks of life.

The Controversial Discussions extended until May 1944 – a total of eleven meetings. They were small gatherings. Male members were often absent, many off at war. Jones excused himself for remaining in the country on grounds of ill health. As hostilities drew to a close, Glover told Jones that he had been intelligent to suggest that the society should hibernate during the war. He and Jones could both see that it was a 'woman ridden Society'. The two of them had made a good team 'until the Klein imbroglio developed'.

When the 'Discussions' ground to a halt, just before D-Day, the result, a classic British muddle-through, was often known as the 'Gentlemen's Agreement' – or, as described by Pearl King, historian of the British Psycho-Analytical Society, an 'armistice'. There were to be parallel training schemes. Candidates would be divided into the 'A' Group, representing the Kleinian part of the society, and the 'B' Group, the Anna Freudians. Each analyst-in-training, when choosing a second supervisor, was to select someone from a third group, the non-aligned Independents. (The Independents included many who became well known in child analysis, Bowlby and Winnicott.)

Among the participants, many thought that the exercise had left them more, not less, polarized. The exasperated Glover resigned from the society and joined its Swiss counterpart. He declared, 'The British Psycho-Analytical Society is no longer a Freudian society.' To him, it was committed to teaching the Klein system of child psychology as part of psychoanalysis, when in fact Kleinianism constituted 'a deviation from psychoanalysis'.

The most evident result of the Controversial Discussions was that neither Klein nor Anna Freud had been expelled. Each had her firm place within the British Society, with her own practitioners and candidates. A split, such as had marred American psychoanalysis, had been avoided.

More practically, and not before time, the rules of the society were redrawn, so that its president would have a limited term of office. Dr Sylvia Payne was elected president in July 1944. Glover stood no chance, having discredited himself by his fiercely anti-Klein chairing.

A more efficient organizational structure was needed, because all expected that after the war a national health service would be set up. How would psychoanalysis fit in? Would medically trained analysts have to choose between full-time NHS work or private practice? Should the London Clinic of Psycho-Analysis apply to be part of the NHS? Would young entrants be put off analytic training?

From The Plat, Jones had plenty of psychoanalytic business to deal with. He was still in active correspondence with the Home Office (Aliens Department) over the conditions for refugees. These were severe. Granting permission for a psychotherapist (Hedwig Schwarz) to work at the London Clinic of Psycho-Analysis, a civil servant wrote that the Secretary of State 'regrets he is not prepared to agree to her doing psychological work in private', nor 'to imply that she will be allowed to establish herself in this country after the war'.

The disharmony of British psychoanalysis was the last thing on Jones's mind. Mervyn became a prisoner of war in October 1944 during the Allied push through the Low Countries after D-Day. It shook his father badly, as did, momentarily, the news of the death of Loe Kann Jones. The momentary flash of the past struck him, he wrote to Anna, 'so vividly I saw her face and heard her speak as if she were alive again'.

His son's capture may have precipitated the severe heart attack Jones suffered in October 1944. He was then sixty-five. As he was carried to the next room, his son Lewis, then eleven, thought his father was going to die. Jones was in bed for six weeks. In December he was moved to University College Hospital, his old training ground. When he had recovered enough to be allowed to go in and out during the day, he used the privilege to take himself to see the new film, *Henry V*. He was unimpressed. The pageantry was splendid, he wrote to Kitty at The Plat, but 'the tasteless Olivier spoiled it.'

His old alma mater put a name to the chronic affliction that made Jones look anaemic: one of his doctors wrote to him that he was living proof that Gaucher's disease was not fatal. The diagnosis was interesting enough to make Jones the subject of an ill-disguised case history in *The Lancet*:

> Patient was a doctor, aged 67, of Welsh descent. From childhood his pallor had attracted notice, and in his early years he was always given iron. When he was a medical student his colour excited repeated comment, but his blood contained Hb [haemoglobin] 90% ... His present complaint was that during the previous two years, while exercising with the Home Guard, he had become more and more inconvenienced by shortness of breath.

But Jones was still president of the International Association. Punctiliously going by the rules, he removed Glover as secretary of the association, a post to which he had been elected in 1938, and replaced him with Anna Freud. When Glover protested, Jones reminded him that, as he had resigned from the British Psycho-Analytical Society, he no longer had any standing in the International Association. Glover was not a refugee, the only category to which the president of the association was allowed to give 'direct' membership. (Jones obviously enjoyed referring to himself in the third person.) In any case, he wrote to Glover, he had thought they were both tired of 'psycho-analytic politics. I hoped that you, like me, were going to enjoy the last period of our lives free from what all our experience has proved to be nothing but poison.'

Victory in Europe saw Mervyn released and flown back to England. Jones, much relieved, could turn his mind to international matters. With the future of Palestine a subject of debate, in 1945 he contributed to a written symposium, 'Gentile and Jew', a paper on 'The Psychology of the Jewish Question'. Describing himself as a social anthropologist, he discussed the aloofness or separation between Jews and Gentiles, and the Jews' resistance to assimilation. The Welsh and the Scots, he observed, were a long way from being assimilated or accepted as Englishmen. But he called attention (in words for which some have not forgiven him – Otto Rank's biographer, E. James Lieberman, calls them a revelation of 'blatant, aggressive bigotry') to what many Gentiles felt to be 'the arrogant pretension to uniqueness inherent in the Jewish religion and philosophy', exemplified by the claim to have 'a specially favoured and more intimate relationship with the Celestial Powers'.

What was the way forward? The creation of a Jewish state – 'the nationalist solution' – might help, but could also have the effect of creating new problems for the bulk of Jews living in other countries. 'To raise the general standard of decent behaviour in general is less spectacular, but in the long run more effective ... In any event it is desirable that it [the nationalist state] be supplemented by all other possible methods of combating the scandal of anti-Semitism.'

In truth, Mervyn observed, Jones deplored the creation in 1948 of the state of Israel, even though he thought of himself as an honorary Jew and liked to pepper his conversation with Jewish words such as '*meshugge*'. 'But the idea of an undiluted Judaism', Mervyn said, 'reminded him of the parochialism of Wales.'

In fact Jones was inching himself back into a new appreciation of his heritage, and would even come out with Welsh words when excited. During the war, his younger children's schools had been evacuated to Aberystwyth. At some point he engaged a Mrs Pritchard to teach Welsh to Nesta, who became fluent. He limped along himself, but never really mastered the language, claiming a lasting grudge against Llandovery College for not having taught it. In a conversation with an old schoolmate, he regretted that, among the many nationalities he had instructed in psychoanalysis, he had never trained a Welshman – even though, he told his friend, 'our temperament is so admirably suited for the work.' As part of this surge of nationalism, Jones joined the Welsh Nationalist Party, Plaid Cymru, founded in 1925, and began to scorn what he contemptuously described as 'the callous English acquiescence in assaults on the Celtic language and culture'.

An unexpected blow came when Jones encountered a new book published by Gollancz in the spring of 1945: *David Eder: Memoirs of a Modern Pioneer*, edited by J. B. Hobman, with 'Foreword by Sigmund Freud' prominently displayed. The foreword consisted of one short paragraph, but it was long enough to demolish Jones's proudest boast, for it described Eder as 'the first, and for a time the only doctor to practise the new therapy in England'. To Anna, Jones stormed that her father had done him a serious injustice. That Freud, in 'one of the last acts of his life', should deprive him of the honour to which he was entitled was incredible. Jones spelled it out for Anna: 'I was indubitably the first person in this country (and, as far as I know, in the whole non-German-speaking world) to assimilate your Father's work [and] to practise psycho-analysis. In the conditions of 40 years ago it was a considerable feat, and I suppose my reputation rests largely on it.' Why had neither Freud nor Anna thought to verify the statement by asking him?

What hurt him all the more was that Professor Gilbert Murray had quoted Freud's claim about Eder in the popular BBC radio programme *The Brains Trust*, thus disseminating the distortion of history over the national airwaves. Jones had already persuaded the *New Statesman* to correct the error, and he hoped that Anna would send a note to any important periodical reviewing the book. He signed himself, 'Yours always sincerely, Ernest'.

Jones turned to his reliable outlet, the *International Journal of Psycho-Analysis*, to give himself what he had described to Anna as 'the honour [of which] your Father has strangely deprived me'. He laid out out his claim to be the first pioneer of psychoanalysis in the English-speaking world. There he credited himself (not inaccurately) with the first paper in English to support psychoanalysis (correcting James Jackson Putnam's attack in the *Journal of Abnormal Psychology*) in 1906.

Reading a draft, James Strachey reminded him to emphasize the importance of F. W. H. Myers and the Society for Psychical Research. The SPR from 1893 had followed the development studies of hysteria and psychotherapy, and had been a very lively (and not at all exclusively spiritualistic) organization when Strachey himself had been an undergraduate at Cambridge from 1905 to 1909. The society had been his own road of approach to psychoanalysis – 'though I was never spooky'.

Strachey, bolstering Jones's claim to England's leadership in psychoanalysis, said that he considered it remarkable that the basic discoveries of psychoanalysis were accessible in print to English readers within six months of their first publication in German.

An ironic reminder that psychoanalysis was truly international came when, as soon as Germany had surrendered, Jones heard from his old irritant in Berlin, Carl Müller-Braunschweig, that the German Psychoanalytic Society now wished to rejoin the International Association. In early July 1945 Müller-Braunschweig described himself as trying to adjust to the new reality, despite 'a kind of paralysis resulting from the terrible things we went through during the war – aggravated by the knowledge that Germany is hated through the world'. His colleague Dr Felix Boehm was among those asking him to resuscitate the German Society and to preside over it. Ought he to write a report on 'the nightmare of the past twelve years'? What was the German Society's position now within the International Association?

From Italy came another request to rejoin the International Association. Nicola Perrotti wrote to announce the resumption of the Italian Psycho-analytical Society, and to ask how it could re-establish normal relations with the IPA.

For the Jones family, there was no question of returning to 42 York Terrace. The house had been damaged by a bomb, partially repaired, and used as a Ministry of Food office, but when it was fully repaired the lease had run out.

Jones was settled in his seventeenth-century house and his twentieth-century library in the new wing. He was well advanced on writing his autobiography. He had contacted his living elder relatives, and had secured information for a detailed family tree. Retracing his childhood had the effect of reviving his Oedipal resentment against his father 'who took a decidedly English view of life' and who had converted 'the name of my birthplace [Rhosfelyn] into an English hybrid [Gowerton]'. For his future readers, Jones interpreted his belated anger as 'no doubt an echo of every child's resentment at the fantasy of his father desecrating his mother'.

He had completed the first eleven chapters, from his childhood origins to his return to London from Toronto, but had reached a painful stopping point: the death of Morfydd Owen in 1918:

> Armistice night, which in happier days I had looked forward to spending with old friends, came and went. I stared at it, and at the German howitzers lining the Mall, but for me, as for so many others, it meant the end of an old world rather than the beginning of a new one.

He also wrote some introductory notes to a new edition of Klein's works, in which he managed to acknowledge her importance in illuminating the early life of infants while distancing himself from both her and Freud. While he disliked and disagreed with Freud's concept of the death instinct, he also recoiled from Klein's 'unsparing presentation of the cutting, tearing, gouging, devouring phantasies of infants', which is 'apt to make most people recoil with a similar exclamation'. He found that she too literally applied Freud's philosophical concept of the 'death impulse'. In that sense, she was too faithful a Freudian.

In 1946 the British Psycho-Analytical Society commissioned a portrait of Jones from the distinguished artist Rodrigo Moynihan. Presenting it, and announcing the establishment of an annual lecture in Jones's name, the president, Sylvia Payne, delivered the address. She gave Jones the credit he craved for being the first person to use Freud's technique outside the German-speaking countries. She paid tribute to his work on the British Medical Association report and on the society's training committee, and was 'astonished at the amount and quality of the work he did, at the Society and International Association congresses'. Moreover, she had noticed, 'The more argumentative the audience, the more Dr Jones enjoyed himself and he inevitably got his own way.'

Under the new regime, headed by Sylvia Payne and encouraged by Rickman, members of the society met with a committee from the Tavistock Clinic to discuss their organizations' relations with each other, particularly as they concerned the new Tavistock Institute of Human Relations, which would apply psychoanalytic principles to social problems. It was agreed that the society's statutory arm, the Institute of Psycho-Analysis, was to be regarded as the centre for training in analytic technique. It was agreed that what was wrong with the pre-war officers of the British Society (that meant Jones and Glover) was they thought only in terms of helping individual patients, and paid no attention to problems of group morale and interpersonal relations.

Having in mid-1944 at last bowed out from leadership of the British Society he had created, Jones gave a valedictory speech in which he traced the evolution of psychoanalysis from the early days when in many countries there was talk of invoking the law 'to prohibit our heinous activities'. He quoted Freud's saying that only Jews could resist such intense social opprobrium, but he supposed that he was the exception that proved the rule.

He spoke of 'the incalculable mass of neurotic misery in the world', and of analysts' duty to inform their medical colleagues of a method of alleviating the suffering. He pointed out the great dissensions that existed among psychoanalysts. It was pretty evident that 'to achieve anything like complete freedom and inner harmony by means of psycho-analysis is even harder than we sometimes think.' He foresaw a future in which the ability to master deep infantile anxieties and achieve mental balance might prove to have a physiological basis. 'Psychoanalysis', he stated, 'is simply the study of mental processes of which we are unaware.' Its future was bound up with its relationship to medicine. He still believed, as he had long argued, that it should be an exception for a non-medical candidate to be admitted to training. Moreover, for medical students, biology should take precedence over psychology in their training on how to deal with the neurotic reactions seen in their patients. Jones concluded with the audacious prediction that the age-old gap between 'mind' and 'body' would disappear: 'It would not be at all surprising that when a common formula is discovered for both, it will be expressed only in mathematical terminology.'

In 1948 Jones was delighted to be accepted as a member of the Athenaeum – not quite the knighthood he hoped for, but a step up the social ladder all the same for a man who had been in *Who's Who* for eighteen years. At his new club, he gave a lunch to celebrate the engagement of Mervyn to Jeanne Urquhart, a fellow Communist Party member. When Mervyn had brought his fiancée to Elsted and announced that he had become engaged to her after knowing her for five weeks, his father said, 'How slow you are!' The lunch, in Lewis's recollection, was spoiled by a guest who insisted on talking about figure skating.

When the time came for the wedding, Jones offered Mervyn the ring he had taken from Morfydd's finger as she was buried. Mervyn was touched. He had noticed that his father kept Morfydd's photograph, 'showing her haunting, mysterious beauty', in his dressing room, and that it was a room his mother seldom entered.

Nineteen forty-eight was a good year for Jones, for it was marked by the appearance of Laurence Olivier's film *Hamlet*, in which Olivier portrayed Hamlet as a man who was taking too long to make up his mind to revenge his father's death. This interpretation was the direct result of Olivier's visit to Jones in 1937. Mindful of Jones's work on Hamlet and the Oedipus complex, when he decided to play Hamlet for his first season at the Old Vic, Olivier, with Tyrone Guthrie and Peggy Ashcroft, went to see Jones and found him 'wonderfully enlightening'. Olivier swallowed the whole Jones line: that the symptoms of Hamlet's repressed Oedipus complex were his cruelty to Ophelia, his spectacular mood-swings and his hopeless inability to do what was required of him. (Olivier also took away with him another of Jones's Shakespearean theories – 'that Iago was subconsciously in love with Othello'. He drew on it when playing Iago at the Old Vic in 1938.)

The success of the film *Hamlet* worked to Jones's advantage. It brought about a new version of his Hamlet essay in book form: *Hamlet and Oedipus*, published in 1949 in New York by W. W. Norton and in London by Gollancz.

That same year saw the publication by Allen & Unwin of his short book *What is Psychoanalysis?* In it he examined people's need in times of insecurity for a strong government to protect them 'from all imagined dangers'. The extreme was 'the clamour for an all-powerful dictator to whom all responsibility for individual lives and personal decisions is given up'. These attitudes were not the same in all countries, he wrote, contrasting 'the Indian desire for independence and self-rule and the startling docility exhibited by the German nation'.

In his first trip abroad since his illness (he had sold the villa in Menton he had acquired before the war), in August 1949 Jones took himself to Zurich for the first post-war congress of the International Association. The diminished numbers showed the toll the war had taken on the ranks of psychoanalysts: there were sixty-four fewer members than had attended the Paris congress in 1938. But Klein, her daughter, Melitta (now moved to New York), and Anna Freud were all there. A ringing address was given by a member of the French Psychoanalytical Society, Jacques Lacan, who was soon to launch his own heretical movement and to establish a new school of literary criticism.

The time had come for Jones to step down from the presidency he had held since 1932. He handed over to the first American to hold the office, Leo Bartemeier. To warm applause, he was awarded the permanent title of honorary president. At the age of seventy, there was nothing left for his superego to do but prod him to begin the major work of his life.

19

A Life for a Life
1950–1958

—◆—

ERNEST JONES WAS not the Freud family's first choice as a biographer, even though he had been approached by the New York publishers Simon & Schuster as early as 1946. By the time of Freud's death, in 1939, three Viennese were on the trail: Ernst Kris, a friend and disciple of Freud's, by then settled in New York, and Siegfried Bernfeld and his wife, Suzanne Cassirer, settled in San Francisco, had done considerable work and published several articles on Freud's early life and background.

By the late 1940s the Freud family agreed that Jones should write the biography. (The decision appears to have been taken by Freud's children Anna, Ernst, Mathilde and Martin; the fifth surviving sibling, Oliver, had gone to America.) They settled on Jones because so many distorted versions of the life were appearing. Two American biographies had appeared, one by the German émigré Emil Ludwig in 1946, the other by Helen Puner, a journalist, in 1949. There had also been *Sigmund Freud*, published in 1924 by Fritz Wittels, an estranged member of Freud's Vienna Psychoanalytic Society. Freud was polite about Wittels' book: 'I value your work though I cannot wholly approve it.'

The Freuds knew Jones well, and appreciated that, as the only surviving member of the Committee, he had been an eyewitness to more than three decades of the development of psychoanalysis. In the end, it may have been Jones's eloquence that got him the job. Anna had been very moved by his funeral eulogy for her father, although she worried that Jones might harbour a simmering resentment at Freud's introduction to the David Eder book.

Jones took on the project thinking it would take ten years. He began receiving visits at The Plat from Arthur Rosenthal, an American publisher who was starting a new firm called Basic Books. There was never any doubt that the Hogarth Press in London would handle the English edition. In March 1950 he approached Bernfeld through a letter saying it was the first of what he hoped would be a lengthy and fruitful correspondence. Bernfeld, in reply, confirmed that he had been collecting material on

Freud's life for years, that he believed that the Puner biography had plagiarized his work, and that he would give Jones full co-operation.

A high priority was to interview Freud's widow, who lived on in her Maresfield Gardens home. In her late eighties, Martha Freud still insisted on going down the passageway leading to the Finchley Road to do her own shopping – always beautifully dressed. (The Frau Professor, as Jones called her, was irritated by Anna's deliberate dowdiness.) She spoke comfortably with Jones, whom she had known for many years, and she too had been moved by his address at the crematorium.

From the Frau Professor, Jones learned many personal details of Freud's courtship of Martha Bernays of Hamburg. He could therefore put in his biography, 'The date of the fateful Saturday, after which they considered themselves engaged, was June 17, one which they never forgot. They even commemorated the 17th of every month for some years.'

Jones listened with the analyst's third ear to the story of Martha's mother whisking her back to Hamburg, believing that if the engagement had to be a long one the lovers were best kept apart. 'Mrs Freud herself described it to me . . .' wrote Jones, 'with an ill-disguised air of admiration at her mother's resolute behaviour.'

At his disposal was also a biographical treasure trove – nearly three hundred revealing letters written by Freud to his friend Wilhelm Fliess in Berlin in the period from 1887 to 1902 during what Jones would describe as the 'passionate relationship of dependency'. How these letters came to survive and reach London was part of the story Jones had to tell. When Freud broke with Fliess, in 1902, he destroyed all the letters Fliess had sent to him. But his own contribution to the correspondence was in Berlin, out of his grasp. After Fliess's death, in 1928, his widow sold the Freud letters to a Berlin dealer, who, fleeing Hitler in the 1930s, sold them to Princess Marie Bonaparte. Freud offered to buy them back, but the Princess resolutely refused and stored the letters in the Rothschild bank in Vienna. That they escaped the Nazi clutches, got to Greece, and eventually reached London required the Princess to use a diplomatic network even more intricate than the one she used to rescue Freud's gold.

After the war, the Princess, working with Anna Freud and Ernst Kris, had been selecting and abridging Freud's letters to Fliess and was preparing a book on the origins of psychoanalysis, with an introduction and notes by Kris. Their approach was academic; their concern to play down the sensational aspects of the dramatic correspondence. They did not, however, put any restraints on Jones.

Jones, as a good Freudian, gave Freud's early years careful attention.

From the as-yet untranslated *Aus den Anfängen der Psychoanalyse* (published in German in 1950 and in English in 1954 as *The Origins of Psycho-Analysis*) he plucked the telling anecdote of the four-year-old Freud on the train as the family moved from Moravia to Leipzig seeing flaming gas jets for the first time and thinking of 'souls burning in hell'. Freud himself later connected this memory with a fear of losing his home (and his mother's breast), but he never really overcame his *Reisefieber*, anxiety at departing on a journey.

With his own knowledge of Freud's autobiographical writings, including the account of his self-analysis, Jones got off to a fast start. By the end of 1950 he had completed the first chapter of the biography and sent it to James Strachey. Strachey liked what he read. He thought it covered the ground completely, and offered only minor suggestions. He wondered about the various ways in which Freud had described the scar on his chin acquired slipping from a stool when he was two. He also called Jones's attention to the specific page in the Fleiss letters in which Freud himself connected his travel phobia with his early journey from Freiberg to Leipzig.

The two men were close collaborators now, as Strachey was preparing the monumental Standard Edition, the translation of the full range of Freud's works, which would extend to twenty-four volumes, published over twenty-one years, and make available in clear English the history and development of Freud's ideas and concepts. This gave Jones much of the essential material he needed for the biography.

Jones, receiving the second volume, complimented Strachey on the 'staggering thoroughness' of his historical and scientific research. He kept a close eye on the preparation of the manuscripts, and made many minor editorial comments – such as pointing out where Strachey used 'that' three times in one sentence.

Jones's old criticisms of Strachey's slowness and indecision were forgotten. Strachey had brought his Bloomsbury light touch to the subject of psychoanalysis, as shown by an amusing piece he wrote for *The Spectator*, 'Some Unconscious Factors in Reading', in which he called attention to the 'remarkable and widespread habit of reading while defecating'. He cited one patient whose reading material was the squares of newspapers provided as toilet paper. Jones sought his advice on matters of style. Where, if anywhere, should he use the historic present? How could he avoid passages of heavy psychological language, other than by printing 'red lines down the side, with a caption, "Skip this; it is unreadable"'?

By May 1951, when Jones sent the opening chapter to Bernfeld, it was clear that he had vaulted gracefully the first hurdle at which many biographies fall – the family history. In fourteen pages, called 'Origins', he traced the Freud line from its putative beginnings in a medieval Jewish settlement in the Rhineland to its flight, in the fourteenth or fifteenth century, to Lithuania, then to Galicia, and in Freud's childhood from Moravia to Leipzig to Vienna. He established that Freud's father, Jakob, was a grandfather at the time of his second marriage and that Sigmund was therefore an uncle at birth. He tucked in analytically relevant facts such as that Freud still wet the bed at the age of two, that he had lost his beloved Nanny when his father had had her arrested for stealing money and toys, and that on the train journey from Leipzig to Vienna Freud had seen his mother naked. Jones, studying the Fliess letters, noted that Freud had used a Latin word (*nudam*) in describing the sight to his friend, and had altered his age at the time from four to two. By the end of the chapter, Jones had established that Freud was his mother's favourite child, endowed with a self-confidence 'that was very seldom shaken'.

Embarking on the biography, Jones was apprehensive. His health was shaky, the material available vast and unsorted. Unlike James Boswell, who in 1772 had told Samuel Johnson of his intention and began collecting materials while Johnson was still alive, Jones had not conceived of the biography before his subject's death. However, he had vast resources of his own on which to draw: the hundreds of letters Freud had written to him personally, his extensive collection of Freud's works, and his thorough knowledge of Freud's works from his own reading, his editing of the *Collected Papers* and his consultation with the Stracheys over the Standard Edition. On his shelves and in his files were also held his correspondence with the Committee and a twenty-year run of the *International Journal of Psycho-Analysis*, filled with perhaps 300 book reviews he himself had written about psychoanalyis and related fields, not to mention his collections of the *Jahrbuch*, the *Zeitschrift* and other associated publications. There were also his own extensive contributions. In 1951 the fifth edition of his *Essays in Applied Psycho-Analysis* appeared, expanded with fresh material such as a merry essay on the anthropological meaning of Christmas that had been commissioned but never used by an American magazine. There was no one alive who knew the field better.

All of Freud's surviving papers were in his Maresfield Gardens house. On repeated visits, Jones carried off large bundles to The Plat, where Kitty and her typewriter were waiting. Never in more than thirty years of marriage had Katherine Jones helped her husband more. Jones could not have written the biography in country isolation at the incredible pace at which the volumes appeared without his wife's able assistance.

Kitty dreaded boredom. At one point she sacked Jones's secretary and handled his correspondence herself in order to fill her time. The children had left home. Her youngest, Lewis, after finishing Stowe (a more distinguished, if more conventional, public school than Mervyn's Abbotsholme) had gone on to the University of Wales at Cardiff to study music. In preparing to become a musician, Lewis was following his mother's bent. His father had no more interest in music than Freud had had.

In any event, Kitty could consider herself part of Freud's inner circle. He had presented her with one of the talismanic gold rings with which he favoured his closest adherents. Among other women ring-holders were Lou Andreas-Salomé, Anna Freud, Marie Bonaparte, Dorothy Burlingham and Gisella Ferenczi.

Throwing herself into the work with enthusiasm, she helped Ernest develop a working system which, according to Mervyn, 'only my parents really understood, and which involved distributing papers among tall pyramids of wire baskets'. Before long, the couple knew the details of Freud's life so well that they would challenge each other to say what Freud had been doing on particular dates.

Confronted with the mountain of material, Jones decided to divide the work into three volumes. Boldly, he prefaced Volume 1 with the admission that 'It is not a book that would have met with Freud's own approval.' In evidence, he cited Freud's destruction of all the correspondence, notes, diaries and manuscripts from his early life – except for the love letters. He used a telling quote from Freud's assurance to his fiancée: 'Yours, my dear one, were never in danger . . . Let the biographers chafe; we won't make it too easy for them. Let each one of them believe he is right in his "Conception of the Development of the Hero".' Jones left to speak for itself Freud's conviction at the age of twenty-eight that he would someday be a hero pursued by biographers.

Jones's second disclaimer was that his own 'hero-worshipping propensities had been worked through even' before he met Freud. He thus left to his readers and reviewers to decide whether he was a biographer guiltless of hagiography.

All biography is a struggle between theme and chronology. Characteristically, Jones chose both. He presented the narrative of Freud's life in a straight time sequence, but placed thematic material in separate chapters at the end of each volume. Volume 1, for example, contains essays on *The*

Interpretation of Dreams and on Freud's theory of the mind, both of which introduced Freud's concept of the Oedipus complex. From the start, Jones, much like Boswell, permitted himself to intrude with his own comments wherever he liked, as he did when recounting his conversations with Freud's widow.

Early in his first volume, he dealt with the question of Freud's Jewishness:

> A Gentile would have said that Freud had few overt Jewish characteristics, a fondness for relating Jewish jokes and anecdotes being perhaps the most prominent one. But he felt himself to be Jewish to the core . . . He had the common Jewish sensitiveness to the slightest hint of anti-semitism and he made very few friends who were not Jews.

Drawing on an autobiographical passage in *The Interpretation of Dreams*, Jones related how Freud's father 'never regained the place he had held in his esteem' after telling his son, aged twelve, that when a Gentile had knocked his new fur cap into the mud, saying 'Jew, get off the pavement,' he had unprotestingly picked it up. Submission, commented Jones, was not in Freud's nature.

Jones treated Freud's fascination with the little-understood drug cocaine as an 'episode' of the years from 1884 to 1887. Freud, he said, did not see any danger in taking the 'magical drug', and had sent some to Martha to redden her cheeks. He urged others to inject it, but felt guilty when he saw them becoming addicted.

In his treatment of the 'Breuer period', identified as 1882 to 1894, Jones revealed the true name of Breuer's patient 'Anna O': Bertha Pappenheim. In his chapter titled 'Marriage', covering 1886, he brushed away rumours (thus also spreading them) of any sexual attraction between Freud and his sister-in-law Minna Bernays. The fact that Freud and Minna used to take holidays alone together had, he said, 'given rise to the malicious and entirely untrue legend that she displaced his wife in his affections'. Jones explained Freud's affinity with his sister-in-law by saying that Freud had always enjoyed 'the society of intellectual and rather masculine women'.

When Martha Freud died, on 2 November 1951, Jones wrote a letter of tribute to *The Times*, as a supplement to her obituary. In it he commemorated the loss of 'a distinguished lady', saying that 'her generous charm, her delightful hospitality, and her complete goodness of heart made her a notable figure. I knew her for 45 years, and to me, as to so many others, her invariable kindliness will remain an abiding memory.'

Hardly a month after her mother's death, Anna Freud read the first chapter of the biography. She wrote breathlessly to Ernst Kris, 'I am simply amazed at his objective, factual and scientific approach to the whole topic.'

An American publisher was breathless too. In February 1952 Jones was about to sign a contract giving Basic Books in New York world rights, excluding Britain and Canada, to the biography. He would receive one thousand dollars for each of the three projected volumes, to be followed by another thousand dollars within twelve months of publication.

Thus emboldened, Jones wrote to Anna to ask if he might see the letters that her mother and father had written during their tortuously long and chaste engagement, from 1882 to 1886. He was aware of what the family knew as 'the *Brautbriefe*', the betrothal letters. Anna had already told Bernfeld about their existence, but had said that she did not want to disturb her mother about them. Martha Freud had indeed threatened to burn them after Freud's death, but her daughters had talked her out of it.

Jones's request caused some consternation among the siblings, as Anna explained: 'The question of the *Brautbriefe* which you raised has aroused quite an emotional upheaval in our otherwise unemotional family.' She said that she and Mathilde felt the letters were too intimate and should be left unread until some future time. But Ernst thought the opposite: that a biographer should be given every possible help. Luckily for Jones, Ernst's view prevailed.

The cache was large: about 1,500 new letters to be read, in addition to the more than 2,500 the Freud family had already let Jones see. They reached him when he had already completed Volume 1. He was faced with considerable rewriting.

It was effort rewarded. Not only did the betrothal letters testify to the deep bond between the young couple, as when Freud told Martha 'now I love you with a kind of passionate enchantment', they were full of humour. Learning that Martha was about to receive 2,500 gulden (about £200) from an aunt, Freud told her, 'You know, it is only poor people who are embarrassed at being given anything; the rich never are.' He provided his fiancée with a sketch (snapped up by Jones as an illustration) of his workroom in the General Hospital of Vienna in 1883. The letters also revealed Freud's agonizingly slow climb to the rank of *Privatdozent* in neuropathology – the status he needed in order to marry.

In his text, Jones enjoyed interpreting Freud interpreting Martha: 'He was constantly reading between the lines of Martha's letters, so that she found no escape in reticence.' Jones could also present, almost as foresight,

Freud's early Anglophilia – acquired from his extensive reading, and confirmed on a visit to his half-brothers in Manchester when he was nineteen. At a time when his prospects in Vienna were poor and he considered emigration, Freud wrote to Martha, 'The thought of England surges up before me, with its sober industriousness, its generous devotion to the public weal, the stubbornness and sensitive feeling for justice of its inhabitants.' Almost pleadingly, he asked, 'Must we stay here, Martha?'

Once the *Brautbriefe* decision had been taken, Jones invited Anna down to Elsted and suggested they could look through the photographs in her large collection. She was happy to accept. She and Dorothy Burlingham were frequent visitors to The Plat. Meanwhile, Jones had to tell Bernfeld, who wanted to know the contents of the letters, that he had promised to keep them private.

When Jones told Anna that there seemed to be some missing, he was right. There were 1,700 more. By August 1952 he told Bernfeld that his wife had been slaving at typing the *Brautbriefe* and selecting passages for inclusion. Only Kitty could decipher the Gothic script in which the letters were written.

Jones himself, along with working six to eight hours a day on the biography and suffering bouts of illness, was still seeing patients. One of these was his old Sussex friend, the Impressionist painter Paul Maze. Maze, nearing seventy, found himself crying all the time and unable to paint, and came to Jones to ask for drugs or hospital treatment. 'You can talk your way out of this,' Jones assured him. Whether the therapist was Jones himself or someone else Maze's family was not sure, but the treatment worked, and Maze resumed painting until his death in 1979.

On 15 November 1952 Jones reported to Bernfeld that Anna had just divulged 520 more letters between Freud and his wife, written after their marriage. She also produced the secret diary that each of the couple kept during their engagement. It appears that as Jones's biography became a reality, Anna saw the importance of making it comprehensive and definitive.

When he told her he planned to dedicate the biography to her, she claimed to be overwhelmed – so much so that she said she had read his letter over and over to see if he really meant it. Jones's book would bring her father as a young man alive to her, she said, and she signed off, 'Very much love, yours, Anna'.

Jones concluded Volume 1 at the start of the twentieth century, with the publication of *The Interpretation of Dreams*, and with his own summary of Freud's theory of the mind as it stood in 1900. He did not claim that Freud had discovered the unconscious. In fact, he said, the idea of unconscious mental processes was much more widely accepted in the late nineteenth century than in the first two decades of the twentieth. To him, Freud's revolutionary discovery was that there are two kinds of mental process. As evidence, he offered Freud's remark that the contrast between 'the ego' and 'the repressed' was more instructive than that between consciousness and the unconscious.

The acknowledgements for assistance with the book rang true: 'Last, and very far from least, I wish to thank my wife for her devoted day-to-day collaboration, without which this book would assuredly not have been written.' He also stated, 'To Siegfried and Suzanne Cassirer Bernfeld's painstaking researches, aided by their friends in Vienna, every student of Freud's early life and environment will be permanently indebted.' Sadly, Bernfeld had died in April 1953, six months before the first volume appeared.

Spending most of his working time writing the biography, Jones faced the fact that his elder son had become a writer – a *real* writer, who wrote for a living.

Mervyn, a journalist and frequent contributor to the *New Statesman*, published his first novel, *No Time to Be Young*, in 1952. Jones, who had been doubtful about anyone making a living from writing, read it and wrote, in a letter signed 'Love from Dad', to tell Mervyn how good he thought the book was: 'The last part where you get on to the human soul shows you do not simply good writing but really great writing.' 'Stick to it,' he said. 'You have chosen the right profession.'

So had he. Even before the first volume of the biography came out, Jones was a minor celebrity, beginning to attract interviews in the press. At the end of July, the imminence of the forthcoming congress in London of the International Psychoanalytic Association drew a reporter from *Time* down to The Plat. The magazine's 'Medicine' section focused on Jones as the International Association's honorary lifetime president, and found him 'a spry Homburg-hatted little Welshman' whom 'Freud called the greatest psycho-analyst in the English-speaking world'. 'He likes to look out of his windows at the rolling Sussex hills, which he calls "maternal mounds". A close student of the Oedipus-complected Hamlet, he is said to have coached Sir Laurence Olivier on the proper gestures to suggest the prince's improper urges.'

The same congress inspired a profile in *The Observer*. With a fine photograph of Jones, it was highly flattering both to Jones and to psycho-analysis: 'The honorary Life President of this International Association, who will read a paper on the opening day, is a studious but vivacious man, slight, but of commanding presence, a man now well advanced in age.' It credited him for the British Medical Association report which had meant not only that no objection was found to the Freudian methods but that only those trained by the Institute of Psycho-Analysis 'could properly use the title psycho-analyst: an invaluable protection against charlatans'.

The Observer noted that the first volume of Jones's three-volume bio-graphy of Freud was about to appear, and that the work was said to be one of his best. This was no small claim, as he had already written, the paper said, over two hundred essays and many books, while in twenty years of editing the international journal 'of his science' he had acquired 'a knowledge, mastered and retained with a scholarly precision, that it would be hard to equal'.

Volume 1 of *The Life and Work of Sigmund Freud*, with its dedication 'To ANNA FREUD, true daughter of an immortal sire', was published in New York and went straight on to the *New York Times* best-seller list. In twelfth place, it appeared below other books whose popularity suggested that Americans wanted to know how to live their lives – Norman Vincent Peale's *The Power of Positive Thinking*, which was in first place, and Alfred Kinsey's *Sexual Behaviour of the Human Female*, in sixth.

Even in his most self-confident moments, Jones cannot have dreamed of such a reception. *Publishers' Weekly* reported that the book's first print-ing of 10,000 was sold out within two weeks, and paper for the second and third printings was already ordered. The enthusiastic reviews instantly established Jones as the principal historian of the psychoanalytic move-ment. In the lead review of the *New York Times Book Review*, Lionel Trilling began, 'It would be difficult to say too much in praise of this first of three volumes of Ernest Jones's life of Sigmund Freud', and went on to pile on praise. Not only did Jones show Freud's achievements, said Trilling, but 'where Freud's conduct was of a kind to do less than credit to himself, when it was extreme or ambiguous or neurotic, Dr Jones makes no bones about characterizing and analyzing it.'

Max Lerner in the *New York Post* declared the publication such an important event that he would devote three of his columns to it. *Time*, devoting several pages to Jones's book, judged that 'stout partisanship in no way dulls the brilliance of Jones's biography, any more than it did in the case of James Boswell's celebrated admiration of Samuel Johnson.'

CBS television devoted an episode of its popular *You Are There* series to Freud.

Praise in Britain – where the book was published by the Hogarth Press as *Sigmund Freud: Life and Work* and subtitled 'The Young Freud 1856– 1900' – was not muted. The *Manchester Guardian* called it 'This entrancing volume'. Taking Jones at his word, it continued, 'The outcome is now Boswellian, for Dr Jones had worked through his hero-worshipping propensities before even meeting Freud.' *The Spectator* looked forward to Jones's next two volumes, although 'it is hard to know how he can improve on the compelling portrait which he has composed for us here.'

The president of the Royal Society gave Jones the next best thing to an FRS. In *The Observer*, Dr E. D. Adrian, OM (later Lord Adrian), master of Trinity College Cambridge, said that few in England had paid serious attention to *The Interpretation of Dreams* because few had heard of Freud. 'It was Ernest Jones who made us take him seriously. It was not done easily: the volume which describes the grudging acceptance of psychoanalysis will be interesting enough, but it can scarcely equal this account of how it all began.'

Not every review was favourable. In the *Irish Times*, Brian Inglis confessed, 'Most of us have hated the word "Freud" at one time or another,' but even so he found the book 'full of surprises and revelations, not least of Freud's courage, integrity and dignity'. *The Economist* admired Jones's devotion and industry, but complained that the writing style occasionally fell into 'a certain clumsiness and abstraction that betrays the Central Europe origin of many of our distinguished psychiatrists'.

Reviews appeared all over the English-speaking world, as well as in Scandinavia, Germany and Switzerland. By Christmas 1953 the book was prominent on book-of-the-year lists, accompanied by advertisements: 'One of the outstanding biographies of the age', *New York Times*; 'A great biography', *New York Herald Tribune*; 'a masterpiece of contemporary biography', *Time* magazine; 'Superb drama', the *New Yorker*.

In retrospect, it is clear that the first volume of Jones's biography appeared just as psychoanalysis was reaching the crest of its post-war wave. While strongest in the United States, the wave swept over Britain as well. Looking back at the Britain of the 1950s, the Nobel laureate Elias Canetti, a Jewish refugee from Germany living in London at the time, wrote: 'It's not sufficient to say that it [psychoanalysis] was embraced with open arms, no, people gobbled it up or prostrated themselves at its feet. This was a subjection so absolute and so servile as you only get in an established master breed. I felt uncouth if I ever said anything against it.'

The eager reception of Jones's book testified not only to the post-war fascination with behaviour and sexuality but also to a pent-up curiosity about what Freud the man was like. That the founder of psychoanalysis should have written, as *Samedi-Soir*'s headline announced, '900 Lettres d'Amour' was as interesting as the information that he showed obvious signs of neurosis.

Welcome academic recognition reached Jones in 1954 when the Bollingen Foundation gave him $2,000 for research and secretarial help, and when he was also made an honorary Doctor of Science by the University of Wales. 'They made a dignified performance of it at the University of Wales,' he relayed to James Strachey, 'so now psycho-analysis is officially recognised as a science.'

He and Kitty kept on at a fiendish pace. It took them only two years to take Freud from the age of forty-five to sixty-two, from 1901 to 1919, the point where 'the world at last was really opening its arms to receive Freud and his work'. There was complicated ground to cover: the trip to Clark University in Worcester in 1909, begun with Freud's attempt before boarding the ship to laugh Jung out of his fanatical teetotalism, only to fall into a dead faint, and including the havoc wreaked on Freud's digestive system by American cooking, with its consequent souring of his attitude towards the United States.

Then came the gradual break with Jung, with its Aryan v. Jewish connotations, and Jones's introduction of himself as a principal player: 'I was in Vienna for June that summer. It was the occasion when I had the idea of the "Committee".' Volume 2 was also to include an account of Anna Freud's trip to England in the autumn of 1914, when war broke out, the war itself and the capture of Freud's son Martin, and finally the post-war psychoanalytic congress in Budapest in 1918 where the treatment of war shock was discussed for the first time. He also included, in the non-narrative part of the biography, more of Freud's famous case histories – including 'Dora', 'Little Hans' and 'the Wolf Man'.

As he wove his text, Jones managed to slip in veiled bits of his own life history, as when describing the trip by Freud and Rank to Budapest in June 1914 'to attend the wedding of an ex-patient, Loe Kann'. 'It is perhaps worth mentioning,' Jones wrote archly, 'because of its being one of the three weddings he ever attended outside his immediate family.' However, he did not think it worth mentioning how fond Freud had become of his wealthy and beautiful patient, nor that she was his own former mistress.

★　　★　　★

The two years devoted to Volume 2 were not spent entirely in research and composition. As many of the people mentioned were still alive – notably Jung – the Hogarth Press's libel lawyer was on the alert. As British libel laws were (and remain) so much stricter than the American ones, Jones was made to understand that only the dead could not be libelled. The burden thus fell on him to provide evidence that certain of those mentioned had died.

The lawyer, Peter Calvocoressi, was in no doubt that Jones had defamed the Freud biographer Helen Puner in his derogatory references to the way she had portrayed Freud's family. One thing, above all, was beyond argument: the statement that 'Jung is crazy' had to go, even if Jones had made it clear that he was quoting Freud's own words. Also, another serious allegation against Jung – that he was anti-Semitic – was risky. When Calvocoressi insisted that the troublesome phrase be watered down, Jones baulked. The likelihood of Jung's suing was so remote that he would undertake to pay all legal costs himself if a case arose. His offer was rejected. Even the phrases about Jung's break with Freud had to be altered to make them less emphatic. The word 'desertion' was even worse than 'defection'; only 'departure' would be acceptable. From New York, Arthur Rosenthal watched with amusement. He saw that Volume 2 might involve some fancy footwork, but hoped it would not have to be resolved by leaving Freud and Jung as fast friends for ever.

It was of no concern to a lawyer that Jones always portrayed himself in a good light in his account of events. When recording, for example, Freud's compliment that Jones had chaired the Berlin psychoanalytic congress very well, he omitted Freud's rebuke contained in the same letter: 'As you ask for my judgment on the way you conducted the Congress I will suppress my habitual frankness with old friends and plainly say that you suffered it to drift occasionally with too weak a hand.'

Perhaps the most astonishing thing about the 534-page *Sigmund Freud: Life and Work: Years of Maturity, 1901–1919* was its appearance just two years after Volume 1. As it went into circulation in September 1955, the second volume got almost as lavish coverage as the first – *Time* gave it six columns, even though puzzled by Freud's persistent antipathy to the United States. On both sides of the Atlantic, the reviewers were respectful: they saw a great biography in the making. Said the anonymous reviewer in *The Times*, 'This is a fine piece of work. Freud emerges as a man like other men but on a grander scale.' For Lionel Trilling, once again in the *New York Times Book Review*, 'the best way to praise it is to say that it is as good as the first volume.' The *Chicago Tribune* declared, 'In every sense this is a Basic Book.'

In London the *Times Literary Supplement* thought Volume 2 brought Freud 'most persuasively to life', and liked Jones's nice phrase about Freud being 'quite peculiarly monogamous'.

The Oxford moral philosopher Stuart Hampshire, writing in *The Observer*, saw the Freud of middle years as 'more than ever single minded, bleak, strong and orderly', climbing mountains, collecting antiquities, and supporting Austria in the First World War. Hampshire liked the way that Jones had brought out the buried life of fantasy and projection revealed in Freud's work.

Like many authors, Jones was sensitive to the slightest criticism, even in an otherwise flattering review, and he did not like Hampshire taking him to task for gullibility, nor his finding psychoanalysis more of a cult than a science. In his review, headlined 'Freud: the Birth of a Creed', Hampshire said that in Jones's pages he could detect 'no suggestion that Freudian theory is one among a set of possible theories'. He disapproved of Jones's uncritical acceptance of pychoanalytic hypotheses as fact: 'Must one accept this claim?' Hampshire nonetheless praised the book as the second volume of 'a great biography', a book of charm which had 'everywhere the authority of first-hand knowledge'.

Readers began to write to Jones with varied queries about Freud. What could he say about Freud's influence on James Joyce? a Leonard Alpert wanted to know. Jones's answer was that he did not know, but in his opinion Joyce was an extremely pathological case.

Much more than after the first volume, the complaints began to come in from those mentioned. The widow of A. A. Brill was so offended by what Jones saw as 'my very mild remarks in Vol. II' (among which were that, around 1914, 'Brill . . . suffered a good deal from suspiciousness') that he was intimidated about what he could say in Volume 3. Freud's personal physician, Max Schur, took issue with Jones's comments on Freud's indiscretion in talking about patients. That was not the Freud that Schur knew: 'For years he referred to me all his patients for physical evaluation and treatment. Never had he given me any detail of the analytic material – beyond the facts essential for the evaluation of the symptoms.' Jones could balance this criticism against his own vivid experience with Loe Kann: from her case, he knew all too well how free Freud could be with the secrets of the consulting room.

To later historians of psychoanalysis, a striking omission from Volume 2 is a mention of the suicide of Victor Tausk. Tausk, a young and attractive Viennese disciple of Freud's, in 1919 managed the feat of shooting and strangling himself at the same time. In *Meeting Freud's Family* Tausk's biographer, Paul Roazen, alleged that Jones had given in to pressure from Anna Freud and had suppressed her father's reactions to Tausk's bizarre death.

Of more concern to students of Jung may be the accusation by the Canadian historian R. Andrew Paskauskas that Jones hid the fact that he himself deliberately engineered the break with Jung in order to advance himself as Freud's chief disciple. In the Paskauskas interpretation of events, Jones formed the Committee *before*, not *after*, Freud's formal break with Jung. However, both Paskauskas and Roazen were writing long after publication of the biography, and long after Jones's death.

In 1956, at a frail seventy-seven, Jones was hard at work on the final volume of his monumental trilogy. The chapter 'London: The End (1938–1939)' gave a dramatic, understated account of his monoplane flight into Vienna in March 1938 to try to talk Freud out of his determination to stay to the end. 'The airfield was stacked with German military planes and the air was full of them assiduously intimidating the Viennese. The streets were full of roaring tanks and also of roaring people with their shouts of Heil Hitler.'

The description of Freud's escape brought in once more a reference to W. C. Bullitt, with whom in 1930 Freud had written an unpublished biography of the American president Woodrow Wilson. Jones expected Bullitt's book to appear much earlier than it finally did (1967), but rightly judged that it would do Freud little credit.

In the chapter 'Fame and Suffering (1926–1933)', Jones depicted Sándor Ferenczi's deterioration and last illness:

> After their meeting in the previous September [1932] Freud and Ferenczi did not again discuss their differences. Freud's feeling for him never changed . . . They continued to exchange letters, the burden of which was mainly Ferenczi's increasingly serious state of health. The medical treatment was successful in holding the anaemia itself at bay, but in March the disease, as it sometimes does, attacked the spinal cord and brain, and for the last couple of months of his life he was unable to stand or walk; this undoubtedly exacerbated his latent psychotic trends.

Two pages later, Jones gave a description of Ferenczi as he lay dying in May 1933:

Then there were the delusions about Freud's supposed hostility. Towards the end came violent paranoiac and even homicidal outbursts, which were followed by a sudden death on May 24 . . . The lurking demons within, against whom Ferenczi had for years struggled with great distress and much success, conquered him at the end.

No lines that Jones ever wrote caused as much anger as these. Although Jones was faithfully following exactly what Freud had written to him, it was Jones who got the blame. After publication of the third volume, many of Ferenczi's friends wrote to Anna objecting to Jones's assessment of Ferenczi's condition in his last years. (Ferenczi died from pernicious anaemia.) The bitterness persists among Ferenczi partisans. Jones's account has been called 'a myth' and 'a travesty of the truth'.

The anger continues also among scholars and followers of Otto Rank, who find Jones's portrait of Rank full of envy and hostility and imputations of insanity – as if Jones were implying that to disagree with the Master were itself a symptom of madness.

In the spring of 1956 Jones underwent an operation for the removal of a growth in the bladder. It was cancer, but, in the fashion of the times, the word was avoided. Still recuperating, and with the third volume of the biography only half finished, Jones accepted an invitation to go to the United States to give lectures celebrating the centenary of Freud's birth.

A fortnight after leaving hospital, with Kitty, he headed for the airport, with his well-used passport. Jones was a small man, grown even smaller with age and illness. Yet his height seemed to increase with successive passports – as did his Welshness. His 1956 passport, carrying the photograph of a very wrinkled face, gave his height as five feet six inches and his birthplace as Llwchwr. In contrast, the passport issued in 1947 had listed his birthplace under its English name, Gower Road, and gave his height as five foot five. So how tall was he? When asked, his son Mervyn answered swiftly, 'Five foot four, like me.'

Jones was, as usual, seemingly inexhaustible. Leaving London for New York on Saturday 14 April, he was ready for an interview with Brendan Gill of the *New Yorker* on Monday morning and another with Harvey Breit of the *New York Times* that afternoon. He had dinner with Edith Jacobson – the former Edith Jacobsohn, once imprisoned in Berlin, now president of the New York Psychoanalytic Society.

There followed a hectic two weeks of travel from Boston to Philadelphia to Chicago, for lectures, television appearances, cocktail parties, banquets and the awarding of a slew of honorary fellowships. The American Psychoanalytic Association made him honorary president. He gave many news-paper interviews, in which he was often asked why Freud so disliked the United States. He said he wished he knew, for it was ironic that Freud's views were accepted more wholeheartedly in America than anywhere else – so much so that the country held two-thirds of the world's analysts.

In Manhattan, Jones gave a lecture at the Town Hall on 'The Nature of Genius', in which he declared (in words that would be unacceptable a decade later) that 'major creative thinking' was 'almost a prerogative of the male sex', a kind of compensation 'for the gift of bodily creation bestowed on women'. 'You leave me no alternative', one woman in the audience protested, 'but to go out and have a baby.' 'Certainly,' responded Jones. 'You won't have difficulty obtaining co-operation.'

To the interviewer from the *New York Post*, he said that he had interrupted the third and final volume of *The Life and Work of Sigmund Freud* to write the series of lectures he was then giving. He also boasted about his textbook on figure skating. (A revised, enlarged and illustrated edition of *The Elements of Figure Skating* had come out in 1952, dedicated 'To My Partner, Katherine' and carrying next to his name his proud new designation 'F.R.C.P.'.) The *Post* described his pleasure in the book: ' "It is *the* standard one on figure skating." He pursed his lips thoughtfully. "Yes," he concluded. "You can quite fairly call it that." '

Jones was astonished that the reporter did not know shorthand. 'Scandalous! I taught it to myself at 12,' he said scornfully. The interviewer found him to be 'a tart little Welshman, thin as a wishbone, as unrelentingly alert as radar'.

In Philadelphia, Jones was equally spirited during an interview with the *Inquirer*, which described him reverentially as 'the world's most renowned psychoanalyst'. When the interviewer referred to a means of 'transportation', Jones burst into laughter. ' "Transportation" is what we provide prisoners being taken to jail,' he explained. He found American intimacy startling, but indulged in a personal description of his blurred cultural identity by explaining that his ready adaptation to opposing cultures derived from the geographical fact that his native parish of Llwchwr stood on the border of two counties in Wales.

He was back from his whirlwind American tour in time to unveil a London Country Council plaque at 20 Maresfield Gardens on the very centenary of Freud's birth, 6 May 1956, and he gave one of the centennial lectures, 'The Nature of Genius'.

Anna Freud was once more full of admiration. 'You were quite marvellous . . . The talk on the wireless was extraordinary in its clarity, lucidity, simplicity and honesty with absence of all frills . . . Also on television I liked you very much.' Even so, when Jones was invited to act as an adviser to John Huston's planned film on Freud, she persuaded him against it. (*Freud*, starring Montgomery Clift, came out in 1962.)

Anna told Jones she wished him a long stretch of time in which to do nothing. He had no such luxury. The third volume of the *The Life and Works*, to be subtitled, *The Last Phase, 1919–1939*, was to come out the following year. In his preface, Jones gave special and deserved thanks to Freud's physician, Max Schur, who had secured the notes of Freud's surgical treatment over sixteen years and had also given him a forty-page essay on Freud's illnesses.

These graphic physical details, deftly presented, gave power and poignancy to the end of the story. Drawing on Schur, Jones was able to say that in August 1939 Freud's wound developed 'an unpleasant odour . . . so that when his favourite chow was brought to visit him she shrank into a far corner of the room'. Thanks to Schur, Jones also had the jewel of Freud's comments: hearing a broadcaster announce on 3 September 1939 that this was to be the last war, he had responded, 'Anyhow it is my last war.'

Jones described how at the end Freud found it hardly possible to eat anything. As he told the story, 'The cancer ate its way through the cheek to the outside and the septic condition was heightened. The exhaustion was extreme and the misery indescribable.' Then, thanks to Schur, Jones recorded Freud's dying plea: 'My dear Schur, you remember our first talk. You promised me then you would help me when I could no longer carry on. It is only torture now and it has no longer any sense.'

It was then, Jones knew, that Schur gave Freud a third of a grain of morphia: 'For someone at such a point of exhaustion as Freud then was, and so complete a stranger to opiates, that small dose sufficed. He sighed with relief and sank into a peaceful sleep . . . He died just before midnight the next day, September 23, 1939. His long and arduous life was at an end and his sufferings over. Freud died as he had lived – a realist.'

A second coronary attack, in June 1957, did not prevent Jones from going to Paris for the Twentieth Congress of the International Psychoanalytic Association at end of July and early August. It was an interesting venue, for the French Psychoanalytical Society had been riven by splits far worse than those of the British Society. Between 1953 and 1954 its vice-president, Jacques Lacan, had walked out and founded his own school of psychoanalysis, the Société Française de Psychanalyse, based on his theory that the human psyche was revealed in the structure of its language.

At the congress, as had become traditional, Jones read the opening paper. As if he knew it would be his valediction, 'The Birth and Death of Moses' was an elegant tour de force. He began by exploring the circumstances leading to Freud's last book, *Moses and Monotheism*: the first draft had been written about 1934, the year after Hitler had seized power. Said Jones, 'The frightful outburst of anti-semitism in Germany raised once more, and in an urgent fashion, the old problem that had always occupied Freud: namely, the meaning of Judaism and its relation to the Gentile world.'

Freud, he continued, had long identified deeply with the figure of Moses, and had studied intently the Michelangelo statue of the prophet in Rome. Then Jones, in an erudite but conversational manner, traced the anthropological and scholarly evidence that had led Freud to decide that Moses was really an Egyptian, not a Jew. Freud then seized upon the interpretations of some passages in biblical scholarship that had Moses slain by the wandering tribe of Jews he commanded. These, according to Jones, fitted so well with Freud's own views on parricide that he was determined to publish his book even though he knew it would offend the Jewish world, as it did. In conclusion, after referring to his own correspondence with Hebrew scholars and to his own research into the question of whether Moses was murdered, Jones distanced himself from Freud's supposition that the subsequent guilt at the murder of Moses was so strong that it permanently affected the mentality of Jews. That, declared Jones, 'is certainly the most temerarious of all his conclusions'.

The use of 'temerarious' – an archaic word for 'blind, reckless, heedless, rash' – allowed Jones to distance himself from Freud's Lamarckian notion that guilt is an acquired characteristic that can be genetically inherited. To prove Freud's thesis, Jones concluded, would require establishing that Jews are burdened with a greater sense of guilt than other people: 'It is an arena into which I do not propose to enter.'

A photograph taken of him with Anna Freud and Marie Bonaparte at the Paris congress shows a jaunty geriatric, with grey-flecked beard and buttoned-up waistcoat. When the time came to thank him for his service to the International Association, he was given an ovation. Sacha Nacht, a Parisian analyst sitting beside Jones, saw silent tears running down his cheeks.

During that trip, Jones suffered a haemorrhage of the eye. He also gave a filmed interview for American educational television. In it he read his concluding words in the about-to-be-published final volume of his biography of Freud:

Man's chief enemy and danger is his own unruly nature and the dark forces pent up within him.

If our race is lucky enough to survive for another thousand years the name of Sigmund Freud will be remembered as that of the man who first ascertained the origin and nature of those forces, and pointed the way to achieving some measure of control over them.

The final volume of his biography was published that autumn. The reviews were excellent and elegiac. Trilling, once more in the *New York Times*, reached a climax of praise: 'There can be no question but that the completed book is what the two earlier volumes promised it would be – one of the important documents in the cultural history of our time.' *The Economist* called the book 'in some ways the most impressive and revealing' of the trilogy, and acknowledged Freud to have been 'one of the great personalities of the recent past'. The *Manchester Guardian*'s reviewer said that the three volumes 'go beyond a biography in the narrow sense. They provide a history of the psychoanalytic movement, written by one best able to judge it.' George Steiner, writing later in *The Reporter*, declared that 'to say that Ernest Jones's *Life and Work of Sigmund Freud* is a modern classic is a truism.'

The reaction to his comments about Ferenczi, on the other hand, was swift. The Hungarian-born analyst Michael Balint, despite a recent weekend visit to The Plat, wrote a strong letter of complaint to Jones's old *Journal*. Jones's picture of a mad Ferenczi, said Balint, contradicted the evidence of those who had known him. He left the contradiction for the next generation to sort out. Jones replied, for the same publication, saying tersely that his comments had been based on evidence supplied by someone who had observed Ferenczi's mental state in his last days.

A fine addition to Jones's collection of admiring reviews came from his elder son. Just before his father's seventy-ninth birthday, Mervyn, by then a drama critic and the author of four novels, wrote to 'Dear Dad' to say that the third volume of the biography was the best of the three:

> It moves very easily and smoothly, and the details never obscure the important elements in the story . . . I could quite easily have read the whole first part at a sitting like a good novel . . . And you've completely mastered the difficult art of writing at one consistent level instead of sometimes for a reader who understands psycho-analysis and sometimes for a reader who doesn't . . .
>
> The narrative part is really a model of how to write a biography
> We all send you warmest wishes for 1958.

Jones did not see much of 1958. Cancer appeared in his liver, and sent him back by ambulance to London, to University College Hospital. Such was Jones's faith in UCH that he trusted its staff would know what to do.

They knew that they could do nothing, and told Kitty that further treatment would be useless. Jones lay in his hospital bed in pain and reverie. He was alarmed to find himself dreaming of people singing hymns – religious music he had not heard since his Sunday-school days in Gowerton. He was alarmed too when, a few days before his death, Mervyn suggested rephrasing a line in the text of *Free Associations*, his uncompleted autobiography. 'No, no, no,' said Jones. 'Makes the sentence clumsy.'

At the conclusion of his epic biography, Jones had written a fine deathbed scene. Now he played it. He asked his doctor to give him something to end the suffering. With his wife at his side, he, in her words, 'took a pill'. On 11 February 1958 he died as he had lived – in charge.

Postscript

Anthony Burgess's novel *The End of the World News*, published in 1982, depicts the end of three eras: one marked by Freud's life, the next by the 1917 Russian Revolution, and the last by the millennium from AD 1000 to 2000. The book opens with Dr Ernest Jones flying into Vienna after the *Anschluss* in March 1938. There are swastikas and military aircraft everywhere. An official with a Nazi brassard is sneering at the proffered passports. He asks Jones why he is coming to Vienna.

> *'Ich komme nach Wien, weil ich Wien liebe.'* Come because like the place.
> . . . Speak good for Englander. Passport says doctor. What does English doctor want here?
> *'Ich bin,'* Jones said, *'kein Engländer. Ich bin Waliser. Ich bin Berater der Psychiatrie. Wien ist das Zentrum der psychoanalytischen Bewegung.'* Welsh. Psychiatric consultant. Vienna centre of psychoanalytical movement.
> . . . Not any longer. Filth of Jew Freud, you mean. Surprised at you, doctor. Welsh are Aryans.
> *'Arisch'*, Jones affirmed . . . Aryan a linguistic term. Not sure what mean by Jew.

When, with great charm, the official stamped Jones's passport, 'Jones smiled something filthy in Welsh and then went to look for a telephone.'

Jones would have been pleased to be thus mythologized, especially by an acclaimed novelist re-creating a scene from the third volume of the Freud biography almost in Jones's own words. The dramatic event featured in *The Times*'s obituary of Jones the day after his death in February 1958:

> It was not only in the world of scientific achievement that Jones was outstanding. He had qualities of leadership, courage, and strength of character which showed themselves at their most brilliant when the Nazis invaded Austria, and Freud himself and the large group of analysts in Vienna were in the gravest danger.
> It was Jones's superhuman efforts which led to a happy outcome and

enabled Freud to end his life peacefully in London, and also enriched
British and American psychiatry by the influx of refugee analysts.

The Times's obituary paid Jones every compliment he could have
wished. It pronounced him 'the natural and undisputed leader from the
beginning' of psychoanalysis in England. It called his study of Hamlet
outstanding, his biography of Freud a masterpiece. The accolades did not
stop there. Even in his hobbies, *The Times* said, Jones was outstanding. It
mentioned his skating and his expertise in chess, and also the 'magnificent
support he received from his wife, Katherine Jokl'.

The *Manchester Guardian* singled out Jones's monumental biography of
Freud: 'It is hard to say who was the more fortunate, the biographer in
having such a subject or the subject in having such a biographer.' The
Sunday Times called him 'a formidable fighter who could claim a brilliant
list of qualifications as his credentials, which partly accounted for his
effectiveness as a "controversialist": By his death we lose a teacher and a
practitioner who made a great professional greater still.' *The Lancet* focused
on his professional standing – 'the most eminent psychoanalyst since the
death of Freud' – while the *South Wales Evening Post*, headlining its
obituary 'The Friend of Freud', recalled Jones's regret that he had trained
students from Chile to Japan but never one from Wales. The *British
Medical Journal* noted his 'gladiatorial' phase, but boasted that it had published several of his papers and extolled him not only as a voluminous
writer but also as a master of lucid but erudite exposition 'of whom it
could be said that whatever he wrote was worth reading'. In an accompanying note Joan Riviere paid tribute to Jones's 'quite exceptional
personality', with remarkable perception, insight and 'a propensity to
recognize evidences of intrinsic worth'.

Jones was cremated at Golders Green Crematorium on 14 February
1958. His ashes were taken to the Gower and placed in the grave at the
Church of St Cadoc in Cheriton, below Llanmadoc, where his little
daughter Gwenith was buried. The same plot in 1983 would also hold
the ashes of Katherine Jones, who died in London after a long and active
widowhood in which she too became a psychotherapist. It was perhaps
owing to Jones's own vigilant campaigning that the Conservative government had in 1957 designated the Gower 'an area of outstanding natural
beauty' – the first stretch of landscape in Britain to receive this protection
against development.

Despite his book sales, Jones did not die a rich man. His wealth at
death was reported at £18,037. 5s. 3d. A not inconsiderable sum at the

time, it represented what he had left after providing for his family in many ways, such as buying a house for Mervyn and his wife. His half-finished, unindexed autobiography, *Free Associations*, was published in 1959. Considering how much of himself Jones put into the Freud biography, the loss of the second half of his autobiography is not very great. He artfully concealed more than he disclosed: hard facts are in short supply, and the manuscript (to his widow's regret) stopped with him at forty. That was before he had achieved his happy marriage and family life, and before he had embarked on his prodigious feats of writing, editing and governing the world of psychoanalysis.

The jury is still out on Ernest Jones, but it ought not to be. His biography of Freud still stands as a monumental work, the essential guide to the life of Freud and the dawn of psychoanalysis. As Freud's first major biographer, he made errors and omissions that those who came later rushed to point out. Indeed, according to Sonu Shamdasani in the *New Oxford Dictionary of National Biography*, 'the larger share of subsequent Freud scholarship has consisted of corrections and revisions of Jones's account.'

A similar pattern of objections and corrections can be found in the wake of many first biographies written about famous figures. The factual errors of the original biographer become more glaring with repeated exposure over time as new letters and new information come to light. Also, social attitudes change with time and reproach the past. As often as not, moreover, the authorized biographer has censored certain parts of the story out of respect for the feelings of family and those others who have allowed access to private material. A conspicuous example is Sir Roy Harrod's fine biography of John Maynard Keynes, published in 1951. Out of consideration for Keynes's family, Harrod omitted any mention of Keynes's homosexuality. A complete story of Keynes's life had to wait until the first volume of Robert Skidelsky's trilogy in 1983, which appeared well after homosexual behaviour had been decriminalized.

Similarly, Richard Ellmann's great biography of James Joyce, first published in 1959, was accused of presenting Joyce's brother Stanislaus in a more favourable light than was Joyce himself, because Stanislaus had given Ellmann access to invaluable material on Joyce's early life. As for Ellmann's acclaimed 1988 biography of Oscar Wilde, a Wilde enthusiast in Germany self-published two hardback editions of corrections to the hundreds of errors he detected in Ellmann's work.

A welcome, measured assessment of Jones's Freud biography appeared in 1979 in a short biography of Jones himself by a fellow South Walian.

In *Ernest Jones*, T. G. Davies, professor of the history of medicine at the University of Wales at Swansea, found Jones too uncritical of Freud and too unwilling to place him in his proper place as one of a series of thinkers who gradually developed the idea of the unconscious. Davies also regretted that Jones had described Freud as psychologically mature while providing a detailed account of Freud's neurotic tendencies. All the same, Davies concluded, 'the description of the last 18 months of Freud's life justifies the biography and shows that Jones was the best biographer Freud could have had.'

'The record', to quote Jones's autobiography, 'is incomplete.' The present is always reshaping the past. Some years after his father's death, sitting in a pub in Llanmadoc, Mervyn Jones fell into conversation with an elderly local. 'Does the name "Freud" mean anything to you?' the man asked. Mervyn allowed that it did. 'Well,' confided the native, 'Freud spent the last years of his life in this village.'

The 'Freud was here' story – still current in Llanmadoc – would seem to fall into the category of what the late Joycean scholar Hugh Kenner called 'Irish Facts' : anecdotes that sound so good that they might as well be true. There is no evidence that Freud ever ventured to Wales. However, as one fascinated by telepathy, he might not have been surprised that his aura should hover over the tiny spot on the globe that his chief disciple loved best. Freud's name is indeed honoured on the Gower. On the plaque hanging on the railings of the Church of St Cadoc to inform visitors of the important grave that lies in its cemetery, Freud's name is engraved – coupled with, but below, that of his disciple and biographer Dr Ernest Jones.

Notes

Full details of books cited in short-title form will be found in the Bibliography

Abbreviations

AF	Anna Freud
AS	Alix Strachey
BM	Brenda Maddox
BPAS	Archives of the British Psycho-Analytical Society, Institute of Psychoanalysis
Brabant	Eva Brabant et al., eds., *The Correspondence of Sigmund Freud and Sándor Ferenczi*: vol. 1, *1908–1914*; vol. 2, *1914–1919*
Brecht	K. Brecht et al., eds., *Here Life Goes on in a Most Peculiar Way*
Brome	Vincent Brome, *Ernest Jones: Freud's Alter Ego*
CGJ	Carl Gustav Jung
Davies, R.	Rhian Davies, *Never So Pure a Sight*
EJ	Ernest Jones
FA	Ernest Jones, *Free Associations* (1959)
Falzeder	Ernst Falzeder et al., eds., *The Correspondence of Sigmund Freud and Sándor Ferenczi*: vol. 2, *1914–1919*; vol. 3, *1920–1933*
Fer	Sándor Ferenczi
Gay	Peter Gay, *Freud: A Life for Our Time* (Norton)
Grosskurth-Kl	Phyllis Grosskurth, *Melanie Klein*
Grosskurth-R	Phyllis Grosskurth, *The Secret Ring*
Hale-JJP	Nathan G. Hale, Jr, ed., *James Jackson Putnam and Psychoanalysis*
Hughes	Athol Hughes, ed., *The Inner World and Joan Riviere*
IJP-A	*International Journal of Psycho-Analysis*
J–I	Ernest Jones, *Sigmund Freud: Life and Work*, vol. 1 (1953)
J–II	Ernest Jones, *Sigmund Freud: Life and Work*, vol. 2 (1955)
J–III	Ernest Jones, *Sigmund Freud: Life and Work*, vol. 3 (1957)
JJP	James Jackson Putnam
JR	Joan Riviere
JS	James Strachey
KJ	Katherine Jokl Jones
KMGDO	*Kent Mail and Greenwich and Deptford Observer*
Leys	Ruth Leys, 'Meyer's Dealings with Jones'

McGuire	William McGuire, ed., *The Freud/Jung Letters*
ME	Max Eitingon
Meisel	James and Alix Strachey, *Bloomsbury/Freud*, ed. Perry Meisel and Walter Kendrick
MJ	Mervyn Jones
MO	Morfydd Owen
Paskauskas	R. Andrew Paskauskas, ed., *The Complete Correspondence of Sigmund Freud and Ernest Jones*
SE	Sigmund Freud, *The Standard Edition of the Complete Psychological Works*
Steiner	Riccardo Steiner, '*It is a New Kind of Diaspora*'

Introduction

1. 'It is statistically demonstrable'. *FA*, 8.
   Beddoe-Jones, *FA*, 10.
   'I only know'. SF to EJ, 23 Mar. 1922, Paskauskas, 464.
   'Whatever he wrote'. Obituary: 'Ernest Jones, M. D. D.Sc. F.R.C.P.,' *British Medical Journal*, 22 Feb. 1958.
   'his expositions'. Roazen, *Freud and His Followers*, 351.
2. 'Freud's Rottweiler'. Robertson, Ritchie, 'A Case of Pen Envy', *Times Literary Supplement*, 27 Oct. 2000, 11.
   'Jones makes trouble'. SF to Fer, 18 July 1925, Young-Bruehl, *Anna Freud*, 475, n. 60.
3. '*Shabbes-Goy*'. *FA*, 200.
   'no more than'. Crick, *The Astonishing Hypothesis*, 3
   'but rather a physician'. Ibid., 14.
   'various wrong tendencies'. EJ to SF, 30 Jan. 1912, Paskauskas, 130.
4. 'irresistible to women'. JR to EJ, 12 Oct. 1919, BPAS.

Prologue

5. 'an eminent psychoanalyst'. Foreign Office telegram to Mr Mack (Vienna), 15 Mar. 1938, National Archives, R 2890/2890/3.
   'the practice of psychoanalysis'. From the magazine *Deutsche Volksgesundheit aus Blut und Boden*, Aug./Sept. 1933, trans. Brecht, 101.
   'Germanic soul'. Clark, *Freud*, 490; quoted also in Cornwell, *Hitler's Scientists*, 160.
   'Nothing can lastingly'. EJ to SF, 18 Sept. 1933, Paskauskas, 728.
6. 'I never left'. J–III, 235.
   'between beloved friends'. J–III, 240; slightly different translation of SF to EJ, 28 Apr. 1938, in Paskauskas, 762.

Chapter 1: The Celt

7. 'He is a Celt'. SF to CGJ, 18 July 1908, McGuire, 165.
   As the population grew. Details of the town's renaming in *FA*, 1.
   Myrddin. *FA*, 2.
10. She taught young Ernest. *FA*, 20.
   'evidently a Celt'. *FA*, 11.
   'a new race . . . all comers'. Edwards, *David Lloyd George*, 1:5.
11. Glendower's death is reported as good news. *2 Henry IV*, III.i.97–8.
   'We have never quarrelled'. Edwards, *David Lloyd George*, 2:210.
12. It was a minister's son. *FA*, 21.
   a gift from Queen Victoria. *FA*, 31.
   'handsome dashing fellow'. Ibid.
   'at the ages of six and seven'. *FA*, 21.
   'Coitus . . . this minute'. *FA*, 21.
14. 'very good . . . too talkative'. Comments from Swansea Grammar School reports,
   EJ archive, BPAS.
   'in the Counties'. Jones's birth certifcate.

Chapter 2: For Wales, See England

15. 'especially for young men'. R. B. Jones, *Floreat Landubriense*, 15.
   ranked a proud third. W. G. Evans, *Llandovery College*, 50.
16. 'never let us forget'. *FA*, 35.
   'The English are notoriously hard to understand'. *FA*, 35.
   'As never man'. EJ's schoolboy notebooks, headed 'The College, Llandovery',
   BPAS.
   dreaming (so he later claimed). *FA*, 36.
17. 'educational work'. W. G. Evans, *Llandovery College*, 51.
   'Those who were late'. A. Pierce Jones, '[Masters] 1892–1908', in R. B. Jones,
   Floreat Landubriense, 99.
   'the depths of cruelty'. *FA*, 39–40.
   'serious vogue'. *FA*, 40.
   'There is plenty of room at the top'. *FA*, 31–2.
19. 'before breakfast'. *FA*, 56.
   'a year or two . . . adoring order'. *FA*, 55.
   'after which I did not resume it'. *FA*, 21.
   'every-day observation'. EJ, 'The Differences between the Sexes in the Development
   of Speech' (1909), 416.
20. 'irregular attendance'. *FA*, 43.
21. 'the Cardiff medical school proper'. *FA*, 45.
   First admitted to Trinity College, Dublin. Parkes, *A Danger to the Men?*, 51.
   'lurid'. *FA*, 46.
   'a red-haired Irishman'. *FA*, 45.
   'upwards and backwards'. Ibid.

Chapter 3: Thus Far and No Further

22. 'Opinionated, tactless, conceited'. *FA*, 86.

a philosophical materialist. *FA*, 49.

23. 'where all the upper class dilettantes go'. Brome, 203.

'gracefully reclined'. This and the following quote from EJ, 'Our Search for Digs', *Magazine of the University College of South Wales and Monmouthshire*, session 1898–9, 62–3. Cardiff University, Library Archives.

Sylvia Plath recounted. Plath, *The Bell Jar*, ch. 6.

'the Holy Trinity'. *FA*, 67.

'some embracing'. *FA*, 68.

24. 'a reaction'. *FA*, 64.

'the little fellow . . . hold him'. *FA*, 69.

25. 'Glamorganites who wander'. *South Walian*, Jan.–Feb. 1903.

26. 'the abdomen, the chest and the brain'. Porter, *The Greatest Benefit to Mankind*, 374.

Jones, in his autobiography. *FA*, 77–8.

27. 'I gave them a good wash'. *FA*, 77.

'an old frock-coat'. *FA*, 75.

'clerking for a full year'. *FA*, 71.

28. 'a lesion in or near the cortex'. 'A Case of Tumor Cerebri in Which Rotation of the Tongue was Present', *Lancet*, 23 Sept. 1901, 848–9.

'the most inspiring teacher'. *FA*, 73.

'General Paralysis of the Insane'. 'Crumbs from the Life of John Rose Bradford', EJ's Notebooks, University College Hospital Archives.

'A Clinical Classification'. Ibid.

Bradford later said. Brome, 25.

'stupid'. EJ to SF, 19 Mar. 1909, Paskauskas, 21.

29. 'despicable race'. EJ to SF, 10 Dec. 1908, Paskauskas, 11.

'opinionated, tactless, conceited'. *FA*, 86.

'Mr Anaesthetist'. *FA*, 93.

'What are the signs'. These questions appear in the final examination papers taken by Jones on 5 April 1900 (midwifery) and on 3, 4 and 6 July (medicine). The papers, in the EJ archives, were set by the Royal College of Physicians in London and the Royal College of Surgeons in England.

'Describe the three best methods'. University of London MB Pass Examination, 28 Oct. 1901, EJ archives, BPAS.

'My darling Ernest'. Mary Ann Jones to EJ, 6 Dec. 1901, BPAS.

30. 'my omnipotence complex'. *FA*, 95.

'irresistible to women'. JR to EJ, 12 Oct. 1919, BPAS.

'she made a dash'. *FA*, 100.

'a love scene'. Ibid.

31. Jones's autobiography suggests. Ibid.

'for the deep sorrow'. W. J. Morris to EJ, 2 Nov. 1902, BPAS.

32. 'more serious enemies'. *FA*, 102. But *Free Associations* is economical with the truth.

Hospital records quoted by T. G. Davies (*Ernest Jones*, 23) and by Brome (29, n. 33) show this to have been the third time he had been absent without the formal leave the hospital's rules required.

He was never to hold. Philip Kuhn to BM, 25 Mar. 2006, maintains that Jones's autobiography rationalizes his failures in losing out to doctors who were actually much better qualified than he.

'My darling Boy'. Thomas Jones to EJ, 20 Dec. 1903, BPAS.

'My dear Genius'. J. F. Jennings to EJ, 28 Jan. 1904, BPAS, CJA/F12/03.

'an exceedingly well read man'. Testimonial from John Rose Bradford, n.d., BPAS.

'In my opinion'. Testimonial from T. D. Acland, 25 Jan. 1904, BPAS.

33. 'that Jones did not get on'. Thomas Jones to EJ, 26 Feb. 1904, BPAS.

'This is most important to you'. Ibid.

Chapter 4: Record Incomplete

35. 'In what I have had to say'. *FA*, xxi.

'Hospital Staff'. H. W. Wagstaff to EJ, 10 May 1904. BPAS.

Dreadnought Seamen's Hospital. Post described in EJ's application to the West End Hospital for Diseases of the Nervous System, Sept. 1907, BPAS.

36. 'years older'. *FA*, 121.

'We shall stay'. Mary Ann Jones to EJ, 4 May 1904, BPAS.

their letterhead. EJ archive, BPAS.

37. performed a double amputation. *FA*, 90.

'chatted as they did up their boots'. W. Trotter to EJ, 19 Mar. 1909, cited in *FA*, 173.

'capable of becoming a guide'. Trotter, *Instincts of the Herd*, 6.

38. Jones recalled. *FA*, 149.

'the beginnings of psycho-analysis'. J–I, 277.

'for motives of'. J–I, 397, n. 1. *SE* 7:3 suggests Oct./Nov. 1905.

The case described. A useful summary of the case of 'Dora' is in Gay, 246–55.

'direct our first'. [Interpretation of Dreams, trans. A. A. Brill, Allen, 1942 ed. p. 256.]

39. 'senseless and worthless'. Freud letter, quoted in Gay, 71.

'I began practising'. *FA*, 152.

'From an interview'. Lancelot Whyte interview quoted in Brome, 44–5. See also EJ, 'Mechanism of Severe Briquet Attack' (1907).

from his correspondence. T. Ellen to EJ, 16 Aug. 1910, BPAS, CJA/F09/02.

'tranquility to a mind'. Ibid.

40. 'I came away'. *FA*, 149–50.

'written in a fluent style'. J. J. Putnam, 'Recent Experiences in the Study and Treatment of Hysteria at the Massachusetts General Hospital, with Remarks on Freud's Method of Treatment by "Psychoanalysis"', *Journal of Abnormal Psychology*, 1 (1906):26–41.

'a manifestation'. Boris Sidis, 'The Psychopathology of Everyday Life (*Zur Psychopathologie des Alltagslebens*)', *Journal of Abnormal Psychology*, 2 (1907), 101.

'The Forces'. Programme for the Third Annual Dinner of the Glamorgan Society, London, 25 Feb. 1905, BPAS.

almost ceased to be a Welshman. *FA*, 63.

41. 'From the point of view of medical knowledge'. *News of the World*, 1 Apr. 1906, 13.

41. 'a very considerable position'. *News of the World*, 25 Mar. 1906, 8.
    'Is it in connection'. *KMGDO*, 23 Mar. 1906, 5.
    'The table-cover'. Ibid.
    'Doctor,' he said. *FA*, 136.
    'I have nothing to say'. *KMGDO*, 23 Mar. 1906, 5.
42. 'He can cut his bloody throat'. *FA*, 136.
    'Harley-St Physician'. *News of the World*, 25 Mar. 1906, p. 9.
    to reconstruct the case against Jones. Kuhn, ' "Romancing with a Wealth of
    Detail" '.
    'acted in a grossly indecent manner'. Ibid., 368, taken from *KMGDO*, 30 Mar.
    1906, 8f.
    'if she complied'. Ibid.
    'she tried to do so'. Ibid., 367.
43. 'Dr Jones spoke'. Ibid., 354, based on *KMGDO*, 13 Apr. 1906, 5a.
    'shameful, disgraceful and disgusting'. Ibid., 355, based on *KMGDO*, 13 Apr.
    1906, 5a.
    'My good woman'. Ibid.
    'I am afraid . . . never occurred'. Ibid.
    'If you try to quieten me'. Ibid.
    'certain marks upon it'. *KMGDO*, 30 Mar. 1906, 83.
44. 'Can one really say it?'. Woolf, *Moments of Being*, 173.
    'Ladies were asked'. Kuhn, 365, from *Cambrian Daily Leader*, 1 May 1906, 8d.
    'In his opinion'. Kuhn, 369, from *Cambrian Daily Leader*, 24 Apr. 1906, 6c.
    'dapper and alert-looking'. Kuhn 360, from *KMGDO*, 30 Mar. 1906, 8e–f.
    'THE MAGISTRATE'. 'Ex-Gowerton Doctor. Assault Charge Dismissed at Green-
    wich', *Cambrian Daily Leader*, EJ archives, BPAS; see also Kuhn, 364, drawn from
    KMGDO.
    'BODKIN'. 'Medical Man's Ordeal', *Daily Post*, EJ archives, BPAS; also Kuhn 372,
    based on *KMGDO*, 5 May 1906, 5f.
45. 'took the unusual step'. *FA*, 137. The letter, surprisingly, does not appear in EJ's
    extensive archive on the case.
    'My dear old chap'. Dyke, [no surname] to EJ, Sunday. n.d., EJ archive. *FA*, 97
    refers to Sir Dyke Duckworth.
    'cheeky courage'. George W. Waugh to EJ, 14 Apr. 1906, EJ archive.
    'Many of your professional brethren'. S. Rowland Fotherill to EJ, 5 May 1906, EJ
    archive.
    'Dr Alfred Ernest Jones'. *Lancet*, 5 May 1906.
    'The Infamous Accusation'. Ibid., 15 May 1906.
    'happily concluded'. 'A Charge Dismissed', *British Medical Journal*, 5 May 1906, 1076.
    'Welsh Doctor Vindicated'. *South Wales Daily Press*, date n.a.
    'Ex-Gowerton Doctor'. *Cambrian Daily Leader*, 1 May 1906.
46. 'two small children'. *FA*, 135.
    'made the panicky decision'. Ibid.
    'baby'. Kuhn, 364, drawn from *Evening Express and Evening Mail*, 1 May 1906, 3b.
    'most disagreeable experience'. *FA*, 135; for date of composition, see MJ's introduc-
    tion, *FA*, ix.

47. 'about the ridiculous charges'. D. Eder to EJ, 30 Apr. 1906, BPAS CEA/F18/06.
   entertain the delegation. *FA*, 130.
   'this unwelcome petticoat influence'. *FA*, 122.
   his own emotional problems. I. Tuckett to EJ, 4 July 1906, BPAS.
   'best wishes'. I. Tuckett to EJ, 11 July 1906, BPAS, CEA/F18/06.

48. Loe's flat. From 1906 'Miss Louise Kann' is listed in *Kelly's Directory* as the occupant
   of 6 Hanover House, St John's Wood High Street.
   'less than candid'. *FA*, xxi.

Chapter 5: Freud to the Rescue

50. as Jung acknowledged. *Diagnostische Assoziatonsstudien* (*Diagnostic Studies in Associ-*
   ation), 1906, quoted in J–II, 34.
   'Such', exclaimed Jones. J–II, 36.
   die Sache. J–II, 54, note I, says, 'Freud always used the expression "*die Sache*" for
   psycho-analysis.'

51. The paper Jones delivered. 'The Clinical Significance of Allochiria', Transactions of
   the First International Congress of Psychiatry, Neurology and Psychology, Amsterdam', *Lancet*, Vol. LXXXV, 830–32.
   'I got back from Amsterdam'. CGJ to SF, 11 Sept. 1907, McGuire, 84–6.
   'The Celt who surprised you'. SF to CGJ, 19 Sept. 1907, McGuire, 88.
   'magnetic passion'. Gay, 50, quoting P. Janet, *L'Etat mental des hystériques* (1892;2nd
   edn, 1911), 132–5.

52. 'splendid isolation'. SF to CGJ, 10 Apr. 1908, McGuire, 141.
   'psychoanalysis'. J–I, 269, dates the first use of the term to a Freud paper of 30 Mar.
   1896.
   'brought the maximum of odium'. J–II, 321.

53. 'free association'. J–I, 265ff.
   'the somewhat estranged offspring'. Michael Howard and W. Roger Louis, eds.,
   Oxford History of the Twentieth Century (Oxford: Oxford University Press, 1998), 68.
   'successor and crown prince'. SF to CGJ, 15 Apr. 1909, McGuire, 218.
   'son and heir'. Bair, *Jung*, 115, quoting Ludwig Binswanger, *Sigmund Freud: Remi-*
   niscences of a Friendship (New York: Grune & Stratton, 1957), 3.
   the only truly original mind. J–II, 37, observation derived from SF to CGJ,
   25 Feb. 1908, McGuire, 126.

54. 'Dr Gross tells me'. CGJ to SF, 25 Sept. 1907, McGuire, 90.
   Sabina Spielrein. See Hayman, *Jung*, 102; Bair, *Jung*, 181.
   'depression'. *American Pocket Medical Dictionary*.

55. 'In that autumn'. EJ to SF, 18 May 1914, Paskauskas, 281.
   his portrait in D. H. Lawrence's novel. See Lawrence, *Mr Noon* (London: Grafton
   Books, 1985), 160.
   'penetrative power . . . ever met'. *FA*, 163–4.
   'many interesting talks'. CGJ to EJ, 23 Nov. 1907, Brome, 47.

56. 'We didn't invite Dr Jones'. J–II, 43.
   'Dr Jones of London'. CGJ to SF, 30 Nov. 1907, McGuire, 101.

'your Englishman appeals to me'. SF to CGJ, 8 Dec. 1907, McGuire, 102.

57. 'fascinating and really important'. J–II, 31.

F. W. H. Myers. J–I, 275.

allied investigators. Richard Noakes, 'Unusual Physics; Negotiating the Borderland between Physical and Psychical Research in Late-Victorian Britain', lecture notes, Royal Institution of Great Britain, 29 June 2004, 6.

'automatic writing'. Abstract by Isador H. Coriat of 'On a Series of Automatic Writings' by Mrs A. W. Verrall, *Journal of Abnormal Psychology*, 1/5 (Dec. 1906): 226–9.

neurasthenia. *American Pocket Medical Dictionary*.

58. 'At this time'. EJ, 'Mechanism of Severe Briquet Attack' (1907).

Campbell challenged him. *FA*, 140.

59. Jones's explanation. Ibid.

'It has come to my knowledge'. Ian Malcolm to EJ, 23 Mar. 1908, BPAS.

60. 'We have come to the conclusion'. Ian Malcolm to EJ, 27 Mar. 1908, BPAS.

'a great opportunity'. Reported in C. Clarke to W. J. Hanna, 29 Oct. 1908, quoted in Cyril Greenland, 'Ernest Jones in Toronto', Part II, 513.

Jones liked what he saw. J–II, 43.

61. From its shape. Ibid.

'What we most need'. *FA*, 181.

'by far the more beautiful'. SF to CGJ, 21 Dec. 1907, McGuire, 104.

'my talkative Viennese'. SF to CGJ, 17 Feb. 1908, McGuire, 119.

'human behaviour'. EJ, 'Rationalisation in Everyday Life' (1909), 166.

62. 'We are doctors'. Stekel, *Autobiography*, 122.

'morose . . . sulky'. *FA*, 159.

63. 'We are still so few'. J–II, 47–8 quotes Freud's letter to Abraham without a date.

'rift in the making'. SF to CGJ, 3 May 1908, McGuire, 145.

'It will be very important'. EJ to SF, 13 May 1908, Paskauskas, 2–3 and n. 3.

64. 'Jones wants to go to Munich'. SF to CGJ, 3 May 1908, McGuire, 146.

'deeply in love . . . time to send me'. EJ to SF, 13 May 1908, Paskauskas, 1–2.

'one of the few Teutonic women'. SF to CGJ, 19 Apr. 1908, McGuire, 141.

65. 'Once you have him'. SF to CGJ, 6 May 1908, McGuire, 147.

'I began to understand'. *FA*, 161.

'quite paranoiac'. EJ to SF, 27 June 1908, Paskauskas, 3.

'I never was in a town'. *FA*, 164.

'quite up to date'. C. M. Campbell to A. Meyer, 2 July 1908, Leys, 460.

'Between ourselves'. *FA*, 163.

66. 'to meet a friend'. *FA*, 164.

'We had a good talk'. EJ to SF, 3 June 1913, Paskauskas, 200–201.

'Jones is an enigma'. CGJ to SF, 12 July 1908, McGuire, 164.

'I tend to think'. SF to CGJ, 18 July 1908, McGuire, 165.

'I find the racial mixture'. Ibid.

67. 'My darling Ernest'. Mary Ann Jones to EJ, 26 Aug 1908, BPAS.

Chapter 6: Hamlet in Toronto

68. 'London'. *FA*, 167.

'Here I am landed'. EJ to SF, 26 Sept. 1908, Paskauskas, 4.

'young, quiet, unobtrusive'. C. K. Clarke to W. J. Hanna, 29 Oct. 1908, quoted in Greenland, 'Ernest Jones in Toronto', Part II, 513–14.

69. 'I am at present busy house hunting'. EJ to SF, 10 Dec. 1908, Paskauskas, 12.

'Dr Ernest Jones'. EJ archive, BPAS.

'Music is rare here'. EJ to SF, 10 Dec. 1908, Paskauskas, 11.

'for there is no one . . . found out'. Ibid.

70. His scientific articles. See the Bibliography.

'services as an occultist . . . spookery again'. CGJ to SF, 2 Nov. 1907, McGuire, 96.

71. crucial importance. G. Stanley Hall, *Adolescence*, 1 (1911), 233, n. 1, and 285, n. 1.

72. 'It might be the best'. SF to EJ, 20 Nov. 1908, Paskauskas, 9.

'Psychical Shock'. EJ to SF, 7 Feb. 1909, Paskauskas, 14.

'we . . . did not regard'. Ibid.

'going to'. Ibid., 13.

Janet's Harvard lectures. Hale-JJP, 14–15 and n. 39.

73. stimulating but exaggerated. Ibid., 1.

'It is an unfortunate feature'. Putnam in *Journal of Abnormal Psychology*, 1 (1906):40.

'I think his real interest'. EJ to SF, 4 Feb. 1919, Paskauskas, 332.

'a good . . . scientific exponent'. EJ to SF, 7 Feb. 1909, Paskauskas, 14–15.

'a large lay circulation'. Morton Prince to EJ, 30 Mar. 1909, BPAS, CPA/823/01.

Freud had already. SF to EJ, 22 Feb. 1909, Paskauskas, 19.

74. 'My wife sends'. EJ to JJP, 27 June 1910, Hale-JJP, 220.

'I think [Jones] has'. SF to A. A. Brill, 22 Feb. 1909.

'In any case'. CGJ to SF, 7 Mar. 1909, McGuire, 208.

75. 'mental twists'. Hale-JJP, 20, drawn from 'The Relation of Character Formation to Psychotherapy', in Prince, *Psychotherapeutics*, 166–86.

Jones had told. EJ to SF, 12 Apr. 1901, Paskauskas, 45

'Greetings from the right side'. EJ to SF, 5 Aug. 1909, Paskauskas, 28.

76. 'What am I to say'. SF to CGJ, 18 June 1909, McGuire, 234.

'such a shifting variety'. Roazen, *Freud and His Followers*, 384.

'Yes, America is gigantic'. *FA*, 131.

'I am inclined'. SF to CGJ, 17 Jan. 1909, McGuire, 196.

'I share Jones's pessimism'. CGJ to SF, 19 Jan. 1909, McGuire, 198.

'You absolutely must'. EJ to SF, 18 May 1909, Paskauskas, 24.

77. 'with plenty of wild chasing'. J–II, 62.

'to see what'. Hale, *Freud and the Americans* Ibid., 4.

'psychic analysis'. Ibid., 20.

'Conference Brings Savants together'. Quoted in ibid., 23.

78. 'and similar childish habits'. Ibid., 22.

'man of great refinement'. *Boston Evening Transcript* quoted Ibid., 20.

'future of psychology'. J–II, 64.

'unsavoury details'. J–II, 157.

'feeling for Jung'. EJ to SF, 23 Dec. 1912, Paskauskas, 184.

79. 'kindly, unassuming'. Putnam, *Addresses on Psycho-Analysis*, 30.

'Shortly put'. EJ to SF, 18 Dec. 1909, Paskauskas, 34.

'but also to further it'. EJ to SF, 17 Oct. 1909, Paskauskas, 29.

'the fact that every psychoneurotic symptom'. EJ, 'The Psycho-Analytic Method of Treatment' (1910), reprinted in *Papers* (3rd edn, 1923), 305.

80. 'This disease'. *Macbeth*, V.i.49.

'The seed'. Greenland, 'Jones in Toronto', Part I, 137–8, discusses the publication of EJ, 'Psycho-Analytic Notes on a Case of Hypomania' (1910) in the *American Journal of Insanity* and its reprinting in the *Bulletin of the Ontario Hospitals*.

81. 'free love'. EF to SF, 20 Apr. 1910, Paskauskas, 52; quoted in Greenland, 'Jones in Toronto', Part II, 117–18.

'pornographic stories'. EJ to SF, 4 May 1910, Paskauskas, 55.

'Jones is now excelling'. SF to Fer, 1 Jan. 1910, Brabant, 118.

'I'll be good'. SF to CGJ, 2 Jan. 1910, McGuire, 283.

Freud had scolded Jones. SF to EJ, 31 Oct. 1909, Paskauskas, 32, and EJ to SF, 18 Dec. 1909, Paskauskas, 34.

82. 'a negro house of prostitution'. Leys, 449.

'hateful pandering'. EJ to A. Meyers, 2 Apr. 1910, Leys, 450.

'The so-called freedom'. CGJ to SF, 5 Mar. 1910, McGuire, 316.

'medical experience'. H. Münsterberg to JJP, 23 Mar. 1910, Hale-JJP, 206.

'the herald of Light'. 'Fair Harvard', Harvard anthem composed by Samuel Gilman, Class of 1811.

83. 'Most of you are Jews'. Wittels, *Sigmund Freud*, 140.

'You are certainly'. JJP to EJ, 10 Oct. 1910, Hale-JJP, 27 and n. 74.

84. 'my excessive interest'. EJ to JJP, 1 July 1910, Hale-JJP, 221.

'Your letters prove'. SF to EJ, 15 Apr. 1910, Paskauskas, 51.

'greatly about this business'. *FA*, 176.

'Tomorrow the geographically most distant'. SF to CGJ, 10 Aug. 1910, McGuire, 343.

'Mutterbindung'. An account of Mahler's analysis with Freud appears in J–II, 88–9, and also in Gustav Mahler, *Letters to His Wife*, ed. Henry-Louis de la Grange, Gunther Weiss and Knud Martner, rev. and trans. Antony Beaumont (London: Faber, 2004).

'Feeling cheerful'. Gustav Mahler to Alma Mahler, 27 Aug. 1910, Ibid., 380.

'associate in psychiatry'. EJ to SF, 6 Nov. 1910, Paskauskas, 73 and 74, n. 9, which distinguishes 'associate in psychiatry' from 'associate professor of psychiatry', which Jones became in the autumn of 1911.

'a beautiful case'. Ibid., 73.

'The originality-complex'. EJ to SF, 19 June 1910, Paskauskas, 61.

Freud's footnote. SF, *The Interpretation of Dreams*, SE, 4:264–6.

86. 'No disconnected and meaningless drama'. EJ, 'The Oedipus-Complex as an Explanation of Hamlet's Mystery' (1910), 82.

'inaccessible to his introspection'. Ibid., 86.

'I never thought'. *2 Henry IV*, IV.iii, 219–20.

'there can be no question . . . horror'. EJ, 'The Oedipus-Complex as an Explanation of Hamlet's Mystery' (1910), 91.

87. 'The Queen his mother'. Ibid., 98.

'the group of mental processes'. Ibid., 97.

'the mother'. Ibid., 96.

'long "repressed"'. Ibid., 99.

'an index'. Ibid., 100.

'and to slay'. EJ, *Hamlet and Oedipus* (New York: Doubleday Anchor, 1949), 100

'an event'. EJ, 'The Oedipus-Complex as an Explanation of Hamlet's Mystery' (1910), 103.

It is only fitting'. Ibid., 113.

Richard Ellmann posits. Richard Ellmann, *James Joyce* (New York, Oxford and Toronto: Oxford University Press, 1982), 340.

'*Amor matris*'. James Joyce, *Ulysses*, Episode 9, 'Scylla and Charybdis' (London: Penguin and Bodley Head, 1986), 170.

88. 'Hamlet was a prime sufferer'. Olivier, *Confessions of an Actor*, 79.

'No malady'. EJ, 'On the Nightmare' (1910), 13.

'The modifications'. Ibid., 17.

89. 'his origin'. EJ, *On the Nightmare* (1931), 98–9. Plath's 1949 Hogarth Press impression, with markings, is in the Special Collections Department, Robert Woodruff Library, Emory University.

'Let me express again'. SF to EJ, 22 May 1910, Paskauskas, 58.

Chapter 7: Perils of the Trade

90. Freud's Worcester lectures. SF, 'The Origin and Development of Psychoanalysis', trans. H. W. Chase, *American Journal of Psychology*, 21/2 and 3 (1910), 181–218; translated as 'Five Lectures on Psycho-Analysis' in *SE*, 11:9–55.

'conclusion that'. Gay, 196.

'very serious personal trouble'. EJ to JJP, 13 Jan. 1911, Hale-JJP, 252.

91. When the patient's friend. EJ to JJP, 5 Feb. 1911, ibid., 255.

recounting the saga. EJ to SF, 8 Feb. 1911, Paskauskas, 88.

'To be slandered'. SF to CGJ, 9 Mar. 1909, McGuire, 141.

92. 'the most hideous excrescence'. EJ to SF, 8 Feb 1911, Paskauskas, 89.

'the art of type-writing'. EJ to SF, 13 July 1911, Paskauskas, 108.

'I am with best love'. SF to EJ, 22 Jan. 1911, Paskauskas, 85.

'Did you accept'. EJ to SF, 17 Mar. 1911, Paskauskas, 97–8.

'mad epidemic of Freudianism'. J–II, 129.

93. 'which astonish'. Morton Prince, 'The Mechanism and Interpretation of Dreams', 129.

'by the psychoanalytic method'. EJ, 'Remarks on Dr Morton Prince's Article: "The Mechanism and Interpretation of Dreams"', 330.

'very courteous criticism'. Morton Prince, 'The Mechanism and Interpretation of Dreams – A Reply to Dr Jones', 337.

'too much the pet of Boston'. EJ to SF, 17 Mar. 1911, Paskauskas, 98.

'Jones is hopelessly lost'. Morton Prince to JJP, 26 Nov. 1910, Hale-JJP, 325.

'Fiona Macprince'. Hale–JJP, 327.

'subterranean psychology'. Lloyd, 'The So-Called Oedipus-Complex in Hamlet', 1377.

94. 'without saying a word'. EJ to SF, 22 May 1911, Paskauskas, 102.
    'ardent supporters'. Ibid., 103.
    'damaged by amateurs'. EJ to JJP, 14 Aug. 1911, Hale, *Freud and the Americans*, 314.
    'the anxiety and the suspense'. EJ to SF, 17 Mar. 1911, Paskauskas, 96.
95. 'Mrs Jones and Ernest Jones'. A. Meyer to Hermann Meyer, 19 May 1911 (original in German), Leys, 465, n. 89.
    'huge doses . . . calculous pyelo-nephritis'. EJ to SF, 13 July 1911, Paskauskas, 110.
    'my enemies'. Ibid.
    'It would be inhuman . . . movement there'. Ibid.
96. intervention by Sir William Meredith. Cited in Friedland, *The University of Toronto*, 242.
    'much good'. EJ to A. Meyer cited in Leys, 465. n. 93.
    'a definite triumph', EJ to SF, 31 Aug. 1911, Paskauskas, 114.
    'Your opinion'. EJ to SF, 17 Oct. 1911, Paskauskas, 116–17.
97. 'putting new life into her'. EJ to A. Meyer, 21 Oct. 1911, Leys, 465, n. 93.
    'I am convinced'. A. Meyer to EJ, 23 Oct. 1911, Leys 465, n. 93.
    'My dear Professor Jones'. SF to EJ, 5 Nov. 1911, Paskauskas, 219.
    'a bad recrudescence'. EJ to SF, 26 Nov. 1911, Paskauskas, 120.
    'I was sorry too'. SF to EJ, 14 Jan. 1912, Paskauskas, 124.
    'for the melancholy pleasure'. Mrs C. F. Blum Chouffet to A. A. Brill, 11 Oct. 1911, BPAS, CBD/F02/02.
98. 'my wife was a patient of mine', EJ to SF, 28 June 1910, Paskauskas 63.
    'consider *unsaid*'. Mrs C. F. Blum Chouffet to A. A. Brill, 11 Oct. 1911, BPAS, CBD/F02/02.
    'sexual anaesthesia'. SF to EJ, 8 Dec. 1912, Paskauskas, 181
    'an old affair'. EJ to SF, 30 Jan. 1913, Paskauskas, 190–1.
    'One of the things'. EJ to SF, 30 Jan. 1912, Paskauskas, 130.
99. 'You have, as it were'. SF to EJ, 9 Aug. 1911, Paskauskas, 112.
    'the home of her heart'. EJ to SF, 15 Mar. 1912, Paskauskas, 135.
    'Perhaps I am influenced'. Ibid., 134.

Chapter 8: Jung, Jones and Jones

100. 'Loe Kann Jones'. Loe Kann to SF, 12 July 1912, Freud Museum.
     'Let us hope'. SF to EJ, 22 July 1912, Paskauskas, 143.
101. 'a formal disavowal'. Ibid.
     deliberate manoeuvre. See Paskauskas, 'Freud's Break with Jung'.
     'Jung abdicates'. EJ to SF, 30 July 1912, Paskauskas, 146.
     'that a small group of men'. Ibid.
     '*strictly secret* . . . my creation'. SF to EJ, 1 Aug. 1912, Paskauskas, 148.
     'a united small body'. EJ to SF, 7 Aug. 1912, Paskauskas, 149.
102. 'Assure your wife'. SF to EJ, 7 Sept. 1912, Paskauskas, 157.
     'strengthened and relieved'. SF to EJ, 22 Sept. 1912, Paskauskas, 162.
     'in a divine'. EJ to SF, 18 Sept. 1912, Paskauskas, 161.
     'Yours in love'. SF to EJ, 8 Nov. 1912, Paskauskas, 172.
     'holy ground . . . heaven'. EJ to SF, 30 Oct. 1912, Paskauskas, 166.

103. 'Your wife shows'. SF to EJ, 28 Oct. 1912, Paskauskas, 164.
'jewel'. SF to EJ, 2 June 1914, Paskauskas, 285.
'I eagerly wanted'. SF to EJ, 8 Nov. 1912, Paskauskas, 171.
'Mrs Jones is doing very well'. SF to Fer, 27 Oct. 1912, Brabant, 419.
'outwardly almost unrecognizable'. SF to Fer, 26 Nov. 1912, Brabant, 433.

104. 'You are right in supposing'. SF to EJ, 26 Dec. 1912, Paskauskas, 186.
'Your wife is splendid'. SF to EJ, 8 Dec. 1912, Paskauskas, 181.
'The physician should be opaque'. SF, 'Recommendations to Physicians Practising Psycho-Analysis', *SE*, 12.118, which says the paper first appeared in 1912.

105. 'I am under the impression'. SF to EJ, 26 Dec. 1912, Paskauskas, 185.
'enjoying her Vienna sojourn'. Ibid., 186.
'She finds all kinds of precautionary measures'. EJ to SF, 29 Dec. 1912, Paskauskas, 188.
'neurotic malaise'. Gay, 163.
he had made. SF to JJP, 8 July 1915, Hale-JJP, 189.
'The nicest case'. SF to EJ, 1 Jan. 1913, Paskauskas, 189.
'behaving quite crazy'. SF to EJ, 16 Dec. 1912, Paskauskas, 186
'*meschugge*'. SF to Fer, 9 Dec. 1912, Brabant, 440.

106. 'He can go jump'. SF to Fer, 30 Dec. 1912, Brabant, 452.
'Meanwhile you remain on top'. CGJ to SF, 18 Dec. 1912, McGuire, 534–5.
'an old affair'. EJ to SF, 30 Jan. 1913, Paskauskas, 190–91.
'Jones left yesterday'. SF to Fer, 2 Feb. 1913, Brabant, 465.
'not only a definite'. EJ, 'A Forgotten Dream' (1912), reprinted in *Papers* (4th edn, 1938), 288–302.

107. 'He [Freud] regards'. Ibid.
'I have a black mark'. EJ to SF, 18 Mar. 1913, Paskauskas, 196.
'an influential and highly respected position'. SF to EJ, 5 Mar. 1913, Paskauskas, 194.
'Now make your heart easy'. SF to EJ, 10 Feb. 1913, Paskauskas, 192.
'write as soon as you can'. Ibid.
'There is more going on'. SF to EJ, 10 Feb. 1913, Paskauskas, 192.
'will bear finding out'. SF to Fer, 4 May 1913, Brabant, 482.

108. 'Jones has had his wife'. SF to Fer, 13 May 1913, Brabant, 486.
'Jones is here'. SF to Fer, 24 May 1913, Brabant, 488.
'*full* love, which I'. EJ to SF, 3 June 1913, Paskauskas, 200.
'not only good'. Fer to SF, 9 July 1913, Brabant, 498.

109. 'seems to fear'. Fer to SF, 17 June 1913, Brabant, 493.
'Be strict'. SF to Fer, 8 June 1913, Brabant, 490.
'father-complex'. EJ to SF, 25 June 1913, Paskauskas, 208.
'omnipotence complex'. Brome, 86 – based on an interview with Michael Balint.
'many interesting discussions'. Fer to SF, 17 June 1913, Brabant, 493.
'the best thing'. EJ to SF, 17 June 1913, Paskauskas, 204.
'drawing towards a close'. EJ to SF, 22 July 1913, Paskauskas, 213.
'I miss him'. Fer to SF, 5 Aug. 1913, Brabant, 503.
'less guilty'. SF to Fer, 9 July 1913, Brabant, 499.

110. 'Both by word and deed'. Thomas E. Brown, 'Psychoanalysis and the Canadian Medical Profession, 1908–1913,' in Shortt, *Medicine in Canadian Society*, 353. Also

an unsubtantiated letter from the Hon. Herbert Bruce to Cyril Greenland, 11 July 1962, said that EJ was 'dismissed from the Faculty . . . because he was a pervert' (Centre for Addiction and Mental Health).

'In those days . . . without intimacy'. *FA*, 227.

111. 'Freudism is'. Quoted in EJ to SF, 30 Mar. 1910, Paskauskas, 49.

'treated by'. BM, *The Married Man*, 44.

'Freud's statement'. SF, foreword to Hobman, *David Eder*.

'for a few symptoms'. EJ to SF, 30 July 1912, Paskauskas, 145.

'especially intelligent'. Ibid.

Dr David Forsyth. In *FA*, 218–19, EJ says that Forsyth was one of four people in Britain to be practising psychoanalysis before the war.

'his personal jealousy'. *FA*, 229.

'generously offered'. EJ to SF, 18 Aug. 1913, Paskauskas, 220.

112. 'I feel more certain'. Herbert Jones to SF, 8 Aug. 1913, Freud Museum.

'the money-side'. Loe Kann to SF, 8 Oct. 1914, Freud Museum.

told Freud about it. EJ to SF, 25 May, 1914, Paskauskas, 284.

'He must be under'. Telegram from Herbert Jones to Loe Kann, quoted in full in her letter to SF, 8 Oct. 1913, Freud Museum.

'I have never been ashamed'. Loe Kann to SF, 8 Oct. 1913, Freud Museum.

113. 'Is Herbert going to consult'. EJ to SF, 15 Feb. 1914, Paskauskas, 262.

'If things go on'. EJ to SF, 9 Jan. 1914, Paskauskas, 254.

'Do me the personal favour'. SF to EJ, 16 Jan. 1914, Paskauskas, 256.

'as a return'. Eder, 'The Present Position of Psychoanalysis', *British Medical Journal*, 2 (1912–15), quoted in Bair, *Jung*, 248 and 729, n. 31.

'in certain quarters'. J–II, 171.

'A purely sexual etiology'. Quoted by Hayman, *Jung*, 158.

'a vulgar person'. EJ to SF, 8 Apr. 1914, Paskauskas, 274.

more than close. Sonu Shamdasani, in the *Oxford DNB* entry on (Alfred) Ernest Jones (1879–1958), says, 'As revealed by their correspondence Jones had an affair with Edith Eder shortly after her analysis with Jung.'

114. 'Dear Ernest'. E. Eder to EJ, 6 Apr. [no year given], BPAS, CEA/Fo1/18/01.

'a most remarkable'. SF to EJ, 2 June 1914, Paskauskas, 285.

'I know from'. SF to AF, 16 July 1914, quoted in Young-Bruehl, *Anna Freud*, 67.

'to lose the dear child . . . dragon'. SF to Fer, 17 July 1914, Falzeder, 2:2.

115. 'surprising murder'. SF to Fer, 28 June 1914, Brabant, 562.

'She is the most gifted'. SF to EJ, 22 July 1914, Paskauskas, 294.

'She has a beautiful character'. EJ to SF, 27 July 1914, Paskauskas, 295.

'The patient overcomes'. EJ to SF, 27 July, 1914, Paskauskas, 296.

116. 'Aug 12 . . . goodbye to Anna'. Entries from EJ's diary, EJ archives, BPAS.

Chapter 9: Comforts of War

117. 'It has generally been decided'. SF to EJ, 22 Oct. 1914, Paskauskas, 300.

'the narrow-minded outlook'. J–II, 195.

'How much must it mean'. JJP to SF, 15 Dec. 1915, Hale–JJP, 182.

'before the leaves'. Kaiser Wilhelm II addressing German troops, August 1914.

118. 'rather a boyish one . . . Prussian'. EJ to SF, 15 Nov. 1914, Paskauskas, 303.

'If there is ever'. EJ to SF, 15 Dec. 1914, Paskauskas, 308.

'The Verein is as doomed'. SF to EJ, 25 Dec. 1914, Paskauskas, 309.

As soldiers with conspicuous symptoms. See Porter, *The Greatest Benefit to Mankind*, 516–19.

119. 'Fate would seem'. Quoted in Gay, 376.

'full fees this month'. Ethel Vaughan-Sawyer to EJ, 4 Dec. 1916, BPAS, CJA/F11/02.

a train driver . . . £1. 10s. 11d. Oksana Newman and Allan Foster, eds., *The Value of a Pound: Prices and Incomes in Britain 1900–1993* (Andover, Hants: Gale Research International, 1995), 7.

120. 'The War Office decided'. EJ to SF, 27 Mar. 1916, Paskauskas, 315–16.

121. 'a valuable officer'. EJ to SF, 15 Jan. 1917, Paskauskas, 321.

'I said the doctors'. D. H. Lawrence to B. Low, 8 July 1916, in Zytaruk and Boulton, *The Letters of D. H. Lawrence*, 2:623.

'I didn't produce'. Ibid.; see also Kinkead-Weekes, *D. H. Lawrence*, 332.

'on social and personal freedom'. Advertisement for *The Signature*, Koteliansky Collection, British Library MS 48966.

122. 'just a few'. D. H. Lawrence to Lady Cynthia Asquith, 14 Oct. 1915, in Zytaruk and Boulton, *The Letters of D. H. Lawrence*, 2:441.

'with his eager assertive manner'. *FA*, 241.

'From the way'. *FA*, 242.

Jones was perhaps. BM, *The Married Man*, 232.

'the dark forces'. *FA*, 242.

123. 'Be sure to read'. BM, The *Married Man*, 215.

'an auto-cycle with side-car'. EJ to SF, 30 May 1916, Paskauskas, 318.

'after five minutes teaching'. *FA*, 242.

'Herbert Jones is better'. EJ to SF, 30 May 1915, Paskauskas, 318.

'Jones has eleven'. SF to Fer, 13 July 1916, Falzeder, 2:134.

124. 'glad to be able'. EJ to SF, 31 Oct. 1916, Paskauskas, 320.

'that is more or less hidden'. EJ, 'The Theory of Symbolism' (1916), 184.

'unconscious symbols'. Ibid., 215.

'Jones's forecast'. J. M. Keynes to JS, 12 July 1929, BPAS, CSC/F03/06.

125. 'the most complete'. Trotter, *Instincts of the Herd*, 201.

'the repressing forces'. Ibid., 80.

'a certain harshness . . . administer'. Ibid., 76.

'You will I am sure'. EJ to SF, 30 May 1915, Paskauskas, 318.

'ψα stands rather isolated in the book. SF to EJ, 14 July 1916, Paskauskas, 319.

126. '12 S.P.R.'. Joan Riviere, diaries, BPAS, CRC/F01.

'Joan Riviere could not'. Hughes, 10.

127. 'Domine well-beloved'. Evelyn Vaughan-Sawyer to EJ, 4 Dec. 1916 (postmark), BPAS, CJA/F11/02.

It's you yourself'. E. Eder to EJ, 6 Apr. 1914(?), BPAS, CEA/F18/01.

'I have recently parted'. EJ to SF, 15 Jan. 1917, Paskauskas, 321.

Chapter 10: A Druid Bride

130. 'You,' she would announce. Bethan Jones, letter, 30 May 1976, *Welsh Music*, 5/3 (summer 1976), 99.

     twenty proposals. This and other details of MO's life are drawn from Rhian Davies, *Never So Pure a Sight*.

131. 'Miss Morfydd Owen'. *Morning Post*, 8 Mar. 1913, cited in R. Davies, 43.

     'I simply *love*'. MO to Kitty Lewis, n.d., R. Davies, 54.

132. 'Bili Museum'. R. Davies, 68.

     At one point. Bethan Jones, letter, 30 May 1976, *Welsh Music*, 5/3 (summer 1976), 99.

133. 'a shy, enigmatic little person'. Quoted in R. Davies, 89.

     a romance with a Russian émigré. R. Davies, 76.

134. 'She is a little monkey'. Lady Lewis to Kitty Lewis, 4 Feb. 1917, K. I. Jones, 'The Enigma of Morfydd Owen', 18.

     'Proposed to Morfydd'. EJ diary, BPAS.

     Eric Hiller. T. G. Davies, *Ernest Jones*, 41.

     'A home needs a mistress'. *FA*, 243.

     'To *Figaro*'. EJ diary, 28 July 1917, BPAS.

135. 'Miss Morfydd Owen'. Programme in R. Davies, 43.

     'Beautiful & beloved'. Ethel Vaughan-Sawyer to EJ, 19 Jan. 1917, BPAS.

     'broken-hearted'. EJ to SF, 22 Jan. 1922, Paskauskas, 454.

     'absolutely unquestionable . . . direct opposite'. JR to EJ, 5 Nov. 1918, Brome, 119.

136. 'admittedly the cleverest'. 'London Welsh Weddings', *Western Mail*, 7 Feb. 1917, quoted in R. Davies, 98.

     'Married 12.15'. EJ diary, BPAS.

     'Dear Eliot'. MO to E. Crawshay-Williams, 16 Feb. 1917, R. Davies, 100–1.

137. 'I got married'. EJ to SF, 20 Feb. 1917, Paskauskas, 322.

     'He regards himself'. SF to K. Abraham, quoted in Ferris, *Dr Freud*, 313n.

     'exceedingly happy'. MO to Kitty Lewis, 7 Sept. 1917, K. I. Jones, 'The Enigma of Morfydd Owen', 19.

     'giving out'. EJ, 'Anal-Erotic Character Traits' (1918), reprinted in *Papers* (5th edn, 1948), 413–17.

138. '500 miles'. EJ diary, Aug. 1917, BPAS.

     Jones claimed. *FA*, 244.

     'Voice: Morfydd Owen Jones'. Programme, R. Davies, 110.

139. 'I feel I have'. MO to Kitty Lewis, n.d., K. I. Jones, 'The Enigma of Morfydd Owen', 20.

     'Of course I know'. JR to EJ, 8 Feb. 1918, CRB/F07/01.

     Her friends considered. K. I. Jones, 'The Enigma of Morfydd Owen', 21.

     'I'm cleaning windows!'. MO to E. Crawshay-Williams, 23 Aug. 1918, R. Davies, 116.

141. 'Telegram Mrs Jones dead'. JR diary entry for 8 Aug. 1918, BPAS, CRC/F01/12.

     'Your telegram came'. Frederick Corder to William Owen, condolence letters, EJ archives, BPAS.

     'My heart goes out'. David Evans to William Owen, condolence letters, EJ archives, BPAS.

'Land of her dream'. M. Jones, 'A Wreath of Rondeaux. For Morfydd Owen', R. Davies, 122.

'a soprano singer'. 'Madame Morfydd Owen', *Western Mail*, 9 Sept, 1918.

'Das Unbeschreibliche'. Cited in R. Davies, 123.

'The death certificate'. Cited in R. Davies, 120.

142. 'My darling wife'. EJ to SF, 4 Oct. 1918, Paskauskas, 324.

'I do not want to console'. SF to EJ, 10 Nov. 1918, Paskauskas, 325.

'Despite the innocent nature'. Ferris, *Dr Freud*, 319.

'how much you have guessed'. Loe Kann to SF, n.d., Freud Museum. There he claimed. *FA*, 245.

'There seems to have been'. SF to EJ, 22 Dec. 1918, Paskauskas, 327.

143. 'I hope you got my cheerful'. EJ to SF, 4 Oct. 1918, Paskauskas, 324.

'Patients naturally expressed'. *FA*, 247.

144. 'terrible experience'. EJ to SF, 4 Dec. 1918, Paskauskas, 326.

His records show. EJ diary, 1918, BPAS.

Chapter 11: Third Time Lucky

145. 'has no grounds whatever'. SF, 'Observations on Transference-Love', *SE*, 12.161.

146. 'centre of gravity'. SF to Fer, 12 Apr. 1919, Falzeder, 2:345.

'More or less the whole world'. SF to Fer, 17 Mar. 1919, Falzeder, 2:335.

'the many men'. EF to SF, 31 Dec. 1918, Paskauskas, 327.

'by reinforcing the view'. EF to SJ, 16 Jan. 1920, Paskauskas, 362.

147. 'The *Aufschwung*'. EJ to SF, 27 Jan. 1919, Paskauskas, 332.

'which were in contradiction'. *IJP-A*, 1 (1920), 116.

'Jung "rump" '. EJ to SF, 9 Jan. 1919, Paskauskas, 328.

148. 'street anxiety'. Paper read by Dr Douglas Bryan, 6 Nov. 1918, reported in *IJP-A*, 1(1920), 117.

'rankling & truthful'. E. Eder to EJ, 28 Jan. 1919, BPAS, CEA/F18/05.

'Circumstances have brought'. Ibid.

149. 'haunted in vain'. J–III, 18.

'turn these stupid'. EJ to SF, 25 Mar. 1919, Paskauskas, 338.

'every minute of the day'. EJ to SF, 25 Mar. 1919, Paskauskas, 338.

150. 'Jones is totally'. SF to Fer, 12 Apr. 1919, Falzeder, 345.

'hungry beggars'. SF to EJ, 18 Apr. 1919, Paskauskas, 340.

Freud sourly. SF to EJ, 10 Nov. 1918, Paskauskas, 325.

'you know how serious'. EJ to SF, 23 Apr. 1919, Paskauskas, 341.

'The first window'. SF to EJ, 18 Apr. 1919, Paskauskas, 340.

'Edited for'. EF to SF, 2 May 1919, Paskauskas, 344.

151. 'having been well loved'. EJ to SF, 10 June 1919, Paskauskas, 348.

'partly on the work'. EJ to SF, 16 July 1920, Paskauskas, 386.

'Dear Hanns'. EJ to H. Sachs, postcard, n.d., BPAS, CSA/F02/01.

'Frl. Jokl'. EJ to Kitty Jokl, 3 May 1919, BPAS.

'This is to certify'. 28 June 1919, BPAS, CJB/F011/09; no author given.

152. 'Dr Kitty'. EJ to Kitty Jokl, 31 July 1917, BPAS, CJB/F01/012.

'The more beautiful'. EJ to SF, 4 Sept. 1919, Paskauskas, 355.

'My very own sweetheart'. EJ to KJ, 19 Sept. 1919, BPAS, CJB/Fo1/13.

153. 'The South!'. KJ memoir. The anecdote is told without exclamation marks in KJ, 'A Sketch of E.J.'s Personality'.

'preventative capsules'. KJ, 'Notes on E.J.' (1965, unpublished), 3.

'never forget'. EJ to KJ, 19 Sept 1919, Brome, 125.

'Did I live'. KJ to EJ, 21 Sept. 1919, BPAS, CJB/Fo1/16.

called 'Kitty'. KJ unpublished family history, property of Jackie Jones/Mervyn Jones.

154. 'strict hard voice'. EJ to KJ, 23 Sept. 1919, BPAS, CJB/Fo1/17.

155. 'calmly . . . fetched'. J–III, 34.

'great and unexpected happiness'. EJ to SF, 12 Oct. 1919, Paskauskas, 356.

'my secretarial wife'. EJ to SF, 7 May 1920, Paskauskas, 378.

'I enjoyed sex'. KJ, 'Notes on E.J.' (1965, unpublished), 3.

'the poor darling'. Ibid.

'C'est pratique'. Ibid.

156. 'Dear friend'. JR to EJ, 12 Oct. 1919, quoted in Brome, 119. The German phrase is taken from Goethe's *Faust*: 'Das Ewigweibliche zieht uns hinan.'

'She was just the same age'. SF to EF, 2 Feb. 1920, Paskauskas, 367.

Freud told Jones. SF to EJ, 12 Feb. 1920, Paskauskas, 370.

157. 'Can you remember . . . soul'. Ibid.

'This girl will'. KJ, 'Notes on E.J.' (1965, unpublished), 8.

'About death'. EJ to SF, 8 Dec. 1919, Paskauskas, 359.

'The grandfather has'. SF to EJ, 8 Mar. 1920, Paskauskas, 372.

'as part of my donation'. EJ to SF, 24 Apr. 1920, Paskauskas, 375.

158. 'You had only one father'. SF to EJ, 2 May 1920, Paskauskas, 376.

'I took my revenge'. EF to SJ, 23 Feb. 1921, Paskauskas, 413.

'deducted by the Government'. EJ to SF, 3 Feb. 1921, Paskauskas, 407.

'does not come'. SF to EJ, 28 Jan. 1921, Paskauskas, 405.

159. 'arrange a little Congress'. Loe Kann to SF, n.d., Freud Museum.

'Isn't it fun . . . practice'. Loe Kann to SF, n.d., Freud Museum.

160. 'German collaborator'. Caine, *Bombay to Bloomsbury*, 367.

'a man of 30'. EJ to SF, 7 May 1920, Paskauskas, 378.

'crushed'. JS to AS, 27 Feb. 1925, Meisel, 220.

'Jones lectured'. JS to A, 7 May 1925, Meisel, 259.

'the unusual experience'. EJ, 'The Early Development of Female Sexuality' (1927).

'the higher sodomy', Caine, *Bombay to Bloomsbury*, 139.

161. 'exceptionally nice'. SF to EJ, 14 July 1921, Paskauskas, 431.

'a torture'. SF to EJ, 12 Oct. 1920, Paskauskas, 393.

'a whole series'. JS to Lytton Strachey, 6 Nov. 1920, Meisel, 30.

'When I am definitely'. EJ to SF, 22 July 1920, Paskauskas, 387.

162. 'I have rather laid'. EJ to SF, 12 Nov. 1920, Paskauskas, 398.

'a Frau Dr Klein'. Fer to SF, 29 June 1919, Falzeder, 2:361.

163. 'and ready to supplant'. SF to EJ, 4 Oct. 1920, Paskauskas, 392.

'It had to be Welsh'. EJ to SF, 17 Oct. 1920, Paskauskas, 394.

'Gwenith is Welsh'. EJ to SF, 28 Oct. 1920, Paskauskas, 396.

Freud congratulated him. SF to EJ, 12 Oct. 1920, Paskauskas, 393.

'will soon be able'. SF to EJ, 21 Oct. 1920, Paskauskas, 395.

'one of the queerest'. SF to EJ, 4 Oct. 1920, Paskauskas, 391.

'The centre of our activity'. Ibid., 392.
'To me it is clear'. EJ to [Who?], 12 Dec. 1910, BPAS, CFC/Fo5/21

Chapter 12: Name-Calling

165. 'It is curious'. AS to JS, 10 Nov. 1924, Meisel, 113.
'I am glad to say'. EJ to SF, 21 May 1921, Paskauskas, 425.
'We are all good Jews'. EJ, *Rundbrief* 1, 21 Dec. 1920, BPAS CFC/Fo5/21.
'If one charges'. EJ, *Rundbrief*, 1 May 1922, p. 122.

166. 'really getting old'. SF to Fer, 8 May 1921, Falzeder, 3:56.
expressed concern. SF to EJ, 2 Oct. 1921, Paskauskas, 440.
'an unmistakably male child'. EJ to SF, 27 Feb. 1922, Paskauskas, 461.
'The name will probably'. Ibid.
'unless you send me'. EJ to SF, 16 Mar. 1922, Paskauskas, 463.

167. 'amplification of your name'. SF to EJ, 23 Mar. 1922, Paskauskas, 464. Although Jones's letter in the BPAS archive spells the name as 'Beddow', the Jones family, and FA10, say the correct spelling is 'Beddoe'.
'So I must continue'. EJ to SF, 1 Apr. 1922, Paskauskas, 465.
orders from 'King George'. EJ to KJ, 20 Sept. 1922, BPAS, CJB/Fo2/010.
'even unqualified ones'. EJ to SF, 15 Dec. 1921, Paskauskas, 447.
'radiant *Mutterglück*'. EJ to SF, 22 May 1922, Paskauskas, 480.

168. 'one of the first'. EJ to B. Low, 12 Feb. 1922, BPAS, CLA/F27/01A.
'in my absence'. D. Eder to EJ, 3 July 1923, CEA/F18/07.

169. 'the only remaining'. EJ, May 1922, *Rundbrief*, 3, 154.
'the political reactions'. Ibid., 78.
'has its personal foes'. SF to EJ, 6 Apr. 1922, Paskauskas, 469.
'should differ so profoundly'. EJ, 'The Island of Ireland' (1922), revised in *Essays on Applied Psycho-Analysis* (1923), 99.
'identification of'. Ibid., 102.
'an abiding rape'. Ibid., 112.

170. 'his worst failure'. EJ to SF, 22 Jan. 1922, Paskauskas, 453.
'half as black'. SF to EJ, 23 Mar. 1922, Paskauskas, 464.
'It is over twelve years'. EJ to SF, 1 Apr. 1922, Paskauskas, 466.

171. 'translating editor'. SF to EJ, 4 June 1922, Paskauskas, 485.
'your personal interference'. SF to EJ, 6 Apr. 1922, Paskauskas, 468.
'Accuracy and plainness'. SF to EJ, 25 June 1922, Paskauskas, 491.

172. Freud explained. SF to EJ, 12 Apr. 1921, Paskauskas, 418–19.
Jones disagreed. EJ to SF, 6 May 1921, Paskauskas, 420–21.
'a series of'. JS to Lady Strachey, 9 Mar. 1921, in Holroyd, *Lytton Strachey*, 2:442n.
'Charity will out'. J–III, 92.

173. 'a Maida Vale Jew'. JR to her mother and sister, 3 Oct. 1922, Hughes, 36.
'full of Jews'. Ibid., 38.
'the material and social leader'. Ibid., 40.
'owed the invitation . . . *food*'. Ibid.
'They live still further out . . . bored'. Ibid., 41–2.
'none of the Committee'. J–II, 181, quoted in Lieberman, *Acts of Will*, 34, n.10.

174. 'that one half'. K. Horney, 'On the Genesis of the Castration Complex in Women', in Horney, *Feminine Psychology*, 38; quoted in Schwartz, *Cassandra's Daughter*, 247.
'the non-repressed ego'. J–III, 92.
'owing perhaps'. SF to EJ, 6 Apr. 1922, Paskauskas, 468.
'a complete restoration'. SF to EJ, 7 Jan. 1923, Paskauskas, 508.
'a disappointment not easy'. Ibid., 507.
'but she is a true Englishwoman'. SF to EJ, 14 Jan. 1923, Paskauskas, 508.

175. 'must know what part'. EJ to SF, 19 Nov. 1922, Paskauskas, 505.
'my domestic happiness'. EJ to SF, 19 Nov. 1922, Paskauskas, 505.
'It is doubtless true'. EJ to SF, 14 Jan. 1923, Paskauskas, 509.

176. 'a swindling Jew'. EJ to KJ, 26 Aug. 1923, Paskauskas, 527, n. 2.
'general way'. EJ to A. A. Brill, 9 Apr. 1923, quoted in Grosskurth-R, 133.
'A Jewish family council'. EJ to KJ, 26 Aug. 1923, Paskauskas, 527, n. 2.
'The word Semitic'. EJ to SF, 12 Sept. 1923, Paskauskas, 526–7.
'Anyone who is so happy'. EJ to Fer, 7 Aug. 1924, Grosskurth-R, 161.
'He doesn't know it'. EJ to KJ, 26 Aug. 1923, BPAS, CJB/Fo2/38.

177. 'practically on his death-bed'. AS to JS, 7 or 8 Nov. 1924, Meisel, 112.
confided to Abraham. EJ to K. Abraham, 8 Apr. 1924, Grosskurth-R, 153.
'the state of mind'. SF to K. Abraham, 31 Mar. 1924, Grosskurth-R, 152.
farewell speech that sounded to Ferenczi. Fer to Otto Rank, 25 May 1924, Grosskurth-R, 157.

178. 'What is the use'. SF to EJ, 25 Sept. 1924, Paskauskas, 552.
later published. As James and Alix Strachey, *Bloomsbury/Freud*.
'Es wäre gewaltsam'. JS to AS, 24 Oct. 1924, Weisel, 95.
'The keeping . . . significance'. Wittels, *Sigmund Freud*, 263.
'a very tiresome hour'. JS to AS, 9 Oct. 1924, Weisel, 83.

179. 'ranks as easily'. EJ to SF, 12 Aug. 1924, Paskauskas, 550.
'Each page'. E. Lloyd to EJ, n.d. Jan. 1924, BPAS, CBB/P26/01.
Jones was helped. King, *No Ordinary Psychoanalyst*, 14–15.
'You will be most amused'. EJ to SF, 12 Aug. 1924, Paskauskas, 550.
'One must perhaps remember'. EF to SJ, 23 June 1922, Paskauskas, 490.

180. That fear, Klein said. Segal, *Introduction to the Work of Melanie Klein*, chapter 1 summarizes Klein's early work.
'Do you know . . . sentimentalist'. AS to JS, 14 Dec. 1924, Meisel, 146.
'absolutely heart-and-soul'. JS to AS, 8 Jan. 1925, Meisel, 175.

Chapter 13: Importing Klein

182. 'a sort of ultra-heterosexual'. AS to JS, 25 Feb. [1925], Meisel, 218.
'She made an extraordinarily'. EJ to SF, 17 July 1925, Paskauskas, 577–8.
'the depressive position'. The concept is described in Rayner, *The Independent Mind*, 16.

183. 'After a woman . . . penis-envy'. SF, 'Some Psychical Consequences of the Anatomical Distinction Between the Sexes' (1927), *SE*, 19:253–4.
'Melanie Klein's works'. SF to EJ, 22 July 1925, Paskauskas, 579.
'Prophylactic child analysis'. EJ to SF, 31 July 1925, Paskauskas, 579.

'Shall we send'. EJ to KJ, 21 July 1925, BPAS, CJB/F03/03.

184. 'Our love has become'. KJ to EJ, 18 June 1923, Brome, 140.

'My real mother'. MJ, *Chances*, 7, 5.

'our sweet, tiny place'. KJ to EJ, 2 Aug. 1926, BPAS, CJB/F03/020.

'our dear Plat'. EJ to KJ, n.d., BPAS, CJB/F03/027.

'the correct turnout'. MJ, *Chances*, 10.

1850. 'Was will das Weib?. J–II, 468.

'The great warmth'. MK to EJ, 24 Oct. 1926, BPAS, CKA/F18/07; also Grosskurth-Kl, 161.

186. 'I believe the prospect'. Ibid.; also Grosskurth-Kl, 160.

'I have the same'. Ibid.

'Is it really'. SF to EJ, 20 Nov. 1926, J–III, 137–8.

187. 'After forty-one years'. Quoted in Gay, 496.

'beyond all doubt'. EJ to SF, 23 Sept. 1926, Paskauskas, 605.

'physicians (doctors of medicine)'. Gay, 499.

'received a not unfavourable impression'. EJ to SF, 30 Sept. 1927, Paskauskas, 631.

Jones favoured Klein. SF to ME, 30 May 1927, Young-Bruehl, *Anna Freud*, 475, n. 58.

188. 'The analysis of a child'. JR, 'Symposium on Child Analysis'. IJP-A, 8(1927) 376.

'the hope that we'. EJ, 'Contribution to the "Symposium on Child Analysis"' Ibid., 391.

189. 'not only adopting'. Fer to SF, 30 June 1927, Falzeder, 3:313.

'his value'. EJ to SF, 20 June 1927, Paskauskas, 620.

'Though we had brought'. EJ to SF, 16 May 1927, Paskauskas, 617.

'so soon . . . resistances'. Ibid., 617–18.

Chapter 14: 'Who then has been sufficiently analysed?'

191. 'medical analysis'. SF to EJ, 6 July 1927, Paskauskas, 620–21.

192. 'a regular campaign'. SF to EJ, 23 Sept. 1927, Paskauskas, 623–4.

'Who then'. SF to EJ, 23 Sept. 1927, Young-Bruehl, *Anna Freud*, 171.

'I can assure you'. SF to EJ, 23 Sept. 1927, Paskauskas, 624.

'Wer ist denn'. SF to EJ, 23 Sept. 1927, BPAS, CF6/F04/008.

'I would not advise'. SF to E. Weiss, 1935, in Edoardo Weiss, *Sigmund Freud as a Consultant* (New York: Intercontinental Medical Book Corps, 1970), 81.

193. 'I did not think', AF to SF, 24 July 1919, Young-Bruehl, *Anna Freud*, 86.

'Is this directed'. SF to EJ, 23 Sept. 1927, Paskauskas, 624.

'the American situation'. EJ to SF, 30 Sept. 1927, Paskauskas, 625.

'two sets'. Ibid., 627.

'of entire devotion'. Ibid., 631.

'behavior of New York'. SF to EJ, 9 Oct. 1927, Paskauskas, 633.

194. 'It was heavenly'. AS to JS, 11 Dec. 1924, Meisel, 144.

'silent but ever-increasing'. 'Bulletin of the International Psychoanalytic Association', *IJP-A*, 9 (1928), 133.

'to become independent'. SF to ME, 30 May 1927, Young-Bruehl, *Anna Freud*, 475, n. 58.

'superficial'. JR, 'Symposium on Child Analysis', 371–3.

'I would like her'. SF to EJ, 9 Oct. 1927, Paskauskas, 633.

defending herself to Freud. SF to ME, 27 Nov. 1927, Young-Bruehl, *Anna Freud*, 171–2.

195.   'I don't believe'. Ibid.

'Lloyd George, no doubt'. Common doggerel, often quoted by Sir John Maddox, FRS.

'shares the common opinion'. EJ, 'The Inferiority Complex of the Welsh', *Welsh Outlook*, March 1929, 128.

'Misfortune and suffering'. Ibid.

'There are few nations'. Ibid, 131.

196.   'nothing but the translation'. EJ, introduction to *Psycho-Analysis* (1928), 7.

'that the first'. SF to EJ, 22 Feb. 1928, Paskauskas, 641.

197.   'you retained'. EJ to SF, 7 Mar. 1928, Paskauskas, 641.

'For nine days . . . as she did'. Ibid., 641–2.

198.   'How do these children'. SF to EJ, 11 Mar. 1928, Paskauskas, 643.

'Only a mother'. Martha Freud to KJ, 19 Mar. 1928, BPAS, CFB/F10/02.

Freud urged him. SF to EJ, 11 Mar. 1928, Paskauskas, 643.

'peculiarly his own child'. KJ, 'Notes on E.J.' (1965, unpublished), 1.

' "Young" and "old" '. SF to EJ, 3 May 1928, Paskauskas, 646.

'My darling husband', KJ to EJ, 23 June 1928, BPAS, CJB/F03/37.

'to investigate'. British Medical Association, *Report of the Psycho-Analysis Committee*, 3.

199.   'all these objects'. Transcript of hearing, 20 Dec. 1928, BMA archives, 8–10. EJ's 'The Theory of Symbolism' (1916) discussed the adoption of new symbols, such as the Zeppelin for the phallus (p. 194), and the use of a room as 'a regular unconscious symbol for woman' (p. 191).

'run on psycho-analytical lines'. Transcript of hearing, 20 Dec. 1928, BMA archives, 11.

'infected with Freudism'. Dr J. S Manson, ibid., 14.

200.   'no other evil'. Moorehead, *Bertrand Russell*, 71.

'A child is nearer'. Ibid., 371.

'ample experience'. British Medical Association, *Report of the Psycho-Analysis Committee*, 22.

'thinking too much'. Ibid., 21.

201.   'the Committee has had'. Ibid., 'Conclusions', 23.

'an invincible opposition'. EJ to SF, 21 Jan. 1929, Paskauskas, 659.

'Jones makes trouble'. SF to Fer, 18 July 1925, quoted in Young-Bruehl, *Anna Freud*, 475, n. 60.

'Since his very first'. SF to ME, 2 June 1925, Young-Bruehl, *Anna Freud*, 172.

'as an interesting adventure'. SF to AF, 25 July 1929, Gay, 500n.

'worked tirelessly . . . the cause'. 'Dr Ernest Jones', *SE*, 21.249–50, quoted in Roazen, *Freud and His Followers*, 350.

202.   'easily recognizable . . . to you'. SF to EJ, 2 June 1929, Paskauskas, 660.

Chapter 15: Skating to the Top

203. 'created a new profession'. EJ quoted in Smith Ely Jelliffe, 'Open Letter to Ernest Jones', *IJP-A*, 20 (1939), 351.
'Psycho-analysis attempts'. EJ, *Psycho-Analysis* (1928), 5.
'certain that man's'. Ibid., 78.
204. 'The Radio'. EJ to SF, 5 May 1932, Paskauskas, 694.
'All staff. Danto, *Freud's Free Clinics*, 215–16.
'revolutionary'. EJ to ME, 18 Oct., 1929, BPAS, CEC/F01/40; see also EJ to SF, 14 Oct. 1929, Paskauskas, 665.
'by carelessness'. King, *No Ordinary Psychoanalyst*, 21.
205. 'an entrancingly beautiful damsel'. *FA*, 36–7.
'control over every fibre'. EJ, *Elements of Figure Skating* (rev. edn, 1952), 5.
'The nature'. Ibid., 15–16.
'Fear . . . has'. Ibid., 16–17.
'with an ample supply'. Ibid., 18.
206. 'to learn to slither'. Ibid., 19.
'into a state'. EJ, 'The Problem of Paul Morphy' (1931), 167. It has been suggested that Jones's chess paper influenced Samuel Beckett's novel *Murphy*, published in 1938, and depicting a chess game played in a mental institution.
'Check-mate'. Ibid., 168.
'In attacking'. Ibid.
207. 'I have always'. SF to EJ, 1 Jan. 1929, Paskauskas, 656.
Like most reputable biologists. This assessment of Lamarckism in the twentieth century was provided by Dr Walter Gratzer of King's College London to BM on 7 Mar. 2006; Huxley's observation on Jewish males is in Walter Gratzer, *A Bedtime Nature: Genius and Eccentricity in Science*. London: Macmillan, 1996, 245.
Jones tried to convince Freud. J–III, 333–6.
208. '"Discomfort" . . . seems'. EJ to SF, 1 Jan. 1930, Paskauskas, 667.
'essential obstacle'. Ibid.
'Every direction'. JR, 'Womanliness as a Masquerade', *IJP-A*, 10 (1929), 303.
'the permanent extinction'. EJ, 'The Early Development of Female Sexuality' (1927), 461.
'Hitherto you have'. EJ to SF, 10 Jan. 1932, Paskauskas, 689.
'the phantasy of the father'. Ibid.
209. 'there is very little'. SF to EJ, 17 June 1932, Paskauskas, 703.
'I can't help looking'. Fer to ME, 20 July 1930, Grosskurth-R, 203.
'Your relationship'. SF to EJ, 4 Jan. 1931, Paskauskas, 681.
210. 'in spite of Mrs'. EJ to SF, 13 June 1932, Paskauskas, 700.
'a completely wild'. Ibid., 701.
211. 'an expression of inner dissatisfaction'. SF to Fer, 18 Sept. 1931, Falzeder, 3:418.
'elimination of impulses'. Gay, 580, based on Fer's *Klinisches Tagebuch* for 14. 1932.
'Isn't Ferenczi'. SF to ME, 18 Apr. 1932, Brome, 174.
'Now, picture'. SF to Fer, 13 Dec. 1931, Falzeder, 3:422.
'after long'. Fer, quoted in Gay, 583.

212. 'Harmless, stupid'. SF to ME, 2 Sept. 1932, quoted in Gay, 583.

'He has completely regressed'. SF to AF, 3 Sept. 1932, quoted in Gay, 583–4.

'to acknowledge one's mistakes'. Ibid., 584.

'I have been'. Fer to SF, 10 Aug. 1927, quoted in Gay, 577.

213. 'Here a great crisis'. EJ to KJ, 5 Sept. 1932, Brome, 176, and BPAS, CJB/F01/25.

Chapter 16: Goodbye to Berlin

214. 'Judapest'. Joyce, *Finnegans Wake*, 150, l. 27

Ferenczi scrawled. Fer to SF, 29 Mar. 1933, Falzeder, 3:447.

'You must be glad'. EJ to SF, 1 Mar. 1933, Paskauskas, 715.

'the Hitler movement'. SF to EJ, 7 Apr. 1933, Paskauskas, 716.

'not inclined'. Ibid.

215. 'Psychoanalysis is'. Brecht, 101.

'Germany is at the present a hell'. J. H. W. van Ophuijsen to EJ, 3 Apr. 1933, BPAS, COA/F06/42; Steiner, 37.

'With the exception'. EJ to SF, 10 Apr. 1933, Paskauskas, 717, n. 4.

216. 'as a member'. *The Times*, 31 Mar. 1933.

Speaking as. Ibid.

'We are having a hectic'. EJ to Smith Ely Jelliffe, 25 Apr. 1933, quoted in Hale, *The Rise and Crisis of Psychoanalysis in the United States*, 125.

217. 'a meeting of modern and traditional'. *The Times*, 31 Mar. 1933.

'Ferenczi takes'. SF to EJ, 29 May 1933, Paskauskas, 721.

'In his last weeks . . . a secret between us'. Ibid.

218. 'degeneration'. EJ to SF, 3 June 1933, Paskauskas, 722.

'It would certainly not'. EJ to A. A. Brill, 20 June 1933, quoted in Masson, *The Assault on Truth*, 153.

'the tendency to prolong'. Fer, in 'Confusion of Tongues', quoted in Zaretsky, *Secrets of the Soul*, 230.

219. 'Fear', Jones expostulated. EJ to J. H. W. van Ophuijsen, 5 Apr. 1933, BPAS, COA/F06/043.

'As you know'. EJ to A. A. Brill, 20 June 1933, quoted in Steiner, 57.

220. 'New York really'. A. A. Brill to EJ, 12 May 1933, Steiner, 56.

'gravest of all'. EJ to SF, 18 Sept. 1933, Paskauskas, 729.

'not been more successful'. Ibid.

with exasperated sarcasm. EJ to P. Federn, 10 Oct. 1933, BPAS, CFD/F03/002.

'request'. *Recollecting Freud*: Roazen, unpublished review, 2005.

221. 'Jones was so upset'. Lieberman, *Acts of Will*, 65.

'the storm of indignation'. EJ to F. Boehm, 28 July 1934, Brecht, 78.

222. 'on the lines of the Nansen passport'. J–III, 322.

he reminded Jones. SF to EJ, 26 May 1935, Paskauskas, 743.

'is more concerned'. This and following quotes from EJ, 'Early Female Sexuality' (1935), 265ff.

castrating symbolism. J–III, 209.

Freud wrote to Jones. SF to EJ, 26 May 1935, Paskauskas, 743.

'our only man'. EJ to SF, 23 Feb. 1937, Paskauskas, 755.

'Mervyn, then nearly eleven'. KJ to EJ, 7 Feb. 1933, BPAS, CJC/F01/34.

224. 'I got back this morning'. EJ to AF, 2 Dec. 1935, Brecht, 130–31.

225. The Jews themselves. EJ, in J–III, 199, says that the remaining Jewish members of the German volunteered to resign and that some thought it would have been better to dissolve the society. See also EJ to AF, 5 Oct. 1935, BPAS, CFA/F02/052, on ME suggesting voluntary resignation.

'Urgently advise'. EJ to T. Benedek, 3(?) Dec. 1935, Brecht, 136.

'I suppose'. EJ to AF, 2 Dec. 1935, Brecht, 131.

then to Brill. EJ to A. A. Brill, 13 Nov. 1935, BPAS, CBD/F04/43.

'I do hope'. P. Roazen to BM, 9 Nov. 2004.

'Heil Hitler!'. M. H. Göring to colleagues, 15 Jan. 1944, Brecht, 147.

'Although it is'. EJ to SF, 27 June 1935, Paskauskas, 745.

226. 'Your recognition'. SF to EJ, 7 July 1935, Paskauskas, 745.

'so attractive'. EJ to SF, 27 Feb. 1936, Paskauskas, 750.

'unmistakable Oedipus situations'. Hughes, 274.

'because of my beautiful eyes'. SF to EJ, 26 May 1935, Paskauskas, 743.

'a branch of pure science'. EJ to SF, 6 July 1936, Paskauskas, 754.

'membership of this Society'. EJ to SF, 2 June 1936, Paskauskas, 752.

227. 'a philosopher'. Bair, *Jung*, 421.

'an American edition'. Ibid., 785, n. 2.

'unremittingly Jewish'. Cornwell, *Hitler's Scientists*, 166.

228. 'the psychology'. EJ, *New Statesman*, 1 Feb. 1956, 230–3.

he wrote to *The Times*. MJ, *Chances*, 11.

'Last Christmas'. *IJP-A*, 18 (1937), 73.

229. 'the consequences'. SF to EJ, 2 Mar. 1937, Paskauskas, 756–7.

Chapter 17: Into an English Garden

230. 'It is important'. EJ to AF, BPAS, CFF/F01/04 – undated but one of a series of letters sent in Apr. 1938.

231. 'had sent a message'. FO 371/21754, stamped C2686, 8 Apr. 1938, National Archives.

'Do you really think'. J–III, 237.

'the harm that'. W. Bragg to Halifax, 25 Apr. 1938, FO 371/21755, stamped C3755, 3 May 1938, National Archives.

232. 'To reassure'. *The Times*, 14 Apr. 1938.

'to ensure'. Ibid., 18 Apr. 1938.

'to have been improperly acquired'. Ibid., 28 Apr. 1938.

234. 'Nobody suggested'. MJ, *Chances*, 6.

'I wish I could . . . obtrude herself'. SF to EJ, 13 May 1938, Paskauskas, 763–4.

235. 'After the Rhine Bridge'. SF to ME, 6 [7?] June 1938, *The Diary of Sigmund Freud, 1929–1939*, trans. and intro. Michael Molnar (London: Hogarth Press, 1992), 237.

'Heil Hitler!'. EJ, obituary of Freud, *IJP-A*, 21 (1940), 3; quoted as 'I am almost tempted to cry out 'Heil Hitler' in J–III, 244.

'the general treatment'. Quoted in Gay, 631.

236. 'influx of foreign Jews'. Ferris, *Dr Freud*, 315.

'living vertically'. Robinson, ' "Now we are free" ', 3.

237. 'an aura, not of fame'. L. Woolf, *Downhill All The Way* (London: Hogarth Press, 1948), 168–9.
     'a screwed up shrunk'. Quoted in Gay, 640.
     'We need your help'. E. Gyömröi-Glück to EJ, 23 Dec. 1938, Steiner, 119.
     'who we think'. Ferris, *Dr Freud*, 390.
238. 'unfavourably on personal grounds'. EJ to AF, 20 Apr. 1938, BPAS, CFF/F01/06; Steiner, 142.
     'Is that what you think?', MJ, *Chances*, 10.
239. 'silly rumour . . . psychiatry'. J–III, 323.
     according to Riccardo Steiner. Steiner, 102.
     'on the mother of all'. EJ, report on Fifteenth International Congress, *IJP-A*, 20 (1939), 116–17.
240. 'But I remember . . . actual translator'. SF to EJ, 1 Nov. 1938, Paskauskas, 764–5.
     Jones replied. EJ to SF, 2 Nov. 1938, Paskauskas, 765.
     'a new recurrence'. SF to A. Zweig, 20 Feb. 1939, J–III, 260.
     'so near to it'. SF to EJ, 7 Mar. 1939, Paskauskas, 769.
241. 'Promise me'. Quoted in Gay, 642–3, in slightly different words from in J–III, 262.
     'regrettable . . . unscientific'. Martin Buber, quoted in Gay, 646.
     Jones reminded Freud. EJ to SF, 14 Nov. 1938, Paskauskas, 766.
     'small and baby-faced'. MJ, *Chances*, 37.
242. 'waved his stick'. Ibid., 40.
     My Own Dearest'. EJ to KJ, 26 Aug. 1939, BPAS, CJC/F03/32.
     'my sweetheart Kitty'. EJ to KJ, 1 Sept. 1939, BPAS, CJC/F02/34.
     'I can so well'. EJ to KJ, 6 Sept. 1939, BPAS, CJC/F02/34.
     'This critical moment'. EJ to SF, 3 Sept. 1939, Paskauskas, 770.
243. 'opened his eyes'. J–III, 262.
     'You promised'. Ibid.
     'friends far away . . . having loved'. J–III, 263–5.
244. 'Ernest makes'. KJ diary, 29 Sept. 1939, Brome, 198.
     Martha Freud herself. Martha Freud to EJ, 5 Oct. 1939, CFB/F10/03.
     'But what of ourselves?'. J–III, 264.

Chapter 18: War within a War

245. 'I've always had'. MJ, *Chances*, 15.
     'That's enough London'. Lewis Jones, interview with BM, 4 Jan. 2005.
246. to attack the officers. King and Steiner, *The Freud-Klein Controversies*, 34
247. 'the existence of such mechanisms'. EJ to AF, 21 Jan. 1942, BPAS, CFF/F02/01.
     'an indigestible morsel'. EJ to MK, 21 Jan. 1942, quoted in Roazen, *Oedipus in Britain*, 86.
     'Dr Schmideberg'. Grosskurth-Kl, 249.
248. One wealthy patient. KJ, 'A Sketch of E. J.'s Personality', 271.
     C. Eleanor Chilton. C. E. Chilton to EJ, 7 Feb. 1939, BPAS, CJD/F01/07. Six letters to EJ on these themes began on 8 Dec. 1924, BPAS, CJD/F01/01.
     One man wrote. Robert E. J. Davis to EJ, 7 June 1941, BPAS, CDA/F03/03.
     Another, who signed. J. T. M. Davies to EJ, 14 Apr. 1941, BPAS, CDA/F03/02.

The girl. EJ to KJ, 6 Sept. 1939, BPAS, CJC/F02/32.

His family recalls. BM conversations with Vanessa Hannam, 2005 and 2006.

249. 'The mind in war'. W. Trotter, *The Times*, 26 Sept. 1939.

'one of the most'. Elliott, 'Wilfred Batten Lewis Trotter (1872–1939)', 328.

The same issue. *IJP-A*, 21 (1939–1940).

'the melancholia that was'. EJ, 'Obituary of Otto Rank', *IJP-A*, 21 (1939–1940), 113.

250. Speaking at last. Grosskurth-Kl, 333.

'woman ridden Society'. Glover to EJ, 28 Jan. 1944, quoted in Grosskurth-Kl, 343.

'Gentlemen's Agreement'. Rayner, *The Independent Mind*, 20–22.

'A' Group . . . 'B' group. See Schwartz, *Cassandra's Daughter*, 223.

251. 'The British Psycho-Analytical Society'. E Glover to EJ, 11 Dec. 1944, Brome, 207.

'regrets he is not'. [Signature illegible] to E. Glover, 15 July 1943, CGA/F32/04.

'so vividly'. Brome, 211.

252. 'the tasteless Olivier'. EJ to KJ, 14 Dec. 1944, BPAS, CJC/F02/051.

one of his doctors. Himsworth to EJ, 8 Feb. 1945, BPAS, CHB/F07/001.

'Patient was a doctor'. *Lancet*, 18 Oct. 1947, 567.

'psycho-analytic politics'. EJ to E. Glover, 8 Jan. 1945, quoted in Grosskurth-Kl, 353.

'blatant, aggressive bigotry'. Lieberman, *Acts of Will*, 407.

'the arrogant pretension'. EJ, 'The Psychology of the Jewish Question' (1945), reprinted in *Essays in Applied Psycho-Analysis* (1951), 1:288–9.

253. 'the nationalist solution . . . anti-Semitism'. Ibid., 299–300.

'*meshugge* . . . Wales'. MJ, *Chances*, 13.

'our temperament'. 'G. J.', 'Dr Ernest Jones', *Llandovery School Journal*, June 1958, reprinted in *Gowr*, 11 (1958), 28–30.

'the callous English acquiescence'. *FA*, 2.

'one of the last acts'. EJ to AF, 28 Apr. 1945, CFF/F02/03.

254. There he credited himself. EJ, 'Reminiscent Notes' (1945), 8–10.

'though I was never spooky'. JS to EJ, 18 July 1945, BPAS, CSD/F03/008.

'a kind of paralysis'. C. Müller-Braunschweig to EJ, 12 July 1945, BPAS, CMA/F23/05.

255. From Italy. N. Perrotti to EJ, 31 Dec. 1945, BPAS, CPA/F07/001.

'who took . . . mother'. *FA*, 2.

'Armistice night'. *FA*, 247.

'unsparing . . . exclamation'. EJ, appendix (1948) in Klein, *Envy and Gratitude and Other Works*, 338

256. 'astonished at'. S. Payne, 'An Address on the Occasion of Presenting His Portrait to Ernest Jones', *IJP-A*, 27 (1946), 6. (Addresses also by W. H. B. Stoddard, J. C. Flügel and J. Rickman.)

'to prohibit'. EJ, 'A Valedictory Address', *IJP-A*, 27 (1946), 7–12.

257. 'How slow'. KJ Notes 2, 1965.

The lunch. Lewis Jones interview with BM, 4 Jan. 2005.

'showing her'. MJ, preface to *FA*, xiii.

'wonderfully enlightening . . . Othello'. Olivier, *Confessions of an Actor*, 79, 82.

'from all imagined dangers'. EJ, *What is Psychoanalysis?* (1949), 120.

Chapter 19: A Life for a Life

259. 'I value your work'. Wittels, *Sigmund Freud*, 13.
he approached Bernfeld. EJ to S. Bernfeld, 23 Mar. 1950, BPAS, CBC/F03/001.
Bernfeld, in reply. S. Bernfeld to EJ, 24 Apr. 1950, BPAS, CBC/F03/02.

260. 'The date'. J–I, 119.
Mrs Freud herself'. Ibid., 120.
'the passionate relationship'. J–I, 316.

261. 'souls burning'. J–I, 14.
Strachey liked. JS to EJ, 15 Dec. 1950, BPAS, CSD/F03/16X.
This gave Jones. Meisel, 317.
'staggering thoroughness'. EJ to JS, quoted in Caine, *Bombay to Bloomsbury*, 366, n. 39.
'remarkable and widespread'. Ibid.
'red lines down the side'. EJ to JS, 10 Feb. 1952, BPAS, CSD/F03/49.

262. 'that was very seldom shaken'. J–I, 15.

263. 'only my parents'. MJ, epilogue to *FA*, 253.
'It is not'. J–I, vii.
'Yours, my dear'. J–I, viii.
'hero-worshipping propensities', J–I, ix.

364. 'A Gentile would'. J–I, 25.
'never regained'. J–I, 25.
'magical drug'. J–I, 89.
'given rise to'. J–I, 168.
'a distinguished lady'. *The Times*, 10 Nov. 1951, BPAS, G13/8D/003.

265. 'I am simply amazed'. AF to E. Kris, 10 Dec. 1951, Young-Bruehl, *Anna Freud*, 307.
'The question of'. AF to EJ, 19 Mar. 1952, CFF/102/14.
'now I love you'. J–I, 147.
'You know'. J–I, 177.
'He was constantly'. J–I, 140.

266. 'The thought of England'. SF to Martha Bernays, 16 Aug. 1882, J–I, 179.
'You can talk'. Vanessa Hannam to BM, 30 June 2004.
'Very much love'. AF to EJ, 25 Nov. 1952, BPAS, CFF/F02/12.

267. 'the ego'. J–I, 437.
'Last . . . indebted'. J–I, x.
'Love from Dad'. EJ to MJ, Brome, 214.
'a spry, Homburg-hatted'. *Time*, 10 Aug. 1953, 37.

268. 'The honorary Life President'. 'Profile: Dr Ernest Jones', *Observer*, 26 July 1953.
Publishers' Weekly. 31 Oct. 1953.
'It would be difficult'. L. Trilling, *New York Times Book Review*, 11 Oct. 1953.
Max Lerner. 'New Light on Freud', *New York Post*, 12 Oct. 1953.
'stout partisanship'. 'Young Doctor Freud', *Time*, 16 Oct. 1953.

269. 'This entrancing volume'. *Manchester Guardian*, 9 Oct. 1953.
'it is hard to know'. 'Conquistador', *Spectator*, 16 Oct. 1953.
'It was Ernest Jones', E. D. Adrian, 'Discoveries of the Mind', *Observer*, 28 Oct. 1953.

'Most of us'. Inglis, *Irish Times*, 2 Jan. 1954.

'a certain clumsiness'. *Economist*, 28 Nov. 1953.

'One of the outstanding' . . . *New Yorker*: advertisement, *New York Times Book Review*, 6 Dec. 1953.

'It's not sufficient'. Canetti, *Party in the Blitz*, 161.

270. '900 Lettres'. 'Freud Révélées', *Samedi-Soir*, 26 Nov. 1953.

'They made a dignified performance'. EJ to JS, 23 July [1954], BPAS, CSD/F01/31.

'the world at last'. J–II, 232.

'I was in Vienna'. J–II, 104.

to attend . . . family. J–II, 119. (The American edition, p. 106, says 'one of the two'.)

271. 'Jung is crazy'. P. Calvocoressi to EJ, 15 Feb. 1955, BPAS.

'As you ask'. SF to EJ, 6 Nov. 1922, Paskauskas, 502–3.

'This is a fine piece of work'. *The Times*, 22 Sept. 1955.

'the best way to praise'. *New York Times Book Review*, 18 Sept. 1955.

272. 'In every sense'. *Chicago Tribune*, 18 Sept. 1955.

'most persuasively'. *Times Literary Supplement*, 28 Oct. 1955.

'more than ever'. *Observer*, 9 Oct. 1955.

'my very mild remarks'. EJ to JS, 7 July 1956, BPAS.

'Brill . . . suffered'. J–II, 197.

'For years'. Max Schur to EJ, 30 Sept. 1955. BPAS, CSA/F01/01.

273. Jones formed the Committee. Paskauskas, 'Freud's Break with Jung.

'The airfield'. J–III, 233.

'After their meeting'. J–III, 188.

274. 'Then there were were the delusions'. J–III, 190.

'a myth'. Bonomi, 'Flight into Sanity', 535.

'a travesty'. Roazen, *Freud and His Followers*, 371; see also Roazen, *Meeting Freud's Family*, 94–9.

'Five foot four, like me'. MJ interview with BM, 19 Jan. 2004.

275. 'major creative thinking'. Fern Marja, 'Freud's Bouncing Boswell at 77', *New York Post*, 6 May 1956.

'It is *the* standard one'. Ibid.

'the world's most renowned'. Helen G. First, 'Freud Biographer Looks at America', *Philadelphia Inquirer*, 24 Apr. 1956.

'You were quite marvellous'. AF to EJ, 10 May 1936, BPAS, CFF/F03/31A.

276. 'an unpleasant odour'. J–III, 261–2.

'Anyhow'. J–III, 262.

'The cancer . . . sense'. Ibid.

'For someone'. Ibid.

277. 'The frightful outburst'. EJ, 'The Birth and Death of Moses' (1958), 1.

'is certainly the most temerarious'. Ibid, p. 4.

'It is an arena'. Ibid.

278. 'Man's chief enemy'. J–III, 472.

'There can be no question'.

'in some ways'. *Economist*, 21 Dec. 1957.

'to say that'. *Reporter*, 7 Dec. 1961.

'go beyond a biography'. *Manchester Guardian*, 6 Dec. 1957.

a strong letter of complaint. *IJP-A*, 37 (1958), 48.

Jones replied. Ibid.

'Dear Dad'. MJ to EJ, 29 Dec. 1957, BPAS.

279. 'No, no, no'. MJ, *Chances*, 147.

'took a pill'. Brome, 218, quoting interview with KJ, 15 Dec. 1980.

Postscript

280. '*Ich komme nach Wien*'. Burgess, *The End of the World News*, 3–4.

281 'It was not only'. 'Dr Ernest Jones – Psycho-analysis in Britain', *The Times*, 12 Feb. 1958.

281. 'It is hard to say'. 'Dr Ernest Jones', *Manchester Guardian*, 12 Feb. 1958.

'a formidable fighter'. 'Psychiatric Pioneer', *Sunday Times*, 16 Feb. 1958.

'the most eminent'. 'Ernest Jones', *Lancet*, 28 Feb. 1958.

'The Friend of Freud'. *South Wales Evening Post*, 12 Feb. 1958.

'gladiatorial'. 'Ernest Jones, M.D. D.Sc. F.R.C.P.', *British Medical Journal*, 22 Feb. 1958.

283. 'the description'. T. G. Davies, *Ernest Jones*, 61.

'The record'. *FA*, xxi.

'Does the name'. Paul Ferris, interview with Mervyn Jones, Llanmadoc, 2 Apr. 1994.

'Irish Facts'. Hugh Kenner, *A Colder Eye*, London: Allen Lane, The Penguin Press, 1989, 19.

Bibliography

Abbreviations

IJP-A	*International Journal of Psycho-Analysis*
Imago	*Imago: Zeitschrift für Anwendung der Psychoanalyse auf die Geisteswissenschaften*, ed. Otto Rank and Hanns Sachs
Jahrbuch	*Jahrbuch für psychoanalytische und psychopathologische Forschungen*, ed. Carl Gustav Jung, directed by Eugen Bleuler and Sigmund Freud
Schriften	*Schriften zur angewandten Seelenkunde*, a monograph series, ed. Sigmund Freud
SE	Sigmund Freud, *The Standard Edition of the Complete Psychological Works*
Zeitschrift	*Internationale Zeitschrift für ärtzliche Psychoanalyse*, ed. Otto Rank, Sándor Ferenczi and Ernest Jones
Zentralblatt	*Zentralblatt für Psychoanalyse: Medizinische Monatsschrift für Seelenkunde*, ed. Wilhelm Stekel and Alfred Adler

Works by Ernest Jones

Note Many of Jones's shorter works, such as obituaries and book reviews, have been omitted for reasons of space.

1904 'The Healing of the Tracheotomy Wound in Diphtheria', *British Journal of Children's Diseases*, 1:153–8
1905 'The Onset of Hemiplegia in Vascular Lesions', *Brain*, 28:527–55
'Multiple Bilateral Contractures Simulating Pseudo-Hypertrophic Muscular Paralysis (An Aberrant Form of the Nageotte-Wilbonchewitch Syndrome)', *Brain*, 28:585–6
'A Case of Extreme Microcephaly, with Ape-Like Movements', *British Journal of Children's Diseases*, 2:214–15
1907 'La vrai aphasie tactile', *Revue neurologique*, 15:3–7
'Eight Cases of Hereditary Spastic Paraplegia', *Review of Neurology and Psychiatry*, 5:98–106
'A Simplified Technique for Accurate Cell Enumeration in Lumbar Puncture', *Review of Neurology and Psychiatry*, 5:539–50
'The Clinical Significance of Allochiria', *Lancet*, 2:830–32
'The Precise Diagnostic Value of Allochiria', *Brain*, 30:490–532
'Mechanism of Severe Briquet Attack as Contrasted with that of Psychasthenic Fits', *Journal of Abnormal Psychology*, 2:218–27

'Alcoholic Cirrhosis of the Liver in Children', *British Journal of Children's Diseases*, 4:1–14, 43–52

'The Occurrence of Goitre in Parent and Child', *British Journal of Children's Diseases*, 4:101–3

1908 'The Symptoms and Diagnosis of Juvenile Tabes', *British Journal of Children's Diseases*, 5:131–40

'The Significance of Phrictopathic Sensation', *Journal of Nervous and Mental Disease*, 35:427–37

'The Variation of the Articulatory Capacity for Different Consonantal Sounds in School Children', *Internationales Archiv für Schulhygiene*, 5:137–57

'Rationalisation in Everyday Life', *Journal of Abnormal Psychology*, 3:161–9

1909 'The Pathology of Dyschiria', *Review of Neurology and Psychiatry*, 7:499–522, 559–87

'The Differential Diagnosis of Cerebellar Tumours', *Boston Medical and Surgical Journal*, 161:281–4

'Psycho-Analysis in Psychotherapy', *Journal of Abnormal Psychology*, 4:140–50; and Morton Prince et al., *Psychotherapeutics: A Symposium*. Boston: Richard D. Badger, 107–18

'Remarks on a Case of Complete Autopsychic Amnesia', *Journal of Abnormal Psychology*, 4:218–35

'Psycho-Analytic Notes on a Case of Hypomania', *American Journal of Insanity*, 66:203–18

'An Attempt to Define the Terms Used in Connection with Right-Handedness', *Psychological Bulletin*, 6:130–32

'The Differences between the Sexes in the Development of Speech' (read at the Sixth International Congress of Psychology, Geneva, 2–7 Aug. 1909), *British Journal of Children's Diseases*, 6:413–16

(with George W. Ross) 'On the Use of Certain New Chemical Tests in the Diagnosis of General Paralysis and Tabes', *British Medical Journal*, 1:1111–13.

[Comments on case reported by] W. G. Heggie, 'Glioma of the Optic Thalamus', *Dominion Medical Monthly*, 33:96–8

'The Pathology of General Paralysis', *Dominion Medical Monthly*, 33:127–36; and *Alienist and Neurologist*, 30:577–88

'Cerebrospinal Fluid in Relation to the Diagnosis of Metasyphilis of the Nervous System', *Bulletin of the Ontario Hospitals for the Insane*, 2:15–39

'A Review of Our Present Knowledge Concerning the Sero-Diagnosis of General Paralysis', *American Journal of Insanity*, 65:653–88

'Modern Progress in Our Knowledge of the Pathology of General Paralysis', *Lancet*, 87/2:209–12

'The Proteid Content of the Cerebro-Spinal Fluid in General Paralysis', *Review of Neurology and Psychiatry*, 7:379–91

1909–10 'The Dyschiric Syndrome', *Journal of Abnormal Psychology*, 4:311–27

1910 'The Oedipus-Complex as an Explanation of Hamlet's Mystery: A Study in Motive', *American Journal of Psychology*, 22:72–113. Trans.: 'Das Problem des Hamlet und der Oedipus-Komplex,' *Schriften*, 10

'The Question of the Side Affected in Hemiplegia and in Arterial Lesions of the Brain', *Quarterly Journal of Clinical Medicine*, 3:233–50

'The Psycho-Analytic Method of Treatment', *Journal of Nervous and Mental Disease*, 37:285–95

'Freud's Theory of Dreams' (read before the American Psychological Association, Boston, 29 Dec. 1909), *Review of Neurology and Psychiatry*, 8:135–43; expanded version in *American Journal of Psychology*, 21:283–308

'The Practical Value of the Word-Association Method in Psychopathology', *Review of Neurology and Psychiatry*, 8:641–72

'Psycho-Analysis and Education', *Journal of Educational Psychology*, 1:497–520

'Some Questions of General Ethics Arising in Relation to Psychotherapy', *Dominion Medical Monthly*, 35:17–22

'Freud's Psychology', *Psychological Bulletin*, 7:109–28

'Simulated Foolishness in Hysteria' (read before the Detroit Society of Neurology and Psychiatry, 3 Feb. 1910), *American Journal of Insanity*, 67:279–86

'The Mental Characteristics of Chronic Epilepsy' (read before the National Association for the Study of Epilepsy, Baltimore, 7 May 1910), *Maryland Medical Journal*, 53:223–9

'A Modern Conception of the Psychoneuroses' (read before a meeting of the Canadian Medical Association, Toronto, 2 June 1910), *Interstate Medical Journal*, 17:567–75

'The Relation between Organic and Functional Nervous Diseases', *Dominion Medical Monthly*, 35:202–7

'On the Nightmare', *American Journal of Insanity*, 66:383–417

'Bericht über die neuere englische und amerikanische Literatur zur klinischen Psychologie und Psychopathologie', *Jahrbuch*, 2:316–37. Trans.: 'Review of the Recent English and American Literature on Clinical Psychology and Psychopathology', *Archives of Neurology and Psychiatry*, 5:120–47

'The Differential Diagnosis of Paraplegia', *Canadian Practitioner and Medical Review*, 35:1–8

1910–11 'The Action of Suggestion in Psychotherapy', *Journal of Abnormal Psychology*, 5:217–254. [Expanded version of Jones (1911), 'The Therapeutic Effect of Suggestion' (read at the first meeting of the American Psychopathological Association, Washington, DC, 2 May 1910, and at the First International Congress of Medical Psychology and Psychotherapy, Brussels, 7–8 Aug. 1910), *Canadian Journal of Medicine and Surgery*, 29:78–87]

[Report on First International Congress of Medical Psychology and Psychotherapy, Brussels, 7–8 Aug. 1910], *Journal of Abnormal Psychology*, 5:290–91

1911 'The Deviation of the Tongue in Hemiplegia' (read at the Thirty-Seventh Annual Meeting of the American Neurological Association, Baltimore, 13 May 1911), *Journal of Nervous and Mental Disease*, 38:577–87

'Remarks on Dr Morton Prince's Article, "The Mechanism and Interpretation of Dreams"', *Journal of Abnormal Psychology*, 5:328–36

'Some Instances of the Influence of Dreams on Waking Life', *Journal of Abnormal Psychology*, 6:11–18

'Reflections on Some Criticisms of the Psycho-Analytic Method of Treatment' (read before the Chicago Neurological Society and Chicago Medical Society (joint meeting), 18 Jan. 1911), *American Journal of Mental Science*, 142:47–57

'The Pathology of Morbid Anxiety' (read before the American Psychopathological Association, Baltimore, 10 May 1911), *Journal of Abnormal Psychology*, 6:81–106

'The Relationship between Dreams and Psycho-Neurotic Symptoms' (read before the Wayne County Society, Detroit, 15 May 1911), *American Journal of Insanity*, 68:57–80

'The Psychopathology of Everyday Life' (read at the Detroit Academy of Medicine, 16 May 1911), *American Journal of Psychology*, 22:477–527

'Syphilis of the Nervous System', *Interstate Medical Journal*, 18:39–47

'Darwin über das Vergessen', *Zentralblatt*, 1:614

1911–12 [Review of Eugen Bleuler, 'Die Psychoanalyse Freuds: Verteidigung und kritische Bermerkungen', *Jahrbuch*, 2(1910), 623–730], *Journal of Abnormal Psychology*, 6:465–70

1912 'The Therapeutic Action of Psycho-Analysis' (read before the Detroit Society of Neurology and Psychiatry, 7 Dec. 1911), *Review of Neurology and Psychiatry*, 10:53–64

'The Value of Sublimating Processes for Education and Re-Education' (read before the American Psychological Association, Washington, DC, 29 Dec. 1911), *Journal of Educational Psychology*, 3:241–56

'A Forgotten Dream (Note on the Oedipus Saving Phantasy)', *Journal of Abnormal Psychology*, 7:5–16

'Zwei interessante Fälle von Versprechen', *Zentralblatt*, 2:33–4

'Analyse eines Falles von Namenvergessen', *Zentralblatt*, 2:84–6

'Ein klares Beispiel sekundärer Bearbeitung', *Zentralblatt*, 2:135

'Unbewusste Zahlenbehandlung', *Zentralblatt*, 2:241–4

'Die Bedeutung des Salzes in Sitte und Brauch der Völker', *Imago*, 1:361–85; 454–88

'Ein ungewöhnlicher Fall von "gemeinsamen Sterben"', *Zentralblatt*, 2:455–9

'Der Alptraum in seiner Beziehung zu gewissen Formen des mittelalterlichen Aberglaubens', *Schriften*, 14:1–149. Trans. in pt 2 of Jones, *On the Nightmare* (1931), 55–240 *Papers on Psycho-Analysis*, 1st edn. London: Ballière, Tindall and Cox

1912–13 'Einige Fälle von Zwangsneurose', *Jahrbuch*, 4:563–606, 5:55–116. Abridged version, 'Analytic Study of a Case of Obsessional Neurosis', in *Papers*, 2nd edn, 1918, 515–39

1913 'The Treatment of the Neuroses, Including the Psychoneuroses', in William A. White and Smith Ely Jelliffe, eds., *The Modern Treatment of Nervous and Mental Diseases by American and British Authors*, 2 vols. Philadelphia: Lea and Faber, 1:331–416. (See Jones, *Treatment of the Neuroses* (1920).)

'Die Beziehung zwischen Angstneurose und Angsthysterie', *Zeitschrift*, 1:11–17. ('The Relation between Anxiety Neurosis and Anxiety Hysteria' (read before the International Society for Medical Psychology and Psychotherapy, Zurich, 9 Sept. 1912)), *Journal of Abnormal Psychology*, 8:1–9

'A Simple Phobia', *Journal of Abnormal Psychology*, 8:101–8

'The Interrelations of the Biogenetic Psychoses' (read at the opening ceremony of the Phipps Psychiatric Clinic, Baltimore, 18 Apr. 1913), *American Journal of Insanity*, 69:1027–32

'Die Bedeutung des Grossvaters für das Schicksal des Einzelnen', *Zeitschrift*, 1:219–23

'Andrea del Sarto Kunst und der Einfluss seiner Gattin', *Imago*, 2:468–80

'Der Gottmensch-Komplex; der Glaube, Gott zu sein, und die daraus folgenden Charactermerkmale', *Zeitschrift*, 1:313–39

'George Meredith über Träume', *Zentralblatt*, 3:54–5

'Hass und Analerotik in der Zwangsneurose', *Zeitschrift*, 1:425–30. Trans.: 'Hate and Anal Erotism in the Obsessional Neurosis' (read before the American Psychopathological Association, Washington, DC, 9 May 1913), in *Papers*, 2nd edn (1918), 540–48.

'[Report on] Internationaler Kongress für Medizin. London, August 1913', *Zeitschrift*, 1:592–7

'The Phantasy of the Reversal of Generations' (read before the Psychiatric Society, Ward's Island, New York, 8 Feb. 1913), in *Papers*, 2nd edn (1918), 658–87. Trans. (abridged): 'Generations-Umkehrungsphantasie', *Zeitschrift*, 1:562–3

1913–14 'The Case of Louis Bonaparte, King of Holland' (read before the American Psychopathological Association, Washington, DC, 8 May 1913), *Journal of Abnormal Psychology*, 8:289–330

1914 'Die Empfängniss der Jungfrau Maria durch das Ohr: Ein Beitrag zu der Beziehung zwischen Kunst und Religion', *Jahrbuch der Psychoanalyse*, 6:135–204. Trans. and rev.: 'The Madonna's Conception through the Ear: A Contribution to the Relation between Aesthetics and Religion', in Jones, *Essays in Applied Psycho-Analysis* (1923), 261–359, and *Essays in Applied Psycho-Analysis* (1951), 2:266–357

'Die Stellungnahme des psychoanalytischen ärztes zu den aktuellen Konflikten' (read before the Fourth International Psychoanalytic Congress, Munich, 8 Sept. 1913), *Zeitschrift*, 2:6–10. Trans.: 'The Attitude of the Psycho-Analytic Physician towards Current Conflicts', in *Papers*, 2nd edn. (1918), 312–17.

[Critique of Jung, *The Theory of Pychoanalysis*], *Zeitschrift*, 2:83–6

'Bemerkungen zur psychoanalytischen Technik', *Zeitschrift*, 2:274–5

'Frau und Zimmer.' *Zeitschrift*, 2:380

'Zahnziehen und Geburt.' *Zeitschrift*, 2:380–81

'Haarschneiden und Geiz', *Zeitschrift*, 2:383

'Die Technik der psychoanalytischen Therapie', *Jahrbuch der Psychoanalyse*, 6:329–42.

'The Unconscious and its Significance for Psychopathology' (read in Jones's absence before the British Medical Association, Aberdeen, 29–31 July 1914), *British Medical Journal*, 2 (1914):966–7; and *Review of Neurology and Psychology*, 12:474–81

1915 'The Repression Theory and Its Relation to Memory' (read before the British Psychological Society, Durham, 30 Jan. 1915), *British Journal of Psychology*, 8:33–47

'Professor Janet on Psycho-Analysis: A Rejoinder', *Journal of Abnormal Psychology*, 9:400–410. Trans.: 'Professor Janet über Psychoanalyse', *Zeitschrift*, 4:34–43

'War and Individual Psychology', *Sociological Review*, 8:167–80

'War and Sublimation' (read before the British Association for the Advancement of Science, Section of Psychology, Manchester, 10 Sept. 1915) in Jones, *Essays in Applied Psycho-Analysis* (1923), 381–90, and *Essays in Applied Psycho-Analysis* (1951), 1:77–87.

1916 'The Theory of Symbolism' (read before the British Psychological Society, 29 Jan. 1916), *British Journal of Psychology*, 9:181–229. Trans.: Hanns Sachs, 'Die Theorie der Symbolik', *Zeitschrift*, 5:244–73, and 8:259–89.

Translation of Sándor Ferenczi, *Contributions to Psychoanalysis*. Boston: R. G. Badger.

'The Unconscious Mental Life of the Child', *Child-Study*, 9:37–41, 49–55

1916–17 Review of Stanley Hall, 'A Synthetic Genetic Study of Fear', *American Journal of Psychology*, *Zeitschrift*, 4:55–60.

1918 'War Shock and Freud's Theory of the Neuroses', *Proceedings of the Royal Society of Medicine*, 11:21–36. Trans.: 'Die Kriegsneurosen und die Freudsche Theorie', in *Zür Psychoanalyse der Kriegsneurosen*. Leipzig: Internationaler Psychoanalytischer Verlag, 1919, 61–82.

'Anal-Erotic Character Traits', *Journal of Abnormal Pscyhology*, 13:261–84. Trans.: Anna Freud, 'Über analerotische Charakterzüge', *Zeitschrift*, 5:69–92

Papers on Psycho-Analysis, 2nd edn. London: Ballière, Tindall and Cox

1919 [Obituary of J. J. Putnam], *Zeitschrift*, 5:233–43. Trans.: 'Dr. James Jackson Putnam', *IJP-A*, 1:6–16

1920 'Recent Advances in Psycho-Analysis' (read before the Medical Section, British Psychological Society, 21 Jan. 1920), *British Journal of Medical Psychology*, 1:49–71; and *IJP-A*, 1:161–85.

Treatment of the Neuroses. New York: Wm. Wood; London: Baillière, Tindall and Cox (based on 'The Treatment of the Neuroses, including the Psychoneuroses' (1913)). Trans.: *Therapie der Neurosen*. Leipzig: Internationaler Psychoanalytischer Verlag, 1921

[Review of A. G. Tansley, *The New Psychology and Its Relation to Life*], *IJP-A*, 1:478–80

1921 'Persons in Dreams Disguised as Themselves', *IJP-A*, 2:420–23

1921–22 'Dream Analysis', in *Encyclopaedia and Dictionary of Education*, London: Pitman, 1:493–4

'Psychotherapy', in *Encyclopaedia and Dictionary of Education*, London: Pitman, 3:1371–2.

1922 Preface to S. Freud, *Beyond the Pleasure Principle*

Preface to S. Freud, *Introductory Lectures on Psycho-Analysis*

[Review of Edward J. Kempf, *Psychopathology*], *IJP-A*, 3:55–65

[Review of D. Forsyth, *The Technique of Psycho-Analysis*], *IJP-A*, 3:224–7

[Review of E. A. Westermarck, *The History of Human Marriage*], *IJP-A*, 3:249–52.

'Notes on Dr Abraham's Article on "The Female Castration Complex"', *IJP-A*, 3:327–8

'Some Problems of Adolescence' (read before a joint meeting of the General, Medical and Education sections of the British Psychological Society, 14 Mar. 1922), *British Journal of Psychology*, 13:31–47

'The Island of Ireland: A Psycho-Analytical Contribution to Political Psychology' (read before the British Psycho-Analytical Society, 21 June 1922), in Jones, *Essays in Applied Psycho-Analysis* (1951), 1:95–112

[Review of S. Freud, *Dream Psychology*], *IJP-A*, 3:114–15

'A Psycho-Analytic Study of the Holy Ghost Concept' (read before the Seventh Congress of the International Psychoanalytic Association, Berlin, 27 Sept. 1922), in Jones, *Essays in Applied Psycho-Analysis* (1951), 2:358–73

1923 '*Essays in Applied Psycho-Analysis*. London: International Psycho-Analytical Press

'The Nature of Auto-Suggestion' (read before the Medical Section of the British Psychological Society, 22 Mar. 1923), *IJP-A*, 4:293–312

'The Nature of Desire', *Journal of Neurology and Psychopathology*, 3:338–41

'Classification of the Instincts' (read before the Seventh International Congress of Psychology, Oxford, 31 July 1923), *British Journal of Psychology*, 14:256–61

Papers on Psycho-Analysis, 3rd edn. London: Ballière, Tindall and Cox

1924 [et al.]. *Glossary for the Use of Translators of Psycho-Analytical Works*. Supplement no. I to *IJP-A*, 5:1–16 (additions and corrections in *IJP-A*, 6)

'Editorial Preface', in S. Freud, *Collected Papers* 1:3–4

[Review of F. Wittels, *Sigmund Freud: His Personality, His Teaching and His School* (1924)], *IJP-A*, 5:481–6.

(ed.) *Social Aspects of Psycho-Analysis: Lectures Delivered under the Auspices of the Sociological Society*. London: Williams and Norgate

'Psycho-Analysis and Anthropology' (read before the Royal Anthropological Society, 19 Feb. 1924), *Journal of the Royal Anthropological Institute*, 54:47–66

'Free Will and Determinism' (read before the Oxford Psychological Society, 27 Oct. 1924), in Jones, *Essays in Applied Psycho-Analysis* (1951), 2:178–89

[Review of R. Laforgue and R. Allendy, *La psychanalyse et les névroses*], *IJP-A*, 5:486–87.

[Review of William McDougall, *An Outline of Psychology* (1923)] *IJP-A*, 5:496–8.

1925 'Mother-Right and the Sexual Ignorance of Savages', *IJP-A*, 6:109–30

Traité théorique et pratique de psychanalyse. Trans.: S. Jankélévich. Paris: Payot. (Translation of *Papers*, 3rd ed (1923))

1926 [Obituary of Karl Abraham], *IJP-A*, 7:155–89; and *Zeitschrift*, 12:155–83. In K. Abraham, *Selected Papers of Karl Abraham*, trans. D. Bryan and A. Strachey. London: Hogarth Press, 1927

'The Psychology of Religion' (read before the Tenth International Congress of Psychology, Groningen, 7 Sept. 1926), *British Journal of Medical Psychology*, 6:264–9.

'The Origin and Structure of the Super-Ego', *IJP-A*, 7:303–11. Trans.: "Der Ursprung und Aufbau des Über-Ichs', *Zeitschrift*, 12:253–62

1927 [Review of S. Freud, *The Question of Lay Analysis* (1926)], *Zeitschrift*, 13:101–7; and *IJP-A*, 8:87–92

[Review of William McDougall, *An Outline of Abnormal Psychology* (1926)], *IJP-A*, 8:421–9

[Contribution to the 'Discussion on Lay Analysis'], *IJP-A*, 8:174–98. Trans.: *Zeitschrift*, 13:171–92

[Contribution to the 'Symposium on Child Analysis'], *IJP-A*, 8:387–91

'La conception du surmoi' (read before the French Psychoanalytical Society, 5 Apr. 1927), *Revue française de psychanalyse*, 1:324–36. Trans.: 'The Development of the Concept of the Superego', *Journal of Abnormal and Social Psychology*, 23:276–85

'The Early Development of Female Sexuality' (read before the Tenth Congress of the International Psychoanalytic Association, Innsbruck, 1 Sept. 1927), *IJP-A*, 8:459–72

1928 *Psycho-Analysis*. London: E. Benn. Rev. edn: London: Allen and Unwin, 1949.

'Psycho-Analysis and Folklore' (read before the Jubilee Congress of the Folk-Lore Society, 25 Sept. 1928), *Scientia*, 55:209–20; and Jones, *Essays in Applied Psycho-Analysis* (1951), 2:1–21

Zur psychoanalyse der christlichen Religion. Leipzig: Internationaler Psychoanalytischer Verlag.

1929 'The Psychopathology of Anxiety' (read before the Psychiatric Section of the Royal Society of Medicine and the British Psychological Society, 9 Apr. 1929), *British Journal of Medical Psychology*, 9:17–25

'La jalousie' (read at the Sorbonne, 21 Mar. 1929), *Revue française de psychanalyse*, 3:228–422

'Fear, Guilt, and Hate' (read before the Eleventh Congress of the International Psychoanalytic Association, Oxford, 27 July 1929), *IJP-A*, 10:383–97.

'Psychoanalysis and Psychiatry' (read at the Psychiatric Institute, Columbia University, 4 Dec. 1929), *Mental Hygiene*, 14:384–98

'Abnormal Psychology', *Encyclopædia Britannica*, 14th edn, 1:50–56

'Freud, Sigmund', *Encyclopædia Britannica*, 14th edn, 9:836–7

1930 'Psycho-Analysis and Biology' (read before the Second International Congress for Sex Research, London, 7 Aug. 1930), in Jones, *Essays in Applied Psycho-Analysis* (1951), 1:135–64

'Psychoanalysis and the Christian Religion' (read before the Lotus Club, Oxford University, 22 Nov. 1930), in Jones, *Essays in Applied Psycho-Analysis* (1951), 2:198–211

1931 'The Problem of Paul Morphy: A Contribution to the Psychology of Chess', *IJP-A*, 12:1–23; and Jones, *Essays in Applied Psycho-Analysis* (1951), 1:165–96

On the Nightmare. London: Hogarth Press and Institute of Psycho-Analysis.

The Elements of Figure Skating. London: Methuen

1933 'The Phallic Phase' (read before the Twelfth Congress of the International Psychoanalytic Association, Wiesbaden, 4–7 Sept. 1932), *IJP-A*, 14:1–33 Trans.: 'Die phallische Phase', *Zeitschrift*, 19:322–57

'The Unconscious Mind', in C. Burt, E. Jones, E. Miller, and W. Moodie, *How the Mind Works.* London: Allen & Unwin, 61–103

[Review of S. Freud, *Why War?* (1933)], *IJP-A*, 14:418–20

1934 'Psycho-Analysis and Modern Medicine' (read before the Paddington Medical Society), *Lancet*, 226:59–62

1935 'Early Female Sexuality' (read before the Vienna Psychoanalytic Society, 24 Apr. 1935), *IJP-A*, 16:263–73

1936 'Psychoanalysis and the Instincts' (read before the British Psychological Society, 22 Mar. 1935), *British Journal of Psychology*, 26:272–88

1938 *Papers on Psycho-Analysis*, 4th edn. London: Ballière, Tindall and Cox

1945 'Reminiscent Notes on the Early History of Psycho-Analysis in English-Speaking Countries', *IJP-A*, 26:8–10

1948 *Papers on Psycho-Analysis*, 5th edn. London: Ballière, Tindall and Cox

'The Psychology of the Jewish Question', in *Essays in Applied Psycho-Analysis*, Vol. 1, 1951, 284–300

1949 *Hamlet and Oedipus.* New York: W. W. Norton; London: V. Gollancz. Reprinted: New York: W. W. Norton, 1971. (Rev. version of 'The Oedipus-Complex as an Explanation of Hamlet's Mystery: A Study in Motive' (1910) and 'A Psycho-Analytic Study of Hamlet', in Jones, *Essays in Applied Psycho-Analysis* (1923), 1–98.)

What is Psychoanalysis? London: Allen & Unwin

1951 *Essays in Applied Psycho-Analysis.* 2 vols, London: Hogarth Press. Reprinted: *Psycho-Myth, Psycho-History: Essays in Applied Psychoanalysis.* 2 vols. New York: Hillstone, 1974

1953 *The Life and Work of Sigmund Freud*, vol. 1: *The Formative Years and the Great Discoveries, 1856–1900.* New York: Basic Books

Sigmund Freud: Life and Work, vol. 1: *The Young Freud, 1856–1900.* London: Hogarth Press. New edn. 1954

1954 'The Early History of Psycho-Analysis', *Journal of Mental Science*, 100:198–210

1955 *The Life and Work of Sigmund Freud*, vol. 2: *Years of Maturity, 1901–1919.* New York: Basic Books

Sigmund Freud: Life and Work, vol. 2: *Years of Maturity, 1901–1919.* London: Hogarth Press. New edn. 1958; repr. 1967

1957 *The Life and Work of Sigmund Freud*, vol. 3: *The Last Phase, 1919–1939.* New York: Basic Books

Sigmund Freud: Life and Work, vol. 3: *The Last Phase, 1919–1939.* London: Hogarth Press

1958 'The Birth and Death of Moses', *IJP-A*, 39:1–4

1959 *Free Associations: Memories of a Psycho-Analyst.* New York: Basic Books. New edn.,
      intro. Mervyn Jones. New Brunswick, NJ: Transaction Publishers, 1990

Works by Other Authors

Abraham, H. C., and E. L. Freud, eds., *The Letters of Sigmund Freud and Karl Abraham,
      1907–1926.* New York: Basic Books, 1965

Albrecht, Adelbert, 'Professor Sigmund Freud', *Boston Evening Transcript,* 11 Sept. 1909, in
      Ruitenbeek, *Freud as We Knew Him,* 22–7

Ambrose, Tom, *Hitler's Loss: What Britain and America Gained from Europe's Cultural Exiles.*
      London: Peter Owen, 2001

The American Pocket Medical Dictionary. Philadelphia and London: W. B. Saunders Co., 12th
      edn, 1922

Appignanesi, Lisa, and John Forrester, *Freud's Women.* London: Weidenfeld & Nicolson, 1992

Bair, Deirdre, *Jung: A Biography.* New York and London: Little, Brown, 2004

Blum, Harold P., 'Freud and Jung: The Internationalization of Psychoanalysis', *Psychoanaly-
      sis and History,* 1/1 (June 1988), 44–55

Bonaparte, Marie, *Female Sexuality.* New York: International Universities Press, 1953

——, Anna Freud and Ernst Kris., eds., *The Origins of Psychoanalysis,* trans. Eric Mosbacher
      and James Strachey, intro. Ernst Kris. London: Imago, 1954

Bonomi, Carlo, 'Flight into Sanity: Jones's Allegation of Ferenczi's Mental Deterioration:
      A Reassessment', *International Forum of Psychoanalysis,* 7 (1988), 2011–206

Boswell, James, *The Life of Dr Johnson* (1795). 2 vols., London: J. M. Dent, 1949

Brabant, E., E. Falzeder and P. Giampieri-Deutsch, eds., *The Correspondence of Sigmund
      Freud and Sándor Ferenczi*: vol. 1, *1908–1914,* trans. Peter T. Hoffer. Cambridge, Mass.:
      Belknap Press of Harvard University Press, 1994

Bragg, Melvyn, *On Giant's Shoulders.* London: Hodder & Stoughton, 1998

Brecht, K., V. Friedrich, L. M. Hermanns, I. J. Kaminer and D. H. Juelich, eds., English
      edn prepared by Hella Ehlers, *Here Life Goes on in a Most Peculiar Way.* Hamburg:
      Kellner, 1993

Breger, Louis, *Freud: Darkness in the Midst of Vision.* New York and Toronto: John Wiley,
      2000

Breit, Harvey, 'A Talk With Ernest Jones', *New York Times Book Review,* 6 May 1956, 292

Brill, A. A., *Selected Papers on Hysteria and Other Psychoneuroses*; Monograph Series, 4. New
      York: *Journal of Nervous and Mental Diseases,* 1909

British Medical Association, *Report of the Psycho-Analysis Committee.* London: British Medi-
      cal Association, July 1929

British Medical Journal, 'A Charge Dismissed', 5 May 1906, 1076

——, 'An Appeal', 10 May 1906, 1200

Britton, Ronald, *Sex, Death, and the Superego: Experiences in Psychoanalysis.* London: Karnac,
      2003

Brome, Vincent, *Ernest Jones: Freud's Alter Ego.* London: Caliban, 1982

——, *Freud and His Early Circle.* London: Heinemann, 1967

Brown, Thomas E., 'Dr Ernest Jones, Psychoanalysis and the Canadian Medical Profession,
      1908–1913', in Shortt, *Medicine in Canadian Society,* 315–60

Burgess, Anthony, *The End of the World News.* London: Hutchinson, 1982

Burlingham, Michael, *The Last Tiffany: A Biography of Dorothy Burlingham*. New York: Athenaeum, 1989

Caine, Barbara, *Bombay to Bloomsbury: A Biography of the Strachey Family*. Oxford: Oxford University Press, 2005

Canetti, Elias, *Party in the Blitz*. London: Harvill, 2005

Chamberlain, Lesley, *The Secret Artist: A Close Reading of Sigmund Freud*. London: Quartet, 2000

Cioffi, Frank, 'Was Freud a Liar?', *Listener*, 7 Feb. 1974, 172–3

Clark, Ronald, *Freud: The Man and the Cause*. New York: Random House, 1980

Cocks, Geoffrey, *Psychotherapy in the Third Reich: The Göring Institute*. New York: Oxford University Press, 1985; 2nd edn, 1997

Cornwell, John, *Hitler's Scientists: Science, War and the Devil's Pact*. London: Viking, 2003

Corrington, Robert, *Wilhelm Reich: Psychoanalyst and Radical Naturalist*. New York: Farrar, Straus, 2003

Crawshay-Williams, Eliot, 'Morfydd Owen', *Wales*, 4 (1958), 50–56

Crick, Francis, *The Astonishing Hypothesis: The Scientific Search for the Soul*. New York: Simon & Schuster, 1994

——, and Christof Koch, 'Towards a Neurobiological Theory of Consciousness', *Seminars in the Neurosciences*, 2 (1990), 263–75

——, and Graeme Mitchison, 'The Function of Dream Sleep', *Nature*, 304 (14 July 1983), 111–14

——, 'REM Sleep and Neural Nets', *Journal of Mind and Behaviour*, 7/2 and 3 (spring and summer 1986), 229–50

Damasio, Antonio, *The Feeling of What Happens: Body and Emotion in the Making of Consciousness*. London: Heinemann, 1999; New York: Harcourt Brace, 1999

Danto, Elizabeth Ann, *Freud's Free Clinics: Psychoanalysis and Social Justice, 1918–1938*. New York: Columbia University Press, 2005

Davies, Lyn, *Morfydd Owen (1891–1918)*, Composers of Wales Monographs. Cardiff: Welsh Music Information Centre, 2004

Davies, Rhian, *Never So Pure a Sight: Morfydd Owen (1891–1918): A Life in Pictures*. Llandysul, Dyfed: Gomer Press, 1994

Davies, T. G., *Ernest Jones: 1879–1958*. Cardiff: University of Wales Press, 1979

Dufresne, T., and Gary Genosko, 'Jones on Ice: Psychoanalysis and Figure Skating', *IJP-A*, 76 (1995), 123–33

Edwards, J. Hugh, MP, *The Life of David Lloyd George with a Short History of the Welsh People*. 4 vols., London: Waverley Book Co., 1917

Ellenberger, Henri F., *The Discovery of the Unconscious: The History and Evolution of Dynamic Psychiatry*. New York: Basic Books, 1970

Elliott, T. R., 'Wilfred Batten Lewis Trotter (1872–1939)', *Obituary Notices of Fellows of the Royal Society*, 3/9 (Jan. 1941), 325–44

Evans, Richard I., *Conversations with Carl Jung and Reactions from Ernest Jones*. Princeton: Van Nostrand, 1964

Evans, W. Gordon, *A History of Llandovery College*. Llandovery: Trustees of Llandovery College, 1981

Falzeder, E., E. Brabant and P. Giampieri-Deutsch, eds., *The Correspondence of Sigmund Freud and Sándor Ferenczi*: vol. 2, *1914–1919*; vol. 3, *1920–1933*, trans. Peter T. Hoffer. Cambridge, Mass.: Belknap Press of Harvard University Press, 1996, 2000

Ferenczi, Sándor, 'Confusion of Tongues between Adults and the Child', in *Final Con-*

tributions to the Problems and Methods of Psychoanalysis. London: Hogarth Press, 1955

Ferris, Paul, 'Dr Ernest Jones', broadcast on the BBC Home Service, 15 Mar. 1959

——, *Dr Freud: A Life.* London: Sinclair-Stevenson, 1994

Flügel, J. C., *The Psychoanalytic Study of the Family.* London: Hogarth Press and the Institute of Psycho-Analysis, 1931

Forrest, Derek, *Hypnotism: A History*, foreword by Anthony Storr. London: Penguin, 1999

Freud, Anna, *The Ego and the Mechanisms of Defence.* London: Hogarth Press, 1979

——, 'Personal Memories of Ernest Jones', *IJP-A*, 60 (1979), 285–7

Freud, Sigmund, *The Standard Edition of the Complete Psychological Works of Sigmund Freud*, trans. from the German under the general editorship of James Strachey in collaboration with Anna Freud assisted by Alix Strachey and Alan Tyson. London: The Hogarth Press and The Institute of Psycho-Analysis. 1953–1974

——, *Beyond the Pleasure Principle*, 1920, *SE*, 18:3–64

——, 'A Case of Hysteria', 1905, *SE*, 7:3–122

——, *The Ego and the Id*, 1923, *SE*, 19:3–66

——, 'Dr Ernest Jones (On His 50th Birthday)', 1929, *SE*, 21:249–50

——, 'Five Lectures on Psycho-Analysis', 1910, *SE*, 11:3–56

——, *The Interpretation of Dreams*, 1900, *SE*, 4–5; trans. A. A. Brill. London: George Allen & Company, 1913.

——, *Moses and Monotheism*, 1939, *SE*, 23:3–137

——, 'Observations on Transference-Love' (Further Recommendations on the Technique of Psycho-Analysis III), 1915, *SE*, 12:157–71

——, *The Psychopathology of Everyday Life*, 1901, *SE*, 6.

——, *The Question of Lay Analysis*, 1926, *SE*, 20:179–258

——, 'Recommendations to Physicians Practising Psycho-Analysis', 1912, *SE*, 12:111–20

——, 'Some Psychical Consequences of the Anatomical Difference between the Sexes', 1925, *SE*, 19:243–58

——, *Totem and Taboo*, 1912–13, *SE*, 13:ix–162

——, and William C. Bullitt, *Thomas Woodrow Wilson, Twenty-Eighth President of the United States: A Psychological Study.* London: Weidenfeld & Nicolson and Boston: Houghton Mifflin, 1967

Friedland, Martin, *The University of Toronto: A History.* Toronto: University of Toronto Press, 2002

Gay, Peter, *Freud: A Life for Our Time.* London: J. M. Dent & Co., 1988, Papermac, 1989; New York: W. W. Norton, 1988

Gilman, Sándor, *Freud, Race, and Gender.* Princeton: Princeton University Press, 1993

G. J., 'Dr Ernest Jones', *Gowr*, 11 (1958), 28–30, reprinted from *Llandovery School Journal*, June 1958

Green, Martin, *Otto Gross: Freudian Psychoanalyst. 1877–1920.* Lewiston, Maine: Edwin Mellen Press, 1999

——, *The von Richthofen Sisters.* New York: Basic Books, 1974

Greenland, Cyril, 'Ernest Jones in Toronto 1908–13', Part I, *Canadian Psychiatric Association Journal*, 6/3 (June 1961), 132–9

——, 'Ernest Jones in Toronto 1908–13', Part II, *Canadian Psychiatric Association Journal*, 11/6 (Dec. 1966), 512–18

——, 'Ernest Jones in Toronto 1908–13', Part III, *Canadian Psychiatric Association Journal*, 12/1 (Feb. 1967), 79–80

Grosskurth, Phyllis, *Melanie Klein: Her World and Her Work*. London: Hodder & Stoughton, 1986

——, *The Secret Ring: Freud's Inner Circle and the Politics of Psychoanalysis*. London: Jonathan Cape, 1991

Guttmann, Giselher, and Inge Scholz-Strasser, eds., *Freud and the Neurosciences: From Brain Research to the Unconscious*. Vienna: Verlag der Osterreichischen Akademie der Wissenschaften, 1998

Hale, N. G., Jr, *Freud and the Americans: The Beginnings of Psychoanalysis in the United States, 1876–1917*. New York: Oxford University Press, 1971

——, *The Rise and Crisis of Psychoanalysis in the United States: Freud and the Americans 1917–1985*. New York Oxford: Oxford University Press, 1995

——, ed., *James Jackson Putnam and Psychoanalysis: Letters between Putnam and Sigmund Freud, Ernest Jones, William James, Sándor Ferenczi, and Morton Prince, 1877–1917*. Cambridge, Mass.: Harvard University Press, 1971

Hall, G. Stanley, *Adolescence: its Psychology and its Relations to Physiology, Anthropology, Sociology, Sex, Crime, Religion and Education*, vol. 1. New York and London: D. Appleton & Co., rev. edn, 1911

Hayman, Ronald, *A Life of Jung*. London: Bloomsbury, 1999

Heimann, Paula, *About Children and Children-No-Longer: Collected Papers 1942–80*, ed. Margret Tonnesmann. London and New York: Tavistock/Routledge, 1990

Hinshelwood, R. D., 'The Organizing of Psychoanalysis in Britain', *Psychoanalysis and History*, 1/1 (1998), 87

Hobman, J. B., ed., *David Eder: Memoirs of a Modern Pioneer*, foreword by Sigmund Freud. London: Gollancz, 1945

Holroyd, Michael, *Lytton Strachey*, vol. 2: *The Years of Achievement, 1910–1932*. London: Heinemann, 1968

Horney, Karen, *Feminine Psychology*. New York: Norton, 1967

——, 'The flight from womanhood', *IJP-A*, 7 (1926), 324–39

Hughes, Athol, ed., *The Inner World and Joan Riviere: Collected Papers 1920–1958*. London: Karnac Books, 1991

Jones, Herbert Davy, *Bassae and Other Verses*. Chicago: Lakeside Press, 1911

Jones, Kitty Idwal, 'The Enigma of Morfydd Owen', *Welsh Music*, 5/1 (winter 1975/6), 8–21

Jackson, D. Joyce, 'Contributions to the History of Psychology: XXXVII. Katherine Jones (1892–1983)', *Psychological Reports*, 57 (1985), 75–83

Jones, Katherine, *In an Outworn Tradition*. London: Brookside Press, 1963

——, 'A Sketch of E. J.'s Personality', *IJP-A*, 60 (1979), 271–3

Jones, Mervyn, *Chances*. London: Verso, 1987

——, 'Correspondence/Gohebiath', *Welsh Music*, 8/3 (autumn 1986), 86

——, 'Your great-grandfather, Ernest Jones', private memoir written for his grandchildren

Jones, R. Brinley, ed., *Floreat Landubriense*. Llandovery: The Trustees of Llandovery College, 1998

King, Pearl, 'Activities of British Psychoanalysts during the Second World War and the Influence of Their Inter-Disciplinary Collaboration on the Development of Psychoanalysis in Great Britain', *International Review of Psycho-Analysis*, 16 (1989), 15

——, 'Early Divergences between the Psycho-Analytical Societies in London and Vienna', in Timms and Segal, *Freud in Exile*, 124–33

——, 'The Life and Work of Melanie Klein in the British Psycho-Analytic Society.' *IJP-A*, 64 (1983), 251

——, ed., *No Ordinary Psychoanalyst: The Exceptional Contributions of John Rickman*. London: Karnac, 2003

——, and Riccardo Steiner, *The Freud-Klein Controversies 1941–45*. London and New York: Tavistock/Routledge, 1992

Kinkead-Weekes, Mark, *D. H. Lawrence: Triumph to Exile 1912–1922*. Cambridge: Cambridge University Press, 1996

Klein, Melanie, *Envy and Gratitude and Other Works, 1946–1963*. London: Tavistock, 1975

——, *The Psycho-Analysis of Children*. London: Hogarth Press, 1975

Kuhn, Philip, 'Family Romances', review of Roazen, *Oedipus in Britain*, in *Psychoanalysis and History*, 3/2 (summer 2001), 227–36

——, ' "Romancing with a Wealth of Detail" or Narratives of Dr Ernest Jones's 1906 Trial for Indecent Assault', *Studies in Gender and Sexuality*, 3/4 (2002), 344–78

Lewis, L. Haydn, 'Morfydd Llwyn Owen (1891–1918), *Welsh Music*, 3/2 (spring 1968), 4–8.

Leys, Ruth, 'Meyer's Dealings with Jones: A Chapter in the History of the American Response to Psychoanalysis', *Journal of the History of the Behavioural Sciences*, 17 (1981), 445–565

Lieberman, E. James, *Acts of Will: The Life and Work of Otto Rank*. New York: Free Press, 1985

Lloyd, James Hendrie, M.D., 'The So-Called Oedipus-Complex in Hamlet', *Journal of the American Medical Association*, 56/19 (13 May 1911), 1377–9

Lothane, Zvi, 'The Deal with the Devil to "Save" Psychoanalysis in Nazi Germany', *Psychoanalytic Review*, 88 (2001), 197–224

McGuire, William, ed., *The Freud/Jung Letters: The Correspondence between Sigmund Freud and C. G. Jung*, trans. Ralph Manheim and R. F. C. Hull. London: Hogarth Press/ Routledge & Kegan Paul, 1974; Princeton: Princeton University Press, 1974

Maddox, Brenda, *The Married Man: A Life of D. H. Lawrence*. London: Sinclair-Stevenson, 1994

Mahony, Patrick J., 'Freud Overwhelmed', *Psychoanalysis and History*, 1/1 (1998), 56–68

Malcolm, Janet, *In the Freud Archives*. New York: Knopf, 1984

Mannin, Ethel, *Confessions and Impressions*. London: Jarrolds, 1935

Masson, Jeffrey M., *The Assault on Truth*. New York: Farrar, Straus and Giroux, 1984

——, ed. and trans., *The Complete Letters of Sigmund Freud to Wilhelm Fliess, 1887–1904*. Cambridge, Mass.: Belknap Press of Harvard University Press, 1985

Marinelli, Lydia, and Andreas Mayer, *Dreaming by the Book: Freud's The Interpretation of Dreams and the History of the Psychoanalytic Movement*, trans. Susan Fairfield. New York: Other Press, 2003

Medawar, P. B., 'Victims of Psychiatry', review of I. S. Cooper, *The Victim is Always the Same*, in *New York Review of Books*, 23 Jan. 1975, 17

Metzel, Jonathan Michel, *Prozac on the Couch: Prescribing Gender in the Era of Wonder Drugs*. Durham, NC, and London: Duke University Press, 2003

Mitchell, Juliet, *Psychoanalysis and Feminism*. London: Allen Lane The Penguin Press and New York: Pantheon Books, 1974

Moore, David, *The Welsh Wars of Independence c.410–c.1415*. Stroud, Glos.: Tempus, 2004

Moorehead, Caroline, *Bertrand Russell*. London: Sinclair-Stevenson, 1992

Morgan, Kenneth O., *Rebirth of a Nation, Wales: 1880–1890*. London: Clarendon Press, 1981

Morgans, Margaret E., 'Gaucher's Disease Without Splenomegaly', *Lancet*, 18 Oct. 1947, 576

Nunberg, Herman, and Ernst Federn, eds., *Minutes of the Vienna Psychoanalytic Society*, trans. M. Nunberg. 4 vols. (1962–1974): vol. 1, *1906–1908*. New York: International Universities Press, 1962

Olivier, Laurence, *Confessions of an Actor*. London: Hodder & Stoughton, 1982

Parkes, Susan M., ed., *A Danger to the Men? A History of Women in Trinity College Dublin 1904–2004*. Dublin: Lilliput Press, 2004

Paskauskas, R. Andrew, 'Ernest Jones: A Critical Study of His Scientific Development', PhD dissertation, Institute for the History and Philosophy of Science and Technology, University of Toronto, 1985

——, 'Freud's Break with Jung: The Crucial Role of Ernest Jones', *Free Associations: Psychoanalysis, Groups, Politics, Culture*, 11 (1988), 7–34

——, ed., *The Complete Correspondence of Sigmund Freud and Ernest Jones 1908–1939*, intro. Riccardo Steiner. Cambridge, Mass., and London: Belknap Press of Harvard University Press, 1993

Payne, Sylvia, 'An Address on the Occasion of Presenting His Portrait to Ernest Jones', *IJP-A*, 27 (1946), 6

Phillips, Adam, *Darwin's Worms*. London: Faber and Faber, 1999

——, *On Flirtation*. Cambridge, Mass.: Harvard University Press, 1994

Pines, Malcolm, 'An English Freud', *Psychoanalytic Psychotherapy*, 5/1 (1990), 1–9

Pinker, Steven, *How the Mind Works*. London: Allen Lane The Penguin Press, 1997

Plath, Sylvia, *The Bell Jar* London: Heinemann, 1963

Porter, Roy, *The Greatest Benefit to Mankind: A Medical History of Humanity from Antiquity to the Present*. London: HarperCollins, 1997

Prince, Morton, M.D., *The Dissociation of a Personality: A Biographical Study in Abnormal Psychology*. New York: Longmans, Green & Co., 1910

——, 'The Mechanism and Interpretation of Dreams', *Journal of Abnormal Psychology*, 5 (Oct.–Nov. 1910), 139–195

——, 'The Mechanism and Interpretation of Dreams – a Reply to Dr Jones', *Journal of Abnormal Psychology*, 5 (Feb.–Mar. 1911), 337–53

——, ed., *Psychotherapeutics*. Boston: Richard G. Badger, 1909

Puner, Helen Walker, *Freud: His Life and His Mind*. New York: Grosset & Dunlap, 1947

Putnam, James Jackson, *Addresses on Psycho-Analysis*. London, Vienna and New York: International Psycho-Analytical Press, 1921

——, *Human Motives*. Boston: Little, Brown, 1915

——, 'Personal Impressions of Sigmund Freud and His Work, with Special Reference to His Recent Lectures at Clark University', *Journal of Abnormal Psychology*, 4 (1909–10), 293–310, 372–9

——, 'Recent Experience in the Study and Treatment of Hysteria', *Journal of Abnormal Psychology*, 1 (1906), 26–41

——, see also under 'Hale, N. G., Jr, ed.'

Rank, Otto, *Myth of the Birth of the Hero: A Psychological Exploration of Myth*. ('Mythus von der Geburt des Helden', *Schriften*, 5 (1909)). Baltimore: Johns Hopkins University Press, 2004

Rayner, Eric, *The Independent Mind in British Psychoanalysis*. London: Jason Aronson, 1991

Richie, Alexandra, *Faust's Metropolis: A History of Berlin*. London: HarperCollins, 1998

Richsher, Charles, and C. G. Jung, 'Further Investigations on the Galvanic Phenomenon and Respiration in Normal and Insane Individuals', *Journal of Abnormal Psychology*, 10 (Dec. 1907-Jan. 1908), 189–91

Riviere, Joan, 'Symposium on Child Analysis', *IJP-A*, 8 (1927), 370–77

Roazen, Paul, 'An Author's Reexamination: Helene Deutsch: A Psychoanalyst's Life', *Psychoanalytic Psychology*, 21/4 (2004), 622–32

——, *Brother Animal: The Story of Freud and Tausk*. New York: Knopf, 1969; London: Allen Lane, The Penguin Press, 1970

——, *Edoardo Weiss: The House that Freud Built*. New Brunswick, NJ, and London: Transaction Publishers, 2005

——, *Freud and His Followers*. New York: Knopf, 1975; London: Allen Lane The Penguin Press, 1976

——, *Helene Deutsch: A Psychoanalyst's Life*. New Brunswick, NJ: Transaction Publishers, 1992

——, *Meeting Freud's Family*. Amherst: University of Massachusetts Press, 1993

——, *Oedipus in Britain: Edward Glover and the Struggle over Klein*. New York: Other Press, 2000

——, 'Oedipus at Versailles', *Times Literary Supplement*, 22 Apr. 2005, 12–13

——, *On the Freud Watch*. London: Free Association Books, 2003

——, 'Recollecting Freud', review of Isidor Sadger's book, edited and introduced by Alan Dundes, trans. J. M. Jacobsen and Alan Dundes. Madison, Wisc.: University of Wisconsin Press, 2005

Robertson, Ritchie, 'A Case of Pen Envy', review of Louis Berger's *Freud* and Lesley Chamberlain's *The Secret Artist*, in *Times Literary Supplement*, 27 Oct. 2000, 11

Robinson, Ken, ' "Now we are free": Freud in England', *Institute of Psychoanalysis News and Events*, annual issue 2006

——, 'Sylvia Payne: Pluralist or Eclectic?', *Bulletin of the British Psychological Society*, 39/8 (2003), 1–11

Rossdale, Polly, and Ken Robinson, *Bloomsbury and Psychoanalysis: An Exhibition of Documents from the Archives of the British Psychoanalytical Society*. London: The Archives of the British Psychoanalytical Society, Queen Mary College, University of London, 2003

Ruitenbeek, Hendrik M., ed., *Freud as We Knew Him*. Detroit: Wayne State University Press, 1973

Sachs, Hanns, *Freud: Master and Friend*. London: Imago, 1945; Cambridge, Mass.: Harvard University Press, 1945

Sadger, Isidor, *Recollecting Freud*, ed. and intro. Alan Dundes, trans. J. M. Jacobsen and Alan Dundes. Madison, Wisc.: University of Wisconsin Press, 2005

Schwartz, Joseph, *Cassandra's Daughter: A History of Psychoanalysis in Europe and America*. London: Allen Lane The Penguin Press, 1999

Scull, Andrew, 'Freud and the Psyche, continued', review of Zaretsky, *Secrets of the Soul*, in *Los Angeles Times Book Review*, 11 July 2004, 8–9

Segal, Hanna, *Introduction to the Work of Melanie Klein*. London: Hogarth Press, 1971

Shamdasani, Sonu, 'Emest Jones', *New Oxford Dictionary of National Biography*. Oxford: Oxford University Press, 2004

——, *Jung and the Making of Modern Psychology*. Cambridge; Cambridge University Press, 2003

——, 'Spielrein's Associations: A Newly Identified Word Association Protocol', *Harvest*, 39 (1993), 164–5

Shorter, Edward. *A History of Psychiatry: From the Era of the Asylum to the Age of Prozac*. New York: John Wiley, 1997

Shortt, S. E. D., ed., *Medicine in Canadian Society: Historical Perspectives*. Montreal: McGill University Press, 1981

Sidis, Boris, review of S. Freud, *The Psychopathology of Everyday Life* (*Zur Psychopathologie des Alltagslebens*) (Berlin: S. Karger, 1904), *Journal of Abnormal Psychology*, 1/2 (June 1906), 101–3

Smith, David L., 'Sigmund Freud and the Crick-Koch Hypothesis: A Footnote to the History of Consciousness Studies', *IJP-A*, 80 (1999), 543–8

Solms, Mark, 'Controversies in Freud Translation', *Psychoanalysis and History*, 1/1 (1998), 28–43

Spotts, Frederic, ed., *Letters of Leonard Woolf*. London: Weidenfeld & Nicolson, 1989

Stekel, Wilhelm, *The Autobiography of Wilhelm Stekel: The Life Story of a Pioneer Psychoanalyst*, ed. E. A. Gutheil. New York: Liveright, 1950

Steiner, Riccardo, '*It is a New Kind of Diaspora': Explorations in the Sociopolitical and Cultural Context of Psychoanalysis*. London: Karnac, 2000

——, *Tradition, Change, Creativity: Repercussions of the New Diaspora on Aspects of British Psychoanalysis*. London: Karnac, 2000

Strachey, James and Alix, *Bloomsbury/Freud: The Letters of James and Alix Strachey, 1924–1925*, ed. Perry Miesel and Walter Kendrick. London: Chatto & Windus, 1986

——, see also 'Freud, Sigmund, *The Standard Edition*'

Sulloway, F. J., *Freud: Biologist of the Mind*. New York: Basic Books, 1979

Tansley, A. G., 'Sigmund Freud, 1856–1939', *Obituary Notices of Fellows of the Royal Society*, 3/9 (Jan. 1941), 246–75

Taylor, Eugene, 'Who Founded the American Psychopathological Association?', *Comprehensive Psychiatry*, 27/5 (Sept.–Oct. 1986), 439–45

Timms, Edward, and Naomi Segal, eds., *Freud in Exile: Psychoanalysis and its Vicissitudes*. New Haven: Yale University Press, 1988

Trosman, Harry, and Ernest S. Wolf, 'The Benfeld Collaboration in the Jones Biography of Freud', *IJP-A*, 54 (1973), 227–33

Trotter, W., *Instincts of the Herd in Peace and War*. London: T. Fisher Unwin, 1917

Turner, Christopher, 'Diary', *London Review of Books*, 3 June 2004, 38–9

Wallas, Graham, *The Great Society*. London: Macmillan, 1914

Who's Who. London: Adam & Charles Black, 1955

Williams, Tom, 'The Relation of Character Formation to Psychotherapy', in Morton Prince et al., *Psychotherapeutics: A Symposium*. London: T. Fisher Unwin, 1910

Wilsey, John, *H. Jones, VC: The Life and Death of an Unusual Hero*. London: Hutchinson, 2002

Wittels, Fritz, *Sigmund Freud: His Personality, His Teaching, and His School*, trans. Eden and Cedar Paul. London: George Allen & Unwin, 1924

Woof, Leonard, *Downhill All The Way*. London: Hogarth Press, 1968.

Woolf, Virginia, *Moments of Being*. Chatto & Windus for Sussex University Press, 1976

Young-Bruehl, Elisabeth, *Anna Freud: A Biography*. New York: Summit Books, 1988: London: Macmillan, 1989.

Zaretsky, Eli, *Secrets of the Soul: A Social and Cultural History of Psychoanalysis*. New York: Knopf, 2004

Zetzel, Elizabeth R., M.D., 'Ernest Jones: His Contribution to Psycho-Analytic Theory', *IJP-A*, 39 (1958), 311–18

Zytaruk, George J., and James T. Boulton, eds., *The Letters of D. H. Lawrence*, vol. 2 (Cambridge: Cambridge University Press, 1981)

Index

in Paris, 65; in Canada, 68–70,
75–6, 85, 90–1, 95, 99, 100, 110;
endorsement of psychoanalysis in
New Haven, 75; at Clark
Conference, 76, 78; commitment
to psychoanalysis, 78; as defender
and interpreter of psychoanalysis,
79–80, 168, 201; as officer of
APA, 83; accusation of sexual
intercourse by patient, 90–1;
income from psychoanalysis, 90,
119, 144, 158, 159, 167;
foundation of American
Psychoanalytic Society, 94; rise to
academic status, 96; international
recognition, 99; in Freud's inner
circle (the Committee), 101, 102;
as co-editor of the *Zeitschrift*, 103;
return to Toronto, 107; analysis by
Ferenczi, 108–9; rejection as
physician, 110, 120–1; return from
Canada to London, 110; as
president of London Psycho-
Analytical Society, 111; primacy in
psychoanalysis, dispute with Eder,
111, 168, 253–4, 259; success in
London, 113; in First World War,
119; established as psychoanalyst in
London, 120; effect on women
patients, 126; as president of
British Psycho-Analytical Society,
147–8; visit to Switzerland post-
First World War, 149; reunion
with Freud and Ferenczi after First
World War, 154; money smuggled
over Austrian border, 155;
donation to 'English Press', 157;
Dutch bank account, 158, 163; tax
avoidance, 158; translation of
Freud's works organized, 160; as
president of IPA, 162, 174, 177,
213; power over psychoanalysis,
163–4; rebuke to Barbara Low,
168; formation of Glossary
Committee, 178; Institute of
Psycho-Analysis founded, 179;
dependence on lay analysts, 186;
on BMA committee on

psychoanalysis, 187, 198–9, 200,
201; London symposium in 1927,
188; Riviere's opposition to Anna
Freud, 194–5; BMA report as
victory over medical
establishment, 201; BBC radio talk
on psychoanalysis, 203–4; growth
of reputation, 203; reduced
number of patients, 209, 237;
asked to stand as president of IPA
by Eitingon, 211; helps Jews to
emigrate from Germany, 215; and
Ferenczi's criticism of
psychoanalysis, 218; negotiations
with DPG, 224–5; choice of
immigrants for Britain, 237; at
Paris congress in 1938, 239;
financial problems, 241; speech at
Freud's funeral, 243–4, 259, 260;
attacked by Rickman, 246; elected
as fellow of Royal College of
Physicians, 249; membership of
Royal College of Physicians, 249;
replacement of Glover by Anna
Freud as secretary of IPA, 252;
annual lecture in Jones's name,
255; meeting with Laurence
Olivier, 88, 257; as member of the
Athenaeum, 257; patients seen
while writing Freud's biography,
266; as celebrity, 267; academic
recognition, 270; honorary
fellowships in USA, 274–5;
lectures in United States for
centenary of Freud's birth, 274–5;
television appearances, 274–5, 276,
277; opening paper at 1957
congress, 277
character: administrative skill, 1;
energy, 1, 26, 83–4, 203, 274,
280–1; literary ability, 1; sharp
tongue, 1, 10, 28–9, 36–7, 62,
198–9; sarcasm, 2, 17, 23, 115,
220, 239; charm, 6, 30;
determination, 6; obstinacy, 6, 15;
cleverness, 13–14, 26; feeling of
inferiority, 13, 109, 160; double
allegiance, 14; as hard worker, 14,